Business Performance Management

PEARSON CUSTOM PUBLISHING

Business Performance Management

Compiled by:

Dr. Ken Yeoh, Barrie Mitchinson, Dr. Alireza Shokri,
Matthew Sutherland and Dr. Nick Creaby-Attwood
Newcastle Business School, Northumbria University

Selected chapters from:

*Managerial Accounting for
Business Decisions*
Third Edition
by Ray Proctor

Management Accounting
Second Edition
by Pauline Weetman

Accounting: Theory and Practice
Eighth Edition
by Michel Glautier, Brian Underdown
and Deigan Morris

*Marketing Metrics:
The Definitive Guide to
Measuring Marketing Performance*
Second Edition
by Paul W. Farris, Neil T. Bendle,
Phillip E. Pfeifer and David J. Reibstein

Marketing Management
by Philip Kotler, Kevin Lane Keller,
Mairead Brady, Malcolm Goodman
and Torben Hansen

*Human Resouce Management:
A Contemporary Approach*
Sixth Edition
by Julie Beardwell and Tim Claydon

Operations Management
Sixth Edition
by Nigel Slack, Stuart Chambers and
Robert Johnston

PEARSON

Harlow, England • London • New York • Boston • San Francisco • Toronto • Sydney • Auckland • Singapore • Hong Kong
Tokyo • Seoul • Taipei • New Delhi • Cape Town • Sao Paulo • Mexico City • Madrid • Amsterdam • Munich • Paris • Milan

Pearson Education Limited
Edinburgh Gate
Harlow
Essex CM20 2JE

And associated companies throughout the world

Visit us on the World Wide Web at:
www.pearsoned.co.uk

Compiled from:

*Managerial Accounting for
Business Decisions*
Third Edition
by Ray Proctor
ISBN 978 0 273 71755 3
Copyright © Pearson Education Limited 2002, 2006, 2009

Management Accounting
Second Edition
by Pauline Weetman
ISBN 978 0 273 71845 1
Copyright © Pearson Education Limited 2006, 2010

Accounting: Theory and Practice
Eighth Edition
by Michel Glautier, Brian Underdown
and Deigan Morris
ISBN 978 0 273 69385 7
Copyright © Guardjust Limited and B. Underdown 2001
Copyright © M. W. E. Glautier, B. Underdown
and D. Morris 2011

*Marketing Metrics:
The Definitive Guide to
Measuring Marketing Performance*
Second Edition
by Paul W. Farris, Neil T. Bendle,
Phillip E. Pfeifer and David J. Reibstein
ISBN 978 0 13 705829 7
Copyright © 2010 by Pearson Education, Inc.
Publishing as FT Press, Upper Saddle River, New Jersey 07458

Marketing Management
by Philip Kotler, Kevin Lane Keller,
Mairead Brady, Malcolm Goodman
and Torben Hansen
ISBN 978 0 273 71856 7
Copyright © Pearson Education Limited 2009

*Human Resouce Management:
A Contemporary Approach*
Sixth Edition
by Julie Beardwell and Tim Claydon
ISBN 978 0 273 72285 4
Copyright © Longman Group Limited 1994
Copyright © Financial Times Professional Limited 1997
Copyright © Pearson Education Limited 2001, 2010

Operations Management
Sixth Edition
by Nigel Slack, Stuart Chambers and
Robert Johnston
ISBN 978 0 273 73046 0
Copyright © Nigel Slack, Stuart Chambers,
Christine Harland, Alan Harrison, Robert Johnston 1995, 1998
Copyright © Nigel Slack, Stuart Chambers, and
Robert Johnston 2001, 2004, 2007, 2010

ISBN 978 1 78134 207 7

Printed and bound in Italy by Rotolito Lombarda S.p.A.

Contents

Preface

This custom text has been compiled to provide students at undergraduate level with an overview of the various approaches, measures and also pertinent issues relating to business performance management. It aims to enhance their understanding of how business performance is conceptualized, evaluated and managed across major functional areas of business – Marketing, Finance (Accounting), Human Resource Management and Logistics & Supply Chain Management. Students who make use of this text are encouraged to reflect on the sheer number of distinctive dimensions by which performance is gauged and managed, not only across functional areas but also within each of those areas.

In addition, it is hoped that students will gain an in-depth understanding of how seemingly unrelated performance measures and dimensions from the different major functional areas are interlinked and mutually influence one another. Ultimately, students are expected to come to the realization that a broad, cross-functional, strategic and all-encompassing approach as well as understanding is essential for the effective management of overall business performance. In this regard, the custom text makes use of the Balanced Scorecard approach as the overarching framework to integrate the many functional area-specific aspects of performance.

Even though this custom text provides a relatively firm foundation of knowledge pertaining to certain aspects of business performance management, students are expected to do significant amounts of additional wider reading and research. This is applicable to both, aspects that are covered within this text or otherwise.

Dr Ken Yeoh

Part 1 Balance Scorecard

Balanced scorecards

Chapter contents

Introduction

Imagine the following conversation between two friends, Claude and Chantal, who want to go and see a Rolling Stones concert in Cologne.

Claude: *'OK, we are going to drive from Rouen to Cologne.'*
Chantal: *'Yes, but which way are we going to go?'*

Claude:	*'Remember last June when we drove from Paris to Brussels?'*
Chantal:	*'Yes, the Johnny Haliday concert. Let's look at how long it took us, how many wrong turnings we made, what our average speed was for each part of the journey and for the whole trip, all the costs involved, how much diesel we used and how much we had left at the end.'*
Claude:	*'I'm glad we calculated all those statistics about the journey. I knew they would come in handy.'*
Chantal:	*'OK, let's use them to plan our journey to Cologne. It would be good to know exactly how long it will take to get there and how much everything will cost.'*

Having made their plans, the two friends commence their journey, driving east at their predetermined speed. Unfortunately, after driving for 45 minutes, they find their road closed for repairs and have to take a diversion; this takes an additional 30 minutes before they return to their chosen route. After another hour's driving they stop for lunch at a service station. Returning to their car, feeling refreshed, they find that the driver's wing mirror has been knocked off and is lying on the floor by the side of the car. There is also a nasty scratch and dent on the front wing! They report this to a policeman in a traffic patrol vehicle parked nearby and record the details to send to their insurance company at a later date. The policeman advises that the mirror must be repaired before the journey is recommenced. This takes an extra hour but the required repairs are achieved; this cost them 150 euros that they had planned to spend on a good hotel in Cologne.

The journey continues and goes well for the next two hours. Unexpectedly, as it is now April, it then starts to snow. All traffic slows down and their average speed drops by 30 kph. Fortunately, the snowstorm only lasts for 20 minutes but the road surface remains wet and speeds increase only a little. They stop to change drivers but, when Chantal exits the passenger seat, she feels dizzy and decides she is not fit to drive. She has had a cold for the last few days but assumed she would be over it by now and has not brought any medication with her. Claude has no choice but to continue driving after a quick wash to freshen up. Two hours later, night falls and Claude feels too tired to drive any further. So, reluctantly, they stop at Aachen for the night. Acknowledging that they will not now get to the Rolling Stones concert, they book into a local motel and watch a movie they both wanted to see on the television in their room.

They do not consider their trip to be a total disaster but they certainly did not achieve their original objective. So, is there anything they could have done to help themselves get to the concert on time? How sensible was it to plan their journey based on what happened in a previous journey to a different destination at a different time? Could they have predicted the snow from available weather forecasts and allowed more time for the journey? Should Chantal have anticipated the return of her cold and bought some appropriate medicine to take with her even though she may not have had to use it?

All analogies break down at some point but this story is not too dissimilar to the way businesses typically used to make their plans for the next financial year. They used previous years' statistics such as profit margins, sales volumes and prices, rates of pay, material and expense costs; these were known from the previous year and it was assumed they would remain valid for the current year. They felt content with this approach because the information was certain and, after all, no-one could accurately predict what these statistics were going to be. So the plan was made and (for companies listed on the Stock Exchange) independent analysts were informed of the predicted profits. Employees were strongly encouraged to meet their budget numbers, often by the use of personal financial incentives, and future changes in the environment were conveniently ignored. These may have included changes in interest rates, innovative competition, widespread flooding, a flu epidemic among employees, decreases in demand due to higher rates of VAT and even terrorist activities. Many resources had been invested in the budgeting process and there was a natural reluctance to abandon it.

However, a better way of achieving corporate objectives has been created, a method that uses more than just recent financial statistics and gives a more rounded approach to the task of managing business performance. It is called the Balanced Scorecard.

Learning objectives

Having worked through this chapter you should be able to:

- describe the theory and structure of the balanced scorecard;
- describe the internal 'lead' and 'lag' relationships between balanced scorecard components;
- explain the different relationships in 'for-profit' and 'not-for-profit' organizations;
- explain the advantage of involving front-line staff in balanced scorecard design and operation;
- draw a diagram to show how corporate strategy can be implemented through the balanced scorecard;
- give examples of how popular strategies would appear on the balanced scorecard;
- explain the flexibility of balanced scorecard design;
- describe the process of cascading scorecards within organizations;
- describe the process of employee involvement in the operation of scorecards;
- create a strategy map in connection with a balanced scorecard;
- appreciate how balanced scorecards are adapted for use by real companies;
- explain how the scorecard approach can help with strategy formulation;
- describe the multiple benefits of operating balanced scorecards;
- explain the role of financial incentives connected to balanced scorecards;
- appreciate the dangers of operating two different performance systems at the same time;
- describe the limitations of balanced scorecards.

Structure and internal relationships

The balanced scorecard was first proposed by Kaplan and Norton in 1992. It is a device to aid managers in their efforts to improve corporate performance in line with corporate goals and was designed to combat the short-termism of traditional accounting systems. To help managers avoid information overload it is recommended that four corporate goals or objectives are chosen for each of four 'perspectives' (or aspects) of organizational activity (16 items in total). The four perspectives are financial, customer, internal business processes and learning/innovation. Each goal (or Critical Success Factor) is monitored by a different performance indicator and a specific target is set for each indicator. These indicators are sometimes referred to as *key performance indicators (KPIs)*. Figure 1.1 illustrates the balanced scorecard structure.

The specific targets set for each indicator should be stretch targets, high but achievable. If they are set either too low or too high, they will demotivate employees and performance will be suboptimal. So, the targets should be set very carefully. But even this is not enough to ensure success. It is good practice for the people responsible for achieving targets to create 'action plans' setting out in detail how they are going to achieve their objectives. A separate action plan should be created for each of the 16 objectives. Also, a single named employee should be designated as responsible for each plan and they should be reviewed on a regular basis at least every six months.

However, it is not essential that each perspective has exactly four objectives; the idea is to keep the amount of monitored information small and, therefore, manageable. Also, if an organization thinks it useful to have five perspectives, there is no reason why it should not do so. For example, one major European oil and gas multinational has a fifth perspective concerned with 'health and safety', which is a very important aspect of their business. Balanced scorecards are essentially flexible and should always be tailored to the requirements of the organization using them.

However, as the number of items monitored is small, it is vital that they and their performance indicators are very carefully chosen. Duplication should be avoided; for example, no indicator should be used more than once on the scorecard. The goals listed should give a broad perspective of activities rather than a narrow one. In the past, it was not unusual for managers to be expected to monitor a much larger number of individual measurements, sometimes more than a hundred! The pressing nature of their other duties meant that they could not do this effectively and strategy implementation was very difficult to achieve. *It was difficult for them to see the forest as a whole because there were so many trees in the way.*

One of the perspectives concerns 'traditional' financial measures but the other three consist of non-financial items. Taken together, the financial, customer, internal business and innovation/learning indicators give a balanced view of corporate performance. Provided the non-financial performance indicators are carefully selected, improvement in them should automatically translate into improved financial performance. This can be thought of in terms of *cause and effect* or *action and result*. Accordingly, the non-financial factors are known as 'lead' indicators and the financial factors as 'lag' indicators. See Figure 1.2. Note that a perspective in the middle of the system may be 'lag' for the one before it but 'lead' for the one after it; the terms are relative. ('Lag'

The financial perspective

Corporate goal	Performance indicator	Target
Survival	Liquid ratio	Increase to 0.8:1.0
Profitability	Return on capital employed	Improve by 5% over the year
Growth	Sales revenue	Increase by 4% a year above inflation
Self-funding	Interest cover ratio	Reduce interest to 10% of operating profit

The customer perspective

Corporate goal	Performance indicator	Target
Responsiveness	Sales order processing period	Reduce to 12 working days
Reliability	On-time deliveries	95% each month
Product quality	Complaints received	2% of goods delivered each month
Image	Ranking by customer	Customer's first or second choice in independent survey

The internal business perspective

Corporate goal	Performance indicator	Target
Satisfied employees	Staff turnover ratio	5% a year maximum
Production efficiency	Output per employee	Increase by 1% every 3 months
Working capital management	Cash-cycle period	Reduce by 1 day every 2 months
Production quality	Value of defective production	Reduction of 2% every 3 months

The innovation and learning perspective

Corporate goal	Performance indicator	Target
Continuing introduction of new products	Proportion of sales from new products	15% of annual sales from products launched in current or previous financial year
Employee development	Number of training hours per employee	16 hours per year minimum for each employee
Market diversification	Number of new markets served	At least one new market entered each year
Product improvement	Spending on research and development	Minimum of 10% a year of after-tax profits

Figure 1.1 **The four perspectives of the balanced scorecard and examples of their application**

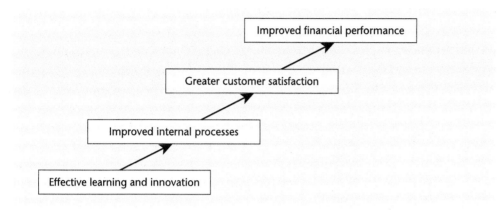

Figure 1.2 **Lead and lag perspectives in a for-profit organization**

indicators are examples of a 'feedback' system but 'lead' indicators are a type of 'feed-forward' system.)

The model is that:

1 Improvements in learning and innovation will automatically lead to improvements in internal business processes.
2 Improvements in internal business processes will automatically lead to improvements in customer satisfaction.
3 Improvements in customer satisfaction will automatically lead to improvements in the financial statistics (profit, return on capital employed, sales revenue, etc.) and, therefore, shareholder value.

This is fundamentally sound but somewhat simplistic as there is a considerable amount of interaction occurring between all perspectives. Note that the model described above assumes the organization to be a 'for-profit' example; in a 'not-for-profit' organization, the lead/lag relationship changes. The ultimate lag perspective becomes that of the customer/client and the financial perspective becomes the first of the lead perspectives. Income is essential for training and innovation to occur *which leads to* improved internal processes *which leads to* improved client satisfaction (see Figure 1.3).

Balanced scorecards are equally useful in both types of organization and many relevant skills are transferable between them. Peter Drucker is on record saying that it would be a good idea for not-for-profit organizations to acquire the performance management skills of commercial ones and for for-profit organizations to acquire the mission-management skills of not-for-profit ones. Whether profit is the main objective or not, all organization can benefit from the use of balanced scorecards.

The indicators included in the scorecard are not generic; they should be reviewed periodically to reflect changes of corporate strategy made in response to the external environment. This is facilitated by a flexible management information system, possibly based on a unified relational database used to warehouse both internal and external data. In summary, the balanced scorecard is driven by organizational strategic objectives rather than a desire for operational control. It is not constrained by the financial year in the way that a budgetary control system is. Note that it is not a strategy in itself but a mechanism designed to help organizations translate their chosen strategies into reality.

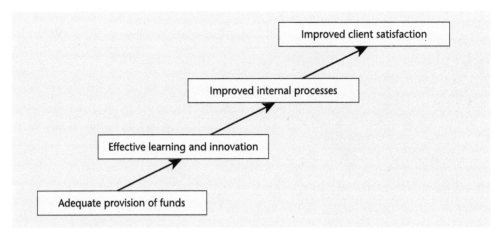

Figure 1.3 **Lead and lag perspectives in a not-for-profit organization**

To summarize the importance of measurement-based balanced scorecards, I quote Melnyk *et al.* (2004):

Strategy without metrics is useless; metrics without a strategy are meaningless.

Practical application

Introducing a balanced scorecard into an organization is a demanding task and involves significant cost. But although it consumes large amounts of resources it usually turns out to be well worthwhile. After all, its basic objective is to improve business performance through effective implementation of corporate strategy.

Balanced scorecards use only a small number of key performance indicators, mostly non-financial; but who decides which ones to use? If the choice is imposed from above, the effectiveness of the initiative will be limited. On the other hand, if front-line operatives are involved in the choice of indicators, the balanced scorecard is more likely to bring about the desired improvements in corporate performance. Front-line staff, rather than higher-level managers, often know best where improvements can be made most effectively. The performance indicators selected should come out of discussions between them and their managers. Genuine consultation here will pay handsome dividends later. Like budgets, balanced scorecards are more likely to be effective if created both top-down and bottom-up.

The choice of balanced scorecard indicators is critical and deserves much thought (see Bourne and Neely's 'Cause and effect' article listed below in Further reading). **Whatever a business decides to measure, it will strive to achieve.** Kaplan and Norton, the inventors of the balanced scorecard, express this succinctly as 'You get what you measure.' For example, suppose a company chooses 'average length of sales order processing' as one of its key performance indicators in the 'customer perspective' of its balanced scorecard. If this is currently taking 18 days and it finds out that its main competitor is taking only 16 days, it may decide to set itself a target of 14 days. If management seeks to achieve this in isolation from other aspects of corporate performance and without consulting the delivery operatives, the company may experience a significant increase in the number of complaints it receives concerning the quality of goods received by customers. It may be that a different method of delivery was adopted in order to achieve the new standard of 14 days but this caused a significant increase in damage to goods in transit. For example, instead of relying on its existing delivery system, the firm may have hired outside contractors to move more goods in less time. Unfortunately, these contractors would not have been as experienced as the firm's own staff and more damage would have occurred.

If the firm's own staff had been consulted, they may have been able to point out that the policy of having only one person per vehicle means that the driver also has to do all the unloading. If there were two employees per vehicle, one hour of unloading time a day could be saved and the number of deliveries increased by 15%. Alternatively, the vehicles could be modified somehow to speed up the unloading process, e.g. the installation of a powered lift at the back of the lorry. The drivers would be very aware of the possibilities but it is unlikely that senior managers would have any ideas in this respect due to their detachment from the unloading process.

The role of the balanced scorecard has developed over time. As well as being a mechanism for monitoring a broad range of performance indicators, it is now also seen as a strategic business tool, a mechanism for clarifying strategy and turning it into action. Because the performance indicators can be changed to suit an evolving environment or revised internal direction, the balanced scorecard can be used to implement new strategic objectives (see Figure 1.4). Where it is used throughout an organization, it not only acts as a mechanism for including employees in the strategy process but also becomes a communication medium for new strategies. This applies just as much to not-for-profit organizations such as the Royal Navy (see Woodley's 'Ship shape' article in Further reading below) as it does to profit-seeking businesses like Tesco.

Figure 1.4 **Strategy implementation through the balanced scorecard**

Extract where JIT is an adopted strategy:

Corporate goal	**Performance indicator**	**Target**
Eliminate stock	Stock value	5% of weekly production materials used value

Extract where TQM is an adopted strategy:

Corporate goal	**Performance indicator**	**Target**
Eliminate product defects	Defective parts per million (DPPM)	Ten per million

Extract where benchmarking is an adopted strategy:

Corporate goal	**Performance indicator**	**Target**
Efficient information system	Number of independent IT systems in use	Three

Extract where ABM is an adopted strategy:

Corporate goal	**Performance indicator**	**Target**
To minimize non-value-added costs	Amount spent on factory security	10% reduction from current cost

Figure 1.5 **Examples of popular strategy implementation**

The goals and their performance indicators can come from the management techniques (e.g. JIT, TQM, benchmarking and ABM) adopted by the organization as their strategy. For example, a company adopting a just-in-time inventory control strategy would have a goal of eliminating stock, and 'stock value' could be one of the selected KPIs (see Figure 1.5 for examples). Most of the performance data will be available internally but sometimes it may have to be obtained via customer surveys, benchmarking, intercompany comparisons, etc. The number of indicators is limited on purpose in order to help management focus on their current priorities. (For a brief description of JIT, TQM and benchmarking, see the appendix at the end of this chapter; for ABM, see the last part of the chapter on ABC.)

Flexibility

One reason why balanced scorecards have been adopted so widely is their flexibility. Kaplan's standard model is an example of how they can be structured but it is not meant to be a rigid format suitable for all organizations. The four perspectives are almost always used but there is no reason why a fifth should not be added if the organization considered it useful. For example, a pharmaceutical company may decide to have a 'Research & Development' perspective as well as a perspective for employee 'Learning & Growth'. Products could be separated from people and scientists from other personnel.

There is no reason why each perspective should highlight exactly four business objectives; three or five may be preferred. Only objectives considered important should be included. However, in order to avoid information overload and the dilution of management focus, it is inadvisable for any balanced scorecard to have more than about 20 objectives in total. Similarly, only one KPI should be chosen to measure performance against objectives. There is almost always a choice of indicators and the decision as to which one to use should always be made carefully.

For example, the various KPIs concerned with the corporate goal of 'improving product quality' could include:

1 defects as a percentage of production, found by quality inspections;
2 number of customer complaints received;
3 market share (measured independently);
4 etc.

Indicator 2, 'number of complaints', will depend on the size of orders placed by individual customers. Only 10 customers may complain in one year compared with 20 customers in the previous year. This looks like a big improvement but the 20 may account for 18% of total sales volume whereas the 10 may represent 25%.

If indicator 3, 'market share', is the chosen indicator, a decrease would be interpreted as a reduction in product quality. But the decrease could be caused by other factors such as a new entrant into the market, possibly using discounts to buy its way in, or by a dent to the brand image caused by association with some sort of political incorrectness such as the use of child labour in the manufacturing process. The point is that a change in market share could have some cause other than a change in product quality.

'Defects as a percentage of production' is probably the best of the above indicators as the link between it and the objective is the most direct and influenced by few, if any, other factors than quality.

Remember, if 'what you measure is what you get' you need to be very careful in deciding what to measure.

Cascading and employee involvement

So far, we have been thinking about balanced scorecards designed for a single semi-autonomous business unit (often referred to as a strategic business unit or SBU) but large organizations often have a holding company and a number of divisions. There is no reason why balanced scorecards should not be used at each of these levels provided appropriate modifications are made. The Group could have its own scorecard and each of the divisions or SBUs could have theirs. Obviously, the objectives, performance indicators and targets must be integrated so that the results achieved at any level help to achieve the targets set at the next level above (see Figure 1.6).

Also, each division may be split into a number of teams, each consisting of a number of employees. In such cases, performance improvement devices for teams and individuals can be created taking as their vision/mission the device at the level immediately above. These 'team/personal scorecards' would not look like the 'standard' balanced scorecards as described above but would be based on them; for example, they would be unlikely to have the four perspectives. These devices would consist of a list of objectives, performance measures and target levels. Titles of these devices include 'personal development matrix' and 'responsibility log' (see Figure 1.7).

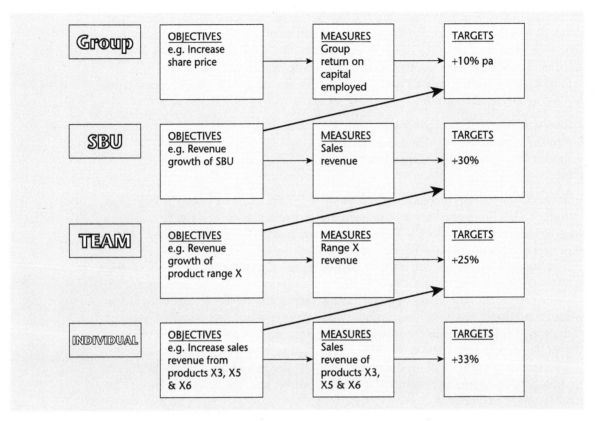

Figure 1.6 **Performance improvement cascade**

Process	Bread making
Responsible manager	**M. Bunn (team supervisor)**
Financial (F1)	**Variable cost**
Current	£124.50/100 kg
Target	£118.00/100 kg
Cause	Waste dough after mixing
Action	Improved-design containers to be purchased
by when	September 30
by whom	A. Spooner, chief mixer
Non-financial (N1)	**Productivity**
Current	310 loaves/hour/operative
Target	350 loaves/hour/operative
Cause	Oven interior rack design is inefficient.
Action	Racks to be dismantled and rebuilt. N.B.: 3-day shutdown needed.
by when	First opportunity is December 27–29.
by whom	Maintenance department plus M. Bunn and D. Nutt
etc.	

Figure 1.7 **Team responsibility log (extract)**

Strategy maps

A strategy map shows the interconnections between business objectives from the different perspectives of a balanced scorecard. It maps the cause and effect relationships
between them, e.g. shortening the sales order processing time should lead to improved
customer satisfaction. Their function is to summarize and make explicit the results of
the many discussions, deliberations and decisions made concerning business strategy.
They are also a very good way of communicating this to everyone in the business and
help to maintain strategic focus. Figure 1.8 is an example of a strategy map with the

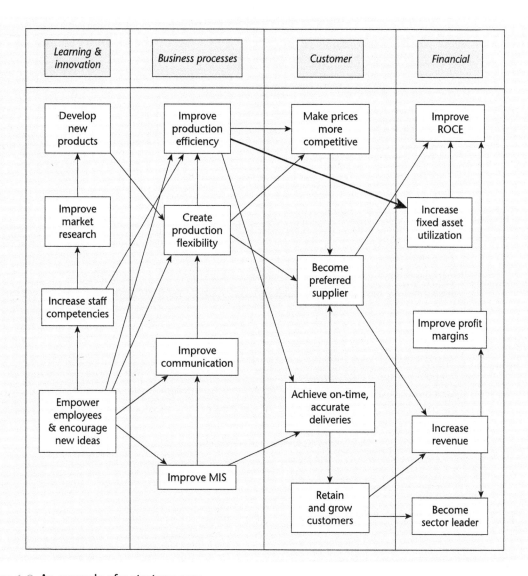

Figure 1.8 **An example of a strategy map**

arrows showing the linkages; note that one of these is thicker than the others. This is to point out that, although most linkages are between adjacent perspectives, they are not restricted to this pattern. An improvement in production efficiency should lead to an improvement in the utilization of fixed assets (assuming the extra capacity created is utilized).

A multinational pharmaceutical company

This example is of a real existing veterinary pharmaceutical company operating internationally in Europe with a multi-million pound turnover. The lead management team were proactive towards managing their performance and decided to investigate the possible use of balanced scorecards. Following a pilot scheme concentrating on the customer/marketing perspective only, it introduced a BSC whose perspectives followed the standard model. However, only two perspectives had 4 objectives; the other had 3 objectives each (14 in total). The 'master' BSC was easily displayed on one side of A4 paper; each perspective had three columns: Objective, Status and Owner (see Figure 1.9). The targets (which incorporated the KPIs) were shown on a separate page, one for each perspective. The whole thing printed out on five pages of paper.

Although this design deviates substantially from Kaplan and Norton's generic model, the main emphasis of monitoring non-financial key success factors is at the heart of the system. The status column consists of blocks of 'traffic-light' colours showing the current state of achievement for each of the key success factors. A green colour signifies that the objective is well on the way to being achieved, red indicates that there is much work still to be done and yellow means that a medium amount of progress has been achieved. Although this approach lacks sophistication, it does make it very easy to see the areas where management should focus their attention. It communicates very effectively.

The company took advantage of the inherent flexibility of the BSC management model to create a scorecard tailored exactly to its own needs. It reviews its choice of key success factors annually but the status and the target levels are updated quarterly. After operating the system described above for a year, it decided to condense the BSC from five pages to one page by showing simplified targets within the four perspectives. Also, the number of objectives was reduced to 2, 3, 3 and 4 (12 in total). The idea of this was to communicate a significant amount of key data as efficiently as possible and in a memorable form.

FINANCIALS	Status (green/yellow/red)	Owner (manager's name)
1.1 Achieve plan		
1.2 Double-digit vet products sales growth		
1.3 Price increase 3%		

INNOVATION	Status (green/yellow/red)	Owner (manager's name)
2.1 XY franchise: new EU regulations		
2.2 Food animals: no timeline slippage		
2.3 Companion animal: 2 submissions/year		
2.4 Affiliates: 3 launches per year		

ORGANIZATION & CAPABILITIES	Status (green/yellow/red)	Owner (manager's name)
3.1 Productivity improvement – Apply new business model		
3.2 Shaping environment: – No barriers to sales		
3.3 Customer service > 98%		
3.4 Regulation & business compliance – No issues		

SALES & MARKETING EXCELLENCE	Status (green/yellow/red)	Owner (manager's name)
4.1 Generics: 20% increase in market share		
4.2 Species teams		
4.3 Marketing plan targets and message kick-off		

Figure 1.9 **Scorecard front page used by multinational veterinary pharmaceutical company**

'Tesco's steering wheel'

Source: CIMA, *Insight*, 2005

'In the 1990s Tesco was third in the UK retail market and losing market share. The recession had hit performance hard and Tesco was purely a food retailer with no operations outside the UK. Tesco subsequently turned around. It became the UK's preferred supermarket (third in the world), reporting a pre-tax profit of £2 billion for the year ending 26 February (a rise of 21 per cent) and 13 per cent growth to £7.6 billion total international sales in 2004.

Tesco then formulated its "steering wheel" approach. This is its own customized balanced scorecard. It communicates strategy-aligned goals and manages strategic performance. It monitors progress and measures success. The organization's core purpose – "to create value for our customers and to earn their lifetime loyalty" – has been delivered on a clear and simple strategy of long-term growth.

This strategy underpins Tesco's four operational elements:

- core UK business;
- non-food business;
- retailing services;
- international operations.

Tesco's steering wheel framework comprises four perspectives – people, customer, financial and operations. Each is driven and monitored by demanding but achievable business targets. Throughout Tesco's retail operations, every store has its own individual steering wheel, to which all staff members' objectives are linked, and which relate strategy to day-to-day work. At every organizational level, where the KPIs are not on track and targets are not being met, the steering wheel group investigates the reasons why, and plans corrective action.

Performance is reported quarterly to Tesco's board and a summary report is sent to the top 2,000 managers in the company to pass on to staff. Further, the remuneration of senior managers is shaped by KPIs, with bonuses based on a sliding scale according to the level of achievement on the corporate steering wheel.

Tesco's values and priorities (concerning customers, staff, business, and compliance issues) are embedded in the steering wheel through appropriate KPIs. These values pervade operations and are instrumental in securing staff commitment to the steering wheel. It is arguable that, by embedding its values in the steering wheel, Tesco transformed its balanced scorecard from a management framework to a cohesive living strategy.'

Successful implementation of a balanced scorecard

Introducing a balanced scorecard into an organization is not merely replacing one system with another. More often than not, it involves a change in corporate culture. It involves increased communication, genuine participation, genuine empowerment, more training and increased costs. Maybe this is why many attempts to introduce balanced scorecards fail. Balanced scorecard systems seem deceptively simple so it is assumed that they are easy to implement.

Two researchers in the Netherlands, Lewy and du Mee, looked into the difficulties of implementation and produced the following 10 pieces of advice:

1 Use the scorecard as the basis for implementing strategic goals, since its visibility makes it the ideal vehicle for doing so.
2 Ensure that your strategy is in place before developing the scorecard, as ad-hoc development will encourage undesirable behaviour.
3 Ensure that the project is sponsored at senior management level.
4 Run a pilot project before full implementation.
5 Scorecards should be designed to meet the specific needs of business units; the generic scorecard should not be used without appropriate adaptation.
6 Introduce the scorecard gradually to each business unit only after its design has been tailored to its needs.
7 Do not use the scorecard as a method of hierarchical control.
8 Do not underestimate the need for training and communication.
9 Do not overcomplicate the scorecard by striving for perfection. It will never be 100% right, so do not delay its implementation by searching for better indicators.
10 Do not underestimate the costs of recording, administrating and reporting.

Strategy formulation

The fundamental role of the balanced scorecard is in strategy interpretation and realization, not in strategy formulation. However, the four-perspective structure can be used as a guide in the formulation process. The four generic questions shown in Figure 1.10 demand thought about the actions necessary to achieve good business performance.

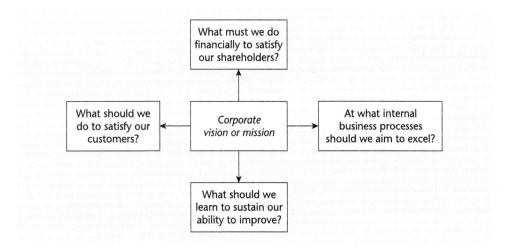

Figure 1.10 **Strategy-guiding questions**

They should be answered in the context of the corporate vision/mission which embodies the long-term aspirations of the business. (The results recorded by the balanced scorecard will also enable the strategy formulators to reflect on the appropriateness of their choices.)

In connection with the International Federation of Accountants (IFAC), the Chartered Institute of Management Accountants has created a 'Strategic Scorecard' to help companies decide their strategy. Like the balanced scorecard, it has four perspectives/dimensions; however, they are very different in nature. They are:

STRATEGIC POSITION	STRATEGIC OPTIONS
STRATEGIC IMPLEMENTATION	STRATEGIC RISKS

The objective is to help top-level managers to ask appropriate and relevant questions which guide them to formulate effective strategy. Although very different, this links to the balanced scorecard through the 'Strategic Implementation' dimension.

Multiple benefits

As discussed above, the major objective of Balanced Scorecards is to align organizational and personal objectives and activities in order for the organization to achieve continuous improvement through effective strategy implementation.

However, Otley (2006) lists the following 12 areas where Balanced Scorecards can make a significant additional contribution to improved business performance:

1 clarifying organizational vision;
2 gaining consensus around the organizational vision;
3 communicating goals and educating employees;
4 setting goals;
5 linking rewards to performance measures;
6 setting targets;
7 aligning strategic objectives;
8 allocating resources;
9 establishing milestones;
10 articulating the shared vision;
11 supplying strategic feedback;
12 facilitating strategy review and learning.

Financial incentives

If the performance of the business is expected to improve when employees meet their personal balanced scorecard targets, it seems sensible to offer them an incentive to do so. If bonuses are awarded on this basis, management is seen to be committed to this performance management system and the degree of success is heightened. Although this sounds straightforward, in practice it can be complicated. Deciding which set of measures to use and their weighting in the bonus calculation is inherently subjective and open to criticism. The danger here is that, after all the hard work of implementing a balanced scorecard system, the employee may be demotivated if he thinks he is being treated unfairly. However, this can be countered by operating a transparent reward system involving consultation and discussion.

An intended consequence of financial incentives is that people will strive to achieve their targets. An unintended consequence is that some will bend, or even break, the rules in order to get their cash bonuses. Human nature is such that, given a choice between behaviour beneficial to shareholders and that beneficial to themselves, most people will choose the latter. There is much evidence of this in traditional budgetary control systems where the playing of 'budget games' is common. When businesses introduce balanced scorecards, they should expect that some 'scorecard gaming' will occur. It would be naïve of them to assume that the new system would change basic human behaviour. When designing the reward system, they should be careful not to make the incentives *too* attractive. Consider the words of W. E. Deming:

> *People with sharp enough targets will probably meet them even if they have to destroy the company to do so.*

A note of caution

It is not unusual for organizations to have a balanced scorecard as well as a traditional budgetary control system. This has been described by Jeremy Hope (co-founder of the Beyond Budgeting movement) as 'similar to driving a car with two steering wheels!' While this is not impossible, extremely high levels of driving skills are essential to avoid things going badly wrong. The risk of accidents is increased.

There are several reasons why these two different strategy implementation devices should not be used simultaneously. First, they may contradict each other, allowing managers to choose which one to follow as best suits them at any particular time. This may let them off the 'responsibility hook'. Secondly, when contradictions do occur, confidence in management systems will diminish and managers will be demotivated. Lastly, significant amounts of resources will be used unnecessarily, maintaining two systems attempting to achieve the same objective, and profits will be adversely affected. Unambiguous clarity of direction is a great help in improving performance.

If both systems are used simultaneously, extra care must be taken to ensure their financial metrics do not contradict each other. However, this raises the 'old chestnut' of the difficulty of using the same numbers as targets and plans. Using both variance analysis and balanced scorecards does seem to cause an excessive use of resources.

Limitations

Choice of strategy

The use of balanced scorecards concerns enabling organizations to gain competitive advantage by implementing corporate strategy resulting in constantly improved performance. This descriptive definition indicates two areas where this management model is vulnerable. The first is getting the strategy right: choosing the activities with the most potential and doing them in the most effective order. Strategy is about doing the right things in the right way. The second critical area is the quality of the information system: choosing the best performance indicators and providing accurate, timely, summarized information in a flexible form.

Getting the strategy right is a perennial problem. Even when the indications are that you have got it right and results are improving, it is dangerous to sit back and become complacent. The business environment is constantly changing and competitors are continually looking for ways of gaining competitive advantage over you. Strategy review and formulation should be a continuous activity of high-level managers. However, it is a fact of business life that they do not always get it right. Business performance depends on the quality of the chosen strategy.

Quality of the information system

Also, the quality of the management information system is crucial; it needs to be appropriate, accurate, up-to-date and user-friendly. The following questions should be asked on a regular basis. Is the information systems strategy appropriate for the operation of the balanced scorecard? Is the hardware network sufficient to support corporate needs? Is the data management system flexible enough to meet frequent changes in information requirements? Is the right data being collected? How reliable is the **external** data collected? Are systems maintenance and modification easy to achieve? The answers to these questions will indicate the effectiveness of the system.

Cause and effect relationships

The nature of the relationships between different perspectives and between different objectives has been described above as one of 'cause and effect'. You may be surprised to know that this is an assumption rather than a fact. Most readers will intuitively have felt comfortable with the relationships discussed earlier, for example that a significant shortening of the sales order processing period automatically always leads to an increase in customer satisfaction or that increased customer satisfaction automatically always leads to increased profits. However, these relationships have never been proved to be those of cause and effect; they could be based on correlation rather than causation. The achievement of corporate objectives indicates that the desired outcomes were likely to be achieved rather than 100% guaranteed.

However, if the cause and effect relationship does not actually exist, use of the balanced scorecard may lead to dysfunctional behaviour and sub-optimal performance. Managers may perform inappropriate actions based on balanced scorecard information. Also, it is worth noting that, if employee reward incentive schemes are based on achieving balanced scorecard targets, any dysfunctional effects are likely to be exaggerated.

Time lags

The information on a single balanced scorecard is divided into four sections by perspective but all of it relates to the same period of time. None of the specific items in any of the four perspectives are causes or effects of specific items in any other perspective. For example, the objectives stated in the 'customer' perspective should lead to different financial performance levels from those shown in the financial perspective of the same scorecard. The latter should be a result of the 'customer' objectives on the previous scorecard.

Also, the complexity of reality may contradict the assumed cause and effect relationships. For example, to gain market share as quickly as possible, a business may adopt a market penetration strategy entailing the initial selling of products at or below variable/marginal cost. This may result in a profit decrease in the next financial period but an over-compensating increase in the period after that.

Subjectivity

Because balanced scorecards are designed and actioned by people, the choice of objectives, performance indicators and target levels will be subjective to some extent. Designers will be influenced by their past experiences and will attempt to project these into a future which will always contain a degree of uncertainty. In other words, their assumptions will not always prove correct.

Semantics and language

It is inevitable that communication within organizations always contains some management-speak jargon. However, words can be interpreted differently by different people. To take a basic example, if an objective was stated as 'increase sales', would this refer to sales volume or sales revenue? If this was not made clear, confusion could easily occur.

Management guru ethos

Peter Drucker (himself a management guru!) said that an important part of a manager's job is to think clearly about the business and that this task was far from easy. He followed this up by saying that adopting management fads/fashions without specific justification was a common excuse for not thinking. Balanced scorecards fit this description as well as other popular management models (TQM, BPR, etc.). Norreklit and Mitchell summarize this very well in their chapter on balanced scorecards in the third edition of *Issues in Management Accounting*:

The world of organizational management is not a well-ordered, rational world. Managerial actions such as introducing new techniques like the balanced scorecard may be motivated by more than the immediate search for profit. They may reflect managers' personal needs to be seen to be changing things, to resemble admirable others, to acquire legitimacy by employing the latest techniques, and to retain flexibility in the ways information is used within their organizations.

The manager's point of view (by Gary Burmiston)

In this increasingly competitive environment, organizations introduce scorecards to answer two vital questions which take up a vast amount of management time:

- What is good performance?
- How do we measure good performance?

Unfortunately, like every other management accounting technique, its 'correctness' is dependent upon how a scorecard is designed, implemented and used.

Many hours of soul searching take place throughout organizations to arrive at that brief, highly focused and insightful report that tells everyone in the company how well it is performing and identifies the areas that need to be addressed to improve performance further.

The reason that many hours are spent is because a good balanced scorecard is not easy to arrive at. Senior managers today can be presented with tomes of information on a daily, weekly and monthly basis and it is part of their job to decipher all the information and identify the key messages, enabling them to make the right decisions. But can the performance of a multinational, multi-billion pound, multi-product company really be distilled into 12 or 15 key performance indicators without losing the intricacies of performance that are important to individuals?

It could be argued that, at the highest level, ROCE should be used to measure an organization's performance and in many cases it is. But, for most people in the organization, ROCE fails on one key issue, its *relevance*.

To measure performance effectively and to expect people across an organization to respond to performance issues, they have to understand how what they do affects the results of the business. It is at this point that ROCE can begin to fall down. An operator on a production line may accept a loss rate of, say, 2% as that is what has been achieved historically and so is accepted as standard performance. But would the impact on ROCE be known if he were to reduce that loss rate to 1.7%? Similarly, would a salesperson know the impact on ROCE if she were to offer an extra discount of 5% to achieve a sale? In both cases the answer is probably 'no'.

Balanced scorecards are used to present information over a wide range of key performance indicators, financial and non-financial, to give an all-round picture of the organization's performance. By giving this all-round picture it is hoped that it becomes relevant to most people within an organization. The word 'hope' is used deliberately as there are frameworks for setting up a balanced scorecard, as highlighted earlier in the chapter, but the key to a successful scorecard is that it picks up on those indicators which truly drive an organization's performance. This is where the debate and management time should be spent.

In a number of organizations I've worked in, the introduction of a balanced scorecard has been a long and protracted affair. There is a desire to keep the performance indicators to a minimum but everyone has their favourites which they feel are important. At one organization, starting from a desire to highlight the top 20 performance indicators to the Board on a weekly basis, the discussions have moved on and the current balanced scorecard currently contains over 50! This is not what Kaplan and Norton envisaged over 15 years ago. The reasons for so many indicators are down to the types of information that is presented and the behaviours demonstrated by senior managers.

Some indicators are there just as background information. These are not needed, but even senior managers and directors like the comfort of knowing. They will argue they get too much information, but try and take information away from them and the debate will really start. Some indicators are there highlighting performance but the ability of managers to act upon and influence them over a short time horizon is limited. Again, it's not really necessary to report on a weekly basis something that takes four months to turn around and is based on an organization's strategic direction.

The best performance indicators are those that can be improved before the next report is issued. Very good balanced scorecards contain only this type of indicator. They succeed in being both relevant to individuals and also demonstrating how decisions are linked to results. Unfortunately, experience shows that such scorecards are in a minority and managers still gain a sense of comfort from too much information, even if they do complain about it.

Once the balanced scorecard has been constructed the key thing to determine is what to compare the actual performance indicators against; what results would suggest the organization is performing well?

Good performance is very subjective and down to the ambition, desires and wants of the senior leaders of an organization. Good performance could be to stand still in a difficult environment, to improve on last year's results, to beat key performance indicators of local competitors, to be seen as best-in-class in their own field or even to be judged to be a world-class company by both peers and non-peers alike.

The key to a good balanced scorecard is being able to compare actual results, in a timely manner, against expectations (whatever they may be) and ensure the right people have the ability to make decisions that can influence those results. Having this will drive improved performance. Reporting numbers which are irrelevant to individuals, who cannot influence them, will not produce any improvement in results.

It is without doubt that a balanced scorecard can be an incredibly powerful and insightful tool for reporting and improving an organization's performance. It is also true that it can be an expensive and resource-sapping total waste of time. The key to getting it right is spending the time to understand the drivers of performance in an organization and making those drivers relevant. By doing so, people at all levels in an organization will know the part they play in its success and are likely to behave in a way that contributes to that success.

Summary

Should balanced scorecards be part of a book on management accounting? After all, three of the four perspectives deal with non-financial information. To answer this question, it is necessary to ask why management accounting exists. The fundamental reason is to provide managers with relevant, timely, accurate information to help them improve company performance. The mechanism is illustrated in Figure 1.4. Why, then, is performance management still perceived by some people as not really directly concerned with **accounting**? To answer this I can do no better than to quote the last words of the seminal text *Relevance Lost: The Rise and Fall of Management Accounting* (Johnson and Kaplan, 1987, Harvard Business School Press, Boston):

> *For too many firms today, however, the management accounting system is seen as a system designed and run by accountants to satisfy the informational needs of accountants. This is clearly wrong. Accountants should not have the exclusive franchise to design management accounting systems. To paraphrase an old saying, the task is simply too important to be left to accountants. The active involvement of engineers and operating managers will be essential when designing new management accounting systems.*

> *Contemporary trends in competition, in technology, and in management demand major changes in the way organizations measure and manage costs and in the way they measure short- and long-term performance. Failure to make the modifications will inhibit the ability of firms to be effective and efficient global competitors.*

To finish, it is worth adding another quote to the above, this time from Charles Darwin, author of the famous theory of evolution, in his book *Origin of the Species*:

> *Those who respond quickly, thrive, those that do not, die.*

The way forward

It is in the interest of all organizations to re-examine and adapt their management systems continuously to ensure their effectiveness. Thoughtless repetition of business activities is no longer an option for successful organizations in the twenty-first century.

The management of business performance is a journey not a destination.

If you have not already done so, you will probably enjoy reading *The Goal* by Goldratt and Cox (2004). This is all about continuous improvement and is all the more interesting being written in the form of a novel.

Fundamentally, business performance management is about continuous improvement and the best advice I can offer for achieving this is: **be open to new ideas.**

Appendix: three popular business performance strategies

In the 'Practical application' section earlier in this chapter, Figure 1.5 illustrated how popular strategies could be incorporated into a balanced scorecard. This appendix gives a brief introduction to these strategies:

- total quality management;
- benchmarking;
- just-in-time.

1 Total quality management

The aim of total quality management (TQM) is to improve continually the quality of the product. 'Quality' is a difficult concept to define and several definitions exist. However, the following is one of the most useful:

A quality product is one that meets the requirements of the customer.

This practical definition is useful in that it enables the degree of quality to be measured or estimated, provided the customer requirements are known. Of course, the operation of TQM has a cost. As much as they would like to, firms cannot spend endless amounts of money on improving quality. To help them decide how much they are prepared to spend on this, they need to understand the various cost elements involved.

The cost of quality is complex (see Figure 1.11) but, in simple terms, it consists of:

- the cost of preventing poor quality occurring in the first place;
- the cost of dealing with poor quality items after they have been produced.

There is a trade-off between the costs of **prevention** and those of **cure**. The more that is spent on prevention and appraisal, the less has to be spent on putting things right, and vice versa. Many firms believe that the cost of conformance is likely to be less than that of non-conformance. This is understandable when you consider some of the costs of external failure (i.e. failure occurring after the product has been received by the customer). These include the loss of customer goodwill and future orders. Although impossible to quantify precisely, these may be justifiably described as **potentially very significant**.

Cost of conformance	Cost of non-conformance
Prevention costs	*Internal failure costs*
– engineering and designing of product for quality	– cost of scrap
– engineering and designing of process for quality	– cost of reworking
– training of employees	– reinspection
– statistical process control	– failure investigation
– preventive maintenance	– cost of lost production
– etc.	– etc.
Appraisal costs	*External failure costs*
– sample preparation	– loss of sales revenue
– sample testing	– warranty claims
– test reporting	– loss of future orders
– purchase and maintenance of test equipment	– loss of customer goodwill
– quality audits	– making good customer losses
– etc.	– product recalls
	– law suits
	– etc.

Figure 1.11 **The component costs of quality**

Unfortunately, customers are not always explicit about their requirements. This being so, the providing firm will have to decide how much to spend on quality. One way of going about this is to ascertain the combined cost of conformance and non-conformance for different degrees of quality (at a given level of production). The point at which the combined cost is at its minimum is the point of optimum quality, from a cost point of view, for the producing firm (see Figure 1.12). However, it should be recognized that some amount of rectification, internal and external, will probably arise when operating at this level of quality.

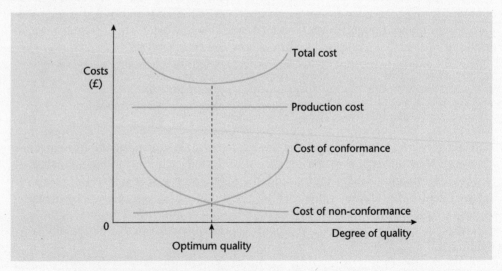

Figure 1.12 **Finding the optimum degree of quality (for a given activity level)**

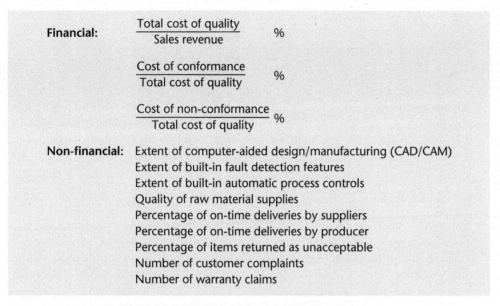

Figure 1.13 Financial and non-financial indicators used in TQM

Of course, the curves drawn in figure 1.12 are based on the assumption that all the costs are known. In reality, many of them are subjective and based on estimates. So how does a firm know if it is improving its quality? It needs to choose some performance criteria that will indicate whether or not this is so. Some of these performance indicators will be financial and others will be non-financial. Figure 1.13 lists a selection of them.

One of the principal aims of TQM in a mass-production environment is to achieve zero defects. Admittedly, this performance standard is a theoretical ideal but it does ensure that the search for quality improvement is ongoing even when significant milestones have been reached. When a firm achieves a failure rate of one item per million for its output it can be justifiably proud of its achievement. However, it should not rest on its laurels but strive for further improvement, say, one defect per 10 million. TQM is not just a technique, it is a managerial philosophy, attitude or 'way of life' embodying the idea of continuous improvement or *kaizen*.

2 Benchmarking

Benchmarking is all about performance measurement and review. Its fundamental aim is the achievement of competitive advantage by learning from the experience of others. The process involves several different organizations comparing certain aspects of their performance with each other. (It can also be used for independent divisions of one company.)

When considering this for the first time, firms are usually wary of participating for fear of competitors having access to confidential information, other participants benefiting more than themselves and company-specific factors reducing the usefulness of the exercise. However, it is possible to overcome these objections by using similar companies which are not direct competitors, concentrating on processes rather than results and looking at problems common to all the participants.

Examples of similar companies not in direct competition are illustrated by the following groups:

- *Retail consumables*: toiletries/household cleaning materials/home decorating supplies/pet food.
- *Retail hardware*: cooking utensils/DIY tools/gardening equipment/car accessories.
- *Charities*: National Society for the Prevention of Cruelty to Children, Royal Society for the Prevention of Cruelty to Animals, Cancer Research, Royal British Legion, Royal National Institute for the Deaf, Royal Society for the Prevention of Accidents.

Topics for discussion and investigation may include the following:

- *Personnel*: roles, responsibilities, organizational structure.
- *Planning and control*: frequency and timeliness of budget reports, reporting level, thresholds for investigating variances, motivation mechanisms, committees, meetings.
- *Information systems*: user-friendliness, access levels, hardware, software, liveware, strategies for information management, e.g. using one company-wide database management system.
- *Communication channels*: briefing/cascading meetings, newsletters, appraisals, suggestion boxes, notice boards, intranet websites, publication of short-term results.
- *Financial management*: debtors collection period, creditors payment period, stock turnover period, gross profitability, overhead types to sales ratios.

The Xerox Corporation was an early adopter of this technique. Together with other members of its benchmarking group, it looked at research and development, factory layout, quality management, marketing, distribution channels, sales order processing and information systems.

The analysis of the information would be along the following lines:

- What things are we doing well?
- Which activities do we need to improve?
- What should we be doing that we are not doing now?

However, it is important that 'better' practices are not blindly followed without thought being given as to why they are successful in other firms. Good practices are not always directly transferable. Hopefully, different participants will obtain different benefits from this exercise. Some may gain insights into improving their information systems while others may become aware of possible improvements to their communication systems. Ideally, the benchmarking process will prove to be mutually beneficial. If nothing else, it usually provides the participants with a greater understanding of their external environment. Benchmarking is increasing in popularity and is not confined by national barriers.

3 Just-in-time

The common perception of just-in-time is that its main objective is the elimination of stocks. Those who operate it know that it embraces much more than this. A more complete list of its objectives includes the achievement of:

- zero defects;
- zero waste;
- zero inventory;
- zero lead times;
- continuous flow processes;
- flexible manufacturing.

The first four of these lend themselves to measurement by performance indicators.

Just-in-time systems are most suitable for high-volume, repetitive manufacturing, although they can be adapted for less repetitive manufacturing. They work best when the manufacturing schedule is stable for reasonably long periods of time (months rather than days). On the production line, the system operates by each workstation requesting materials to work on from the previous workstation. This is referred to as a 'pull' system and no workstation is allowed to 'push' its output down the line to the next operation. The mechanism by which this is achieved is the 'kanban' system. A kanban is simply a request for some output from the previous station. It is often in the form of a container **sent by** one station and used to transport the work-in-progress from the previous station to the requesting station. In this way, work is pulled down the line.

Just-in-time is active in the following four areas of manufacturing:

- product design;
- process design;
- human/organization elements;
- manufacturing planning and control.

Product design uses value engineering to reduce the number of components used. It builds in achievable quality at appropriate levels. Where possible, it uses modular designs with parts common to other products and enables manufacturing to take place in flexible production cells with self-directed work teams.

Process design aims to make use of flexible manufacturing cells. It builds in preventative maintenance schedules and reduces machine set-up times to a minimum. In common with TQM, it uses computer-aided design/manufacturing (CAD/CAM), built-in fault-detection features and automatic process controls. Stock-holding areas are eliminated so that any unrequested work-in-progress is immediately seen as a problem demanding a solution. There is a famous saying, 'Inventory is like water in a river, it hides problems that are like rocks.' Get rid of the water and the rocks can no longer be ignored.

The human element is a holistic approach encouraging the use of **all** the employees' skills. This implies continuous training in new skills, including problem solving, and a flexible, multi-skilled labour force. The difference between direct and indirect labour is reduced – if not eliminated – and teamwork is encouraged. Employees are encouraged to use their brains as well as their bodies to achieve production goals. Computing power is made available to employees at the point of work to help them monitor their own performance and create solutions to their problems. This approach is sometimes known as *total employee involvement* or *empowerment*. Decision making is devolved to the people at the sharp end of the production process, leaving managers to tackle more strategic issues.

Manufacturing planning and control aims at continuous, rapid-flow, small-batch manufacturing but strictly within the confines of a 'pull' system. The use of kanbans encourages paperless, visual systems to control workflow. JIT software is commonly available to assist in the production planning process and this is usually interfaced with a materials resource planning (MRP) program. One advantage of this approach is that it reveals the costs of the 'hidden factory', i.e. those jobs and systems that are not really necessary and add no value to the products under a JIT environment. For example, in non-JIT manufacturing it is not unusual for 'progress chasers' to be employed to expedite specific orders for certain customers. This activity is unnecessary when production is planned and continuously monitored. Another very important aspect is the supplier relationship. The concept of the right-quality raw materials being delivered to the right place at the right time is central to JIT. It is common for raw materials not to be inspected on delivery. If defects do occur, the supplier is expected to rectify the situation immediately. If necessary, the manufacturer will send a team of its own employees to help with this process. It is no longer seen as essential to buy materials at the lowest possible price. The quality and reliability of supplies are more important. The two parties work together in a kind of partnership to their mutual benefit.

This has several implications for the management accounting information system. Traditional variance analysis can actually work against the successful operation of JIT. Purchasing the cheapest materials will give the most favourable price variance, but the low price may be due to the poor quality of the materials. Asset utilization ratios can be positively misleading as they encourage continuous usage of machinery producing for stock. Direct labour hours are no longer an appropriate basis for the apportionment of overheads. New performance indicators are required to monitor and enforce the JIT system.

Further reading

Atkinson, A., Banker, R., Kaplan, R. and Young, S. (2001) *Management Accounting*, 3rd edition, Prentice Hall, Harlow. See chapter 'Management accounting and control systems for strategic purposes: assessing performance over the entire value chain'.

Bauer, K. (2005) 'KPIs: avoiding the threshold McGuffins', *DM Review*, Vol. 15, Issue 4, April.

Bourne, M. and Neely, A. (2002) *'Cause and Effect'*, Financial Management, September.

CIMA (2005), 'Making your balanced scorecard work harder', *Insight*, June. www.cima-global.com/insight

Davis, S. and Albright, T. (2004) 'An investigation of the effect of balanced scorecard implementation on financial performance', *Management Accounting Research*, Vol. 15, 135–53.

DeBusk, G. K., Brown, R. M. and Killough, L. N. (2003) 'Components and relative weights in utilization of dashboard measurement systems like the balanced scorecard', *The British Accounting Review*, Vol. 35, 215–31.

Dilla, W. N. and Steinbart, P. J. (2005) 'Relative weighting of common and unique balanced scorecard measures by knowledgeable decision makers', *Behavioral Research in Accounting*, Vol. 17.

Drucker, Peter, (2006) *Managing the Non-Profit Organisation: Principles and Practices*, HarperCollins.

Gering, M. and Rosmarin, K. (2000) 'Central beating: succeeding with the balanced scorecard means moving on from central planning', *Management Accounting*, June.

Horngren, C., Bhimani, A., Datar, S. and Foster, G. (2002) *Management and Cost Accounting*, 2nd edition, Prentice Hall Europe, Harlow. See Chapter 19, 'Control systems and performance measurements'.

Kaplan, R. and Norton, D. (1996) *The Balanced Scorecard*, Harvard Business School Press, Boston, MA.

Kaplan, R. and Norton, D. (2001) *The Strategy-focused Organization: How Balanced Scorecard Companies Thrive in the New Business Environment*, Harvard Business School Press, Boston, MA.

Kaplan, R. and Norton, D. (2001) 'Transforming the balanced scorecard from performance measurement to strategic management', *Accounting Horizons*, 15, 87–104.

Melynk, S. A., Stewart, D. M. and Surink, M. (2004) 'Metrics and performance management in operations management: dealing with the metrics maze', *Journal of Operations Management*, Vol. 22, 209–17.

Norreklit, H. (2000) 'The balance on the balanced scorecard: a critical analysis of some of its assumptions', *Management Accounting Research* 11(1), 65–88.

Norreklit, H. and Mitchell, F. (2007) 'The Balanced Scorecard' – Chapter 9 in the book *Issues in Management Accounting*, 3rd edition, edited by Hopper, T., Northcott, D. and Scapens, R. FT Prentice Hall, Harlow.

Otley, D. (2006) 'Trends in Budgetary Control and Responsibility Accounting', Chapter 13 of *Contemporary Issues in Management Accounting*, edited by Bhimani, A., Oxford University Press, Oxford.

Prickett, R. (2004) 'Balanced Scorecard provides ROI', *Financial Management*, December/January, p. 4.

Smith, M. (1999) *Management Accounting for Competitive Advantage*, LBC Information Services, Pyrmont, Australia.

Smith, M. (2000) 'Strategic management accounting: the public sector challenge', *Management Accounting*, January.

Smith, M. (2005) 'The balanced scorecard', *Financial Management,* February.

Ward, A. (2005) 'Implementing the balanced scorecard at Lloyds TSB', *Strategic HR Review*, Vol. 4, Issue 3, March/April.

Whittle, N. (2000) 'Older and wiser', *Management Accounting*, July/August.

Williams, K. (2004) 'What constitutes a successful balanced scorecard?', *Strategic Finance*, Vol. 86, Issue 5, November.

Woodley, P. (2002) *Ship Shape*, Financial Management, June.

Chumpy Lighting Ltd

Introduction

Chumpy Lighting Ltd manufactures a wide variety of light bulbs which it sells to lighting shops and builders merchants through wholesale distributors. It also sells direct to the big UK supermarkets. It is situated in a small town a few miles from the city of Durham in the north-east of England where it has been making light bulbs for domestic use for more than 40 years. Five years ago, it diversified into bulbs for industrial lighting, using its wholesale distributors, in an attempt to grow its revenue. It currently employs 550 people and has an annual turnover of £125 million, making it the fifth largest producer of light bulbs in the UK.

Just over six months ago, it was taken over by a multinational electrical products company, Eindnacht GmbH, based in Germany. Since then, the new owner has been reviewing the operations of its UK acquisition. Last week, the managing director of Chumpy Lighting received a confidential report from its parent company detailing the review's findings. In summary, most comments were critical and highlighted areas where Chumpy's performance has been declining. In conclusion, Eindnacht has given them two years in which to demonstrate a significant improvement in performance. If this does not happen, the manufacturing will be transferred to other Eindnacht factories in mainland Europe.

The managing director, Harriet Thompson, summoned her fellow directors yesterday to an extraordinary management meeting to discuss the report and the demands made by their new owners.

Organizational structure of Chumpy Lighting Ltd

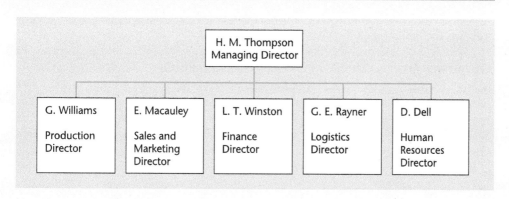

Summary of Eindnacht's report on Chumpy Lighting Ltd

Products

Chumpy Lighting serves two distinct lightbulb market segments, domestic and industrial. No new products have been launched in either sector in the last two years. Twelve years ago, in response to a growing market, the 'Alpha' range of 20 different low-energy long-life domestic bulbs was introduced. A significant investment in new plant and machinery was made to produce this range. The traditional tungsten filament light bulbs were phased out over two years from the introduction of the alpha range which now accounts for 100% of domestic bulb production. The 'Beta' range of industrial bulbs was introduced five years ago in an attempt to achieve increased sales and profits. There are now 154 different bulbs in this range.

Production

On the basis of 'number of bulbs produced', the alpha and beta ranges account for 73% and 27% of production respectively. Production facilities are used Mondays to Fridays from 08.00 to 17.00 with operatives allowed a morning and afternoon break of 15 minutes each and a one-hour lunch break. The factory is closed for five weeks each year during which holidays must be taken.

The last new product, the 'Everlasting Halogen Spotlight' (EHS) bulb, aimed at the industrial security sector, was launched by Chumpy Lighting just over two years ago. Unfortunately, due to a manufacturing fault, the EHS was prone to overheating and had a high failure rate. On several occasions, the EHS exploded causing potential physical danger to anyone in the vicinity at the time. Fortunately, only one serious injury occurred and a damaging legal case was only avoided by a significant out-of-court settlement being made to the injured person. Although much negative publicity was avoided, negative rumours concerning product safety circulated in the industry. A product recall had to be performed and the EHS production process had to be redesigned to correct the fault. This resulted in a five-month gap before the EHS was re-launched. It is estimated that this and the attendant bad publicity caused a 5% fall in annual sales revenue from the beta range for that year in addition to the very significant cost of the recall operation.

Marketing and sales

It is estimated that the domestic bulb market is worth approximately three times as much as the industrial bulb market.

Domestic: Apart from the last year, spending on advertising and promotion has shown very little variation in monetary terms (indicating a reduced spend in real terms). During this period, sales volumes have increased by an average of 2% a year. However, the market size of low-energy long-life domestic bulbs has increased by 8% a year on average over the same period. Selling price increases have generally matched general inflation at around 2% a year except for an increase of 5% two years ago in an attempt to boost revenue. Superficial changes and new packaging were introduced at this point in an attempt to reposition the alpha bulbs. Unfortunately, this strategy does not seem to have worked; the loss in volume caused by the price increase appears to have countered the extra revenue gained from higher prices in an increasingly competitive market.

Industrial: During the first three years of its life, the 'Beta' range of industrial bulbs approximately doubled its sales each year until the EHS recall. Due to an increased spend on advertising and promotion, sales have now recovered to the level immediately prior to this incident. For the last decade or so, this market sector has increased by about 3% a year.

Customer satisfaction

Domestic: Retailers (via our wholesalers) tell us that their domestic customers think the alpha range bulbs look dated and overpriced compared with those of their competitors. The wholesalers themselves are not too happy with the 35 days' average time it takes to deliver their orders. Apparently, there is only one other manufacturer who is slower than Chumpy so the company is not the automatic first choice of most suppliers. Sales order processing times are approximately twice as long as the 21 days taken by the company's best competitor.

Industrial: A telephone survey of 'heavy' customers showed a decrease in confidence regarding the product quality of 'beta' bulbs over the last two years although their prices are seen as reasonable.

Employee satisfaction

The anonymous Employee Satisfaction Survey commissioned by Eindnacht raised some issues of concern. The level of motivation is low and the staff turnover rate is currently 6% a year (5% last year).

Production efficiency is driven by the current production bonus scheme which is based on the number of bulbs produced by each operative in given time periods. Quality inspection takes place later, in the receiving area of the warehouse. Over the last three years, the proportion of rejected bulb production has increased from 3.6% to 5.4% with a commensurate increase in the cost of wastage.

Financial performance

Although sales revenues have increased for three of the last four years, operating profit has fallen slightly each year over the same period. Also, the Return on Capital Employed has reduced from 14% to 11% a year. The ROCE required of its subsidiary companies by Eindnacht GmbH is a minimum of 18% a year.

Summary

Chumpy Lighting's present management has been given two years to meet the standards set by its parent company, in particular to reach an 18% return on its capital employed. If this is not achieved, the UK site will face closure and production will be relocated, probably to mainland Europe. There will be an interim review after 12 months to gauge the extent of progress made.

Extracts from management meeting

Mr Winston, Finance Director

A RoCE of 18% is asking a lot! That's not far off double of last year's 11%. There's going to have to be a huge joint effort from all of us; efficiency is certainly going to have to improve significantly. And the quality of our bulbs – that's going to be fundamental.

Mr Williams, Production Director

OK, I'm already working on that. I keep trying to impress the importance of bulb quality to our workforce. They all say they understand but then they work as fast as they can to maximize their bonuses. If we scrapped the bonus scheme, the output quantities would plummet; we couldn't keep up with demand.

Ms Macauley, Sales and Marketing Director

You can't do that. We would lose sales by the thousands. Word would get round that we can't supply and we would lose even more. We've got to maintain our supplies to our customers, especially the big ones. Our quality control means that the bulbs we send out are OK; well, most of them anyway.

Mr Williams, Production Director

Most of our machinery is 12 years old or more now, breakdowns are common and maintenance costs are increasing all the time. Even more important, our technology is well out-of-date. Our best machine can only turn out 300 bulbs an hour and I know that our competitors are all using much more modern and efficient equipment. We need to invest in some new machinery. That will give us the efficiency you want – with fewer operatives – and the cost per unit should come down at the same time. That should help with our profitability.

Mrs Dell, Human Resources Director

Are you saying we will need fewer operatives? Morale is not very high at the moment and redundancies won't do anything to improve it. We've lost two of our best supervisors in the last three months; it takes time to train good people and they are a bit thin on the ground right now. When rumours of redundancies start going round, it's usually the best people who leave first.

Frankly, I think our production bonus scheme aimed at individual operatives is out of date. I'd like to introduce more team-working with teams competing against each other and league tables of performance published monthly for all to see. You would have to empower them to devise their own methods but this has the effect of boosting morale. The received wisdom is that this can dramatically increase productivity. It would also get round the problem of finding good supervisors as you wouldn't need them any more. You could let each team select its own leader, which would again be good for morale.

Mr Winston, Finance Director

Well, if we are going to reach 18% RoCE, we are going to have to get our costs down somehow, and quickly. What about reviewing our suppliers? I can't remember when we last had a price decrease from any of them. Except for one, they are all based in the UK; I'm sure we can get our material costs down by sourcing from China or eastern Europe.

Mr Williams, Production Director

That's all very well but what about reliability? It's no use paying less if they send you rubbish.

Ms Thompson, Managing Director

Yes, I understand that but plenty of other businesses do it. I think a review of material sourcing is a good idea. It's essential that we become more competitive. We need to act on several fronts, and with the minimum of delay. We may be able to improve our profitability by undercutting our competitors. If we can get more volume by bringing our prices down, the contribution from each extra sale is pure profit. If a 10% reduction in cost and selling price gave us a 25% increase in volume, I reckon that would add a few percentage points to our profitability right away.

Ms Macauley, Sales and Marketing Director

I'd like to agree with you but, in my experience, a 10% price reduction would soon be matched by our competitors and we would just start a price war which would do none of us any good. I think we are going to have to be more subtle than that. We need to work on our image and increase sales that way, get customers to think of us as their first choice supplier . . . and get some new customers too.

Mr Rayner, Logistics Director

We could make our wholesalers happier if we delivered in the strict order we received our sales orders in. But you know as well as me that when one of the big supermarkets places one of their huge orders, we have to give it priority or they won't come back – we know that for a fact. So all the other orders in progress are put on one side until we get theirs out of the way. It's only the relationships we've built up with the wholesalers over many years that keeps them coming back. If I were them, I'd certainly be looking elsewhere; and I think more and more of them are doing just that. Isn't there any way we could increase our productivity without increasing costs? An extra delivery lorry wouldn't do any harm either.

Mr Williams, Production Director

We looked at working a two-shifts-a-day system a few years ago and decided we couldn't justify it. Maybe we should look at it again. Perhaps we could introduce weekend working or some sort of more complex flexible working arrangements.

Ms Macauley, Sales and Marketing Director

There is one avenue we haven't explored yet – the Internet. Selling directly to the public is a very different approach. Although we would probably end up poaching some of our own sales from the supermarkets, it could give us access to many more new customers and a much bigger market. But it would need a significant investment in the necessary technology and, in view of the timescale, we would have to buy in some expertise. In the circumstances, I think this is a risk we have to take. If we do it right, it could secure our future.

Mr Winston, Finance Director

That sounds great but I am somewhat concerned about the effects of all this expansion on cash flow. Our liquid ratio is now at an all-time low of 0.7:1.0. I think we ought to get it back up to 1.0:1.0. We must avoid the overtrading trap or we really will be done for.

Ms Thompson, Managing Director
Well, if we want to stay in business, we need to do something and we need to do it soon. If the figures don't show a significant improvement in a year's time, it's going to be bad news all round.

Tasks:

1 Create a balanced scorecard for Chumpy Lighting Ltd in the form of a diagram; show clearly your chosen perspectives, objectives, key performance indicators and target performance levels. Summary draft action plans should also be shown.
2 From your balanced scorecard, create a Strategy Map for Chumpy Lighting Ltd. Start by identifying the cause and effect relationships between the objectives.

Review questions

1   Describe the theory and structure of the balanced scorecard.
2   Describe the internal 'lead' and 'lag' relationships between balanced scorecard components.
3   Explain the different relationships in 'for-profit' and 'not-for-profit' organizations.
4   Explain the advantage of involving front-line staff in balanced scorecard design and operation.
5   Draw a diagram to show how corporate strategy can be implemented through the balanced scorecard.
6   Give examples of how popular strategies would appear on the balanced scorecard.
7   Explain the flexibility of balanced scorecard design.
8   Describe the process of cascading scorecards within organizations.
9   Describe the process of employee involvement in the operation of scorecards.
10   Explain how a strategy map can be created from a balanced scorecard.
11   Explain how the scorecard approach can help with strategy formulation.
12   Describe the multiple benefits of operating balanced scorecards.
13   Explain the role of financial incentives connected to balanced scorecards.
14   Describe the limitations of balanced scorecards.

The answers to all these questions can be found in the text of this chapter.

Part 2 Accounting

## Chapter 2

Performance evaluation and feedback reporting

This case study shows a typical situation in which management accounting can be helpful. Read the case study now but only attempt the discussion points after you have finished studying the chapter.

Overall performance – Shell scorecard

Shell uses a number of key performance indicators to evaluate the overall performance of Shell from a financial, efficiency, social and sustainable development perspective and collectively they represent the Shell scorecard. In addition, Shell monitors and manages the businesses by means of detailed parameters. The scorecard highlights four key performance indicators which together provide a summarised overview of Shell's performance. These are measured on a quarterly and annual basis. As explained on page 86 in the Directors' Remuneration Report, the scorecard is also used to determine remuneration for staff, Senior Management and Executive Directors.

Total shareholder return (25 per cent scorecard weighting)
Total shareholder return (TSR) is measured as the sum of the difference between the share price at the start of the year and the share price at the end of the year, plus the cash value of dividends paid during the calendar year (gross and reinvested quarterly). The TSR is compared against other major integrated oil companies and provides therefore a benchmark of how Shell is performing against its industry peers.

Net cash from operating activities (25 per cent scorecard weighting)
Net cash from operating activities is a measure that reflects Shell's ability to generate cash for investment and distributions to shareholders. The Consolidated Statement of Cash Flows on page 117 shows the components of cash flow. The net cash from operating activities for scorecard purposes is adjusted for taxes paid on divestments.

Operational excellence (30 per cent scorecard weighting)

Within each of the different businesses, operational performance is measured by means of detailed parameters that are combined into a business dashboard. The four key operational indicators for the businesses are production for Exploration & Production and Oil Sands, LNG sales for Gas & Power, refinery availability for Oil Products and technical plant availability for Chemicals (both corrected for uncontrollable incidents such as hurricanes). In 2008 the measure for Oil Products was changed from 'unplanned downtime' to refinery availability to provide focus on two critical areas namely turnaround management and reliability.

Sustainable development (20 per cent scorecard weighting)

As well as measuring financial performance and efficiency, Shell uses various indicators to evaluate Shell's contribution to sustainable development. This Report discusses on pages 64–68 the priorities with regards to staff and environmental data such as greenhouse gas emissions, use of flaring and energy use in its businesses and assets. Safety remains a key topic for Shell and is measured by the number of injuries and fatal accidents, as discussed on page 69. The main metric for assessing our performance in the area of sustainable development is total recordable case frequency (TRCF). See page 69 for further discussion of TRCF.

Source: Royal Dutch Shell, Annual Report, 2008, p. 56.

Discussion points

1 What is the mix of financial and non-financial performance measures mentioned in this extract?

2 How easy would it be to measure the performance of an individual against these targets?

Learning outcomes

After studying this chapter you should be able to:

- Distinguish feed forward control from feedback control.

- Explain the main features of performance reports.

- Explain how performance evaluation is carried out.

- Explain the use of benchmarking in performance evaluation.

- Explain and give examples of non-financial performance indicators.

- Explain the nature and use of the Balanced Scorecard.

- Understand how management may set standards of performance and reward achievement of standards.

- Describe and discuss examples of research into performance measurement.

2.1 Introduction

This management accounting text has been based throughout on the view that those who manage a business have a need and a desire to make informed judgements and decisions. In a continuing cycle of management action, there will be a judgement, from which a decision will be formed, followed by evaluation of that decision and a new judgement based on that evaluation. The stage at which the decision is evaluated requires management accounting to exercise its score-keeping function by devising quantitative measures of performance. It also calls on management accounting to direct attention to those areas most urgently requiring a judgement and a further decision.

Planning is sometimes referred to as **feed forward control**. This means making predictions of outputs expected at some future time and then quantifying those predictions, in management accounting terms. The budgetary process is an example of a management accounting approach which has a feed forward (or planning) aspect. Feed forward control systems are very effective, if carried out well, because they anticipate problems rather than wait for them to happen.

Budget variance analysis is a technique for control in comparing the actual outcome with the standard expected. This is sometimes referred to as **feedback control**. This is useful for looking back at what went wrong (or what went well) and for taking corrective action to ensure that a problem does not continue.

This chapter considers in more depth feedback control, which involves comparing outputs achieved against outputs desired and taking corrective action if necessary. To provide this type of control it is essential to identify the responsibility for the costs and for taking whatever action is required. The term **responsibility centre** is used to identify the unit to which a feedback report is to be made. A responsibility centre could be a cost centre where the individual manager has responsibility only for costs, a profit centre where the individual manager has responsibility for costs and revenues, or an investment centre where the individual manager has responsibility for costs, revenues and investment in assets.

Definitions

> **Feed forward control** means making predictions of outputs expected at some future time and then quantifying those predictions, in management accounting terms.
>
> **Feedback control** involves comparing outputs achieved against outputs desired and taking corrective action if necessary.
>
> **A responsibility centre** is an area of responsibility which is controlled by an individual. It might be a cost centre, a profit centre or an investment centre.

In any control process, whether feed forward or feedback, there are three essential elements:

1 There must be objectives which state the aim or purpose of the control.
2 There must be a model which can be used to predict an expected outcome.
3 There must be power to act in order to take corrective action.

In addition, for feedback control there must be the ability to measure the actual outcome on the same basis as the predicted outcome.

For a feedback control system to be effective, the following basic principles should be observed:

(a) the benefits from the system should exceed the costs of implementing it;
(b) the performance criteria being measured should be reported promptly so that rapid action may be taken;

(c) reports should be as simple as possible and readily understood;

(d) reports should highlight the significant factors requiring management attention;

(e) the reporting framework should be integrated with the organisational structure so that responsibility is identified correctly.

The operation of feedback control will be explored in this chapter in relation to short-term decision making. First, in this chapter we discuss the nature of the report to be written for performance measurement purposes.

2.2 Preparing performance reports

There are three basic questions in relation to report preparation:

1 To whom should the report be addressed?
2 What should be reported?
3 How frequently should the report be presented?

2.2.1 To whom should the report be addressed?

In the context of the management of responsibility centres, the report should be addressed to the manager in charge of the responsibility centre. That could be a cost centre, a profit centre or an investment centre. If the report is to have meaning for the manager concerned, it must include only those costs which may be controlled by the manager of the responsibility centre.

The level of detail in the report will be influenced by the managerial position of the person to whom it is addressed. Reports to senior management will be condensed so that those managers can see the broader picture. They will of course also have access to the more detailed reports, should they so wish.

2.2.2 What should be reported?

The report should be designed to identify clearly those items that are controlled by the manager of the particular responsibility centre. If the responsibility centre controls the price and quantity of an item, then both should be reported and the combined effect quantified. If the responsibility centre controls quantity but not the price of an item, then the report should be designed to emphasise the quantity aspects of transactions in the reporting period.

It could be that, despite a lack of direct responsibility, it would be helpful for the manager of the responsibility centre to be aware of all the costs incurred as a result of the activity of the centre. If that information is felt to be useful, then it could be included in the report, but subheadings would be required to make clear the distinction between controllable and non-controllable costs.

The design of the report is extremely important because the manager of the cost centre, profit centre or investment centre will not use the report effectively if it does not provide useful information in a helpful manner. Managers should be consulted on design of reports, and there should be trial periods of experimentation with a new design of report before it comes into routine use. Graphs, bar charts and pie diagrams may be ways of communicating more effectively than through tables of figures alone.

2.2.3 How frequently should the report be presented?

The frequency of reporting should be related to management's information needs. There may be a need for information on a daily basis. Computers provide on-screen access to information so that the traditional concept of a reporting period, with a printed report at the end of each period, may no longer be appropriate in all circumstances. There is, however, a danger in reporting all items too frequently. Reports have to be read and acted upon, and reporting which occurs too frequently could result in too much time being spent on the review activities.

The question of frequency of reporting is perhaps best answered in terms of the frequency of the cycle of review and corrective action. If daily action is required in an operation, then daily provision of information about the activity will allow corrective action at the earliest possible opportunity. If a monthly review cycle is more appropriate, then the reporting system should be designed to provide monthly summaries. It is vitally important that, whatever the frequency chosen, the reports are produced in a timely manner.

If a computer is in use to record costs and quantities, then the program used should be such that the reports required are generated as part of the process so that there is no delay in transferring information for reporting purposes.

2.3 Performance evaluation

Performance evaluation requires the management accountant to carry out the following process:

- Decide on what to measure.
- Plan how to report.
- Consider the behavioural aspects.

2.3.1 What to measure

In looking at what to measure, we will draw on aspects of management accounting which lead to a measure of performance. Because each management accounting technique serves a different purpose, the decision on what to measure will also depend on the intended purpose and will be discussed in the context of specific applications.

2.3.2 How to report

In planning how to report, the general principles applied will be those of responsibility and the separation of **controllable costs** and **non-controllable costs**. All costs are controllable at some level of management, but they may not be controllable at a lower level. Breaking down cost into the separate elements of quantity and price, the extent of control may vary for each element. There will be those in the organisation who have authority to acquire resources, thus controlling quantity and price. There will be others whose job it is to make use of the resources acquired, in which case they will control only the quantity element of cost. There will be others again whose job is to find the best price for resources. They will control only the price element of cost.

It is important to distinguish controllable from non-controllable costs when seeking to establish responsibility for costs. Frequently, the responsibility will be shared, and it is important that the sharing is correctly identified.

Definitions   A **controllable cost** is a cost which is capable of being regulated by a manager within a defined boundary of responsibility.

A **non-controllable cost** is one which is not capable of being regulated by a manager within a defined boundary of responsibility, although it may be a cost incurred so that the responsibility may be exercised.

Performance reporting is partly concerned with planning and control, so the idea of controllable and non-controllable costs is important. However, it is also applied in decision making, and further classifications into relevant/non-relevant and avoidable/unavoidable costs may therefore also be used within the same report.

When a decision is taken there is usually more than one option available. **Avoidable costs** are those costs that may be saved by not taking a particular option. **Unavoidable costs** will not be saved by such an action.

Definitions   An **avoidable cost** is one which may be eliminated by not taking a particular option.

An **unavoidable cost** will not be eliminated by taking a particular action.

2.3.3   Behavioural aspects

Performance evaluation has behavioural aspects because measurement of performance has a direct impact on the organisation's perceptions of how its staff are performing and on the individual staff member's perception of his or her relative performance. As a general guide, favourable reactions to performance reporting are likely to be maximised if staff are made aware in advance of how the performance measures will be calculated and how the responsibility for costs will be allocated. If the individual has control over quantities and prices, then that person should be regarded as having control over, and responsibility for, that item. If the individual has control over quantities but not prices, then it may be appropriate to report the cost to that individual but only regard responsibility as extending to the quantity aspects. If the individual has no control over quantity or price, then no responsibility for the cost of that item can be identified, although there may be a separate question of whether that item should be reported to the individual in order to heighten awareness of the impact of non-controllable costs.

Activity 2.1

You are the team leader for a group of social workers who specialise in dealing with the needs of elderly persons in their homes. You have been told by your line manager that your team's budgeted spending limit will be exceeded by the end of the year if you continue with the present level of activity. The major items of cost are: team members' salaries, travel to clients' homes for visits and a charge from the local authority for the provision of office facilities. Salaries have increased because of a national pay award not allowed for in the budget. Travel costs have increased over budget because of fuel price increases. The local authority has kept the charge for office facilities within the budget. Your line manager has some discretion to make savings under one expense heading to match overspending under another. How will your team explain its performance in the end-of-year report?

Budgets may be used for cost control by way of variance analysis. There also needs to be a concern with the human implications of variance analysis. It may be that the variance analysis approach is seen as a means of managerial review of subordinates, in which favourable variances receive praise and adverse variances are seen as a cause for corrective action to be taken. That approach may have undesirable consequences for a number of reasons:

1   Employees may reject standards because they were not adequately consulted in setting them.
2   Those under review may divert their efforts into minimising the adverse variances rather than making positive steps towards overall performance improvement.
3   Negative feedback may reduce motivation, leading to reduced effort and lower performance levels.

Those who are concerned at these negative aspects of variance analysis have suggested that there may be a need for accounting systems which are less evaluative in approach. The emphasis should perhaps move to learning and improvement rather than stressing personal responsibility, accountability and past achievement. Later in this chapter there are some ideas about performance measurement using non-financial measures which may be more relevant than financial measures at the individual manager level. First, however, a case study is used to illustrate the traditional variance analysis approach to performance evaluation and control.

Activity 2.2

You are the financial manager of a school where some teaching departments are spending more than their budget allowance on materials and others are being frugal and spending less. It is six months into the financial year and you would like to give a warning to the overspenders, but also find out why there are underspenders. Suggest two ways of dealing with this problem, of which one way would probably create friction between yourself and the teachers, while the other would encourage the teachers to work with you in controlling the overall budget for the school.

2.3.4   Case study: evaluating and reporting performance

Fiona McTaggart now explains a situation where she prepared performance reports using flexible budgets and also shows how the performance report appeared in each case.

FIONA: *My client was in a manufacturing business which produced hand-crafted cane furniture. I was asked to devise a monthly performance reporting system which would provide performance measurement of the manufacturing activity. Three levels of reporting were required. The managing director required a brief summary of any matter requiring executive action but did not want all the details each month. The furniture supervisor needed a much more specific analysis of the performance of the activity as a whole and the relative performance of each employee. There was also a proposal to give each employee a personal performance statement that showed some indication of the average performance of the activity as a whole, without giving individuals access to information which was best kept personal to each employee.*

The budget was set at the start of the year based on average monthly output of 300 chairs and 80 tables. In practice the actual monthly output varied around this average. I recommended a three-column form of report which would show the original budget for one month's output, the flexible budget showing the costs expected for the actual level of output achieved and the actual costs incurred.

I made a list of all the costs incurred in making cane furniture. The main direct costs were materials and skilled labour. Although the employees were employed on full-time contracts, it was useful to identify separately the time they spent in productive activity making the furniture, which I classed as a direct cost, and the time they spent in non-productive activity, which I classed as an indirect cost.

I then listed all the indirect costs and subdivided them according to various levels of responsibility. Each employee was responsible for a portion of indirect materials used in

*fastening the cane together and was also responsible for a portion of equipment mainten-
ance and depreciation. This indirect cost was allocated in proportion to the output produced. It might sound rather hard that the employee's responsibility for cost increased as
the output increased, but it was decided in discussion that staff needed to be aware of the
costs incurred when productive output takes place. Individual employees would not be
regarded as being responsible for unproductive time unless they directly caused it as a
result of their individual actions.*

*The furniture supervisor was responsible for control of the total costs allocated to the
individual operative staff, plus the cost of non-productive time (to the extent that this was
in the control of the supervisor), and the overhead costs of heating and lighting the workshop area.*

*The managing director had ultimate responsibility for all costs, including the cost of
administration, providing adequate working conditions, the employer's share of employment costs and any non-productive work due to causes beyond the control of the furniture
supervisor.*

*Exhibit 2.1 shows how the performance report was designed. There were three separ-
ate parts to the report. The first was for individual members of staff. The second was for*

Exhibit 2.1
Monthly performance report: (a) employee report; (b) supervisor's report;
(c) managing director's report

Part A: Employee report	Name..............*Employee X*...............			
Date of statement	....			
	Budget	Flexible budget	Actual	Variance
Output: target/actual	100 chairs 20 tables	110 chairs 18 tables	110 chairs 18 tables	
Direct materials	. . .	. . .	. . .	. . .
Direct labour	. . .	. . .	. . .	. . .
Controllable indirect costs	. . .	. . .	. . .	. . .
Indirect materials	. . .	. . .	. . .	. . .
Total controllable costs for employee X	. . .	. . .	. . .	. . .
Cumulative controllable costs for year to date	. . .	. . .	. . .	. . .
Maintenance	. . .	. . .	. . .	. . .
Depreciation	. . .	. . .	. . .	. . .
Total for exployee X	. . .	. . .	. . .	. . .
Cumulative for year to date	. . .	. . .	. . .	. . .
Matters for attention Action planned				

Exhibit 2.1 **continued**

Part B: Supervisor's report	Name...			
Date of statement	....			
	Budget	Flexible budget	Actual	Variance
Output: target/actual	300 chairs 80 tables	320 chairs 76 tables	320 chairs 76 tables	
From Part A Controllable costs for each employee				
Costs of employee X	. . .	. . .	. . .	. . .
Costs of employee Y	. . .	. . .	. . .	. . .
Costs of employee Z	. . .	. . .	. . .	. . .
Total controllable costs				
Overheads				
Controllable indirect costs	. . .	. . .	. . .	. . .
Non-productive time	. . .	. . .	. . .	. . .
Heating & lighting	. . .	. . .	. . .	. . .
Matters for attention Action planned				

(In practice, this report would also include cumulative totals for the year to date, as shown on Part A, but they are omitted here so that the main features are more readily seen.)

the furniture supervisor, who also had access to the individual staff reports, and the third was for the managing director, who had access to the more detailed reports if these were required.

Each report set out the variances from flexible budget for each element of cost. At the foot of the report was a section for highlighting matters for attention and a space below for the person receiving the report to write a comment. In the case of individual employees, a comment was expected on any action planned in response to matters noted. This action plan would be discussed and agreed with the supervisor. In the case of the report to the supervisor, the comment was expected to show the action planned for the production activity as a whole, or for individual employees where there was a particular problem. In the case of the report to the managing director, the comment was expected to confirm discussions with the supervisor but also to note any action on indirect costs regarded as the managing director's responsibility.

We had a trial run of this reporting format for three months, to iron out any wrinkles, and during that time there were some difficulties in getting the overhead responsibility allocation right. Everyone denies responsibility for indirect costs but, at the end of the day, they have to be incurred and are an unavoidable consequence of business activity. It was eventually agreed that the direct cost allocation would remain, but that, for employees and the

Exhibit 2.1 **continued**

Part C: Managing director's report	Subject: *Cane furniture production*			
Date of statement	....			
	Budget	Flexible budget	Actual	Variance
Output: target/actual	300 chairs 80 tables	320 chairs 76 tables	320 chairs 76 tables	
From Part B				
Total employee controllable costs	. . .	. . .	. . .	. . .
Total indirect costs for which supervisor is responsible	. . .	. . .	. . .	. . .
Other overheads				
Administration	. . .	. . .	. . .	. . .
Employment costs	. . .	. . .	. . .	. . .
Abnormal non-productive time	. . .	. . .	. . .	. . .
Total				
Matters for attention Action discussed with supervisor				
(In practice, this report would also include cumulative totals for the year to date, as shown on Part A, but they are omitted here so that the main features are more readily seen.)				

supervisor, the emphasis would be on responsibility for the volume aspects of the allocation, with any external price increases being regarded as non-controllable or else a matter for discussion with the purchasing section.

Fiona's description has concentrated very much on the two questions of what to measure and how to report. Since she is describing the early stages of designing and implementing a new system, there is no information on the behavioural aspects of how the reporting system operated in practice. There is a description of the trial run and the extent to which the views of participants were taken into account in the design of the final report. The case study would need to be followed up after a period of, say, three months of operation, to find out how effectively the new system was achieving satisfactory control.

Activity 2.3

Read the case study again and identify the points at which Fiona McTaggart's actions match the principles of reporting set out in this chapter.

Real world case 2.2

The annual report of Punch Taverns 2008 included the following statement:

These financial results and the Company's share price performance have had a marked effect on remuneration; thus demonstrating the strong connection between performance and reward for the Company's Executive Directors:

– Executive Directors have received no annual bonuses for the current financial period.

The long-term incentive awards scheduled to vest in November 2008 have not met their performance conditions and have therefore lapsed. This demonstrates the strong connection between performance and reward for the Company's Executive Directors.

Contrast that statement with the 2004 annual report:

The bonuses for 2004 were been paid in the basis of the level of satisfaction of the performance targets. The table below shows the principal performance targets used for 2004.

Chief Executive Officer	*Finance Director*	*Chief Operating Officer*
EBITDA	EBITDA	EBITDA
Internal Financial Measures	Internal Financial Measures	Internal Financial Measures
Pubmaster Integration	Pubmaster Integration	Pubmaster Integration
EPS Growth	Debt Management	Operational Targets
Investor Relations	Investor Relations	Divisional Targets

(Note: EBITDA – earnings before deducting interest, taxation, depreciation and amortisation.)

Source: Punch Taverns, Annual Report 2008, p. 34 and Annual Report 2004, p. 30.

Discussion points

1 Why are there some targets that are similar and some that are different for each post-holder?

2 The detailed results of these ratios do not appear in either the 2004 annual report or the 2008 report. What are the possible reasons for confidentiality?

2.4 Benchmarking

Benchmarking is the name given to the process of measuring the organisation's operations, products and services against those of competitors recognised as market leaders, in order to establish targets which will provide a competitive advantage.

The stages of benchmarking are:

1 Decide what area of activity to benchmark (e.g. customer services, business processes in particular departments, quality of employees, standard of training).

2 Select a competitor who is reputedly the best in the area of activity to be bench-marked. Major companies in one country may target an international competitor rather than a domestic company. In some benchmarking situations the competitor may agree to an exchange of information because both parties believe they can benefit from the exchange.

3 Decide on the appropriate measurements to be used in defining performance levels.

4 Determine the competitor's strengths and compare these with the company's own record.

5 Use the information collected as the basis for an action plan. To be effective, this action plan must involve all grades of employee working in the area of activity.

The management accountant has a role throughout this process because the emphasis is on improving profit and measuring performance. The management accounting role starts with directing attention, by producing the performance measures and showing the relationship with profit improvement. It moves into problem solving as the information on comparative performance measures is collected and has to be transformed into an action plan for the organisation. It then takes on the score-keeping aspect as the achievement of total quality is monitored.

2.5 Non-financial performance measures

Within an organisation, people are employed to carry out specific activities. The only aspect of their work over which they have direct control may well be the volume and the quality of tasks they undertake. Applying revenues and costs to these activities may be important for the organisation as a whole, but will have little meaning for the individual employee who does not sell the goods or services directly and does not purchase the input materials.

To ensure that the motivation of employees is consistent with the profit objectives of the organisation, it may be necessary to use **non-financial performance measures** to indicate what is required to achieve the overall financial targets. Using non-financial performance measures does not mean that the financial performance measures may be disregarded. They are ways of translating financial targets and measures into some-thing that is more readily identifiable by a particular employee or group of employees.

The non-financial performance measures should cover both quantity and quality.

2.5.1 Quantity measures

It is necessary to convert the accounting numbers to some measure of quantity which relates more closely to individual members of an organisation. If the employees are involved in the entire productive process, then the financial target may be converted to units of product per period. That approach may be more difficult when a service activity is involved or a group of employees is involved in only part of a production process.

As an illustration of the problems of performance measurement in a service business, take an example of a school where activities are subdivided by subject area. The primary measure of activity will be the number of pupils taught, but the individual departments will have no control over that number. If teaching staff are appointed on permanent contracts, so that salary costs are largely fixed costs, then the cost per student will vary depending on the number of students taught in any period. A performance measure of cost per student may be attractive to the management accountant but will have little impact on the staff of the history department whose main aim is to ensure that their pupils achieve high grades in the end-of-year examinations.

For them, examination success rates are the prime performance measure and they will be concerned to ensure that fluctuations in pupil numbers do not affect that success rate. A performance report on the history department would therefore emphasise first of all the non-financial performance, in terms of examination success, but would then additionally report the cost implications so that the consequences of achieving a high, or a low, success rate could be linked to the cost of that activity.

2.5.2 Quality measures

The ultimate measure of quality is customer satisfaction. Companies will invest time and effort in measuring customer satisfaction, perhaps by questionnaire survey or possibly by telephone interview. Indirect measures of customer satisfaction may be found in complaints records, frequency of repairs under warranty and level of goods being returned as unwanted.

Another important aspect of quality is the process undertaken by the organisation. This is so important that an external agency (often the auditors) may be employed to provide independent certification of the quality of the process and the controls within the process.

Finally, quality is measured also in terms of the inputs to the process, where inputs may be materials, labour and capital equipment. Quality of inputs may be controlled directly by imposing standards on suppliers, or may be monitored by reviewing the rate of return of unsatisfactory goods, the non-productive time incurred because of faulty equipment, or the reliability of delivery dates and quantities.

Some examples of non-financial performance measures are:

1 In respect of demand for products:
   (a) number of enquiries per advertisement placed; and
   (b) percentage of customers who remember the advertisement.
2 In respect of delivering the products:
   (a) error-free deliveries as a percentage of total deliveries;
   (b) number of complaints as a percentage of units sold; and
   (c) time between receiving customer order and supplying the goods or service.

An electricity supply company provided the following information about non-financial performance over a one-year period:

Restore supply in 3 hours	Target	80%
	Performance	**83.8%**
Restore supply in 24 hours	Target	99%
	Performance	**99.9%**
Moving a meter inside 15 working days	Target	95%
	Performance	**96.7%**
Reply to telephone calls within 10 seconds	Target	90%
	Performance	**91.1%**

2.5.3 Key performance indicators

There has been increased interest from regulatory bodies in encouraging businesses to report externally the key performance indicators (KPIs) that are used internally. These are now found in some descriptions of reward schemes for directors and senior managers. The UK government planned for, but then rejected, compulsory reporting of KPIs. However, market pressure is likely to encourage companies to disclose more KPIs.

Activity 2.4

Write out five non-financial performance measures which could be reported by an organisation which delivers parcels to the general public and to businesses.

2.6 The Balanced Scorecard

Section 2.5 has illustrated some of the non-financial measures of performance that may be used alongside the financial measures. There is a danger of creating increasingly long lists of performance measures with no way of balancing the perspectives resulting from these different aspects of performance. Kaplan and Norton (1992) put forward an idea which they called the **Balanced Scorecard** as a way of linking performance measures. It focuses on the key goals of the organisation and the measurement of performance in achieving those goals.

They suggested that performance measurement can be viewed by asking four questions:

- How do our customers see us? (Customer perspective)
- How do our shareholders see us? (Financial perspective)
- How do we see ourselves? (Internal business perspective)
- Can we learn and grow to improve and create value? (Learning and growth perspective)

2.6.1 Presenting the scorecard

For each of these four questions the organisation should set major goals and define performance measures which demonstrate that the goals are being achieved. It might be reasonable to set three or four goals in each case. This would lead to a scorecard that would fit on a single sheet of paper. There is no specific form for the scorecard. Figure 2.1 shows an example. Here we see the management strategy being applied to set the goals for each section of the scorecard, and the performance measures being used to give feedback to management on how well the goals have been achieved.

Fiona now gives an example of work she has carried out to create a Balanced Scorecard system in a service business.

FIONA: *I have recently worked on designing a Balanced Scorecard for a company which owns a chain of hotels in major towns and cities around the country and wanted to evaluate the relative performance of the separate hotels. The hotels are designed to a standard model of 'no-frills' value for money and comfort, with secure parking for cars. Customers are likely to stay for one or two nights, either as business customers looking for convenience and reasonable pricing, or as families and tourists on short-stay visits. As this was the first attempt at creating a scorecard, we used only three goals for each aspect of the Balanced Scorecard. It was important to involve all staff in setting up the scorecard so we established focus groups in each city or town to give their input to the goals and measurements. Each focus groups included an operations manager, catering and cleaning staff and a regular customer. The result is set out in Exhibit 2.2.*

2.6.2 Scorecard in strategic management

Kaplan and Norton soon realised that the Balanced Scorecard was more than a performance report. It was a useful tool in the system of strategic management. They set out five principles for a strategy-focused organisation:

Figure 2.1
Creating a Balanced Scorecard

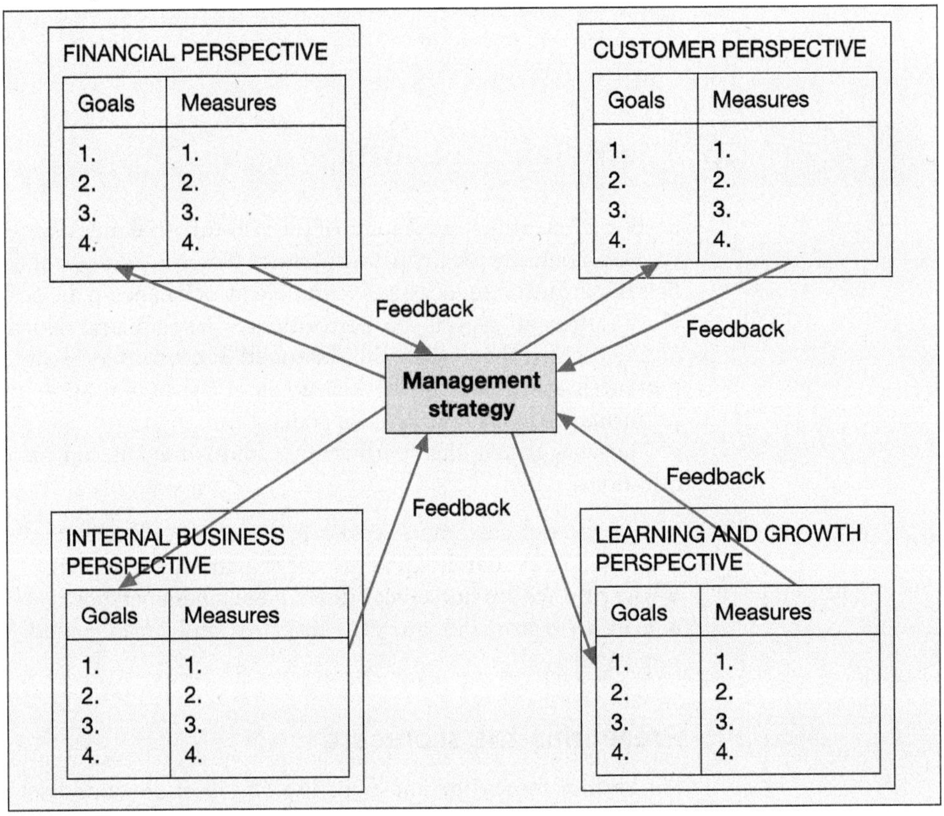

1 Translate the strategy into operational terms.
2 Align the organisation to the strategy.
3 Make strategy everyone's everyday job.
4 Make strategy a continual process.
5 Mobilise leadership for change.

This makes the Balanced Scorecard a tool of forward planning for change, as well as being a retrospective view of past performance. An important aspect of using the Balanced Scorecard is the involvement of employees in all stages of setting the scorecard and monitoring the outcome. It is flexible so that the Balanced Scorecard can be designed to be relevant to the organisation and its operations or procedures.

2.6.3   Criticisms of the Balanced Scorecard[1]

The Balanced Scorecard has attracted some criticisms.

- It is biased towards shareholders and fails to give adequate attention to the contribution of other stakeholders, particularly employees and suppliers.
- Because it does not give attention to the role of employees, it fails to consider aspects of human relations within the organisation. The Balanced Scorecard cascades down the organisation with little involvement from senior managers. This may lead to employee dissatisfaction.
- It does not help the organisation to define specific performance measures and does not help define how to use performance targets.
- It does not deal with strategic uncertainties.

To avoid these problems it is suggested that the scorecard should be used for implementing strategic goals, because of its visibility, but only after the strategy is set in place. The project must be supported actively by senior management and the scorecard must be explained when it is introduced. It must be tailored to the needs of the organisation rather than using a more general package. It must not be over-complicated and there must be sufficient time and resources for communication and training.

Exhibit 2.2

Creating a Balanced Scorecard for a hotel chain

Financial perspective	
Goal	*Measure*
1 To reduce unfilled room rate by 3% over the previous year, by offering discount for a third-day stay.	Marginal revenue from additional room occupancy, compared with marginal costs of creating that occupancy, with estimate of revenue lost on third-day discount.
2 To control fixed overhead costs within 3% overall increase on previous year.	Cost records – monthly update of fixed overhead actual cost against target.
3 To control variable costs per room per night at 50% of room charge.	Cost records – monthly report on variable room costs compared to room rents received.

Customer perspective	
Goal	*Measure*
1 To increase market share by 5% over 12 months.	Market share surveys published in trade journals, plus reports commissioned from benchmarking organisations.
2 That 50% of customers return for a second visit.	Customer satisfaction questionnaire left in bedroom plus follow-up telephone enquiry.
3 That 90% of customers express general satisfaction with the service, especially cleanliness and staff courtesy.	Customer satisfaction questionnaire left in bedroom plus follow-up telephone enquiry.

Internal business perspective	
Goal	*Measure*
1 To improve customer satisfaction by improving checkout times.	Number of checkouts completed between 7 a.m. and 9 a.m. each day.
2 To improve the cycle of laundry delivery and return from 4 days to 3 days, on average.	Records of laundry despatch and return.
3 To identify and implement one innovative practice.	Staff suggestion box – list of staff suggestions and note of actions taken to review and implement each.

Learning and growth perspective	
Goal	*Measure*
1 To achieve 60% participation of relevant staff in a vocational training programme.	Staff records of attendance and achievement in vocational training programme.
2 To empower staff in setting personal goals that are consistent with organisational goals.	Record of annual appraisal reviews where appraising manager confirms that personal development plans are consistent with organisational goals.
3 To improve internal communication process by weekly bulletin to staff.	Record of bulletin issues and staff feedback on relevance and usefulness.

Imagine that you are planning to start a business operating a taxi service. Write a Balanced Scorecard containing two goals and two measurements of achieving the goals for each of the four sections of the Balanced Scorecard (Customer perspective, Financial perspective, Internal business perspective and Learning and growth perspective).

2.7 Management use of performance measurement

This chapter has concentrated largely on how the management accountant may provide measures of performance. For such measures to have relevance in a managerial context, they should satisfy three criteria:

- There should be well-defined performance measures which represent a range of performance from bad to good.
- There should be defined standards of performance which indicate what is good and what is not good.
- There should be rewards attached to successful attainment of targets and penalties attached to non-attainment of targets.

Sections 2.7.1 to 2.7.3 present a case study bringing together the use of benchmarking and performance standards to achieve the objectives and strategy of the organisation. Section 2.7.4 explains a performance measurement method called 'Six Sigma' which is intended to improve results. Section 2.7.8 explains some of the particular features of performance measurement in public-sector organisations.

2.7.1 Performance measures

Fiona McTaggart describes a recent experience in establishing performance measures through benchmarking:

FIONA: *I have recently completed a project advising a parcel delivery business on establishing a performance measurement system for distribution depots spread across the country. The business has a series of warehouse depots at locations convenient to major towns. Parcels are carried by lorry from one depot to another so that the delivery targets are met with careful attention to cost control. The non-financial performance measure which most concerns customers is meeting targets. Other companies in competition with this company are also performance conscious and will publicise their performance in meeting delivery targets. The financial performance measure which most concerns management is cost containment in a competitive business. Depot managers find they are expected to have regard to customer delivery targets and cost control.*

My first task in advising the company was to contact a benchmarking expert in order to find out as much as possible about the competition. The expert had plenty of information on non-financial targets, including surveys undertaken by consumer organisations. The expert also had a broad outline of the cost structure of the leading operator in the field, which regards itself as a very well-controlled business.

Fiona emphasises here the importance of a **strategic-management** approach, looking beyond the organisation, and of understanding the effective limits on targets where there is an established leader in the field. In the next section she explains how the targets were set at a level which would be acceptable to depot managers while meeting customers' expectations.

2.7.2   Standards of performance

Standards may be set by an inward-looking process which builds on the management perception of the performance required to achieve desired goals. Demonstrating that such targets are achievable may require reference to the performance of previous time periods and of similar units elsewhere in the organisation. The competitive position of the organisation requires that standards are set by reference to performance in other organisations. That may be relatively difficult or relatively easy to obtain, depending on the relative secrecy or openness of the sector.

Fiona McTaggart continues her description:

FIONA: *After collecting all the information available, senior management decided they wanted depot managers to concentrate on: (a) performance as a profit centre; (b) delivery targets; and (c) sales and customer care. The system is now in place.*

Performance as a profit centre requires targets for sales and costs. Each depot had initial targets set by reference to average performance over the past three years. The national reporting of target achievement is achieved by concentrating on percentages above and below target.

Delivery targets are reported according to the depot which last handled a parcel before it reached the customer. However, where a delivery target is not met, it is permissible for the depot manager to produce a summary of documentation showing where a previous depot in the chain caused a delay. These summaries are reviewed by head office and a supplementary report prepared showing bottleneck situations.

Customer care is monitored by customer feedback questionnaires. These are sent out by head office and collected there. The questions concentrate on delivery target time, condition of parcel, attitude of company personnel and perceived value for money. Depot summary reports are prepared.

Weekly reports are provided for depot managers which summarise the performance of the specific depot and show rankings against other depots. A narrative commentary by the managing director makes specific mention of the highest and lowest performers and explains how well the company is performing in relation to competitors.

Fiona has indicated that a mixture of financial and non-financial performance measures is used to create a part of the Balanced Scorecard. In the next section she comments on the rewards and penalties.

2.7.3   Rewards and penalties

If there are no rewards and no penalties it may be difficult to motivate employees in relation to performance targets. One view is that self-satisfaction in personal attainment is sufficient reward. Equally it could be argued that personal shame in not achieving a target would be sufficient penalty. However, more may be required.

Rewards and penalties are often difficult to administer because they involve human relations. The input of the individual must be seen in the context of the contribution of a team. Achieving a goal of the organisation may require team effort where it is difficult to identify the relative contributions of each member of the team. That may be overcome in relation to rewards by ensuring that no team member is deprived of a reward. Application of penalties, however, is more difficult because employment law generally seeks to protect employees against unjust treatment.

Rewards and penalties are linked to motivation. It has been suggested by experts in the theory of motivation that there are different needs at different levels of employment. Initially the employee is seeking the basic satisfaction of food and shelter which a paid job provides. A secure job provides safety in the longer term. Working in an organisation with clear goals provides the security of membership of a group.

Developing personal potential in meeting performance targets leads to rewards of respect and praise. Taking a lead in meeting the goals of the organisation is evidence of realising one's potential. Studies of motivation have at various times emphasised achievement, recognition, challenge and promotion as aspects of rewards which motivate. Fairness (equity) is also seen as important, as is meeting expectations.

Fiona McTaggart completes her description of performance measurement in a transport company:

FIONA: *As I have already mentioned, the managing director writes a weekly letter to all depot managers noting in particular the best and worst performers. That gives a sense of achievement to some managers and perhaps shames others into moving up from the bottom of the league tables. There is also a real reward of an all-expenses-paid weekend break holiday for the best-performing manager over the year. The difficulty with league-table-type performance is that someone necessarily has to be bottom of the league, so while this system is motivating in a competitive sense, it has some negative aspects in that the performance measures are relative to other depots rather than relative to achievable targets. I have pointed out to the managing director that there may be some demotivating aspects to this system, but he is very keen on competition and survival of the fittest.*

Fiona has indicated that using performance targets for motivation is not an easy matter and depends very much on the personalities involved.

2.7.4   Six Sigma

Six Sigma is an approach to performance measurement that was initially developed by Motorola but is now advertised more widely by consultants. In statistics the standard deviation from the mean of a normal distribution (the bell-shaped curve) is usually represented by the Greek letter sigma σ. We know that 99.9 per cent of the area under the bell-shaped curve lies within three standard deviations either side of the central mean value. So we can say with 99.9 per cent confidence that a value lies within a total of six standard deviations, or 'six sigma'. The easy way to summarise this is to say 'we want to get things right 99.9 per cent of the time'.

If managers want to improve a particular aspect of a business, they choose a goal, measure how well the business is achieving at present, and then define improvements that will achieve the Six Sigma standard. The aim is to eliminate waste without destroying value.

It could be thought that mysterious titles like 'Six Sigma' are a veneer over a very obvious way to make improvements, but it is felt to have value because it emphasises a basic idea of continuous improvement.

2.7.5   Performance management in the public sector

The public sector covers central government, local government and bodies funded from public funds, such as the National Health Service and the many executive agencies. In all cases there is keen attention paid to performance management.

A long-established approach to measuring value-for-money in the public sector is to examine economy, efficiency and effectiveness.

- An economy measure involves considering and controlling the costs of inputs.
- An efficiency measure relates the costs of inputs to the benefits of outputs.
- An effectiveness measure asks whether the outputs of a programme achieve the desired outcomes of a programme.

Many bodies providing a public service set and report their own performance measures. Examples are shown in Exhibit 2.3.

Real world case 2.3

The UK government provides some of its services through executive agencies which are managed like private businesses but have to meet targets set by the Secretary of State and Ministers of State. The Driving Standards Agency (DSA) is one of these agencies, responsible for setting and operating driving tests. The following information is extracted from the 2008–09 annual report and accounts.

Appointments and waiting times

		2006–07	2007–08	2008–09
Appointments will be available within 9 weeks at 90% of permanent car driving centres (measured quarterly)	✓	99%	96%	95.5%
National average waiting time will be no longer than:				
Six weeks for a car	✗	5.5	6.4	6.1
Four weeks for a motorcycle	✗	3.5	3.7	4.7
Three weeks for vocational	✓	3.3	3.2	2.2

Financial target

DSA has been set a financial target of achieving a return on capital employed (ROCE) of 3.5 per cent of average annual net assets in the five-year period to 2008–09, having taken into account previous years' surpluses. After taking into account interest receivable, the actual level of ROCE achieved in the year was minus 2 per cent. Overall, cumulatively, the Agency is £8.1m ahead of its cumulative target having achieved a cumulative 5.9% ROCE.

Year	Return £m	Net assets £m	ROCE %
Brought forward from 2003–04	8.9		
2004–05	0.4	45.6	0.8%
2005–06	8.8	51.1	17.1%
2006–07	5.7	63.7	8.9%
2007–08	2.0	74.8	−2.6%
2008–09	2.0	97.1	−2.0%
Total	19.7	332.3	5.9%

Capital expenditure

Overall capital expenditure was £24.6m compared to a plan of £45.8m. Most of the slippage was attributable to the MPTC (Multi-Purpose Test Centres) project as bringing sites to fruition was challenging due to planning and site remediation issues. The MPTC project remains the most significant investment with £12m spent in the year. This brings the total capital investment to £51m, with £20m remaining to be spent in 2009–10 and subsequent years in order to complete the programme.

Source: Annual Report and Accounts 2008–09, DSA, pp. 10, 43, www.dsa.gov.uk.

Discussion points

1 What view might customers take of the achievements against the targets?

2 What is the possible link between delay in capital expenditure and achieving target waiting times?

Exhibit 2.3
Examples of performance measurement targets

An ambulance trust

During the year we were able to maintain response time performance above the national targets of reaching 75 per cent of life threatening calls attended within eight minutes and 95 per cent attended within 19 minutes. We also achieved financial balance. This is a great achievement and is entirely due to the professionalism and dedication of all our staff, and our community lay responders.

A service providing official documents in response to telephone and postal enquiries

● Answer 80 per cent of our telephone calls in 10 seconds, 90 per cent in 20 seconds and 95 per cent in 30 seconds.
● Achieve an abandon call rate of no more than 2 per cent of call volumes answered.
● Average time to answer of 6 seconds.
● Process standard written post order requests within an average of 2 working days of receipt.
● Deliver a service that achieves a benchmarked satisfaction score of 83.1 per cent.
● Achieve a fair outcome for customers when things go wrong and achieve less than 1 per cent of complaints received against overall dispatches.

A train operating company

Punctuality: 90 per cent of all trains Monday to Saturday in the published timetable to arrive within 10 minutes of their scheduled time at their final destination.
Reliability: 99 per cent of all trains Monday to Saturday in the published timetable to run.

Activity 2.6

How useful are performance targets of the type set out in Exhibit 2.3? How easy or difficult would it be for the organisations involved to be selective in presenting actual results that fall within the target? Is the achievement of the performance target sufficient to ensure a good quality of customer service?

2.8 What the researchers have found

Section 2.8.1 reports investigation of the benefits of the Balanced Scorecard. Section 2.8.2 explains the French view that their *tableau de bord* pre-dates the US creation of the Balanced Scorecard. Section 2.8.3 indicates steps to be taken in developing measures of corporate performance. Section 2.8.4 notes criticisms of performance targets in the public service.

2.8.1 Benefits of the Balanced Scorecard

Davis and Albright (2004) investigated whether bank branches implementing the Balanced Scorecard outperformed branches in the same banking organisation. They found evidence of superior performance in branches operating the Balanced Scorecard. The bank researched was in the southeastern United States. The southern division contained seven branches. The president of the southern division of the branch decided to implement the Balanced Scorecard after learning about it in a graduate management course. The researchers selected four branches in the southern division and compared them with five branches in the northern division that had not implemented the Balanced Scorecard. Nine key financial measures identified by the group management as performance measures were used to make comparisons.

The branches using the Balanced Scorecard outperformed the others. The researchers explained their reasons for believing that their findings could be attributed to the use of the Balanced Scorecard. However, it is possible that a division with a more enthusiastic managing director would achieve better results in any event. Perhaps the most persuasive evidence was the note that the managing director of the northern division later asked the managing director of the southern division to help set up a Balanced Scorecard.

2.8.2   American Balanced Scorecard vs French *tableau de bord*

Bourguignon *et al.* (2004) explain that the Balanced Scorecard is received with less enthuasiasm in France than in some other countries, because French companies have used the *tableau de bord* for more than 50 years. The authors show that the main differences between the two systems may be explained by differences in ideology. The US approach is built on contracts where individuals choose to be committed and to have a general moral claim to fairness. US managers create hierarchies of management. In France social hierarchy, obedience, legitimacy and security are matters of education and honour, not of management devices. The *tableau de bord* is designed for each manager's view of strategy. It does not require the rigid classifications imposed by the US model. The French authors emphasise learning from the *tableau de bord*. The US system focuses on rewards from the Balanced Scorecard.

2.8.3   Trends in corporate performance management

A Technical Briefing published by CIMA (2002*a*) reviews a range of initiatives in performance measurement. It lists the factors required for a successful performance management system as:

- It must be integrated with the overall strategy of the business.
- There must be a system of feedback and review.
- The performance measurement system must be comprehensive.
- The system must be owned and supported throughout the organisation.
- Measures need to be fair and achievable.
- The system needs to be simple, clear and understandable.

    It also lists some common issues raised with performance measurement systems:

- Key drivers of success are not easily measured.
- Behaviour is not in line with strategic objectives.
- The system conflicts with the culture of the organisation.
- The development process is too time-consuming or difficult.

    The Technical Briefing also summarises research into Value-based Management (as a broad-based heading which included Economic Value Added but also other methods of evaluating shareholder value); the Balanced Scorecard; Benchmarking; Strategic Enterprise Management and the Performance Prism (a three-dimensional view of performance devised at Cranfield School of Management, described on its website: www.performanceprism.com).

2.8.4   Criticisms of performance targets in public service

Performance targets are now widely used in the public service arena as a means by which government relaxes direct control of an activity, but still retains indirect control. CIMA (2002*b*) Technical Briefing explains how the modernised government agenda has applied to the executive agencies. These are agencies that carry out government policy under delegated day-to-day management. Key themes in setting targets are economy, efficiency and effectiveness. However, the critics say that the targets create the kind of bureaucracy that the agencies were set up to eliminate. It is suggested that staff spend more time on meeting and recording targets than they spend on the main activity of the agency. Rigid measurement systems provide areas for inventiveness in meeting targets and also encourage neglect of areas that are not being measured. There is also a danger that the targets are short-term because they are set by politicians who have a short-term perspective.

2.9 Summary

Key themes in this chapter are:

- **Feed forward control** means making predictions of outputs expected at some future time and then quantifying those predictions, in management accounting terms.

- **Feedback control** involves comparing outputs achieved against outputs desired and taking corrective action if necessary.

- A **responsibility centre** is an area of responsibility which is controlled by an individual. It might be a cost centre, a profit centre or an investment centre.

- The key questions to ask in designing a performance report are:
  - To whom should the report be addressed?
  - What should be reported? and
  - How frequently should the report be presented?

- The key stages in performance evaluation are:
  - decide on what to measure;
  - plan how to report; and
  - consider the behavioural aspects.

- It is important to distinguish **controllable costs** from **non-controllable costs** when seeking to establish responsibility for costs.

- **Benchmarking** is the name given to the process of measuring the organisation's operations, products and services against those of competitors recognised as market leaders, in order to establish targets which will provide a competitive advantage.

- A **Balanced Scorecard** has four perspectives: Customer perspective; Financial perspective; Internal business perspective; and Learning and growth perspective.

- **Non-financial performance measures** should cover both quantity and quality of performance. The measures should be related to the procedures under consideration. **Six Sigma** is explained as an example of a quantified performance target based on remaining within the 'tails' of the normal distribution. Performance management in the public sector focuses on economy, efficiency and effectiveness.

References and further reading

Bourguignon, A., Malleret, V. and Nørreklit, H. (2004) 'The American Balanced Scorecard versus the French Tableau de Bord: the ideological dimension', *Management Accounting Research*, 15: 107–34.

CIMA (2002a) *Latest Trends in Corporate Performance Measurement*, Technical Briefing. CIMA Publishing, download available on website www.cimaglobal.com.

CIMA (2002b) *Performance Management in Executive Agencies*, Technical Briefing, CIMA Publishing, download available on website www.cimaglobal.com.

Davis, S. and Albright, T. (2004) 'An investigation of the effect of Balanced Scorecard implementation on financial performance', *Management Accounting Research*, 15: 135–53.

Kaplan, R.S. and Norton, D.P. (1992) 'The Balanced Scorecard: measures that drive performance', *Harvard Business Review* (January–February): 71–9.

Kaplan, R.S. and Norton, D.P. (2001*a*) 'Transforming the Balanced Scorecard from performance measurement to strategic management: part I', *Accounting Horizons*, 15(1): 87–104.

Kaplan, R.S. and Norton, D.P. (2001*b*) 'Transforming the Balanced Scorecard from performance measurement to strategic management: part II', *Accounting Horizons*, 15(2): 147–60.

Merchant, K. and van der Stede, W. (2003) *Management Control Systems: Performance Measurement, Evaluation and Incentives*. Harlow: Pearson Education.

Simons, R. (1999) *Performance Measurement and Control Systems for Implementing Strategy: Text and Cases* (international edition). Upper Saddle River, NJ: Prentice Hall.

Smith, M. 'The Balanced Scorecard', *Financial Management* (2005), February: 27–8.

QUESTIONS

The Questions section of each chapter has three types of question. '**Test your understanding**' questions to help you review your reading are in the 'A' series of questions. You will find the answer to these by reading and thinking about the material in the textbook. '**Application**' questions to test your ability to apply technical skills are in the 'B' series of questions. Questions requiring you to show skills in '**Problem solving and evaluation**' are in the 'C' series of questions. The symbol [S] indicates that a solution is available at the end of the book.

A   Test your understanding

A2.1   Define 'feedback control' (section 2.1).

A2.2   Define 'feed forward control' (section 2.1).

A2.3   Define 'responsibility centre' (section 2.1).

A2.4   What are the three basic questions to be asked in relation to report preparation (section 2.2)?

A2.5   How does an organisation decide on the frequency of internal reporting (section 2.2.3)?

A2.6   What is required of the management accountant in carrying out performance evaluation (section 2.3)?

A2.7   Define a 'controllable cost' (section 2.3.2).

A2.8   Define a 'non-controllable cost' (section 2.3.2).

A2.9   Define an 'avoidable cost' (section 2.3.2).

A2.10 Define an 'unavoidable' cost (section 2.3.2).

A2.11 What are the behavioural aspects of performance evaluation (section 2.3.3)?

A2.12 Explain what is meant by 'benchmarking' (section 2.4).

A2.13 Explain the meaning of 'non-financial performance measures' (section 2.5).

A2.14 Give two examples of quantitative non-financial performance measures (section 2.5.1).

A2.15 Give two examples of qualitative non-financial performance measures (section 2.5.2).

A2.16 What are the four main aspects of a Balanced Scorecard (section 2.6)?

A2.17 Give one example of a goal and one example of a matching measurement for each of the four main aspects of a Balanced Scorecard (section 2.6).

A2.18   What are the benefits and problems of linking rewards and penalties to a performance measurement system in an organisation (section 2.7.3)?

A2.19   What is the 'Six Sigma' approach to performance measurement (section 2.7.4)?

A2.20   What have researchers found about the benefits of using a Balanced Scorecard (section 2.8.1)?

A2.21   What have researchers described as the factors required for a successful performance management system (section 2.8.2)?

B   Application

B2.1
Suggest six non-financial performance measures for a company which offers contract gardening services to companies which have landscaped sites surrounding their offices. Give reasons for your choice.

B2.2
Suggest three financial and three non-financial performance measures for a business which provides training in the workplace for updating wordprocessing and computing skills. Each training course lasts two weeks and there is a standard fee charged per trainee.

B2.3
Design a Balanced Scorecard for a restaurant business which owns three restaurants in the same town. Include three goals and three measurements of performance for each of the four aspects of the Balanced Scorecard, and write a short note justifying your choices.

B2.4 [S] [CIMA question]
A manufacturing company pays its employees a constant salary for working 35 hours each week. The production process is highly specialised and the quality of output is a critical factor. All completed units are inspected. Currently about 10% of output fails to meet the expected specification.

The managing director has forecast increasing sales and is keen to reduce the labour cost per unit of production. He has suggested three possible ways of achieving this:

1   improve direct labour productivity
2   increase the number of hours worked
3   reduce the rate of rejections

Which of the above suggestions would enable the company to reduce the labour cost per unit?

A   Suggestion 2 only.
B   Suggestions 1 and 2 only.
C   Suggestions 1 and 3 only.
D   Suggestions 2 and 3 only.

CIMA Paper P1 – Management Accounting – Performance Evaluation November 2008, Question 1.3

B2.5 [S] [CIMA question]
Which of the following is the best description of 'management by exception'?

A   Using management reports to highlight exceptionally good performance, so that favourable results can be built upon to improve future outcomes.
B   Sending management reports only to those managers who are able to act on the information contained within the reports.
C   Focusing management reports on areas which require attention and ignoring those which appear to be performing within acceptable limits.
D   Appointing and promoting only exceptional managers to areas of responsibility within the organisation.

CIMA Paper P1 – Management Accounting – Performance Evaluation November 2008, Question 1.5

C Problem solving and evaluation

C2.1 [S]

Standard pine benches are assembled and packed in the bench assembly department of Furniture Manufacture Ltd. The department is treated as a cost centre. Control reports prepared every month consist of a statement comparing actual costs incurred in the department with the level of costs which was budgeted at the start of the month.

For the month of June Year 6 the following control report was produced, and received favourable comment from the directors of the company.

Bench Assembly Department Control Report for June Year 6

	Budgeted cost			Actual cost	Variance[1]	
	Fixed	Variable	Total			
	£	£	£	£	£	
Direct labour	–	36,000	36,000	30,000	6,000	(F)
Indirect labour	6,000	8,000	14,000	14,000	–	
Indirect materials	–	4,000	4,000	3,500	500	(F)
Power	3,000	12,000	15,000	9,000	6,000	(F)
Maintenance materials	–	5,000	5,000	3,000	2,000	(F)
Maintenance labour	5,000	4,000	9,000	15,000	6,000	(A)
Depreciation	85,000	–	85,000	75,000	10,000	(F)
Production overhead	–	20,000	20,000	15,000	5,000	(F)

Note: 1 (F) = favourable; (A) = adverse.

Due to a power failure, the level of production achieved was only 75% of that expected when the budget was prepared. No adjustment has been made to the original budget because the departmental manager claims that the power failure which caused the loss of production was beyond his control.

Required
Prepare a memorandum to the directors of the company:

(1) Explaining the weaknesses in the existing form of control report.
(2) Presenting the control report in such a way as to give a more meaningful analysis of the costs.
(3) Assessing the performance of the Bench Assembly Department during the month.

C2.2 [S]

Dairies Ltd operates a milk processing and delivery business. The retail distribution of milk is controlled by a regional head office which has overall responsibility for five geographical distribution areas. Each area is run by an area manager who has responsibility for ten depots. At each depot there is a depot manager in charge of 20 drivers and their milk floats. Milk is bottled at a central processing plant and sent to depots by lorry.

All information regarding the operation of each depot and each area office is sent to the divisional head office accounting department. This department produces weekly reports to be sent to each depot manager, each area manager and the manager of the distribution division.

A pyramidal system of reporting is in operation whereby each manager receives an appropriate weekly report containing the financial information on the operations for which he is responsible.

Required
(1) Explain what is meant by responsibility accounting.
(2) List, giving reasons, the information which should be contained in the weekly reports to each of the three levels of manager specified.

C2.3

You are the management accountant at the head office of a company which owns retail shoe shops throughout the country. The shops are grouped into areas, each having an area manager.

Goods for sale are bought through a central purchasing scheme administered by head office. Shop managers have discretion to vary sales prices subject to the approval of the area manager. It is the responsibility of shop managers to record on a wastage sheet any shoes which are discarded because of damage in the shop. Shop managers have total control over the number of staff they employ and the mix of permanent and casual staff, subject to interview in the presence of the area manager. Shop managers also arrange for cleaning of the premises and are responsible for heat and light and other overhead costs.

The head office accounting system has produced the following information with regard to the Southern area:

	Shop A £	Shop B £	Shop C £	Area target %
Turnover	450,000	480,000	420,000	100
Costs:				
Cost of goods sold	355,000	356,000	278,000	69
Wastage	5,000	4,000	2,000	
	360,000	360,000	280,000	
Salaries and wages:				
Branch manager	15,000	16,000	16,000	
Bonus for manager	1,000	1,500	1,500	
Permanent assistants	9,000	7,000	7,000	
Bonus for assistants	450	480	420	
Casual workers	3,000	4,000	5,000	
	28,450	28,980	29,920	6
Heat, light, cleaning and other overheads	7,600	8,500	8,200	2
Operating profit before area office recharges	53,950	82,520	101,880	
Area office recharges	3,000	3,000	3,000	
	50,950	79,520	98,880	22

Further information
(a) The Southern area has an overall operating profit target of 20% of sales. The area office has a target allowance of 2% of sales to cover its expenses other than those recharged to shops.
(b) Details of area office expenses are:

	£
Area manager's salary	18,000
Area manager's bonus	3,000
Other office expenses	2,400
	23,400
Area office recharges	(9,000)
	14,400

(c) It is the policy of the company to disclose sufficient information to motivate and inform the appropriate level of management or staff, but to avoid reporting excessive detail, particularly where such detail would unnecessarily disclose information about wages or salaries of individual employees.

Required
Prepare three separate reports including comments on and interpretation of the quantitative performance data as follows:

(1) To the area manager on the overall performance of the area and the relative performance of each shop within the area.
(2) To the manager of shop A on the performance of that shop relative to the rest of the area and to the area target.
(3) To the employees of shop B showing them how their shop performed relative to the rest of the area.

Case studies

Real world cases

Prepare short answers to Case studies 2.1, 2.2 and 2.3.

Case 2.4

Lightwave Radio Ltd produces a range of products at its assembly plant. Due to recent rapid expansion the company's system of management control is now inadequate. The board has established a working party drawn from all disciplines of management to develop the structure for a new computer-based management control and reporting system.

As chief accountant, you represent the finance department on the working party and believe that the management reporting system should be based on the division of the production process into a series of cost centres.

Required

(a) Explain the essential features of a cost centre.
(b) Identify the main features you would expect to find in a cost control report prepared for use at individual cost centre level.
(c) List three objections or questions which you might anticipate receiving from other members of the working party, and explain how you would answer each.

Case 2.5

You are the managing director of Combine Ltd, a company engaged in the manufacture and sale of refrigerators and freezers. The board of directors has agreed to reorganise the company into two divisions – the domestic refrigerator division and the industrial freezer division. At the next board meeting the measures to be used to monitor management performance are to be discussed.

Prepare a five-minute presentation to your fellow directors which explains:

- the key factors to be considered in the design of financial performance measures for the divisional managers; and
- the use of non-accounting measures for appraising short-term divisional management performance.

Suggest three examples of non-accounting measures which could be used to monitor sales performance in the company.

Case 2.6

Obtain the annual report of a large listed company. Look throughout the report for mention of non-financial performance indicators. Having read the report, prepare a list of non-financial performance indicators which you think would be useful to readers in understanding more about the company. For each indicator suggested, you should give a reason. The aim should be to have a table of indicators covering no more than one side of A4 paper in printed form.

Note

1. Smith (2005).

## CHAPTER 3

Budgeting for planning and control

Setting the scene

While some proposed management accounting techniques seem to be little used in practice, this cannot be said of budgeting. Surveys have shown that 99 per cent of all companies in Europe operate formal budgeting systems. Most management accountants spend a considerable amount of time preparing, revising and monitoring budgets and most organisations have clear and well proven budgeting routines.

(Kennedy and Dugdale (1999) Getting the most from budgeting, *Management Accounting* (UK), February)

Learning objectives

After studying this chapter you should be able to:

1   explain how strategic planning relates to budgeting;

2   identify the budgets that make up the overall budget;

3   prepare operating budgets for a manufacturing enterprise;

4   describe zero-based budgeting;

5   appreciate the difference between traditional budgeting and activity-based budgeting.

The process of budgeting focuses on the short term, normally one year, and provides an expression of the steps which management must take in the current period if it is to fulfil organizational objectives. However, many organizations prepare three-year plans, with a detailed budget covering the first year, and a summarized one covering each of the following two years. The focus of this chapter is on the preparation of the budget for the first year.

Objectives of budgeting

Long-range planning involves the selection of the mission statement (i.e. the reason for the organization being in business) and the determination of a suitable plan for attaining its objectives. Budgets are the quantitative expressions of these plans stated in either physical or financial terms or both. Therefore, the long-range plan is the guide for preparing the annual budgets and defines actions that need to be taken now in order to move towards long-term objectives. Indeed, the budget represents the first one-year span of the long-range plan.

The reader will recall that one important feature of planning is the coordination of the various activities of an enterprise, and of its departments, so that they are harmonized in the overall task of realizing corporate objectives. For example, if the marketing function were to increase sales massively over a short period of time, the manufacturing function would have to increase output substantially – probably through the use of costly overtime labour, or by buying goods from an outside supplier at high prices. Conversely, excessive production may force the marketing function to sell at unrealistically low prices in order to avoid excessive investment in stock. The function of budgeting is to coordinate the various activities of an organization in order to achieve company rather than divisional or departmental objectives. Therefore it is necessary to establish objectives for each section of the organization which are in harmony with the organization as a whole.

As a plan of action, budgets can be used to control by comparing actual outcomes as they happen with the planned outcomes. If the actual differs significantly from the planned, actions can be taken to put the plan back on track if necessary.

The need for flexibility

Because business conditions are always changing, it is necessary to view the budgeting process as a guide to future action, rather than a rigid plan which must be followed irrespective of changing circumstances. The latter approach may place the manager in a straitjacket in which he or she is forced to take decisions which are not in accordance with company objectives. For example, a departmental manager may find, due to changing conditions, that he has not spent all his budget on a particular item. In order to spend all his budget allowance, so as to prevent the possibility of a cut in his allowance next year, he may squander funds which could have been put to better use in other sections of the organization. This used to be the case in government organizations, in that if money was not spent, the next year's budget would be reduced regardless of whether the money was needed that year. Towards the end of the government financial year, many managers would ensure that any expense heading which was under-spent was spent by the year end.

More importantly, management must plan for changing business conditions, in order that appropriate action may be taken to deal with changes that may occur should any of the assumptions underlying plans be affected by such changes. This implies that contingency plans should be available to deal with changes which were unforeseen at the time when the budget was originally prepared.

Some firms relate their budgets to changing conditions by means of a rolling budget which is prepared every quarter, but for one year ahead. At the end of each quarter the plans for the next three quarters are revised, if this is necessary, and a fourth quarter is added. By this process the budgets are kept continually up-to-date.

Flexibility is also required if budgetary control is to be effective. Indeed the type of budget which may be suitable for planning may be inappropriate for control purposes. Therefore, budgets should be established for control purposes which reflect operating conditions which may be different from those envisaged in the planning stages. This is essential if individual managers are to be held responsible only for those deviations over which they have control. Such a requirement is called for by the use of a responsibility accounting system.

The organization of budgeting

The budgeting process itself requires careful organization. In large firms, budgeting is often in the hands of a budgeting committee which acts through the budget officer whose function it is to coordinate and control the budgeting process for the whole organization. Departmental budget estimates are requested from divisional managers, who in their turn collate this information from estimates submitted to them by their own departmental managers. Hence, budget estimates are based on information which flows upwards through the organization to the budget committee. The budget committee is responsible for coordinating this information, and resolving any differences in consultations with the managers involved. The final budget proposal is presented to the board of directors for its final approval.

Steps in budgeting

The first stage of a budgeting exercise is the determination of the 'key' factors or constraints which impose overall limits to the budget plan. Among these factors are the productive capacity of the plant, the finances available to the firm, and, of course, the market conditions which impose a total limit on the output the firm is able to sell. Normally from a management point of view, the critical question is 'what is the firm able to sell in the budget period?', and this question summarizes all the limits to the budget plan. It is for this reason that the sales budget is at once the starting point and the fulcrum of the budgeting process.

Figure 3.1 illustrates how the various resources and activities of an enterprise are coordinated. A similar exercise would be carried out in a non-manufacturing organization or service organization. The areas which would not feature in some service organizations would be finished goods stock budget, material usage budget, raw materials budget and materials purchases budget. It is necessary to adapt the budget process to the industry and type of organization. For example in the health service, each service (acute, maternity, diagnostic and paramedic, etc.) would prepare an expense budget based on staff and the forecast of patients to be treated. Some materials costs would be incurred (drugs, bed sheets, etc.) but the major expense would be salaries. Next, the service costs would be accumulated into an expenditure budget while concurrently the money available to run the service would be cascading from the Department of Health downwards towards the area health authorities and then down to the hospitals. Ultimately a master budget would be prepared and submitted to the governing body.

The arrows indicate the flow of relevant information. Once the level of sales is established, selling and distribution cost may be ascertained. The production budget itself is determined by the sales forecast, the desired level of stock of finished goods and plant capacity. From the production budget may be estimated the production costs, and the cost schedules for materials, labour and overheads.

In addition, the budgeting process for capital expenditure reflects decisions taken in developing the long-range plan. The capital expenditure budget is concerned with expenditure during the budget period on the maintenance and improvement of the existing productive capacity. Associated with this budget are research and development costs for improving methods of production and product improvement as well.

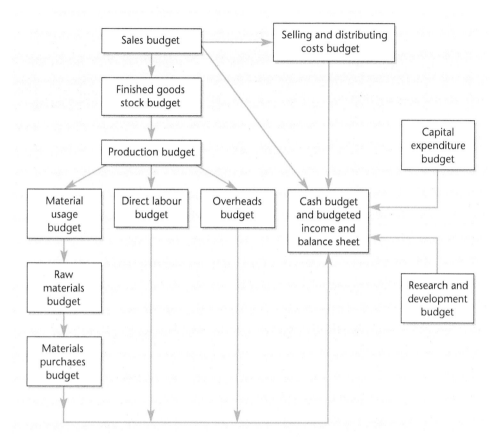

Figure 3.1

From a financing point of view, the cash surplus or deficits arising out of the overall budget are revealed by the cash budget which incorporates all cash revenues and cash expenditures. This enables the firm to arrange its financial needs accordingly.

Finally, the projected results in terms of the overall net profit and the changes in the structure of the firm's assets and liabilities are expressed in the budgeted profit and loss account and the budgeted balance sheet at the end of the budget period.

This description of the manner in which the budget coordinates the various activities of the firm is a simplified one. Budgetary planning is an activity which is of critical importance to the firm, and the problems involved are often complex and difficult ones to resolve. A firm's sales policy, for example, cannot be considered in isolation from its pricing policy and its cost structure. The firm's planned costs in relation to the required output may be too high to reach the profit target. If this should be the case, pricing and advertising policies may require further scrutiny, both planned and development costs may have to be reduced, and the final product itself may have to be modified. The role of the budget committee is, therefore, a very important one: not only has it to harmonize all the divisional budgets into an overall planning framework, but it has to deal with the numerous adjustments which may have to be made if the overall budget fails to meet some of the firm's stated objectives. Hence, the role of the budget committee is not only important in a practical sense: it affects important and sensitive areas of policy making and management.

Forecasting sales

A major problem in budgeting is forecasting sales, for many factors affecting sales are outside the firm's control, for example the behaviour of the firm's competitors and the future economic climate.

The importance of an accurate sales forecast cannot be overemphasized. If the sales forecast is too optimistic, the firm may be induced to expand its capital expenditure programme and incur costs which may not be recoverable at a later date. In the meantime the production target may be set too high, resulting in the pile-up of stock of finished goods, which in itself has important financial consequences. Moreover, an optimistic sales forecast may disguise a deteriorating sales position, so that the necessary economies are not made which would produce a satisfactory profit. If, on the other hand, the sales forecast is pessimistic, the firm will miss the opportunity of larger current profit and may be misled as to its future prospects. The firm may, as a result, not undertake the necessary capital expenditure which would place it in a good position to exploit the market.

The sales forecast is the initial step in preparing the sales budget. It consists of not only analysing the market for the firm's products, but also forecasting the levels of sales at different prices. Hence, the study of the firm's pricing policy is an integral aspect of sales forecasting. Once the sales forecast is completed, the sales budget may be derived from the target sales established both as regards price and sales volume.

There are various methods of forecasting sales, for example:

1 *The salesforce composite method*. This method places responsibility upon individual salespeople for developing their own sales forecasts. The advantage of this method is that if participative budgeting is to be encouraged, the sales staff should assist in the preparation of the sales forecast.
2 *The analysis of market and industry factors*. This method recognizes the importance of factors not within the knowledge of the salesforce, such as forecasts of the gross national product, personal incomes, employment and price levels, etc. The salespeople's estimates are modified by the information so obtained.
3 *Statistical analysis of fluctuations through time*. Sales are generally affected by four basic factors: growth trends, business cycle fluctuations, seasonal fluctuations and irregular variations in demand. A time series analysis of sales is a statistical method of separating and analysing the historical evidence of the behaviour of sales to identify these several effects and their impact on sales. The results of this analysis are applied to the sales forecast, and are means of testing the quality of the forecast.
4 *Mathematical techniques for sales forecasting*. Of recent years, mathematical techniques have been applied to the study of the relationship between economic trends and a firm's sales pattern through time, to arrive at a projection of future sales. These techniques usually involve the use of computers. One such technique is known as exponential smoothing, which is really a prediction of future sales based on current and historical sales data, weighted so as to give a greater importance to the latest incoming information.

An illustration of the budgeting process

Once the sales forecast is known, a firm may begin to prepare the budget. We believe that the reader will obtain a better understanding of budgeting if we work through a simple example. In the following example, we focus on the technical problems of budget construction, and we assume that the problem of changing price levels is not present. This assumption allows us to treat asset values as remaining constant.

Example 3.1 The Edco Manufacturing Co Ltd manufactures two products, A and B. A formal planning system had been introduced some time ago as a means of steering the company into more profitable levels of operation. Considerable progress had already been made in streamlining production and reducing costs. The budgeting process normally began in October, prior to the end of the accounting year on 31 December.

The Edco Manufacturing Co Ltd
Forecast results for the year ending 31 December 20X0
Income statement

	£
Sales	135,000
Cost of goods sold	80,000
Gross margin	55,000
Selling and administrative expenses	25,000
Income before tax	30,000
Tax at 40%	12,000
Income after tax	18,000

Balance sheet

	Cost	Depreciation	
	£	£	£
Non-current assets			
Plant and machinery	250,000	30,000	220,000
Current assets			
Inventories:			
Raw materials		1,650	
Finished goods		6,025	
		7,675	
Debtors		20,000	
Cash		5,325	
		33,000	
Less: Creditors: amounts falling due within one year			
Creditors	5,000		
Tax	12,000		
		17,000	
Net current assets			16,000
Total assets *less* current liabilities			236,000
Capital and reserves			
Called-up share capital			210,000
Income statement			26,000
			236,000

The expected results for the current year ending on 31 December 20X0 were as shown above. From these forecast results, the expected performance for the current year may be calculated as follows:

$$\text{return on stakeholders' equity: } \frac{£18,000}{£236,000} = 7.6\%$$

$$\text{return on capital employed: } \frac{£30,000}{£236,000} = 12.7\%$$

The following additional information was obtained for the purpose of preparing the budget for the year ending 31 December 20X1.

The sales forecast

	Product A	Product B
Expected selling price per unit	£11	£14
Sales volume forecast		
1st quarter	1,500 units	2,000 units
2nd quarter	1,000	2,000
3rd quarter	1,000	2,000
4th quarter	1,500	2,000
Total for the year	5,000	8,000

Factory costs forecast

Two departments are concerned with production: the preparation department and the machining department. The following analysis relates to the production of these departments:

1 Direct costs

	Direct labour required per unit of product (in labour hours)		Departmental wage rate	Direct labour cost per unit of output	
	A	B		A	B
Preparation department	$\frac{1}{5}$	$\frac{1}{2}$	£2 per hour	£0.40	£1.00
Machining department	$\frac{1}{2}$	$\frac{1}{2}$	£2 per hour	£1.00	£1.00
				£1.40	£2.00

2 Raw material requirement forecast

The standard quantities of the two raw materials, X and Y, which should be used in the manufacture of the two products, and the prices of these raw materials have been estimated as follows:

Standard quantities:
Raw material X – 2 units for each unit of product A
Raw material Y – 3 units for each unit of product B

Estimated costs:
Raw material X – £0.50 for each unit of X
Raw material Y – £0.30 for each unit of Y

3 Overhead costs

Factory overheads are classified into fixed and variable costs. The fixed overhead costs are deemed to be incurred in equal amounts quarterly for the purpose of allocation, whereas the variable overheads vary according to the level of production. The following estimates are available:

Fixed overheads:

Depreciation	£10,000 per annum
Rates and insurances	4,000
Supervisory salaries	6,000
	£20,000

Variable overheads

	Cost per unit of output	
	A	B
	£	£
Indirect labour		
Indirect material		
Repeairs and maintenance	£0.50	£1.00
Power		

Using activity-based costing, some of the fixed and variable overheads may be allocated on the basis of cost drivers, instead of on the basis of cost per unit, or cost per labour hour.

Inventory forecasts

Finished goods

Product A – estimated opening inventory:	750 units
Product B – estimated opening inventory:	1,000 units

It was planned that the closing inventory level at the end of each quarter should be maintained at a level equal to half the expected sales for the next quarter for both products.
  For the purposes of calculating the expected income, the closing inventory is to be valued on a variable costing basis, as follows:

	A	B
Raw materials	£1.00	£0.90
Direct labour	1.40	2.00
Variable overheads	0.50	1.00
Total variable costs per unit	**£2.90**	**£3.90**

Raw materials
Raw material X – estimated opening inventory: 1,500 units
Raw material Y: 3,000 units

Administrative and selling costs forecast

	£	£
1 Administrative costs		
Office salaries	18,000	
Stationery	1,000	
Other	1,000	
		20,000
2 Selling costs		
Salaries	15,000	
Advertising	5,000	
		20,000
Total		40,000

Cash flow forecast

1 Sales receipts

50 per cent of sales received in cash during month of sales
50 per cent of sales received in cash in the following month

2 Cash expenditure

(a) *Production costs*: Direct labour, direct materials and variable overheads paid in the month in which incurred. Fixed overheads paid in equal amounts quarterly.
(b) *Administrative and selling costs*: Paid in equal amounts quarterly.
(c) *Other costs*: Tax outstanding amounting to £12,000 will be paid off in equal instalments quarterly over the year.

Capital expenditure: Expenditure on the acquisition of assets is planned as follows:

	£
1st quarter	10,000
2nd quarter	15,000
3rd quarter	8,000
4th quarter	20,000
	53,000

Sundry creditors balance

The amount outstanding to sundry creditors will remain constant at £5,000 throughout the year.

PREPARING THE BUDGET FOR THE YEAR ENDING 31 DECEMBER 20X1

The task of preparing the overall budget involves a sequence of steps:

Step		
	1	The sales budget
	2	The production budget
	3	The direct materials usage budget
	4	The materials purchases budget
	5	The budgeted direct labour costs
	6	The overhead costs budget
	7	The closing inventory budget
	8	The selling and administrative costs budget
	9	The capital expenditure budget
	10	The cost of goods sold budget
	11	The cash budget
	12	The budgeted income statement
	13	The budgeted balance sheet

Step 1 The sales budget

The sales budget is prepared from the sales forecast as follows:

	1st quarter	2nd quarter	3rd quarter	4th quarter	Total
Units					
Product A	1,500	1,000	1,000	1,500	5,000
Product B	2,000	2,000	2,000	2,000	8,000
Value					
Product A (£11)	£16,500	£11,000	£11,000	£16,500	£55,000
Product B (£14)	28,000	28,000	28,000	28,000	112,000
	£44,500	£39,000	£39,000	£44,500	£167,000

Step 2 The production budget

The production budget is designed to plan the resources required to produce the output envisaged by the sales forecast. A precondition for an agreement as to the size of the sales budget is the adequacy of the productive capacity of the plant to provide the required output. If existing capacity is inadequate, decisions will have to be made as to the advisability of introducing overtime working, of subcontracting production, or of hiring or purchasing additional plant and equipment. If, on the other hand, the sales forecast falls short of productive capacity, sales promotion schemes may be considered as a means of closing or reducing the gap. With the tendency of business people to use inventory levels as buffers to insulate an efficient rate of production from variations in sales, the production budget is also dependent upon the planned levels of closing inventory.

Using the information given in our example, the following production budget may be prepared:

	1st quarter	2nd quarter	3rd quarter	4th quarter	Year
Product A					
Desired closing inventory (units)	500	500	750	750	750
Add: Sales	1,500	1,000	1,000	1,500	5,000
Total required	2,000	1,500	1,750	2,250	5,750
Less: Opening inventory	750	500	500	750	750
Production required	1,250	1,000	1,250	1,500	5,000
Product B					
Desired closing inventory (units)	1,000	1,000	1,000	1,000	1,000
Add: Sales	2,000	2,000	2,000	2,000	8,000
Total required	3,000	3,000	3,000	3,000	9,000
Less: Opening inventory	1,000	1,000	1,000	1,000	1,000
Production required	2,000	2,000	2,000	2,000	8,000

Step 3 The direct materials usage budget

The rate of usage of raw materials is known, so that the direct materials usage may be budgeted by multiplying the usage rate by the production required.

	1st quarter	2nd quarter	3rd quarter	4th quarter	Year
Material X (2 units for A)	2,500	2,000	2,500	3,000	10,000
Material Y (3 units for B)	6,000	6,000	6,000	6,000	24,000

Step 4 The materials purchase budget

The purpose of this budget is to determine both the quantities and the values of raw material purchases necessary to meet the production levels stipulated in the production budget. The information required for this budget is found in the direct materials usage budget, inventory forecasts and raw materials purchase prices.

	1st quarter	2nd quarter	3rd quarter	4th quarter	Year
Raw material X					
Desired closing inventory	1,000	1,000	1,500	1,500	1,500
Add: Material usage (Step 3)	2,500	2,000	2,500	3,000	10,000
Total required	3,500	3,000	4,000	4,500	11,500
Less: Opening inventory	1,500	1,000	1,000	1,500	1,500
Purchases required (units)	2,000	2,000	3,000	3,000	10,000
Price per unit	£0.50	£0.50	£0.50	£0.50	£0.50
Total purchases (value)	£1,000	£1,000	£1,500	£1,500	£5,000

	1st quarter	2nd quarter	3rd quarter	4th quarter	Year
Raw material Y					
Desired closing inventory	3,000	3,000	3,000	3,000	3,000
Add: Material usage (Step 3)	6,000	6,000	6,000	6,000	24,000
Total required	9,000	9,000	9,000	9,000	27,000
Less: Opening inventory	3,000	3,000	3,000	3,000	3,000
Purchases required (units)	6,000	6,000	6,000	6,000	24,000
Price per unit	£0.30	£0.30	£0.30	£0.30	£0.30
Total purchases (value)	£1,800	£1,800	£1,800	£1,800	£7,200
Total purchases (X plus Y)	£2,800	£2,800	£3,300	£3,300	£12,200

Step 5 Budgeted direct labour costs

This budget is based upon calculations of the labour requirements necessary to produce the planned output. The direct labour costs are computed by multiplying the labour requirements by the forecast of wage rates payable during the budget period.

	1st quarter	2nd quarter	3rd quarter	4th quarter	Year
Production (Step 2 – units)					
Product A	1,250	1,000	1,250	1,500	5,000
Product B	2,000	2,000	2,000	2,000	8,000
Labour hours					
Preparation department					
Product A ($\frac{1}{5}$)	250	200	250	300	1,000
Product B ($\frac{1}{2}$)	1,000	1,000	1,000	1,000	4,000
Total	1,250	1,200	1,250	1,300	5,000
Machining department					
Product A ($\frac{1}{2}$)	625	500	625	750	2,500
Product B ($\frac{1}{2}$)	1,000	1,000	1,000	1,000	4,000
Total	1,625	1,500	1,625	1,750	6,500
Direct labour costs					
Preparation department					
Labour hours	1,250	1,200	1,250	1,300	5,000
Wage rate/hour	£2	£2	£2	£2	£2
Direct labour cost	£2,500	£2,400	£2,500	£2,600	£10,000
Machining department					
Labour hours	1,625	1,500	1,625	1,750	6,500
Wage rate/hour	£2	£2	£2	£2	£2
Direct labour cost	£3,250	£3,000	£3,250	£3,500	£13,000
Total direct labour cost	£5,750	£5,400	£5,750	£6,100	£23,000

Step 6 The overhead costs budget

Having disposed of the direct costs of production in the form of materials and direct labour, we now come to the preparation of the estimates of the overhead costs of production. These costs are divided into the two categories mentioned earlier. We are told that the fixed overheads are incurred in equal amounts quarterly, and we may calculate the total variable costs per quarter by multiplying the expected variable costs per unit by the planned quarterly output.

	1st quarter	2nd quarter	3rd quarter	4th quarter	Year
Production (Step 2)					
Product A (units)	1,250	1,000	1,250	1,500	5,000
Product B (units)	2,000	2,000	2,000	2,000	8,000
Variable costs					
Product A (£0.50 per unit)	£625	£500	£625	£750	£2,500
Product B (£1.00 per unit)	2,000	2,000	2,000	2,000	8,000
Total	2,625	2,500	2,625	2,750	10,500
Fixed costs					
Depreciation	2,500	2,500	2,500	2,500	10,000
Rates and insurance	1,000	1,000	1,000	1,000	4,000
Supervisory salaries	1,500	1,500	1,500	1,500	6,000
Total	5,000	5,000	5,000	5,000	20,000
Total overhead costs	£7,625	£7,500	£7,625	£7,750	£30,500

Step 7 The closing inventory budget

The closing inventory budget consists of an estimate of the value of planned closing inventory of raw materials and planned inventory of finished goods. It is arrived at by calculating the budgeted unit cost of inventory and multiplying the result by the planned inventory level.

1 Budgeted closing raw material inventory

Raw material	X	Y	
Closing inventory (units)	1,500	3,000	
Cost per unit	£0.50	£0.30	
Value of closing inventory	£750	£900	
Total			£1,650

2 Budgeted finished goods inventory

We are told that the accountant values the inventory of finished goods on a variable costing basis, and that the unit cost of Products A and B has been calculated to be £2.90 and £3.90 respectively. These values are applied to the budgeted closing inventory figures as follows:

Product	A	B	
Closing inventory (units)	750	1,000	
Cost per unit	£2.90	£3.90	
Value of closing inventory	2,175	3,900	
Total			£6,075

Step 8 The selling and administrative expenses budget

Selling expenses		
Salaries	£15,000	
Advertising	5,000	£20,000
Administrative expenses		
Office salaries	18,000	
Stationery	1,000	
Other expenses	1,000	20,000
Total		£40,000

Step 9 The capital expenditure budget

Capital budgeting is an aspect of long-range planning and control. The annual capital expenditure budget must be seen, therefore, as a one-year slice of the long-term capital budget. The purpose of the annual capital expenditure is to make provision in the current budget for the planned capital expenditure in the current year. This information has been provided as follows:

Capital expenditure	
1st quarter	£10,000
2nd quarter	15,000
3rd quarter	8,000
4th quarter	20,000
Total for the year	£53,000

Step 10 The cost of goods sold budget

The reader will recall that all the previous budgets mentioned have dealt with the various aspects of the production process, in unit and value terms, including the expenses associated with selling and administration and the valuation of closing stock. The purpose of this budget is to bring all these items together to arrive at an estimate of the cost of the goods sold. This estimate will be used in the budgeted profit and loss account. It is compiled as follows:

Opening raw materials inventory (balance sheet 31.12.20X0)	£1,650
Add: Materials purchases (Step 4)	12,200
Raw materials available for production	13,850
Less: Planned closing inventory of raw materials (Step 7)	1,650
Cost of raw materials to be used in production	12,200
Cost of direct labour (Step 5)	23,000
Factory overhead costs (Step 6)	30,500
Cost of goods to be manufactured	65,700
Add: Opening inventory of finished goods (balance sheet 31.12.20X0)	6,025
	71,725
Less: Planned closing inventory of finished goods	6,075
Budgeted cost of goods sold	£65,650

Step 11 The cash budget

The cash budget consists of the estimates of cash receipts and cash payments arising from the planned levels of activities and use of resources which are considered in the various budgets we have examined. The cash budget is a complete survey of the financial implication of expenditure plans of both a current and a capital nature during the year. Moreover, by comparing the anticipated outflows of cash with the expected inflows, the cash budget enables management to anticipate any deficits so that the necessary financing arrangements may be made, and to decide upon a policy for placing any cash surpluses.

As its name implies, the cash budget deals only with 'cash' flows – it excludes expenses of a non-cash nature, such as depreciation. The cash budget is one of the last budgets to be prepared because it depends upon the other budgets which form part of the budgeting process.

Note that the cash budget is planned through time: the time profile of cash receipts and cash payments is critical to the analysis of a firm's cash needs at any given point of time.

In practice, determining the level of cash which is required at any point in time may not be an easy matter. The dilemma of cash management lies in the conflict of liquidity with profitability. If a firm holds too little cash in relation to its financial obligations, a liquidity crisis may occur and may lead to the collapse of the business. On the other hand, if a firm holds too much cash it is losing the opportunity to employ that cash profitably in its activities. Idle cash balances usually earn very little profit for the firm. A reasonable balance must be found, therefore, between the financial objectives of maintaining a degree of liquidity and of minimizing the level of unproductive assets. The problem of ascertaining optimal balances of physical stocks has for long attracted the attention of operational researchers, and certain of the ideas which they have developed may have applicability as regards the holding of optimal cash balances. Such techniques include just-in-time (JIT) inventory purchase systems, developing supply chains, where there is a direct link between suppliers and purchasers so that inventory needs are known almost immediately. Boots Company installed a computer system costing £75 million which saves £400 million per annum on inventory. It does this by linking the sales system to the inventory system to the resupply system so that only the relevant amount of inventory is resupplied.

	1st quarter	2nd quarter	3rd quarter	4th quarter	Total
	£	£	£	£	£
Opening cash balance	5,325	10,900	11,450	15,275	5,325
Receipts					
Debtors (balance sheet)	20,000	–	–	–	20,000
50% of current sales (Step 1)	22,250	19,500	19,500	22,250	83,500
50% of previous quarter (Step 1)	–	22,250	19,500	19,500	61,250
Total receipts	42,250	41,750	39,000	41,750	164,750
Total cash available	47,575	52,650	50,450	57,025	170,075
Payments					
Purchases (Step 4)	2,800	2,800	3,300	3,300	12,200
Direct labour (Step 5)	5,750	5,400	5,750	6,100	23,000
Factory overheads (Step 6) (excluding depreciation)	5,125	5,000	5,125	5,250	20,500
Selling and administrative expenses (Step 8)	10,000	10,000	10,000	10,000	40,000
Capital expenditure (Step 9)	10,000	15,000	8,000	20,000	53,000
Tax (balance sheet)	3,000	3,000	3,000	3,000	12,000
Total payments	36,675	41,200	35,175	47,650	160,700
Closing cash balances	10,900	11,450	15,275	9,375	9,375

The effects of inflation on business enterprises are manifested in a growth in monetary terms, which may be in some direct relationship with the rate of inflation, while at the same time undergoing no growth at all in real terms, or even shrinking in profitability and value. The financing problem resulting from the monetary growth associated with inflation lies in the need to finance higher levels of inventory and debtors. If a firm is unable to finance the higher level of working capital required from adjustments to its prices and sales revenues, it must either borrow or reduce its level of activity. In effect, the rapid inflation which business firms experienced in the 1970s caused severe liquidity problems and many cases of insolvency.

The problems of cash budgeting under conditions of inflation require that special attention be given to the timing of cash inflows and outflows, which should be adjusted for changes in specific price changes affecting the firm. In this connection, adjustments to budget figures for changes in the general purchasing power of money will not reflect the impact of inflationary changes as they affect individual firms.

Among the special problems associated with budgeting under conditions of inflation is the loss of purchasing power exhibited by holdings of net monetary assets. This implies that losses in the value of net monetary items should be minimized in a manner consistent with the overall objectives of the firm by the reduction of holdings of net monetary assets. In effect, particular attention should be given to cash and debtor balances, and the impact of changes in selling prices on cash inflows should be carefully monitored. At the same time, gains resulting from the impact of inflation on creditor balances should encourage more aggressive borrowing policies.

Step 12 The budgeted income statement

The purpose of the budgeted income statement is to summarize and integrate all the operating budgets so as to measure the end result on the firm's profit.

	£
Sales (Step 1)	167,000
Cost of goods sold (Step 10)	65,650
Gross income	101,350
Selling and administrative expenses (Step 8)	40,000
Net income before tax	61,350
Tax (40%)	24,540
Net income after tax	36,810

Step 13 The budgeted balance sheet

The final stage is the projection of the budgeted results on the firm's financial position at the end of the year. The following balance sheet reflects the changes in the composition of assets and liabilities as a result of the planned activities:

Budget balance sheet as at 31 December 20X1

Non-current assets	Cost	Depreciation	
	£	£	£
Plant and machinery	303,000	40,000	263,000
Current assets			
Inventory			
Raw materials	1,650		
Finished goods	6,075		
		7,725	
Debtors		22,250	
Cash		9,375	
		39,350	
Less: Creditors: amounts falling			
Due within one year			
Creditors	5,000		
Tax	24,540		
		29,540	
Net current assets			9,810
Total assets *less* current liabilities			272,810
Capital and reserves			
Called-up share capital			210,000
Retained earnings			62,810
			272,810

Evaluating the budget proposals

As a means of comparing the planned performance for the coming year with the results of the current year, the planned performance may be interpreted as follows:

Return on shareholders' equity: £36,810 ÷ £272,810 = 13.5% (previous 7.6%)
Return on capital employed: £61,350 ÷ £272,810 = 22.5% (previous 12.7%)

It is evident, therefore, that the firm is expected to make considerable improvements in the forthcoming period. If the budgeted results are considered to be satisfactory, the final stage is a recommendation that the budget proposal be accepted by the board of directors as its policy, and as conforming with its view of the future.

Budgeting systems

In this section we consider briefly three budget approaches: (1) zero-based budgeting; (2) feed-forward control; and (3) flexible budgeting.

Zero-based budgeting

The traditional approach to budgeting is the incremental approach which starts with the previous year's budget and adds or subtracts from that budget to reflect changing assumptions for the coming year. For example, if the previous year's budget expenditures for a department were £1 million, the department might request a 5 per cent increase (£50,000) to provide the same level of service for the coming year. The typical justification for increased expenditures is the increased cost of inputs (labour and materials, and so on). Any inefficiencies in the previous year's budget tend to be perpetuated by this almost automatic acceptance of that document as the starting point of the new plan.

One method developed to overcome the shortcomings of incremental budgeting is zero-based budgeting, by which all levels of management start from zero (a clean sheet of paper) and estimate the resource requirements to fund the year's activities. Managers must defend their budget levels at the beginning of each year. Thus, unlike incremental budgeting, the zero-based approach requires past budget decisions to be re-evaluated each year. Thus resource requirements are more likely to be adjusted to changing business conditions.

Feed-forward control

Feedback systems aim to highlight deviations from the budget plan as soon as possible so that remedial action may be taken. A feed-forward system differs from a feedback system in that it seeks to anticipate, and thereby to avoid, deviations between actual and desired outputs. The aim is to improve forecasting procedures. Therefore, once effective forecasting procedures have been established, the significant comparisons are no longer between planned and actual costs, but between forecasts, as follows:

1 *Latest forecast vs previous forecast*. This comparison becomes the prime action mover, and leads to the following questions:
   (a) Why has the forecast changed?
   (b) How does the latest forecast affect the net cash flow?
   (c) What actions should be taken to improve the situation?

2 *Actual vs previous forecast*. This comparison leads to the following questions being asked:
   (a) Was the previous forecast effective as regards identifying the events now facing the firm?
   (b) If not, why was the previous forecast wrong?
   (c) Are the errors in forecasting due to excessive pessimism or optimism, and can these errors be corrected?

Flexible budgeting

So far, we have discussed functional budgets and cash budgets. Another type of budget which takes into account changes in the volume of activity is the flexible budget. Most budgets assume a certain level of activity and this level of activity is used in the preparation of the budget. For example, in the Edco Manufacturing case above it was assumed that 1,250 units of output would be produced in the first quarter. However, actual production might be greater or less than 1,250 units. To compare the actual costs of, say, 1,300 units with the budgeted costs of 1,250 units would render the comparison meaningless. In a situation where the actual production was greater than budget, this would tend to show overspends on variable costs as these costs would increase with activity, but the budgeted value of these costs would remain at the 1,250 units level. Conversely, if no production was produced, then the financial report would show a saving on the variable costs as these would be set at the 1,250 units level, whereas the actual costs would be zero.

To overcome this weakness in reporting, flexible budgets are prepared which reflect the changes in production levels by multiplying the variable costs per unit by the actual activity levels. These are then compared with the actual costs and a meaningful variance is calculated. Any fixed costs are isolated in the report and shown separately.

Activity-based budgeting (ABB) and activity-based management (ABM)

The initial interest in activity-based costing (ABC) related to product or service costing, but that an ABC system offers more than just accurate product-cost information. It also provides information about the cost and performance of activities and resources. Activity-based management (ABM) is a term which has developed from the early approaches to ABC, and is designed to denote much wider use of the concept by management than just for product costing. Having undertaken ABC for product costing the information can be used for ABM. ABM is based on the premise that since people are involved in activities, and activities consume resources, the control of activities allows the control of costs at their sources. Activity-based budgeting (ABB) is an important element of ABM. It is a planning and budgetary tool which provides an understanding of the linkages between the drivers behind the activities. ABB defines the activities underlying the financial figures in each function and uses the level of activity to determine how much resource should be allocated, how well it is managed and how to explain variances from budget.

Traditional budgeting systems tend to view the organization vertically in functional blocks of cost and focus on resources bought by function or department. Most cost reports typically show wages, salaries, rent and so on by department in line with the functional organization structure. These reports reveal little about how the resources are being used to add value to the customer, what drives the level of resources required and whether the right amount of resources is in place. Alternatively, a business can be viewed as a series of linked activities, or processes, which ultimately add value to the customer. In adopting this view, ABM helps management to understand the activities, their cost and how they link together to form a simple chain of value-creating activities for a business. In doing so, ABM focuses on activity outputs rather than resource inputs.

ABB provides the foundation for a more effective control of overhead. ABC product costs give enhanced visibility to the components of overhead, providing greater segmentation and one which indicates the sources and purpose of resource consumption. This additional detail, together with the gathering of cost-driver information, provides management with valuable feedback which will aid the operational control of their manufacturing processes. ABM and ABB take the unit cost driver rates and multiplies by activity volume to give a spending amount: budget volumes for budgeted spending and actual volume for actual spending. Example 2 below indicates the type of report which can be produced with ABB, showing both budgeted and actual activity volumes and spending at those volumes. This activity-based budget report directs attention at the use of resources in the overhead area. It shows differences from budget for both expenditure and cost-driver levels. It highlights areas for investigation (Innes and Mitchell, 1993).

Example 3.2

Budget report

Activity	Cost driver	Unit cost	Original budget volume	£000	Actual budget volume	£000
Purchasing	Orders	£25/order	1,000	25	1,200	30
Set-ups	Set-ups	£150/set-up	200	30	300	45
Handling	Movements	£250/movement	400	100	500	125
Inspection	Inspections	£140/inspection	500	70	550	77
				225		277

Note: Great care must be taken in constructing and using activity-based budgets, because the *units costs/cost driver* assume that all the costs are stictly proportional to volume. This is certainly not true in the short term, and probably not completely true, either, in the long term.

In view of the fact that activities are linked across departments forming cross-functional processes, ABB permits managers to recognize the horizontal flow of products, services and activities through an organization by focusing attention on the organization as a whole. ABB ensures that there is an optimum allocation of scarce resources across the business. For example, consider the case of a conflict between two departments of a firm, the purchasing and warehouse functions. The purchasing department was buying from a supplier which delivered weekly, and the warehouse section held high staff levels solely to cater for this event. Although the change to smaller daily deliveries caused an increase in purchase prices, it eased the workload on staff in the warehouse and provided overall a substantial cost saving to the company.

In providing an understanding of the costs of activities, their importance to the organization and how efficiently they are performed, ABM allows managers to focus on those activities that might offer opportunities for cost savings. The process view of organizations allows management to focus on value-added and non-value-added activities that are not adding value, but are causing costs to be incurred.

Summary

Budgeting is an activity which should be seen as being concerned with the implementation of a yearly segment of the long-range plan. The budget expresses this plan in financial terms in the light of current conditions.

We have seen that the process of budgeting can be applied to any organization, such as retailing, local government, health service, leisure, banking, insurance and farming, to name but a few. Some steps (finished goods stock) are not relevant but the process is fundamentally the same. Budgets may be evaluated by means of financial ratios such as the return of shareholders' equity and the return on capital employed.

Activity-based budgeting directs cost control to the source of overhead costs (the activities) rather than their consequences (the production).

Self-assessment questions

1   Outline the series of steps that are implied in orderly budgeting.

2   Discuss the importance of the sales forecast.

3   State the various methods used for forecasting sales.

4   Examine the relationship between the sales budget and the production budget.

5   Comment on the significance of the cash budget.

6   Describe (a) zero-based budgeting; (b) feed-forward control; and (c) flexible budgeting.

7   How does an activity-based budgeting system differ from a traditional system?

1 Dafa Ltd is a trading company dealing in a single product. It is preparing its annual budget for the twelve months ending 30 June 20X1. So far, the following budgets have been prepared:

	July–Sept	Oct–Dec	Jan–Mar	April–June
Sales (at £3 per unit)	15,000	18,000	21,000	12,000
Purchases (at £2 per unit)	12,000	14,000	10,000	8,000
Sundry expenses				
Distribution	500	800	1,100	200
Administration	1,000	1,000	1,000	1,000
Depreciation	500	500	500	500
	2,000	2,300	2,600	1,700

Notes:

(a) Sales are made on one month's credit. It may be assumed that debtors outstanding on sales at the end of each quarter are equivalent to one-third of sales in that quarter, and that this is received the following quarter.
(b) All purchases are for cash. No credit is received.
(c) Distribution and administration expenses are paid in cash as incurred.
(d) The company has no expenses apart from those given.
(e) Opening balances at 1 July 20X0 are:

Debtors   £3,000
Cash   £2,000
Inventory   1,000 units

Required:

Complete Dafa Ltd's annual budget by preparing:

(a) a debtors' budget
(b) a cash budget, *and*
(c) an inventory budget to show the number of units in inventory at the end of each quarter.

2 A small private company, after several years of unprofitable trading, was taken over by a new management on 31 December.

The accounts for the following year were summarized thus:

	£
Direct materials	78,000
Direct wages	31,200
Variable overheads	15,600
Fixed overheads	30,000
Income	1,200
Sales	156,000

The balance sheet as at the end of the first twelve months of trading was as follows:

	£	£	£
Non-current assets			24,000
Current assets			
Inventory		26,000	
Debtors		26,000	
		52,000	
Less: Creditors: amounts falling due within one year			
Bank overdraft	26,500		
Creditors	19,500		
		46,000	
Net current assets			6,000
Total assets *less* current liabilities			30,000
Capital and reserves			
Called-up share capital			40,000
Income statement			(10,000)
			30,000

The budgeted sales for the second year of trading are as follows:

	£
1st quarter	42,000
2nd quarter	45,000
3rd quarter	48,000
4th quarter	51,000

It is anticipated that the ratios of material consumption, direct wages and variable overheads to sales are unlikely to change; that the fixed overheads (incurred evenly during the year) will remain at £30,000 per annum; and that creditors can be held at three months' direct material usage. Both inventory and debtors can be maintained at two months' sales.

Bank interest and depreciation, the latter at 10 per cent per annum on fixed assets, are included in the overheads.

Required:

Prepare quarterly budgets for the second year of operation to indicate to management:

(a) Whether the results are likely to be satisfactory.
(b) Whether the overdraft facilities (which are normally limited to £25,000) are sufficient, or whether further capital must be introduced.

3* Jones is considering whether to open up his own wholesaling business. He makes the following estimates about the first six months' trading:

(a) Sales on credit	– For first two months £50,000 per month.
	– Thereafter £80,000 per month.
	– One month's credit allowed to customers.
(b) Gross margin	– The cost of goods bought for resale is expected to be 75 per cent of the selling price.
(c) Closing inventory	– £75,000.
(d) Purchases creditors at end	– £50,000.
(e) Wages and salaries	– Paid for period £40,000.
	– Owing at end of period £2,500.
(f) Warehouse expenses	– Cash paid for rent, rates, lighting, heating, etc. £50,000.
	– In addition £5,500 of warehouse expenses will be owing at end of six months.
	– Of the cash paid, however, £3,500 will be rent and rates paid in advance.
(g) Furniture, fixtures and fittings	– Amounting to £50,000 to be purchased on opening of business and will be subject to 10 per cent p.a. depreciation.
(h) Delivery vehicles	– Three vans costing £2,000 each will be purchased at once and will be subject to 25 per cent p.a. depreciation.
(i) Loan interest	– Long-term loans can be raised at an interest rate of 10 per cent p.a.
(j) Jones	– Expects to draw from the business accounts his own 'wages' at a rate of £300 per month.

Required:

(a) A budgeted cash account for the period on the basis of the above information (see part (c) below).
(b) Budgeted income statement for the period and balance sheet as at the end on the basis of the above information (see part (c) below).
(c) Advise Jones as to how much capital should be introduced initially into the business. Jones, however, has only £50,000 available as capital. Complete the accounts on the assumption that he accepts your advice.
(d) Jones asks you whether the business appears to be a worthwhile one. Give a brief reply to this question.

4 The Astra leisure complex is a medium-sized company specializing in the leisure industry. The complex comprises a swimming pool, a diving pool, a leisure pool, a sauna, a sports hall (suitable for basketball, five-a-side football, etc.) and a conference hall. The complex also has a bar and a restaurant.

The managing director of the business, who has been recently appointed, is surprised to discover that there is no budgeting system at the complex.

Required:

(a)   List five main reasons why a formal system of budgeting should be introduced.

(b)   Identify which functional budgets will be required. For each functional budget named, propose which member of the organization should be responsible for its preparation and justify your choice. Draw an organization chart to illustrate your answer.

(c)   Explain how computer applications could be used to advantage in the proposed budgeting system.

5* Rutland Furnishings Company is a small carpet and upholstery cleaning business with both commercial and domestic customers.

The balance sheet of the company at 31 October 20X0 was:

	£	
Non-current assets (NBV)		
Freehold premises		32,000
Fixtures, fittings, equipment		4,000
Motor vehicles		12,000
		48,000
Current assets		
Inventory	3,200	
Debtors	20,000	
	23,200	
Current liabilities		
Creditors	4,000	
Bank overdraft	8,200	12,200
Net working capital		
		11,000
		£59,000
Capital		£59,000

The company allows credit to its commercial customers but domestic customers are expected to pay cash. On the basis of past performance, the company expects sales in the coming six months to be:

November	December	January	February	March	April
£16,000	£16,000	£20,000	£40,000	£12,000	£12,000

The proportions of cash and credit sales are usually:

Month of sale	Cash sales (%)	Credit sales (%)
November	30	70
December	45	55
All other months	20	80

Customers who are on extended credit normally pay in the month following sale. The company's invoice price is made up of 55 per cent wages, 25 per cent materials and 20 per cent profit. Wages are paid in the month incurred.

Half the materials purchased each month are subject to a 3 per cent cash discount for immediate payment and it is company policy to take advantage of this discount. The firm pays the remainder of the purchases, without discount, in the month after purchase. Goods are normally purchased in the month they are sold except December when owing to a supplier's shut-down, half December's goods are purchased in November.

Expenditure on petrol and other expenses is £2,600 per month. Additionally, the fixtures, equipment and motor vehicles are depreciated at 25 per cent per annum on a reducing balance basis.

Required:

(a) Prepare a cash budget for the six months November to April.
(b) Prepare an income statement for the same period.
(c) Prepare a balance sheet at 30 April 20X1.
(d) The company proposes to purchase a new industrial cleaner costing £10,000 in January. Given the overdraft facility is £9,500, what action should the management take?

References   Innes, J. and Mitchell, F. (1993) *Overhead Cost*, Academic Press.

Kennedy, A. and Dugdale, D. (1999) Getting the most from budgeting, *Management Accounting (UK)*, February.

## CHAPTER 4

Behavioural aspects of performance evaluation

Setting the scene

Do management accounting and control systems benefit organizations? Nobel Laureate Herbert Simon and his colleagues, among others, say they do. Such systems, they believe, play three roles: score-keeping, attention-directing and problem-solving. Robert Simons, writing in the March 1992 *CA Magazine* concurs. Management accounting, he says, consists of 'identification, measurement, accumulation, preparation, interpretation, and the communication of information that helps executives in filling organizational objectives'. In fact, most writers agree that financial controls, such as budgeting systems, aid in planning, co-ordinating and controlling any organization's complex flow of inter-related activities, and in motivating workers. But research also suggests there is a dark side to management accounting, that the system can do more harm than good.

(Mackintosh, 1994)

Learning objectives

After studying this chapter you should be able to:

1 explain what is meant by 'management style';

2 contrast 'Theory X' with 'Theory Y';

3 describe possible management reactions to budgets;

4 identify three possible levels of cost performance;

5 define 'management by objectives';

6 explain what is meant by 'contingency theory'.

Traditionally, accountants have followed economists in assuming the main organizational problem to be the maximization of profits and the optimization of resource allocation to this end. Consequently, accountants have tended to regard organizations in purely technical terms, subjecting human resources to the same analysis as that applied to other economic resources in the search for maximizing productivity and profits.

For more than two decades, social progress, political change and the internationalization of corporate organizations have created a strong awareness of the uniqueness of human resources, and in particular, of the way in which the behaviour of both management and workers affects the realization of organizational objectives. Both management and workers are recognized as having variable performance patterns depending directly on management styles and organizational culture. Much of the early work in this area was concerned with the evaluation of managerial perform-ance, and the reaction of workers to management style and organizational culture. In the 1970s and 1980s the success of Japanese organizations was attributed to charac-teristics of national and corporate culture which exerted a strong influence on how organizations worked. This prompted research into the influence of organizational culture on business performance.

In this chapter, we review briefly some of these developments.

Managerial style and organization culture

According to Horngren and Foster (1987) managerial style is 'the set of behaviours exhibited by key managers in an organization'. Of particular interest is the con-trast between authoritarian as against participative management styles in relation to decision making and the context in which performance is evaluated.

Again, according to these authors, organization culture is 'the set of beliefs and values shared by members of the organization'. This encompasses the prevalent inter-personal relationships and other significant constraints on social behaviour.

The considerable success of Japanese industry has underlined the importance of culture as a key factor, and points to a definition of this concept in an organizational setting that arguably is much broader than the definition adopted by Horngren and Foster. In effect, culture may be deemed to determine the manner in which both workers and management interact, and also the manner in which management deci-sions are made. Accordingly, management style may be viewed as subsumed in the concept of organization culture.

Much of the international comparison of the relative success of business organi-zations made currently tends to find substantial cause for disparity precisely in different national cultures as they find their expression in business enterprises. How far this may be substantiated as against the weight of other success factors is an open question. Nevertheless, the existence of the belief is in itself symptomatic of the importance attached to culture.

Despite all the research, there is considerable controversy about the influence of culture as an organizational success factor. Moreover, something that works in one culture may not work in another. There was considerable surprise when Carlos Ghosn succeeded in restoring the fortunes of Nissan despite conspicuously ignoring some of the hallowed traditions of Japanese corporate culture. For these reasons, we shall concern ourselves with the traditional accounting concern of evaluating man-agement performance, as expressed in the literature of the English-speaking nations.

The objectives of performance evaluation

The objectives of performance evaluation may be stated as follows:

1 to assess how effectively the responsibilities assigned to managers have been car-ried out;
2 to identify areas where corrective actions should be taken;
3 to ensure that managers are motivated towards achieving organizational goals;
4 to enable comparisons to be made between the performance of different units of an organization, to discover areas where improvements may be made.

In our analysis of the process of control, we have so far discussed two important pre-requisites for performance evaluation:

1 identifying areas of responsibility over which individual managers exercise control (responsibility accounting), and
2 the setting of standards of performance to be used as yardsticks for the evaluation of performance.

In this chapter, we address ourselves to some of the behavioural problems of budgets as measures for evaluating performance.

Leadership styles and the problem of control

There is a tendency for firms to expect desired results merely from the use of appropriate techniques, thereby failing to recognize that success in organizational control depends upon the actions of responsible individuals and their appreciation of the importance of sound interpersonal relationships McGregor has characterized the two extremes of interpersonal relationships or management styles as 'Theory X' and 'Theory Y' (McGregor, 1960). According to McGregor, these extremes are conditioned by the manager's view of mankind.

Theory X

The Theory X view of man, as summarized below, is supportive of an authoritarian leadership style:

1 Management is responsible for organizing the elements of productive enterprise – money, materials, equipment and people – in activities directed to economic ends.
2 As regards people, management is concerned with directing their efforts, motivating and controlling their actions, and modifying behaviour to fit the needs of the organization.
3 Without this active intervention by management, people would be passive – and even resistant – to organizational needs. Therefore, they must be persuaded, rewarded, punished, controlled. In short, their activities must be directed, and therein lies the function of management. This view is often summed up by the assertion that management consists of getting things done through other people.

Theory Y

By contrast, Theory Y is supportive of a more democratic and participative leadership style:

1 Management is responsible for organizing the elements of productive enterprise – money, materials, equipment and people – in activities directed to economic ends.
2 People are not by nature passive or resistant to organizational needs. They appear to have become so as a result of negative experiences of organizational needs.
3 The motivation, the potential for development, the capacity for assuming responsibility, the readiness to direct behaviour towards organizational goals are all present in people. Management does not put these qualities in people. It is the responsibility of management to make it possible for people to recognize and develop these human characteristics.

4 The essential task of management is to arrange organizational conditions and methods of operation so that people can achieve their own goals best by directing their efforts towards organizational objectives.

There is evidence that the Theory X leadership style is widely prevalent and clearly operational. Those who prefer the assumptions of Theory Y claim that the Theory X leadership style has a human cost in the frustration and the lack of personal development which result from its application to people. The trend in behavioural research suggests that benefits may be derived from leadership and organizations based on the assumptions of Theory Y. These assumptions recognize, in particular, that the basic motivating forces affecting people at work include biological, egoistic and social factors.

As people, employees at whatever organizational, level have certain needs which condition their own objectives. They are seeking *compensation* for their efforts to enable them to provide some desired standard of life for themselves and their families. They need outlets for their physical and intellectual energies which provide both *stimulation* and *satisfaction*. They seek *self-realization* in a sense of their own worth and usefulness. They are pursuing further *growth* and greater *personal effectiveness*. They seek the *recognition* of their fellows, whether their organizational equals, superiors or subordinates. They appreciate their *identification* with a worthwhile and successful undertaking.

In order to maximize employees' contribution to organizational activities, it follows that these personal needs and goals should be capable of realization in the tasks in which they are employed. An awareness of the nature of personal needs, therefore, is an important aspect of control.

The effects of budgets on people

Research suggests that there is a great deal of mistrust of the entire budgetary process at the supervisory level (Argyris, 1953). There is a tendency for traditional budgets to provide the following responses.

Reactions to pressure

The evaluation of a manager's performance in terms of the departmental budget is one of the few elements in performance appraisal which is based on concrete standards. There is little room for manipulation or escape if results are not going to turn out as expected in the budget. If budget pressure becomes too great, it may lead to mistrust, to hostility and eventually to poorer performance levels as reaction sets in against budgetary control.

The problem of distinguishing between controllable and non-controllable costs is an important cause of tension among managers. The task of the manager of a department or expense centre, for example, is to attain goals with the minimum cost. One of the initial difficulties which arises in evaluating performance applies to all levels of management, namely, the treatment of factors beyond their control. This problem is aggravated when the responsibility for an activity is shared by two or more individuals or functions. Labour inefficiency, for example, may be due to excessive machine breakdowns (maintenance function), inferior materials (purchasing function), defective materials (inspection function) or poor-calibre personnel (personnel function).

Establishing standards of performance in itself is not an easy task. It demands the clear definition of goals and responsibilities, the delegation of authority, the use of satisfactory surrogates for the activities concerned, effective communication of information and an understanding of the psychology of human motivation.

Overemphasis on the short run

One of the dangers facing organizations which evaluate the effectiveness of managers in terms of profit is that too much emphasis is given to achieving short-term profitability at the expense of the long term. Short-term increases in profits gained at the expense of reductions in research and development or the failure to maintain adequate standards of maintenance are two examples of short-term cost savings which are detrimental to the firm in the long term.

Poor-quality decision making by top management

Excessive reliance on the profit performance of divisions may also affect the quality of decisions made by top management. If the managerial competence of divisional managers is assessed mainly on the basis of their ability to hit agreed profit targets, they may be motivated to make wrong decisions. For example in order to reduce IT costs charged by a centralized department, a manager may decide to acquire his own server. He now makes no demands on the central IT facility and so receives no charge; his own performance is improved; since no savings are made in the budget of the central service provider the performance of the total company is worse. Moreover, if reported profits are used as part of an early-warning system, it may trigger action by top management which is not warranted. Therefore, although profit budgets are indispensable for planning purposes, great care should be taken in utilizing them for control. The attainment of profit targets is dependent on many factors, some of which are entirely outside the control of a divisional manager. The uncertainty attached to profit forecasts, in particular, limits the usefulness of profit targets for the evaluation of the performance of a divisional manager. The process of formulating the divisional profit forecast also introduces bias in the evaluation of performance. Divisional profit targets are usually based on the divisional manager's forecast of future events. Therefore, it is the ability to forecast the future successfully, rather than the ability to manage successfully, which forms the basis on which that manager's performance is evaluated. This consideration also affects the validity of comparisons between the performance of different divisions. For example, it is easier to determine an attainable profit goal for a division whose major constraint is productive capacity, where sales are limited only by output, than for a division which sells in a highly competitive market.

Another problem arising from the use of profit budgets in evaluating divisional performance stems from the fact that an annual budget covers too short a period in which to obtain a realistic picture. The effects of decisions in some instances may take several years before being reflected in profits. Thus, the decision to introduce a new product is one of several decisions whose impacts on divisional profits are not fully realized for some years. The more complex and innovative the division the longer will be the time period necessary for the evaluation of performance. In the light of these considerations, the use of annual profits may give a completely inaccurate view of divisional performance.

Poor communication

Where a Theory X style of management exists, negative attitudes may be generated against organizational goals leading to the falsification of budget results and an unwillingness to transmit information – the hiding of bad news. Managers will feel that their own survival justifies these tactics.

The prevalence of negative behaviour in an organization which practises management by domination may be aggravated by the response of top management, when it is realized that information which is needed for decision making is not transmitted. Their immediate reaction may be to impose even tighter controls, which reinforces the negative attitudes held by subordinate managers leading to the transmission of even less accurate and useful information. The progressive tightening of the managerial reins may well result, therefore, in a progressive deterioration of the information flow.

The communication of information is of central importance to the processes of planning and control, as it provides the link between various levels of management and the various decision points. Any reluctance on the part of subordinate managers to communicate information is a serious impediment to the efficiency with which planning and control decisions are made. It is not a sufficient condition for success that an organization should have accounting control systems and that it should have stipulated standards of performance. These control methods will not operate successfully and standards of performance will not be attained if the style of management adopted fails to secure a high degree of motivation and goal congruence within the organization.

Departmental focus

The budget process which involves defining areas of responsibility, measuring and comparing performance, concentrates the manager's entire attention on his/her own department. This narrow departmental focus obscures important relationships between departments, so that interdepartmental dependencies are ignored or overlooked in the quest for optimizing departmental results. Consequently, economies which would result from greater interdepartmental collaboration are lost to the organization.

The stifling of initiative

The planning and control aspects of budgeting may be overemphasized with the result that opportunities for the exercise of personal initiative are excluded. Budgets which appear to be straitjackets discourage managers from deviating from budget commitments even when circumstances indicate that opportunities for new actions exist.

Bias in budgeting

In the last analysis, the process of setting targets involves making subjective judgements. As a result, bias may inevitably be found in the budgeting process in a conscious or unconscious form. Managers may inflate costs and reduce expected revenues when setting budget targets, thereby making them easier to achieve. In this way, the introduction of conscious bias is a deliberate means of ensuring that their performance as managers will be highly evaluated.

The introduction of bias into estimates that find their way into budgets typifies the behavioural responses of individuals to organizational pressures. Take the example of a salesman threatened with the possibility of redundancy as a result of falling sales. He may negotiate sales targets that are at the low end of expected outcomes so that the chances of exceeding them are good. Whereas a stretch target might have encouraged him to do even better.

The presence of bias in setting budgets may be met either through the process of counter-biasing, which leads to gamesmanship in budgeting, or by reducing ignorance about the objectives of the firm in relation to personnel. The reduction of conflict between the firm's objectives and the objectives of managers and personnel is discussed later in this chapter, in the context of the system known as management by objectives.

Budget information and performance evaluation

According to Hopwood (1974), budget information may be used in three different ways for the purposes of assessing managerial performance:

1 Budget-constrained evaluation, where the manager's performance is primarily evaluated on the basis of the ability to continually meet budgets on the short-term basis.
2 Profit-conscious evaluation, where the manager's performance is evaluated on the basis of the ability to increase the general effectiveness of the operations of his/her unit in relation to the long-term objectives of the firm. In this case, budget information will be used with a degree of flexibility.
3 Non-accounting evaluation, where budget information plays a relatively small part in the evaluation of the manager's performance.

A summary of the effects of these different styles of managerial evaluation on managerial behaviour is given below:

	Budget-constrained	Profit-conscious	Non-accounting
Involvement with costs	High	High	Low
Job-related tension	High	Medium	Medium
Manipulation of accounting reports	Extensive	Little	Little
Relations with supervisor	Poor	Good	Good
Relations with colleagues	Poor	Good	Good

The need for several measures of performance

While the use of standard costs and flexible budgets plays an important role in the control of activities and in the evaluation of performance, undue attention to cost control tends to diminish the importance of other goals. For example, non-financial goals for a factory manager might include productive efficiency, the quality of the product, production schedules, the maintenance of satisfactory relations with employees. What importance will be given to these if the budget requires him to minimize costs?

The evaluation of performance therefore requires both financial and non-financial measures of performance. It is evident that some organizational and departmental goals may conflict, such as, for example, the need to minimize costs and to maintain product quality. Emphasis on specific goals will therefore mean that other goals may not be attained. The objectives of performance evaluation, which we have stipulated, require a balanced view of performance covering the various areas of managerial responsibility. If management uses only conventional measurement of revenues, expenses, profit, cost variances and output, it is possible that short-run economic gains may be achieved at the expense of long-run goals. The failure to appreciate the impact of control techniques on individuals responsible for organizational activities may adversely affect employee morale, loyalty, trust and motivation.

The importance of participation

The active participation by managers in the planning process not only enhances their personal sense of involvement in the organization, but improves the efficiency of the planning process. Moreover, such participation establishes a common understanding of purpose, and promotes the acceptance of organizational objectives and goals at all levels. Likewise, the control process is aided by the active participation of managers in the investigation of variances, the evaluation and selection of appropriate solutions and the development of related policies.

The degree of effort expended by members of an organization in attempting to achieve designated goals is particularly dependent upon their personal aspiration level. The aspiration level may be defined as that level of future performance in a familiar task which individuals explicitly undertake knowing their past performance level. For example, a manager's aspiration level as regards costs is the spending level which s/he accepts as realistic and with which s/he will strive to comply. Hence, we may identify three potential levels of cost performance:

1 the budgeted level;
2 the aspiration level;
3 the actual level.

Since the aspiration level is the real inner goal acceptable to the manager, the purpose of participation is to bring the aspiration level in harmony with the budgeted level (or vice versa). Clearly, a budgeted level significantly at variance with the aspiration level will have a negative effect on managerial behaviour.

It follows that managers should be motivated and not pressurized into achieving their budgetary goals. This may be achieved by recognizing the importance of aspiration levels in the planning stage and the timely communication of results as a basis for improving performance, where necessary. The purpose of participation in the control process is, therefore, to motivate managers and to generate in each participant the desire to accomplish or even improve his/her level of performance.

Management by objectives

From the foregoing discussion of the problem of controlling the activities of an organization and evaluating managerial performance, it follows that several conditions must be satisfied if the accounting function is to play a useful role.

1 Divisional and departmental goals must be clearly identified and defined, and appropriate measurements selected by which to express them and evaluate managerial performance. Where objectives are too vague or too ambiguous to be susceptible to clear definition in conventional terms, surrogates should be sought which will enable them to be defined and measured.

2 There should be participation by all levels of management in the control process, thereby ensuring good communication between supervisor and subordinate.

3 A style of management is required which pays particular attention to the human element in organizations, and in so doing provides an environment conducive to the effective employment of all resources.

The aim of management by objectives is to provide a framework for administering a control system which embraces these three conditions. By translating organizational objectives and goals in such a way that they become the personal objectives and goals of all management personnel, management by objectives seeks to create a high degree of goal congruence within an organization. The unity of personal and organizational objectives encourages managers to take actions which are in the best interest of the organization.

Some organizational goals are too remote from individual managers, and therefore have little significance for them, for example, goals relating to the return on capital employed or overall growth targets envisaged in the long-range plan. Management by objectives seeks to establish personal targets at all levels as a means of overcoming this problem. Relating personal goals to department and divisional goals and thence to organizational goals, achieves integration between them which may be depicted as follows:

Personal goals → Divisional goals → Organization goals

Management by objectives involves the following processes:

1 The review of long-term and short-term organizational objectives and goals.

2 The revision, if necessary, of the organizational structure. An organizational chart is required to illustrate the titles, duties and the relationships between managers.

3 Standards of performance necessary to fulfil key tasks are set by individual job holders in agreement with their immediate supervisors. Unless job holders participate in setting performance standards, they will not feel committed to them. The standards of performance which result from systems of management by objectives are not 'ideal', nor are they minimum acceptable levels of performance. They indicate what are agreed to be 'satisfactory' levels of performance. As far as possible, they should be expressed in quantitative terms. The purpose of management controls is to make it possible for supervisors to offer help and guidance to their subordinates rather than acting as watchdogs. A divisional profit goal in this sense is not only a target for the divisional manager, for it may also act as a means whereby top management may help to solve divisional problems should they become apparent through the failure to reach a stipulated figure.

4 Results are measured against goals. An important aspect of this stage is the use of periodic performance appraisal interviews, in which supervisor and subordinate jointly discuss results and consider their implications for the future. The performance appraisal interview is essentially a discussion between manager and subordinate about objectives and their achievement. Performance appraisal should

evaluate managers not merely in terms of current performance as expressed in tangible results; it should also enable their performance as managers, their personal qualifications and character and their potential for advancement to be assessed. It is an integral part of the process of managing by results by which both parties to the interview assess their efficiency as managers. The managers assess their own role as coaches to the subordinates; the subordinates consider their role in supporting the managers.

5 Long- and short-term organizational goals are reviewed in the light of current performance.

These stages in management by objectives are illustrated in Figure 4.1.

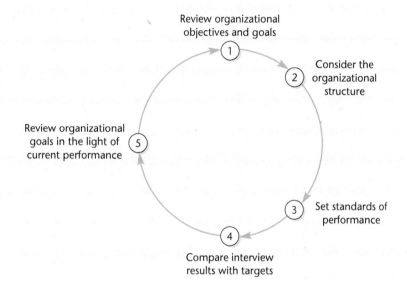

Figure 4.1

Organization theory

Some of the assumptions upon which we have so far relied have been necessary for the purpose of facilitating the examination of the basic aspects of accounting for planning and control. If an accounting system is to be effective in providing information for planning and control purposes, it should be capable of adapting to organizational and environmental factors peculiar to individual enterprises. Different enterprises may require different methods of control, depending on the internal and external influences affecting their own activities. Hence, some assumptions may be more applicable to some organizations than to others. In this respect, organization theory attempts to provide a framework for understanding the influences which bear upon organizations and is important, therefore, for clarifying issues of importance to the accountant.

Approaches to organization theory

By regarding the organization as a logical and rational process, the classical approach focuses in some detail on the organizing function of management. Hence, the classical theory is concerned with the structure of organizations and the determination of the tasks necessary to attain organizational objectives. By contrast, the human relations approach stresses people rather than structures, their motives and behaviour rather than the activities which need to be harnessed for achieving organizational goals. This approach originated in the Hawthorne experiments, which revealed that social and human factors in work situations were often more important than physical factors in affecting productivity. This series of experiments, first led by Harvard Business School Professor Elton Mayo at the Hawthorne Plant of the Western Electric Company in Cicero, Illinois from 1927 to 1932 started out by examining the physical and environmental influences of the workplace (e.g. brightness of lights, humidity) and later, moved into the psychological aspects (e.g. breaks, group pressure, working hours, managerial leadership). The ideas that this team developed about the social dynamics of groups in the work setting had lasting influence – the collection of data, labour–management relations, and informal interaction among factory employees. Four general conclusions were drawn from the Hawthorne studies:

1 The aptitudes of individuals are imperfect predictors of job performance, the amount produced being strongly influenced by social factors.
2 Informal organization affects productivity. The Hawthorne researchers discovered a group life among the workers.
3 Work-group norms affect productivity.
4 The workplace is a social system of interdependent parts.

The human relations theory asserts that since the most important factors are individual needs and wants, the structure of organizations should be geared to individuals rather than the individual being geared to the structure.

Finally, there has developed the contingency approach which starts with the premise that there is no single organizational design that is best in all situations. According to this approach, there are four factors or forces of particular significance in the design of an organizational structure: forces in the manager; forces in the environment; forces in the task; and forces in the subordinates.

1 *Forces in the manager*. This refers to factors relating to the personalities of managers and their influence on the design of the organizational structure. Managers tend to perceive organizational problems in a unique way, which is a function of background, knowledge, experience and values. These factors shape organizational decisions in such areas as strategy, organizational structure and style of management. Accordingly, organizations do not have objectives – only people have objectives. In this analysis, these objectives will differ from manager to manager.
2 *Forces in the environment*. Some studies suggest that the most effective pattern of organizational structure is that which enables the organization to adjust to the requirements of its environment (Burns and Stalker, 1961). These studies indicate that organizations with less formal structures are best able to cope with uncertain and heterogeneous environmental conditions. Conversely, highly structured

organizations will be more effective in stable environmental conditions. Hence, bureaucratic structures, as implied in classical theory, are more appropriate to stable conditions, whereas more democratic and participative structures are required to enable organizations to adapt to a changing environment.

3 *Forces in the task*. Empirical studies indicate that technology has an important impact on the design of an organizational structure. For example, Woodward (1965) has found that organizational structures varied according to the technology involved. According to Woodward, fewer managers are required under systems of unit production than under systems of mass production. The technology associated with unit production systems may also require relatively higher levels of operative skill, and there is evidence to suggest that skilled workers feel more involved in their jobs and are more anxious for an opportunity to participate in decision-making relating to their jobs than unskilled workers. This makes it possible to delegate more authority to lower levels in an organization and has important implications for devising schemes based on 'management by objectives'.

4 *Forces in the subordinates*. This refers to the psychological needs such as the subordinate's desire for a measure of independence, for the acquisition of skills and the motivation for assuming responsibility. The desire to participate in decision-making is not uniform among employees, and as implied earlier it is much stronger among skilled workers and employees with a professional background than it is among unskilled workers. Hence, organizations employing relatively more skilled than unskilled employees will be faced with a greater desire for a democratic structure.

Agency theory

According to Antle (1989), agency models are highly stylized logical tools for discovering basic relationships. They extend the traditional intellectual boundaries of accounting by assuming that its problems have psychological, sociological, economic and political dimensions. Heretofore, these problems have been recognized to some extent in articles dealing with the behavioural aspects of performance evaluation, which have been discussed earlier in this chapter.

Specifically, agency theory re-examines extant basic assumptions about human behaviour in organizations, by considering behaviour in terms of a model in which protagonists are acting out a principal and agent relationship. This relationship grants the agent delegated powers to act on behalf of the principal. The theory considers how to structure the relationship so that the agent acts in the best interests of the principal.

Agency theory is claimed to be particularly relevant when focusing on financial reports generated by agents whose performance is in part evaluated on the basis of those reports. If the choice of accounting method rests with the agents, as is normally the case in so far as management information systems are concerned, agency theory assumes that the information reported through these systems will reflect management preferences over what is reported.

Williamson's (1964) seminal work on the existence of managerial discretion as highly significant in organizational decision making shed new light on the manner in which personal interests influenced decisions. Williamson's thesis conflicted with the traditional view assumed in accounting theory that the interests of shareholders and managers are joined in the maximization of shareholders' wealth. Agency theory addresses the problem of information reporting for assessing managerial behaviour where management holds private information and does not communicate it, or communicates only the information that it wants to communicate.

From the foregoing, it is evident that agency theory considerably extends the debate over the assessment of managerial performance. It shifts this debate from one in which performance is seen as a reactive problem to be examined in the light of managerial styles to the much wider issue of the vested interests that exist in organizations and that are not adequately recognized in extant theories of the firm.

Summary

The budget process alone is not sufficient to maintain adequate management control. Too often, organizations tend to expect results from budgetary control and fail to recognize its behavioural implications. As a result, pressures are created leading to mistrust, hostility and actions detrimental to the long-term prospects of an organization. It follows that accountants should work more closely with behavioural scientists and that they should learn more about the behavioural implications of organizational control.

Participation schemes may be introduced into organizations with due consideration for the psychological problems entailed. One such scheme is management by objectives. Management by objectives differs from the conventional budgetary control theory in that it enables the precepts of Theory Y to be put into practice by creating an environment which allows employees to develop as individuals and to exercise responsibility through self-control. Self-control is found to induce stronger work motivation, for by giving individual managers greater freedom of action, it affords them a greater measure of satisfaction and pleasure which a sense of accomplishment confers.

Being concerned with the provision of information for planning and control, the accountant should find a knowledge of organization theory particularly useful in understanding the internal and external influences which affect the nature of organizational activities and the environment in which decisions are made. These influences have implications for the design of control systems, and the significance of contingency theory lies in the identification of their sources.

New considerations in the assessment of managerial behaviour have been inspired by protagonists of agency theory, which looks at the impact of discretionary managerial behaviour on management information.

Self-assessment questions

1 State what you understand by 'managerial style'.

2 What is meant by 'organization culture'?

3 List the objectives of performance evaluation.

4 Explain 'Theory X'.

5 Contrast 'Theory X' with 'Theory Y'.

6 Comment on possible managerial reactions to budgets.

7 Describe three possible levels of cost performance.

8 Define 'management by objectives'.

9 What do you understand by 'contingency theory'?

Problem (*indicates that a solution is to be found in the Lecturer's Guide*)

1* The following extract is taken from a conversation between the chairman of Westway Engineering Company and James Brown, accountant, on the day Brown took up his appointment with the company.

> Chairman: 'We apply a system of payment by results to foremen as well as to operatives. For each department, budgeted allowances are set for the expenditure which should be incurred over varying levels of output. The greater the saving on budgeted expenditure for a department, the greater the bonus received by the foreman concerned. For example, this report shows how the bonus the foreman of our assembly department had built up suffered a severe jolt last month.'

He hands the following report to Brown.

Westway Engineering Company – Assembly Department Foreman: W Rodgers

		For month		Year to date
	Budget allowance	Actual	(Over) under budget	(Over) under budget
	£	£	£	£
Direct material	4,000	5,000	(1,000)	(3,000)
Direct labour	10,000	12,000	(2,000)	(3,500)
Indirect labour	5,000	4,500	500	1,000
Indirect material	2,000	1,700	300	(1,000)
Power	6,000	6,500	(500)	(2,000)
Maintenance	7,000	10,000	(3,000)	4,000
Depreciation	5,000	4,000	1,000	2,000
Insurance	100	80	20	500
General expense	10,000	8,500	1,500	4,500
			(3,180)	2,500

> Chairman: 'Since the new accounting system was installed a year ago, there appears to have been a general deterioration in morale. The relations between a number of staff certainly need improving. Two months ago an error was made on an order, and the goods were returned for correction, a process which cost £700. None of the departmental foremen were prepared to accept the cost of the error, which was finally charged to general factory loss. Because of the incident two foremen stopped talking to each other.'

Required:

Discuss what improvements should be made in the accounting system in operation at Westway's.

References

Antle, R. (1989) Commentary on intellectual boundaries in accounting research, *Accounting Horizons*, June 1989.

Argyris, C. (1953) Human problems with budgets, *Harvard Business Review*, January–February.

Burns, T. and Stalker, G.M. (1961) *The Management of Innovation*, Tavistock Publications.

Hopwood, A. (1974) *Accounting and Human Behaviour*, Accountancy Age Books.

Horngren, C.T. and Foster, G. (1987) *Cost Accounting: A Managerial Emphasis*, 6th edn, Prentice Hall.

McGregor, D.M. (1960) *The Human Side of the Enterprise*, McGraw-Hill.

Mackintosh, N.B. (1994) *CA Magazine*, September.

Williamson, E.O. (1964) *The Economics of Discretionary Behaviour: Managerial Objectives in a Theory of the Firm*, Prentice Hall.

Woodward, J. (1965) *Industrial Organization: Theory and Practice*, Oxford University Press.

Part 3 Marketing

5

INTRODUCTION

In recent years, data-based marketing has swept through the business world. In its wake, measurable performance and accountability have become the keys to marketing success. However, few managers appreciate the range of metrics by which they can evaluate marketing strategies and dynamics. Fewer still understand the pros, cons, and nuances of each.

In this environment, we have come to recognize that marketers, general managers, and business students need a comprehensive, practical reference on the metrics used to judge marketing programs and quantify their results. In this book, we seek to provide that reference. We wish our readers great success with it.

5.1 What Is a Metric?

A metric is a measuring system that quantifies a trend, dynamic, or characteristic.[1] In virtually all disciplines, practitioners use metrics to explain phenomena, diagnose causes, share findings, and project the results of future events. Throughout the worlds of science, business, and government, metrics encourage rigor and objectivity. They make it possible to compare observations across regions and time periods. They facilitate understanding and collaboration.

5.2 Why Do You Need Metrics?

"When you can measure what you are speaking about, and express it in numbers, you know something about it; but when you cannot measure it, when you cannot express it in numbers, your knowledge is of a meager and unsatisfactory kind: it may be the beginning of knowledge, but you have scarcely, in your thoughts, advanced to the stage of science."—William Thomson, Lord Kelvin, Popular Lectures and Addresses (1891–94)[2]

Lord Kelvin, a British physicist and the manager of the laying of the first successful transatlantic cable, was one of history's great advocates for quantitative investigation. In his day, however, mathematical rigor had not yet spread widely beyond the worlds of science, engineering, and finance. Much has changed since then.

Today, numerical fluency is a crucial skill for every business leader. Managers must quantify market opportunities and competitive threats. They must justify the financial risks and benefits of their decisions. They must evaluate plans, explain variances, judge performance, and identify leverage points for improvement—all in numeric terms. These responsibilities require a strong command of measurements and of the systems and formulas that generate them. In short, they require metrics.

Managers must select, calculate, and explain key business metrics. They must understand how each is constructed and how to use it in decision-making. Witness the following, more recent quotes from management experts:

> "... every metric, whether it is used explicitly to influence behavior, to evaluate future strategies, or simply to take stock, will affect actions and decisions."[3]

> "If you can't measure it, you can't manage it."[4]

5.3   Marketing Metrics: Opportunities, Performance, and Accountability

Marketers are by no means immune to the drive toward quantitative planning and evaluation. Marketing may once have been regarded as more an art than a science. Executives may once have cheerfully admitted that they knew they wasted half the money they spent on advertising, but they didn't know which half. Those days, however, are gone.

Today, marketers must understand their addressable markets quantitatively. They must measure new opportunities and the investment needed to realize them. Marketers must quantify the value of products, customers, and distribution channels—all under various pricing and promotional scenarios. Increasingly, marketers are held accountable for the financial ramifications of their decisions. Observers have noted this trend in graphic terms:

> "For years, corporate marketers have walked into budget meetings like neighborhood junkies. They couldn't always justify how well they spent past handouts or what difference it all made. They just wanted more money—for flashy TV ads, for big-ticket events, for, you know, getting out the message and building up the brand. But those heady days of blind budget increases are fast being replaced with a new mantra: measurement and accountability."[5]

5.4   Choosing the Right Numbers

The numeric imperative represents a challenge, however. In business and economics, many metrics are complex and difficult to master. Some are highly specialized and best suited to specific analyses. Many require data that may be approximate, incomplete, or unavailable.

Under these circumstances, no single metric is likely to be perfect. For this reason, we recommend that marketers use a portfolio or "dashboard" of metrics. By doing so, they can view market dynamics from various perspectives and arrive at "triangulated" strategies and solutions. Additionally, with multiple metrics, marketers can use each as a check on the others. In this way, they can maximize the accuracy of their knowledge.[6] They can also estimate or project one data point on the basis of others. Of course, to use multiple metrics effectively, marketers must appreciate the relations between them and the limitations inherent in each.

When this understanding is achieved, however, metrics can help a firm maintain a productive focus on customers and markets. They can help managers identify the strengths and weaknesses in both strategies and execution. Mathematically defined and widely disseminated, metrics can become part of a precise, operational language within a firm.

Data Availability and Globalization of Metrics

A further challenge in metrics stems from wide variations in the availability of data between industries and geographies. Recognizing these variations, we have tried to suggest alternative sources and procedures for estimating some of the metrics in this book.

Fortunately, although both the range and type of marketing metrics may vary between countries,[7] these differences are shrinking rapidly. Ambler,[8] for example, reports that performance metrics have become a common language among marketers, and that they are now used to rally teams and benchmark efforts internationally.

5.5   Mastering Metrics

Being able to "crunch the numbers" is vital to success in marketing. Knowing which numbers to crunch, however, is a skill that develops over time. Toward that end, managers must practice the use of metrics and learn from their mistakes. By working through the examples in this book, we hope our readers will gain both confidence and a firm understanding of the fundamentals of data-based marketing. With time and experience, we trust that you will also develop an intuition about metrics, and learn to dig deeper when calculations appear suspect or puzzling.

Ultimately, with regard to metrics, we believe many of our readers will require not only familiarity but also fluency. That is, managers should be able to perform relevant calculations on the fly—under pressure, in board meetings, and during strategic deliberations and negotiations. Although not all readers will require that level of fluency, we believe it will be increasingly expected of candidates for senior management positions, especially those with significant financial responsibility. We anticipate that a mastery of data-based marketing will become a means for many of our readers to differentiate and position themselves for career advancement in an ever more challenging environment.

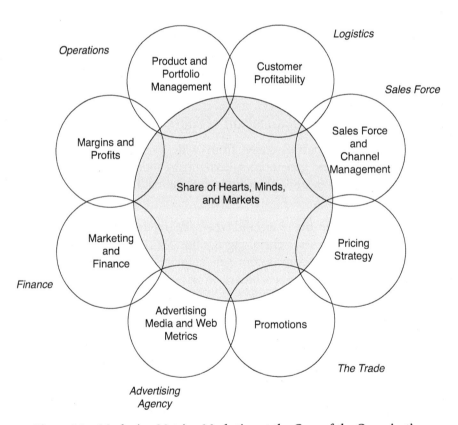

Figure 5.1   Marketing Metrics: Marketing at the Core of the Organization

Reference Materials

Throughout this text, we have highlighted formulas and definitions for easy reference. Within each formula, we have followed this notation to define all inputs and outputs.

$—(Dollar Terms): *A monetary value. We have used the dollar sign and "dollar terms" for brevity, but any other currency, including the euro, yen, dinar, or yuan, would be equally appropriate.*

%—(Percentage): *Used as the equivalent of fractions or decimals. For readability, we have intentionally omitted the step of multiplying decimals by 100 to obtain percentages.*

#—(Count): *Used for such measures as unit sales or number of competitors.*

R—(Rating): *Expressed on a scale that translates qualitative judgments or preferences into numeric ratings. Example: A survey in which customers are asked to assign a rating of "1" to items that they find least satisfactory and "5" to those that are most satisfactory. Ratings have no intrinsic meaning without reference to their scale and context.*

I—(Index): *A comparative figure, often linked to or expressive of a market average. Example: the consumer price index. Indexes are often interpreted as a percentage.*

$—Dollar.   %—Percentage.   #—Count.   R—Rating.   I—Index.

References and Suggested Further Reading

Abela, Andrew, Bruce H. Clark, and Tim Ambler. "Marketing Performance Measurement, Performance, and Learning," working paper, September 1, 2004.

Ambler, Tim, and Chris Styles. (1995). "Brand Equity: Toward Measures That Matter," working paper No. 95-902, London Business School, Centre for Marketing.

Barwise, Patrick, and John U. Farley. (2003). "Which Marketing Metrics Are Used and Where?" Marketing Science Institute, (03-111), working paper, Series issues two 03-002.

Clark, Bruce H., Andrew V. Abela, and Tim Ambler. "Return on Measurement: Relating Marketing Metrics Practices to Strategic Performance," working paper, January 12, 2004.

Hauser, John, and Gerald Katz. (1998). "Metrics: You Are What You Measure," *European Management Journal*, Vo. 16, No. 5, pp. 517–528.

Kaplan, R. S., and D. P. Norton. (1996). *The Balanced Scorecard: Translating Strategy into Action*, Boston, MA: Harvard Business School Press.

Table 5.1   Major Metrics List

Metric	Metric
Share of Hearts, Minds, and Markets	Channel Margins
Revenue Market Share	Average Price per Unit
Unit Market Share	Price Per Statistical Unit
Relative Market Share	Variable and Fixed Costs
Brand Development Index	Marketing Spending
Category Development Index	Contribution per Unit
Decomposition of Market Share	Contribution Margin (%)
Market Penetration	Break-Even Sales
Brand Penetration	Target Volume
Penetration Share	Target Revenues
Share of Requirements	
Heavy Usage Index	*Product and Portfolio Management*
Hierarchy of Effects	Trial
Awareness	Repeat Volume
Top of Mind	Penetration
Ad Awareness	Volume Projections
Knowledge	Year-on-Year Growth
Consumer Beliefs	Compound Annual Growth Rate (CAGR)
Purchase Intentions	Cannibalization Rate
Purchase Habits	Fair Share Draw Rate
Loyalty	Brand Equity Metrics
Likeability	Conjoint Utilities
Willingness to Recommend	Segment Utilities
Customer Satisfaction	Conjoint Utilities and Volume Projections
Net Promoter	
Willingness to Search	*Customer Profitability*
	Customers
Margins and Profits	Recency
Unit Margin	Retention Rate
Margin (%)	Customer Profit

Table 5.1 *Continued*

Metric	Metric
Customer Lifetime Value	Residual Elasticity
Prospect Lifetime Value	*Promotion*
Average Acquisition Cost	Baseline Sales
Average Retention Cost	Incremental Sales/Promotion Lift
	Redemption Rates
Sales Force and Channel Management	Costs for Coupons and Rebates
Workload	Percentage Sales with Coupon
Sales Potential Forecast	Percent Sales on Deal
Sales Goal	Pass-Through
Sales Force Effectiveness	Price Waterfall
Compensation	
Break-Even Number of Employees	*Advertising Media and Web Metrics*
Sales Funnel, Sales Pipeline	Impressions
Numeric Distribution	Gross Rating Points (GRPs)
All Commodity Volume (ACV)	Cost per Thousand Impressions (CPM)
Product Category Volume (PCV)	Net Reach
Total Distribution	Average Frequency
Category Performance Ratio	Frequency Response Functions
Out of Stock	Effective Reach
Inventories	Effective Frequency
Markdowns	Share of Voice
Direct Product Profitability (DPP)	Pageviews
Gross Margin Return on Inventory Investment (GMROII)	Rich Media Display Time
	Rich Media Interaction Rate
Pricing Strategy	Clickthrough Rate
Price Premium	Cost per Click
Reservation Price	Cost per Order
Percent Good Value	Cost per Customer Acquired
Price Elasticity of Demand	Visits
Optimal Price	

Continues

Table 5.1　*Continued*

Metric	Metric
Visitors	Earnings Before Interest, Taxes, Depreciation, and Amortization (EBITDA)
Abandonment Rate	
Bounce Rate	Return on Investment (ROI)
Friends/Followers/Supporters	Economic Profit (aka EVA®)
Downloads	Payback
	Net Present Value (NPV)
Marketing and Finance	Internal Rate of Return (IRR)
Net Profit	Return on Marketing Investment (ROMI); Revenue
Return on Sales (ROS)	

5.6　Marketing Metrics Survey

Why Do a Survey of Which Metrics Are Most Useful?

From the beginning of our work on this book, we have fielded requests from colleagues, editors, and others to provide a short list of the "key" or "top ten" marketing metrics. The intuition behind this request is that readers (managers and students) ought to be able to focus their attention on the "most important" metrics. Until now we have resisted that request.

Our reasons for not providing the smaller, more concentrated list of "really important" metrics are as follows. First, we believe that any ranking of marketing metrics from most to least useful will depend on the type of business under consideration. For example, marketers of business-to-business products and services that go to market through a direct sales force don't need metrics that measure retail availability or dealer productivity.

The second reason we believe that different businesses will have different rankings is that metrics tend to come in matched sets. For example, if customer lifetime value is important to your business (let's say, financial services), then you are likely to value measures of retention and acquisition costs as well. The same notion applies to retail, media, sales force, and Web traffic metrics. If some of these are important to you, others in the same general categories are likely to be rated as useful, too.

Third, businesses don't always have access (at a reasonable cost) to the metrics they would like to have. Inevitably, some of the rankings presented will reflect the cost of obtaining the data that underlie the particular metrics.

Fourth, some metrics might be ranked lower, but ultimately prove to be useful, after managers fully understand the pros and cons of a particular metric. For example, many believe that Economic Value Added (EVA) is the "gold standard" of profitability metrics, but it ranks far below other financial performance measures such as ROI. We believe one reason for the low ranking of EVA is that this metric is less applicable at the "operating level" than for overall corporate performance. The other reason is that the measure is relatively new, and many managers don't understand it as well. Customer Lifetime Value is another metric that is gaining acceptance, but is still unfamiliar to many managers. If all these metrics were well understood, there would be no need for a book of this type.

In summary, while we believe the rankings resulting from our survey can be useful, we ask readers to keep the above points in mind. We report in Tables 5.2 and 5.3 the overall ranking of the usefulness of various metrics as well as the different rankings for different types of businesses and different categories of metrics. Although no business is likely to be exactly like yours, we thought readers might find it useful to see what other marketers thought which metrics were most useful in monitoring and managing their businesses. For a look at the complete survey, see Appendix A.

Survey Sample

Our survey was completed by 194 senior marketing managers and executives. More than 100 held the title of Vice President/Director/Manager or "Head" of Marketing, some with global responsibility. Most held titles such as VP of Marketing, Marketing Director, and Director Sales and Marketing. There were 10 presidents and C-level managers with heavy marketing responsibilities, and the remaining respondents included product/project/category managers, trade marketing managers, pricing managers, key account managers, development managers, and assistant/associate vice presidents.

Industries represented in our survey are too diverse to easily summarize. No more than 10 responses from a single industry were recorded, and the respondents listed their markets as aerospace, automobiles, banking, chemicals, consumer goods, construction, computers, consulting, education, industrial distribution, investments, government, health care, housing, insurance, information technology, manufacturing, materials, medical devices, paints, pharmaceuticals, retailing, software, telecommunications, and transportation. Roughly 20% of respondents did not provide a specific industry.

Survey questions asked respondents to rate the usefulness of particular metrics in monitoring and managing their businesses. Note that this survey asks managers to give ratings with respect to how these metrics are actually used but does not inquire about the reason. Nor did the survey offer guidance concerning the meaning of "useful"—that was left as a matter of interpretation for survey participants.

Financial metrics are generally rated very high in usefulness compared to any true marketing metrics. This is not surprising given that financial metrics are common to almost every business.

Table 5.2 Survey of Senior Marketing Managers on the Perceived
Usefulness of Various Marketing Metrics (n = 194)

Group			All Who Responded to Question		Customer Relationship			What Does Your Business Sell?			Who Are Your Customers?		
			194		Contract	Frequent Purchase	Infrequent Purchase	Products	Services	Mixed	End Consumers	Business	Mixed
# of People in Group					65	69	41	105	36	31	44	85	48
Metric	Question Number		% Saying Very Useful	Rank	Rank	Rank	Rank	Rank	Rank	Rank	Rank	Rank	Rank
Net Profit	Q8.10#1		91%	1	1	1	1	1	1	1	1	1	1
Margin %	Q8.3#2		78%	2	10	2	3	2	6	2	2	3	6
Return on Investment	Q8.10#3		77%	3	4	5	2	3	5	3	3	2	8
Customer Satisfaction	Q8.2#12		71%	4	2	17	11	13	3	5	19	6	4
Target Revenues	Q8.4#2		71%	5	8	12	5	12	8	3	13	7	6
Sales Total	Q8.6#3		70%	6	7	10	8	10	8	8	16	3	12
Target Volumes	Q8.4#1		70%	7	5	6	11	8	13	10	8	7	10
Return on Sales	Q8.10#2		69%	8	12	12	3	9	17	8	4	17	2
Loyalty	Q8.2#8		69%	9	70	71	98	4	11	17	13	5	16
Annual Growth %	Q8.4#7		69%	10	13	3	11	7	11	15	8	10	10
Dollar Market Share	Q8.1#1		67%	11	13	7	7	5	13	21	8	11	13

Continues

Table 5.2   *Continued*

Group		All Who Responded to Question	Customer Relationship			What Does Your Business Sell?			Who Are Your Customers?		
			Contract	Frequent Purchase	Infrequent Purchase	Products	Services	Mixed	End Consumers	Business	Mixed
# of People in Group		194	65	69	41	105	36	31	44	85	48
Metric	Question Number	% Saying Very Useful / Rank	Rank	Rank	Rank	Rank	Rank	Rank	Rank	Rank	Rank
Customers	Q8.5#1	67% / 12	5	16	11	19	4	5	26	13	3
Unit Margin	Q8.3#1	65% / 13	17	9	5	11	21	10	13	12	13
Retention Rate	Q8.5#3	63% / 14	3	26	26	28	2	5	76	9	5
Sales Potential Forecast	Q8.6#2	62% / 15	11	18	11	17	18	10	23	14	18
Unit Market Share	Q8.1#2	61% / 16	23	4	16	5	54	30	8	18	17
Brand Awareness	Q8.2#1	61% / 17	23	7	16	14	33	10	4	25	9
Variable and Fixed Costs	Q8.3#6	60% / 18	15	11	32	15	8	30	19	21	13
Willingness to Recommend	Q8.2#10	57% / 19	9	32	26	30	6	19	36	16	29
Volume Projections	Q8.4#6	56% / 20	23	14	21	16	31	24	45	15	27
Sales Force Effective	Q8.6#4	54% / 21	21	22	21	25	31	15	42	23	18
Price Premium	Q8.8#1	54% / 22	28	27	8	23	33	17	56	19	25

Marketing Spending	Q8.3#7	52%	23	51	15	16	18	67	21	6	46	21
Average Price per Unit	Q8.3#4	51%	24	23	19	21	22	33	38	27	26	25
Penetration	Q8.4#5	50%	25	39	25	26	30	54	24	39	24	32
Top of Mind	Q8.2#2	50%	26	33	25	26	30	33	30	39	27	21
Compensation	Q8.6#5	49%	27	17	30	52	32	18	46	42	20	58
Return on Marketing Investment (ROMI)	Q8.10#8	49%	27	47	32	8	26	45	24	19	39	
Consumer Beliefs	Q8.2#5	48%	29	33	35	21	47	21	10	30	29	24
Contribution Margin %	Q8.3#9	47%	30	56	21	21	29	46	24	45	32	36
Net Present Value	Q8.10#6	46%	31	31	37	26	39	27	20	39	41	20
Market Penetration	Q8.1#6	45%	32	17	41	58	38	41	38	45	35	33
Sales Funnel, Sales Pipeline	Q8.6#7	44%	33	17	60	32	54	21	21	74	21	58
Relative Market Share	Q8.1#3	44%	34	36	38	40	32	33	65	58	41	27
Purchase Habits	Q8.2#7	43%	35	39	35	43	27	41	80	30	29	69
Inventories	Q8.7#7	43%	36	62	20	48	20	109	59	24	45	46
Likeability	Q8.2#9	43%	37	28	54	38	47	21	46	45	37	39
Effective Reach	Q8.9#6	42%	38	48	40	32	37	46	44	7	61	46
Economic Profit (EVA)	Q8.10#4	41%	39	31	63	26	50	27	30	71	36	38
Impressions	Q8.9#1	41%	40	36	61	26	50	41	24	19	64	29
Customer Profit	Q8.5#4	41%	41	16	69	52	59	18	54	73	28	46
Optimal Price	Q8.8#5	41%	42	39	47	36	36	46	46	45	49	36

Continues

Table 5.2   *Continued*

Group		All Who Responded to Question		Customer Relationship			What Does Your Business Sell?			Who Are Your Customers?		
				Contract	Frequent Purchase	Infrequent Purchase	Products	Services	Mixed	End Consumers	Business	Mixed
# of People in Group		194		65	69	41	105	36	31	44	85	48
Metric	Question Number	% Saying Very Useful	Rank	Rank	Rank	Rank	Rank	Rank	Rank	Rank	Rank	Rank
Payback	Q8.10#5	41%	42	51	51	20	54	27	43	67	34	44
Incremental Sales or Promotional Lift	Q8.8#8	41%	44	66	24	52	24	96	65	24	50	51
Consumer Knowledge	Q8.2#4	40%	45	36	57	43	64	21	30	58	37	51
Contribution per Unit	Q8.3#8	40%	46	71	29	48	39	62	46	63	54	29
Break-Even Sales	Q8.3#10	40%	46	51	39	43	43	40	59	58	41	46
Customer Lifetime Value	Q8.5#5	39%	48	23	77	40	69	21	30	76	46	33
Price Elasticity	Q8.8#4	39%	48	71	31	38	35	72	54	34	56	39
Purchase Intentions	Q8.2#6	39%	50	54	67	19	62	41	30	45	32	79
Growth CAGR	Q8.4#8	38%	51	45	32	74	41	54	72	83	31	45
Internal Rate of Return	Q8.10#7	38%	52	44	63	36	66	27	29	71	53	35
Effective Frequency	Q8.9#7	37%	53	56	52	43	45	67	44	12	74	46

Visitors	Q8.9#15	37%	54	39	58	58	60	46	38	53	51	62
Average Acquisition Cost	Q8.5#7	36%	55	21	95	43	77	13	38	83	41	43
Share of Voice	Q8.9#8	36%	55	66	43	52	45	62	64	33	72	39
Visits	Q8.9#14	36%	57	39	58	66	61	46	38	53	55	51
Workload	Q8.6#1	36%	58	50	48	66	53	54	59	79	40	58
Repeat Volume	Q8.4#4	36%	59	56	46	58	50	54	65	64	52	58
Clickthrough Rate	Q8.9#10	35%	60	33	61	77	63	33	54	29	67	51
Baseline Sales	Q8.8#7	34%	61	71	42	56	42	72	80	45	56	69
Total Distribution	Q8.7#4	34%	62	84	43	48	44	96	59	28	66	69
Net Reach	Q8.9#4	34%	62	62	48	66	58	72	51	37	62	62
Brand Penetration	Q8.1#7	34%	64	62	54	62	47	62	75	30	69	62
Out of Stock %	Q8.7#6	33%	65	86	27	88	34	109	86	18	64	85
Average Retention Cost	Q8.5#8	33%	66	30	98	40	82	13	51	91	48	51
Product Category Volume	Q8.7#3	33%	67	84	45	57	57	92	58	62	62	51
Cost per Customer Acquired	Q8.9#13	32%	68	48	72	66	70	54	51	74	60	51
Average Frequency	Q8.9#5	31%	69	76	48	71	54	83	75	16	77	86
Channel Margin	Q8.3#3	30%	70	66	80	48	70	83	37	67	82	39
Direct Product Profitability	Q8.7#9	30%	71	76	56	62	67	72	54	66	69	62
Recency	Q8.5#2	29%	72	56	74	71	75	33	80	94	59	62
Cost per Thousand Impression	Q8.9#3	28%	73	62	81	62	70	62	75	38	83	75

Continues

Table 5.2 *Continued*

Group	Question Number	All Who Responded to Question — % Saying Very Useful	All Who Responded to Question — Rank	Customer Relationship — Contract (Rank)	Customer Relationship — Frequent Purchase (Rank)	Customer Relationship — Infrequent Purchase (Rank)	What Does Your Business Sell? — Products (Rank)	What Does Your Business Sell? — Services (Rank)	What Does Your Business Sell? — Mixed (Rank)	Who Are Your Customers? — End Consumers (Rank)	Who Are Your Customers? — Business (Rank)	Who Are Your Customers? — Mixed (Rank)
# of People in Group			194	65	69	41	105	36	31	44	85	48
Pageview	Q8.9#9	28%	74	45	84	88	87	54	46	56	83	69
Cost per Click	Q8.9#11	27%	75	56	86	77	79	46	65	53	88	75
Brand Equity Metrics	Q8.4#10	26%	76	76	76	77	68	72	89	58	90	74
Markdowns	Q8.7#8	26%	77	96	52	84	65	106	80	34	90	86
Cannibalization Rate	Q8.4#9	24%	78	88	65	95	74	83	97	78	76	91
Abandonment Rate	Q8.9#16	24%	79	56	90	95	90	62	71	81	87	68
Ad Awareness	Q8.2#3	23%	80	76	88	77	78	72	80	64	104	75
Cost per Order	Q8.9#12	23%	81	71	91	74	90	67	65	95	73	75
Gross Rating Points	Q8.9#2	23%	82	88	91	58	84	67	80	42	99	92
Break-Even Number of Employees	Q8.6#6	23%	83	66	96	71	100	46	59	85	69	96
Hierarchy of Effects	Q8.1#11	23%	84	81	83	84	80	72	86	92	83	69

Metric	Code											
Numeric Distribution %	Q8.7#1	97	89	69	103	106	73	62	75	108	85	22%
All Commodity Volume	Q8.7#2	104	78	69	89	83	75	93	67	96	85	22%
Penetration Share	Q8.1#8	79	75	95	75	72	84	74	93	76	87	22%
Brand Development Index	Q8.1#4	79	94	80	75	83	89	94	79	91	88	21%
Prospect Lifetime Value	Q8.5#6	97	67	98	104	46	95	66	106	81	89	21%
Percentage Sales on Deal	Q8.8#12	92	79	87	72	83	92	87	82	91	89	21%
Willingness to Search	Q8.2#13	100	79	85	107	72	86	77	102	71	91	20%
Trial Volume	Q8.4#3	103	79	90	97	96	82	108	72	90	92	19%
Net Promoter Score	Q8.2#11	109	58	106	107	61	94	103	101	55	93	19%
Facings	Q8.7#5	110	99	45	107	72	81	105	66	99	94	19%
Redemption Rates	Q8.8#9	92	94	82	104	96	92	100	69	102	95	19%
Cost of Coupons/ Rebates	Q8.8#10	79	102	87	97	96	87	90	77	102	95	19%
Category Development Index	Q8.1#5	79	92	99	86	83	97	103	87	95	97	18%
Reservation Price	Q8.8#2	99	86	100	89	72	96	84	93	99	98	17%
GMROII	Q8.7#10	100	94	87	89	96	98	99	84	102	99	16%
Percent Good Value	Q8.8#3	62	109	100	72	67	107	77	108	91	99	16%
Percentage Sales with Coupon	Q8.8#11	86	105	93	89	96	98	90	88	109	99	16%
Price per Statistical Unit	Q8.3#5	79	94	104	65	83	104	90	102	91	102	16%
Conjoint Utilities	Q8.4#11	89	94	107	89	92	101	108	99	81	103	14%
Residual Elasticity	Q8.8#6	92	92	109	97	92	102	77	109	98	104	14%

Continues

Table 5.2   *Continued*

Group			All Who Responded to Question		Customer Relationship			What Does Your Business Sell?			Who Are Your Customers?		
# of People in Group			194		Contract	Frequent Purchase	Infrequent Purchase	Products	Services	Mixed	End Consumers	Business	Mixed
Metric	Question Number	% Saying Very Useful	Rank		65	69	41	105	36	31	44	85	48
					Rank	Rank	Rank	Rank	Rank	Rank	Rank	Rank	Rank
Percent Time on Deal	Q8.8#13	14%	105		102	96	95	105	96	89	97	102	104
Conjoint Utilities & Volume Projection	Q8.4#12	13%	106		87	99	108	103	92	89	103	105	89
Pass-Through	Q8.8#15	11%	107		102	107	100	108	83	97	102	108	100
Share of Requirements	Q8.1#9	10%	108		102	102	105	106	106	106	108	99	108
Average Deal Depth	Q8.8#14	10%	109		110	105	100	109	96	97	105	107	104
Heavy Usage Index	Q8.1#10	6%	110		101	110	107	110	96	110	110	110	104

Table 5.3   Ranking of Metrics by Category

Metric	Section in Survey	Question Number	% Saying Very Useful	Ranking in Survey Section
Dollar Market Share	1	Q8.1#1	67%	1
Unit Market Share	1	Q8.1#2	61%	2
Market Penetration	1	Q8.1#6	45%	3
Relative Market Share	1	Q8.1#3	44%	4
Brand Penetration	1	Q8.1#7	34%	5
Hierarchy of Effects	1	Q8.1#11	23%	6
Penetration Share	1	Q8.1#8	22%	7
Brand Development Index	1	Q8.1#4	21%	8
Category Development Index	1	Q8.1#5	18%	9
Share of Requirements	1	Q8.1#9	10%	10
Heavy Usage Index	1	Q8.1#10	6%	11
Customer Satisfaction	2	Q8.2#12	71%	1
Loyalty	2	Q8.2#8	69%	2
Brand Awareness	2	Q8.2#1	61%	3
Willingness to Recommend	2	Q8.2#10	57%	4
Top of Mind	2	Q8.2#2	50%	5
Consumer Beliefs	2	Q8.2#5	48%	6
Purchase Habits	2	Q8.2#7	43%	7
Likeability	2	Q8.2#9	43%	8
Consumer Knowledge	2	Q8.2#4	40%	9
Purchase Intentions	2	Q8.2#6	39%	10
Ad Awareness	2	Q8.2#3	23%	11
Willingness to Search	2	Q8.2#13	20%	12
Net Promoter Score	2	Q8.2#11	19%	13
Margin %	3	Q8.3#2	78%	1
Unit Margin	3	Q8.3#1	65%	2
Variable and Fixed Costs	3	Q8.3#6	60%	3

Continues

Table 5.3 *Continued*

Metric	Section in Survey	Question Number	% Saying Very Useful	Ranking in Survey Section
Marketing Spending	3	Q8.3#7	52%	4
Average Price per Unit	3	Q8.3#4	51%	5
Contribution Margin %	3	Q8.3#9	47%	6
Contribution per Unit	3	Q8.3#8	40%	7
Break-Even Sales	3	Q8.3#10	40%	8
Channel Margin	3	Q8.3#3	30%	9
Price per Statistical Unit	3	Q8.3#5	16%	10
Target Revenues	4	Q8.4#2	71%	1
Target Volumes	4	Q8.4#1	70%	2
Annual Growth %	4	Q8.4#7	69%	3
Volume Projections	4	Q8.4#6	56%	4
Penetration	4	Q8.4#5	50%	5
Growth CAGR	4	Q8.4#8	38%	6
Repeat Volume	4	Q8.4#4	36%	7
Brand Equity Metrics	4	Q8.4#10	26%	8
Cannibalization Rate	4	Q8.4#9	24%	9
Trial Volume	4	Q8.4#3	19%	10
Conjoint Utilities	4	Q8.4#11	14%	11
Conjoint Utilities & Volume Projection	4	Q8.4#12	13%	12
Customers	5	Q8.5#1	67%	1
Retention Rate	5	Q8.5#3	63%	2
Customer Profit	5	Q8.5#4	41%	3
Customer Lifetime Value	5	Q8.5#5	39%	4
Average Acquisition Cost	5	Q8.5#7	36%	5
Average Retention Cost	5	Q8.5#8	33%	6
Recency	5	Q8.5#2	29%	7
Prospect Lifetime Value	5	Q8.5#6	21%	8
Sales Total	6	Q8.6#3	70%	1

Metric	Section in Survey	Question Number	% Saying Very Useful	Ranking in Survey Section
Sales Potential Forecast	6	Q8.6#2	62%	2
Sales Force Effective	6	Q8.6#4	54%	3
Compensation	6	Q8.6#5	49%	4
Sales Funnel, Sales Pipeline	6	Q8.6#7	44%	5
Workload	6	Q8.6#1	36%	6
Break-Even Number of Employees	6	Q8.6#6	23%	7
Inventories	7	Q8.7#7	43%	1
Total Distribution	7	Q8.7#4	34%	2
Out of Stock % (OOS)	7	Q8.7#6	33%	3
Product Category Volume (PCV)	7	Q8.7#3	33%	4
Direct Product Profitability (DPP)	7	Q8.7#9	30%	5
Markdowns	7	Q8.7#8	26%	6
Numeric Distribution %	7	Q8.7#1	22%	7
All Commodity Volume (ACV)	7	Q8.7#2	22%	8
Facings	7	Q8.7#5	19%	9
Gross Margin Return on Inventory Investment (GMROII)	7	Q8.7#10	16%	10
Price Premium	8	Q8.8#1	54%	1
Optimal Price	8	Q8.8#5	41%	2
Incremental Sales or Promotional Lift	8	Q8.8#8	41%	3
Price Elasticity	8	Q8.8#4	39%	4
Baseline Sales	8	Q8.8#7	34%	5
Percentage Sales on Deal	8	Q8.8#12	21%	6
Redemption Rates	8	Q8.8#9	19%	7

Continues

Table 5.3 *Continued*

Metric	Section in Survey	Question Number	% Saying Very Useful	Ranking in Survey Section
Cost of Coupons/ Rebates	8	Q8.8#10	19%	8
Reservation Price	8	Q8.8#2	17%	9
Percent Good Value	8	Q8.8#3	16%	10
Percentage Sales with Coupon	8	Q8.8#11	16%	11
Residual Elasticity	8	Q8.8#6	14%	12
Percent Time on Deal	8	Q8.8#13	14%	13
Pass-Through	8	Q8.8#15	11%	14
Average Deal Depth	8	Q8.8#14	10%	15
Effective Reach	9	Q8.9#6	42%	1
Impressions	9	Q8.9#1	41%	2
Effective Frequency	9	Q8.9#7	37%	3
Visitors	9	Q8.9#15	37%	4
Share of Voice	9	Q8.9#8	36%	5
Visits	9	Q8.9#14	36%	6
Clickthrough Rate	9	Q8.9#10	35%	7
Net Reach	9	Q8.9#4	34%	8
Cost per Customer Acquired	9	Q8.9#13	32%	9
Average Frequency	9	Q8.9#5	31%	10
Cost per Thousand Impression (CPM)	9	Q8.9#3	28%	11
Pageview	9	Q8.9#9	28%	12
Cost per Click (CPC)	9	Q8.9#11	27%	13
Abandonment Rate	9	Q8.9#16	24%	14
Cost per Order	9	Q8.9#12	23%	15
Gross Rating Points	9	Q8.9#2	23%	16
Net Profit	10	Q8.10#1	91%	1
Return on Investment (ROI)	10	Q8.10#3	77%	2

Metric	Section in Survey	Question Number	% Saying Very Useful	Ranking in Survey Section
Return on Sales (ROS)	10	Q8.10#2	69%	3
Return on Marketing Investment (ROMI)	10	Q8.10#8	49%	4
Net Present Value (NPV)	10	Q8.10#6	46%	5
Economic Profit (EVA)	10	Q8.10#4	41%	6
Payback	10	Q8.10#5	41%	7
Internal Rate of Return (IRR)	10	Q8.10#7	38%	8

## Chapter 6

▽ Introduction to marketing

IN THIS CHAPTER, WE WILL ADDRESS THE FOLLOWING QUESTIONS:

1 Why is marketing important and what is the scope of marketing?

2 How do we understand markets and customers?

3 How is marketing practised?

4 What are the European marketing realities, company and consumer challenges?

5 What is the philosophy of marketing?

6 How is marketing in a post modern world and retro marketing practised?

7 What is an overview of marketing management?

Marketing management is a challenging and rewarding career choice because it is a core management function central to all company efforts. Successful marketing of products and services both locally and globally in a dynamic, networked, demanding marketplace is a vital skill needed by every company. If we think about it marketing profoundly affects our day-to-day lives. It is embedded in everything we do – from the clothes we wear, to the food we eat, the restaurants we visit, the websites we click on, the advertisements we see, the service we receive, the price we pay and so on.

Marketing managers need to understand consumer needs and the effect all marketing mix variables have on their consumers. Low-cost airlines are a great example of companies that give the customer what they want – low-cost travel.

Source: Steven May / Alamy Images

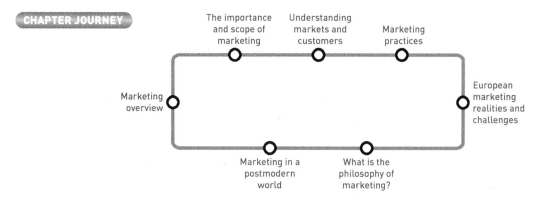

CHAPTER JOURNEY

The importance and scope of marketing

Understanding markets and customers

Marketing practices

Marketing overview

European marketing realities and challenges

Marketing in a postmodern world

What is the philosophy of marketing?

Marketing managers oversee a wide range of internal and external activities to ensure business success and customer satisfaction, activities that will be covered in this text.

Take the Ryanair example below.

Ryanair is Europe's most successful low-cost airline, carrying over 65 million consumers, with 563 routes connecting 26 European countries. Ryanair and other low-cost airlines such as easyJet and German Wings have opened up the skies to more passengers and have completely revolutionised air travel. Since 1994, low-cost airlines have successfully matched a market need by capturing the imagination of overcharged Europeans travellers, tired of costly tickets but good service offered by national 'flag carriers' such as British Airways, Air France and Lufthansa. Consumers all over Europe are happy to have €1 flights to Riga or €5 flights to Warsaw or even free flights to the major European capitals such as London, Paris, Rome, Berlin, Barcelona, Amsterdam and Copenhagen.[1] Led by chief executive Michael O'Leary Ryanair focuses its company effort on its low-cost marketing strategy, and uses a range of technologies both internally and externally. It researches the market and understands its consumers, markets and competitors. Ryanair understands the consumer segments, and chooses to target the price-conscious consumer. It is positioned as the low-cost, low-service alternative to the full service airlines. Marketing is designed to create the strong brand that is Ryanair in the minds of the European consumer. To manage its brand image Ryanair uses the 7Ps of the marketing mix:

- **Product/service:** Ryanair's service offering is basic and low frills – an unassigned economy seat on an aircraft.
- **Pricing:** It competes on rock-bottom prices.
- **Place/global supply network and channels:** Ryanair operates from the lowest-cost airports, manages a network of suppliers and uses only one direct channel to market.
- **Promotion/communication:** Promotion is minimal and inexpensive, focusing on Internet marketing;
- **Process:** Ryanair has eliminated all unnecessary service processes on board as well as for bookings and check in;
- **Physical evidence:** Ryanair's planes have very basic and minimal interiors.
- **People:** Ryanair's staff are focused on the low-cost, no frills marketing strategy. It implements its marketing programme and manages its return to investors as a core focus (Chapter 7). In total, Ryanair is an excellent example of a company that understands both its consumers and the need for a total company marketing effort in creating a strong brand in a market dominated by major brands.

Marketing and a marketing department are critical ingredients for business success. It is the role of the marketing manager and the marketing department to plan, manage and execute the marketing strategy throughout the company with innovation, intuition and creativity. Marketing is organised effort, activity and expenditure designed first to acquire a customer and second to maintain and grow a customer at a profit. In this chapter, we lay the foundation for your study of marketing by providing an overview of the main marketing issues facing European companies in a rapidly changing marketing environment.

▽ The importance of marketing

Marketing is a significant dimension of any business in today's highly competitive environment and financial success is often dependent on marketing ability. Finance, operations, accounting, administration and other business functions will not really matter if companies do not understand consumer needs and identify sufficient demand for their products and services for them to make a profit.

Companies of all kinds – from consumer product manufacturers (such as Nokia or Ericsson in Sweden), to health care insurers (e.g. Bupa in the United Kingdom), from car manufacturers (e.g. BMW or Porsche in Germany) to banks (such as Société Générale in France or RaboBank in Holland), from non-profit organisations (Amnesty International, which was founded by a British lawyer) to industrial product manufacturers (e.g. Airbus – a French, German, English and Spanish conglomerate) – all have to use marketing to understand their core customers and grow their businesses. The 2007 survey of the 'Top Ten CEO Challenges' acknowledges the importance of marketing.[2] The CEOs cited excellence of strategy execution as their top challenge. The report highlighted the fact that marketing challenges differ globally, with European CEOs focusing on getting new, more responsive ideas out sooner. Therefore execution in terms of speed, flexibility and adaptability to change is a more dominant theme in Europe (3rd place) than in Asia (8th place) and the United States (10th place). All CEOs recognised the importance of marketing to building brands and a loyal customer base, two core assets that make up a large percentage of the value of a company.

Marketing is a complex set of tasks as well as a philosophy of business and it has been the Achilles heel of many formerly prosperous companies. Some companies had to confront new competitors: the Spanish clothing company Zara entered Benetton's target market, while H&M has been competing with Gap in many markets. There are also new consumer concerns. The Dutch company Philips, by being the first to focus on energy-efficient, environmentally friendly consumer and business lighting, has overtaken many national light bulb brands in Europe. Consumers also have more choice. The German discount supermarket Lidl has Euro 9 billion in non-domestic European sales, and now plans to target Hungary, Estonia, Lithuania, Croatia and Slovenia, where its main rival Aldi has no presence. Lidl has had a dramatic effect on established supermarkets such as Spar, Kaiser and Edeka in its domestic market. Its policies of 'hard discounting' – offering goods at prices even lower than normal discount stores, and supplying only own brands characterise its marketing strategy. Lidl has more than 400 stores in Britain, and a nationwide survey by the consumer magazine *Which?* in 2007 reported that British consumers rated Lidl and Aldi higher than Tesco, Asda, Morrison's and Sainsbury's. Marketing managers have to rethink and reorient their marketing efforts to deliver customer satisfaction within competitive markets.

Even market leaders such as Nokia, BMW and Carrefour recognise that they cannot afford to relax their marketing effort as their leadership is challenged by fast and agile competitors and changing consumer tastes. Just ask Ford or Gap, both of whom lost 19 per cent and 15 per cent of their brand value respectively, according to Business Week/Interbrands annual ranking of the 100 Best Global Brands 2008.[3] The big brand winners were Google, Zara and BMW, companies that really understand marketing and how to satisfy changing consumer needs.

As Rupert Murdoch, chief executive of the world's largest media company – News Corp, the owner of *The Times*, ITV and BSkyB in the UK and a host of TV stations across Europe including bTV in Bulgaria, B1 TV in Romania, Fox Televizija in Serbia, Fox Turkey, TV Puls in Poland and LNT in Latvia, noted: 'The world is changing very fast. Big will not beat small any more. It will be the fast beating the slow.' Take the example of Benetton, founded in Italy in 1965.

▽ Benetton

Benetton, which for years had enjoyed great success with a unique brand of clothing and provocative advertising, had to rethink its marketing strategy when new fast fashion competitors such as Zara and H&M entered the young fashion market and started capturing market share and brand loyalty through a comprehensive marketing strategy. Zara understood the new patterns of consumer behaviour of teenagers and young adults – markets that craved new styles quickly and cheaply and were happy with 'disposable clothing'. Zara studied the marketing mix variables and saw that global supply network management service process and physical evidence such as store layout and design were more important than traditional marketing expenditure on advertising. Zara's advertising budget is 0.03 per cent of its revenues,[4] which is very different to Benetton that focused on creative advertising, spending €80 million on advertising alone. Benetton has now seen the errors of its ways, investing over €160 million in modernising its global supply chain. It can now deliver new styles to its worldwide stores once a week rather than once a month, which was its traditional delivery strategy. According to Vincenzo Scognamiglio, the head designer of Benetton, 'Time is my enemy.' Zara and H&M have very lean supply chains capable of replenishing shelves in days rather than months. Managing your supply network can be as important as style in the increasingly cut-throat business of mass market cloths.[5,6]

Marketing means understanding customer and consumer needs and making marketing choices to match these needs. Zara prospered due to its focus on rapid delivery of fashion styles to the market while Benetton floundered due to its over-focus on advertising. Advertising is not everything, marketers needs to use the full range of the marketing mix variables to succeed.

Source: Sipa Press/Rex Features (left); David Pearson/Alamy (right)

Awareness of changing consumer and business trends and the use of marketing expertise to react to and change before, or with these trends, is a major marketing skill set for the future generation of marketers. BMW prides itself on being the world's number one car manufacturer in the luxury niche market and also on its marketing ability to react to changing consumer lifestyle segments and match these segments with products. In 2000 BMW commissioned consumer research that identified four new market segments: Upper liberals; Postmoderns; Upper conservatives and Modern mainstreams, and then redesigned its product range to provide cars to match these predicted new segments. The strategy succeeded and in 2006 BMW had profits in excess of €4 billion. Changing a product range to match expected changes in future customer segments requires immense marketing skill. If BMW had got this wrong it could have been disastrous, but BMW was right and have the profits to reflect that.

Making the right decisions isn't always easy. Marketing managers must make major strategic or long-term decisions along with tactical or short-term decisions. *Strategically* they must consider which features to design into new services or products, what kind of price to offer customers, what channels to use to distribute their services and products, how much to spend on communications including advertising, sales, or the Internet, and which other media is most appropriate. *Tactically* they must also decide on details as diverse as the exact wording or colour for new packaging, managing ongoing research, the colour of the wallpaper in reception and the format for answering the phone. For many companies the role of the marketing department has being confined to tactical issues, ignoring the strategic role of marketing in the overall success of the company. The companies at greatest risk are those that fail to carefully monitor their customers and competitors and who fail to continuously match their value offerings to customer needs. They take a short-term, sales-driven view of their business and ultimately they fail to satisfy their stockholders, employees, suppliers and supply network members and – most importantly – their customers. Skilful marketing is a never-ending pursuit. As Jay Conrad Levinson[7] author of *Guerrilla Marketing* noted: 'Marketing is not an event, but a process . . . It has a beginning, a middle, but never an end, for it is a process. You improve it, perfect it, change it, even pause it. But you never stop it completely.'

▽ The scope of marketing

To prepare to be a marketing manager, you need to understand what marketing is, how it works, what is marketed, and who does the marketing.

What is marketing?

Marketing is about identifying and meeting human and social needs. One of the shortest definitions of marketing is the process of 'meeting needs profitably'. This has been called balanced centricity – which is a focus on the customer but also on the company and its objectives.[8] When the Swedish company IKEA noticed that people wanted good furniture at a substantially lower price, they created well-designed, low-priced furniture. When Nokia realised that phone design was crucial and began to design its own range of clam shell phones the company captured part of a growing market. These companies demonstrated marketing savvy and expertise in turning a private or social need into a profitable business opportunity. Marketing is a revenue-generating function of a business, and the ultimate test of marketing success is a profit level that allows a company to prosper in the long run.[9]

There is much debate about a definition of marketing. A definition must be generic enough to cover a large variety of products and services in both consumer and business-to-business markets. It must be applicable to different marketing contexts and be able to change. In 2007 Professor Christian Gronroos, of the Hanken Swedish School of Economics in Finland, proposed a definition that encompasses recent research into customer value, relationship marketing, services marketing and the promise concept.[10]

Marketing is a customer focus that permeates organisational functions and processes and is geared towards marketing promises through value proposition, enabling the fulfilment of individual expectations created by such promises and fulfilling such expectations through support to customers' value-generating processes, thereby supporting value creation in the firm's as well as its customers' and other stakeholders' processes.[11]

Managing exchange processes between businesses and consumers and business-to-business calls for a considerable amount of work and skill. **Marketing management** is the art and science of choosing target markets and getting, keeping and increasing customers through creating, managing, communicating and delivering superior customer value.

We can distinguish between a *social* and a *managerial* definition of marketing. A social definition shows the role that marketing plays in society; for example, one marketer has said that marketing's role is to 'deliver a higher standard of living'. Here is a definition that reflects the role of marketing in society: Marketing is a *societal process* by which individuals and groups obtain what they need and want through creating, offering and freely exchanging products and services of value with others. **Social marketing** is an umbrella term used to describe how, in different ways, marketing can encourage positive social behaviour, and includes 'critical marketing', and 'green or sustainable marketing'.[12] This can be explained as follows. There are two dimensions to marketing and its role in society: 'On the one hand, social marketing encourages us to use our skills and insights as marketers to progress social good. On the other hand, it facilitates the control and regulation of conventional marketing through critical studies of its impact on the health and welfare of society'.[13] Social marketing is most often used to define the ways in which policy makers can use the techniques of marketing to change human behaviour for the better – whether it is concerned with obesity, gambling, smoking or drink-driving.

What is included in marketing?

Some business people who don't understand marketing think of marketing as 'the art of selling products', or simplistically equate it with advertising. Both of these are marketing tactics visible to the consumer. Many people are surprised when they hear that selling is *not* the most important part of marketing and that not all companies have large advertising budgets. Selling and advertising are only the tip of the marketing iceberg. Most of what occurs in marketing happens before the customer sees an advertisement (which is just the tangible representation of the marketing strategy), hears about a new product or service or meets a sales representative. Just like an iceberg, over 80 or 90 per cent of marketing occurs out of the sight of the consumer. Advertising, sales and so on are the final rather than the beginning stages of marketing.

The main focus of marketing is on what occurs below the waterline rather than above it. These are all the decisions that marketers make before the product or service comes to the market, and afterwards to maintain its position in the market. Non-marketers are inclined to think that marketing is only what occurs above the line.
Source: Ralph A. Clevenger / Corbis

Peter Drucker, a leading management theorist, describes the process of marketing this way: 'The aim of marketing is to know and understand the customer so well that the product or service fits him/her and sells itself.' Ideally, marketing should result in a customer who is ready to buy. All that should be needed then is to make the product or service available.[14]

When Sony designed its PlayStation 3 game system, when Apple launched its iPod, and when Toyota introduced its Prius hybrid car, these companies were swamped with orders because they had designed the 'right' product or service, based on executing and managing carefully designed and complete marketing programmes.

Innocent drinks has successfully marketed a product to customers who are looking for a healthier diet. Eight years after launching Innocent drinks the company has a turnover of £75 million. It has captured a 71 per cent share of the £169 million UK smoothie market, with over 2 million smoothies sold per week. Innocent drinks is expanding into other European countries including Ireland, Holland, France, Denmark and Belgium. Innocent's vision, in the words of co-founder Richard Reed, is 'to be Europe's favourite little juice company'.

Understanding markets

Marketing managers can market seven entities: services, products, events, experiences, people, places and ideas. Let's take a quick look at these categories.

Services A growing proportion of economic activity focuses on the provision of services. The current list of Fortune 500 companies contains more service companies and fewer manufacturers than in previous decades. The European economy, as a mature economy, consists of a 70–30 services-to-product GDP ratio. Services are everywhere. The top ten European companies and European service companies are shown in Table 1.1. Services include airlines, hotels, car hire, hairdressers and beauticians, maintenance and repair, accountants, bankers, solicitors, engineers, doctors, software programmers and management consultants to name but a few. Many market offerings consist of a variable mix of products and services. At a fast-food restaurant, for example, the customer consumes both a product and a service.

According to the World Trade Organisation (WTO), the services sector accounts globally for €1 trillion of world trade. Over two-thirds of the workforce in Europe are employed in services and between 60 and 70 per cent of the gross value-added figure achieved by European states can be attributed to services. Within Europe, an ageing population will have a future need for nurses, home health care, physical therapists and social workers. Double-income families need childcare, education, house cleaning and gardening services. There will also be an increased demand for business-to-business services that already account for over 55 per cent of total employment in Europe, equating to over 55 million people.

Table 6.1 The top European companies

The top 10 European firms (in terms of revenue)	The top 10 European service providers (in terms of revenue)
1 Royal Dutch Shell (Netherlands)	1 ING Group (Netherlands) [insurance]
2 BP (Britain)	2 AXA (France)
3 DaimlerChrysler (Germany)	3 Crédit Agricole [banking]
4 Total (France)	4 Allianz (Germany)
5 Volkswagen (Germany)	5 Fortis (Belgium/Netherlands) [banking]
6 ENI (Italy)	6 HBSC holdings
7 Siemens (Germany)	7 BNP Paribas (France) [banking]
8 Carrefour (France)	8 UBS (Switzerland) [banking]
9 E.ON (Germany)	9 Assicurazioni Generali (Italy) [insurance]
10 Tesco (Britain)	10 Deutsche Bank (Germany)

Current marketing thought argues that all companies are in fact service companies and that we need to use a services perspective for marketing as the main or dominant focus.[15, 16] This text takes a service-dominant logic perspective as an underlying concept. That means that the 7 Ps of the marketing mix – product/service, price, promotion, place; and the three extra service mix elements – process, physical evidence and people – are used for both products and services. In other words all businesses are considered service businesses using all 7Ps of the marketing mix. The 7Ps are used throughout this text as the default for both products and services. The service-dominant logic will be explored in greater detail throughout the text. This perspective acknowledges the importance of the customer experience of exchange, whether with a product or service. It also acknowledges that the company alone does not offer value to a consumer; value is in fact created when the company and the customer work together; often called **co-creation**.

Products The manufacture of physical products was the traditional cornerstone of economic activity in Europe. Marketing has always oriented towards the marketing of products, reflecting its historical development in the agricultural sector. European companies manufacture and market billions of fresh, canned, bagged and frozen food products, and millions of cars, refrigerators, television sets, machines and various other mainstays of a modern economy.

Services and products The service-dominant logic suggests that the separation between products and services is not a clear one. The 'servicisation' of products refers to the relative importance of the service dimension in a given product offering. Thinking in marketing has moved from a strategy that conceives of either a product or a service to one which sees both product and service dimensions in any market offering.[17] Many products have a service component and many services have product components. Take for example a physical product such as a car. We purchase a car, which provides the service of getting from one place to another. But the car comes with its own need for services such as insurance, finance, repairs and even a petrol station. The Swedish car manufacturer Volvo has built a service into its cars that alerts the driver if they are falling asleep. What a great service! Another example is a mobile phone provider such as Nokia. The company provides a product (mobile phone handsets) but also a service (networks). Nokia sees itself as a service or solutions provider – 'connecting people'.

Events Music shows such as the U2 Zoo tour, the Hurricane music festival in Germany, the Frankfurt book fair and major trade fairs or international summits, for example the global health conference, are all global marketing events that take months to plan and market. Global sporting events such as the Olympics and the World Cup Football are marketed to both companies and fans. Event marketing is big business, as evidenced by the estimated loss of £2 billion to the British economy when the England team failed to qualify for Euro 2008. The 2006 Football World Cup was one of the most watched events in television history, with over 26 billion viewers over the course of the tournament. The final attracted an estimated audience of 715.1 million people who watched Italy claim their fourth World Cup title.

Experiences By managing several services and products, a firm can create, stage and market experiences. Alton Towers – the most popular theme park in the United Kingdom – or Disneyland Resort Paris or Legoland in Denmark, Germany and England, all represent this kind of experiential marketing, allowing customers to visit a fairy kingdom, a pirate ship, a Lego town or a haunted house, complete with hotel accommodation and food. There is also a growing market for customised experiences, such as spending a week at a Samba Soccer camp, on a yoga retreat in Kitzbühel, Austria, or skiing on Mount Blanc in the Alps.[18]

People Celebrity marketing is a major business. Artists, musicians, chefs, CEOs, financiers and other professionals can all become celebrities through clever marketing. Some people have done a masterful job of marketing themselves and becoming global celebrities – think of David Beckham, Bono, Jordan and Carla Bruni. Within the United Kingdom, chefs such as Gordon Ramsay, Jamie Oliver and Nigella Lawson have all become household names, with their own brands of restaurants, cookbooks and kitchen utensils. Similarly, Spanish actors Penélope Cruz and

Celebrity: Kate Moss surrounded by a bevy of other models wearing her Topshop designs.

Source: Rex Features

Antonio Banderas, who were national celebrities in their native Spain, became global celebrities after working in Hollywood in English-speaking films. Celebrity culture is embedded in contemporary European culture, with nearly 3 million celebrity magazines sold each week in Britain, compared with 7.5 million in the United States, a country with five times the population.[19] Kate Moss, the English supermodel, launched her 5th line of clothing for Topshop in March 2008. Topshop credits the use of her name and designs with boosting Topshop sales by more than 10 per cent.[20] Another example is Virgin's CEO Richard Branson, who was famous as a CEO but became a global celebrity after he attempted to circumnavigate the globe in a hot air balloon. Management consultant Tom Peters, himself a master at self-branding, has advised each person to become a 'brand'.

Places Cities, states, regions and whole nations compete actively to attract tourists, factories, company headquarters and new residents.[21] Europe is the most visited region in the world.[22] Six European countries are in the world's top ten destinations for holiday makers, as can be seen from Table 1.2.

Place marketing includes a full marketing programme to attract both tourism and inward economic investment, often called foreign direct investment (FDI). Ireland's extraordinary economic growth in the past decade, leading the country to be called the 'Celtic Tiger', attracted an estimated 30 per cent of the global spend on FDI. The 'Cool Britannia' campaign tried to promote Britain as a cool place to visit and in which to invest.

Ideas Social marketing uses the tools and techniques of marketing to change people's behaviour. Whether it is to encourage people to drive slowly, to think about recycling, to stop smoking or eat healthily, marketing can be instrumental in getting people to think differently. In relation to campaigns against drink-driving in Europe, the European Safety Council runs the 'Safe and Sober' Campaign, while the UK's government body Drink Aware,[23] markets the idea

Table 6.2 Europe is the most popular tourist destination according to World Tourism Organization figures

Rank	Country	Continent	International tourist arrivals (2006) in millions	International revenues from tourism (2006) in € millions
1	France	Europe	54.4	29.57
2	Spain	Europe	40.29	35.22
3	United States	North America	35.19	59.7
4	China	Asia	34.16	23.36
5	Italy	Europe	28.30	26.26
6	United Kingdom	Europe	20.74	23.23
7	Germany	Europe	16.26	22.61
8	Mexico	North America	14.74	N/A
9	Austria	Europe	13.98	11.51
10	Russia	Europe	13.78	N/A

Source: United Nations World Tourism Organization (2007) International tourist arrivals by country of destination, *UNWTO World Tourism Barometer*, 5(2), June, p. 8. Copyright © UNWTO Publications. Reproduced with permission.

of alcohol restraint in its 'Respect alcohol, respect yourself' campaign. The '5 a day' campaign by the UK's Department of Health encourages consumers to think about eating five portions of fruit and vegetables a day. It has successfully encouraged supermarkets such as Marks & Spencer and Tesco to display a '5 a day' sign on products that contribute to this objective.

Marketing's role in creating demand

Marketers must have a variety of skills, one in particular being the ability to stimulate demand for their company's services and products. However, this is too limited a view of the tasks that marketers perform and the skills that they must have. Just as production and logistics professionals are responsible for supply management, marketers are responsible for demand management along with their other roles. Marketing managers seek to influence the level, timing, and composition of demand to meet the organisation's objectives. Eight states of market demand are possible:

1 **Full demand:** Consumers buy all services or products brought to market.

2 **Overfull demand:** There are more consumers demanding the service or product than can be satisfied.

3 **Irregular demand:** Consumer purchases vary on a seasonal, monthly, weekly, daily or even hourly basis.

4 **Declining demand:** Consumers begin to buy the service or product less frequently or not at all.

5 **Negative demand:** Consumers dislike the service or product and may even pay a price to avoid it.

6 **Nonexistent demand:** Consumers may be unaware of or uninterested in the product or service.

7 **Latent demand:** Consumers may share a strong need that cannot be satisfied by an existing product or service.

8 **Unwholesome demand:** Consumers may be attracted to services or products that have undesirable social consequences.

In each case, marketers must identify the underlying cause(s) of the demand state and then determine a plan of action to shift the demand to a more desirable state.

Figure 6.1 The health
care market is an
example of a
contemporary
network

Source: H. J. Schau, M. F.
Smith and P. I. Schau
(2005) The healthcare
network economy: the
role of Internet information
transfer and implications
for pricing, *Industrial
Marketing Management*, 34,
147–56. Reproduced with
permission.

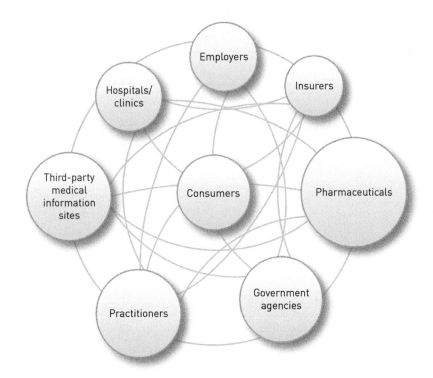

Markets Traditionally, a 'market' was a physical place where buyers and sellers gathered to buy and sell products and trade services. Economists describe a *market* as a collection of buyers and sellers who transact a particular service or product or product or service class (such as the housing market, the airline market or the gaming market).

Each nation's economy and the global economy in general consist of complex interacting sets of markets linked through exchange processes. This is referred to as the **network economy,** a term that will be used throughout this text. A network economy is driven by a dynamic and knowledge-rich technology dominant environment, meaning that the hierarchical stand-alone organisations of the twentieth century have changed into a variety of networks such as:

1 **internal networks:** are designed to reduce hierarchy and open firms to their environments;

2 **vertical networks:** maximize the productivity of serially dependent functions by creating partnerships among independent skill-specialised firms;

3 **intermarket networks:** seek to leverage horizontal synergies across industries; and

4 **opportunity networks:** are organised around customer needs and market opportunities and designed to search for the best solutions to them.

Marketing outcomes within the network economy are dependent on and face competition from a strategic network of companies rather than from competition among individual companies.[24] Marketing increasingly will be responsible for creating and managing new marketing knowledge, education, real-time market information systems, intrafirm integration, conflict resolution, technology forecasting, risk and investment analysis, transfer pricing of tangibles and intangibles, and the coordination of the network's economic and social activities. So managing a network of companies is a core marketing requirement. The health care network diagram (Figure 6.1) reflects not only the linkages between companies within the network but also the growing participation by the consumer in these networks.

Marketers often use the term **market** to describe various groupings of customers who buy their products or services. They view other companies with similar or substitute products and services as constituting the industry, and groups of buyers as constituting the market. They talk about need markets (the health food market), product or service markets (the shoe market or the holiday travel market), demographic markets (the youth market), and geographic markets (the French market).

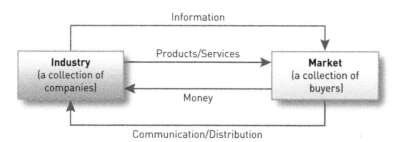

Figure 6.2 A simple marketing system

They extend the concept still further to describe other, not immediately obvious markets such as voter markets, labour markets and donor markets.

Figure 6.2 shows the relationship between the industry and the market. Companies and buyers are connected by four flows. The company distributes products and services to the market; and in return it receives money or payment and information, such as customer attitudes and sales data. The inner loop shows an exchange of money for products and services; the outer loop shows an exchange of information.

Consider the following key customer markets: consumer, business, global and non-profit.

Consumer markets Consumer purchases are generally made by individual decision makers or a decision-making unit, either for themselves or for others with whom they have relationships. The consumer market is made up of companies marketing consumer products and services as diverse as soft drinks (Red Bull), make-up (L'Oréal), air travel (AirFranceKLM), shoes (Clarks) and car insurance (the Automobile Association).

Consumer markets are enormous. Consumer purchasing power within the European Union has grown to the point where it is slightly larger than that of the United States.[25] Germany, with a population of 82 million, is Europe's largest consumer market with consumer purchasing power estimated to be €1495 billion, or 19.5 per cent of Europe's €7681 billion. A pan-European study by MB-Research ranked the United Kingdom second with €1180 billion and France third with €1076 billion, followed by Italy (€943 billion) and Spain (€536 billion).[26] (See Figure 6.3.)

There has been much debate about the high consumption levels in Europe and how this generation is the one 'born to consume' or what has been called the 'McLuxury Generation'. The champagne-growing region of Rheims in France has been expanded for the first time in over 80 years, as world consumption increased by 5 per cent in 2007, to a record 339 million bottles.[27] Consumers are smarter, they expect more, they approach purchase decisions with greater scrutiny and have access to more data for comparison. It is suggested that consumers are 'self-indulgent, pleasure-seeking individualists, dominated by marketers and advertisers, and sheep-like in their mimicking of others'. . . with the new religion of worshipping at the cathedral of the shopping mall'![28] Alternatively consuming can be seen as a sign of love and affection as we purchase for others to show affection and affiliation.[29]

In Tesco in the United Kingdom, the average number of product lines has exploded from 5000 in 1983 to over 40,000 in 2002. Only 20 years ago the average UK consumer could choose between three TV channels; now there are around 300 channels broadcasting to UK subscribers. The café chain Coffee Republic offers 11 different types of coffee, four added toppings, three types of milk and sugar, three types of cup size – in all 6000 different ways to have a cup of coffee. A visit to any chemist will yield 14 different types of dental floss and over 20 different toothpastes.[30] We live in a time of 'choice explosion'.[31]

Take the Internet. Customers can now log on to the Internet and choose from over 100,000 CDs rather than having to travel to a shop that can physically stock perhaps only 25,000 CDs. This changes choice, this changes distribution, this changes the service aspects and this changes the marketing programmes that marketers need to use. Information technology changes space–time–place relations; we have yet to grasp the scope of this disruption.[32] Take iTunes. As of January 2008, 50 million customers had downloaded over 4 billion songs since the service first launched in April 2003. This reflected an increase of 1 billion since July 2007 when there were

Figure 6.3 European purchasing power in 2007

Source: Michael Bauer Research (2007) European purchasing power in 2007: who's on top? 31 August (retrieved from www.english.mb-research .de/content/view/). Reproduced with permission.

Purchasing power in Europe 2007

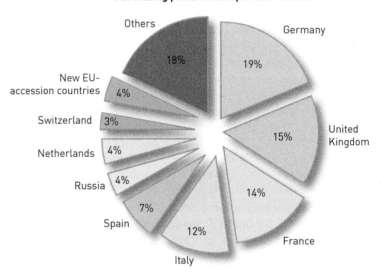

Purchasing power in Europe: €7.7 trillion

3 billion downloads.[33] A new single-day record was set when 20 million songs were downloaded on the 25 December 2007.

Business markets The term business, business-to-business or industrial marketing focuses on understanding business buying centres and on how businesses purchase in different ways to consumers. Business markets are now networked organisations operating in a complex environment. Nowadays the focus is on neither consumer or business markets but on recognising that the lines between the two are blurring in four important ways:[34]

1 A blurring of value chains through outsourcing and other relationships that allows networks of companies and customers to operate. When Apple set up its iTunes online music store, it brought together recording companies with music and customers who wanted to download music tracks for €0.99 – a mix of consumer and business-to-business marketing for Apple.

2 A blurring of relationships with customers, as customers are invited to participate with companies in the design and delivery processes. The decline in travel agencies as customers book directly with airlines and hotels is an example.

3 A blurring of functions within the firm as marketing and other functions are more integrated through technology.

4   A blurring of products, services and customer experience, moving from an 'industrial' base to a knowledge-based society.

Pharmaceutical firms have long focused on business markets such as doctors, hospitals, clinics and insurance providers. In recent years, however, they have recognised the need to combine this approach with extensive campaigns to build consumer awareness and demand for new drugs and treatments. Rather than relying on channels to drive awareness, these companies work from the consumer side and the industrial side simultaneously to create sales in the middle.

Global markets Globalisation characterises the climate of business and society in the twenty-first century. This text is oriented towards global companies and each chapter explores both global and local marketing issues. We have more global organisations than at any other time in the history of the world. Singapore is ranked first in overall globalisation, followed by Hong Kong, with the Netherlands ranked third, followed by Switzerland, Ireland and Denmark. Global companies face unique and additional decisions and challenges. They must decide which countries to enter; how to enter each (as an exporter, licenser, joint venture partner, contract manufacturer or solo manufacturer); how to adapt their product and service features to each country; how to price their products and services in different countries; how to adapt their communications to fit different cultures; and how to manage their service process, people and technology across the globe and within a network of companies. They make these decisions in the face of different requirements for buying, negotiating, owning and disposing of products and services; different cultures, languages and legal and political systems; and currencies that might fluctuate in value. Yet the pay-off for doing all this additional marketing can be huge. Having a global mindset is important. The struggle is often summarised as the attempts of an organisation to be local while staying global – the concept of glocalisation. Getting to a global mindset requires individual managers to demonstrate a glocal mentality, which features three components:[35]

1   Think globally.

2   Think locally.

3   Think globally and locally simultaneously.[36]

Many leading European football clubs – including Manchester United, Real Madrid and Juventus – have both a local and a global marketing strategy. They all have loyal local supporters but also a worldwide fan base. Both have to be managed well. Take Real Madrid:

> The popular Spanish football club Real Madrid became a global brand through the marketing expertise of Florentino Perez, the man who is credited with turning Real Madrid from an 'old-fashioned soccer club' into a star-studded global marketing brand when he took over the football club in 2000. He said that he wanted to be in every country in the world through their Real Madrid brand marketing and through sales of football shirts, club merchandise and image rights aligned with their leading players. Perez spent €316 million on 17 new players, including Zinedane Zidane, David Beckham, Christiano Ronaldo and Luis Figo, earning his collection of superstars the title of 'Los Galacticos'. Perez's pledge each season was that the world's best will play for Madrid. The club increased its revenue by 17 per cent to €327 million, particularly in the Asian market. During a 17-day tour of Asia in 2003 the club sold €135,000 worth of jerseys in Japan in one day of the club's promoted training sessions.[37]

Non-profit, voluntary and government markets Companies marketing their services and products to non-profit organisations such as churches, universities, charities and government agencies need to understand marketing as much as private, profit-making companies. There is no agreed definition for the non-profit sector, which has been called the third sector, as opposed to the public sector and the business sector. It is variously termed the independent sector in Scandinavian countries; civil society in central and eastern Europe; the charitable sector or voluntary sector in the United Kingdom and Ireland; or the 'économie sociale' in France. Whether these organisations are co-operatives, mutual societies, associations or foundations they are united in that they do not operate solely for financial gain but for some non-profit objective. For example Médecins Sans Frontières (MSF), founded in France, is an international humanitarian aid organisation that provides emergency medical assistance to populations in danger in more than 70 countries. MSF's objective is to provide aid to as many people as it can. In relation to government markets much government purchasing calls for bids or tenders as dictated by the European Union, and governments often favour the lowest bid in the absence of extenuating factors.

Marketplaces, marketspaces and metamarkets

The *marketplace* is physical, such as a shop you spend money in, the bank you visit or the restaurant you eat in.[38]

The *marketspace* is digital, as when you shop on the Internet, conduct your banking online or when you use an ATM or a kiosk for booking, ordering or confirming.[39]

The *metamarket*, proposed by Mohan Sawhney, describes a cluster of complementary products and services that are closely related in the minds of consumers, but spread across a diverse set of industries.[40] The car metamarket consists of car manufacturers, new and used car dealers, financing and insurance companies, mechanics, spare parts dealers, service shops, car magazines, classified car adverts in newspapers, and car sites on the Internet. In purchasing a car, a buyer will get involved in many parts of this metamarket, and this creates an opportunity for *metamediaries* to assist buyers in moving seamlessly through these groups, although they are disconnected in physical space. Metamediaries are intermediaries that bring together collections of companies or people. One example is Auto Trader, the world's largest car marketplace (www.autotrader.com), which provides a website where a car buyer can study the stated features and prices of different cars and easily click to other sites to search for the lowest price or nearest dealer, for financing, for car accessories, and for used cars at bargain prices. Auto Trader also has features that link to the car's history and links directly to classified advertisements or auction-style listings. Metamediaries also serve other metamarkets, such as the home ownership market, the parenting and baby care market, and the wedding market.

Autotrader.nl is a meta-intermediary website that helps prospective car buyers navigate the car metamarket.

Source: European Auto Trader BV

How is marketing practised?

Marketing practice can be viewed from many perspectives. The traditional view is the Kotlerian marketing management view of managing the marketing mix after selecting target market(s) and positioning.[41] The marketing mix was suggested by McCarthy, who classified marketing activities as *marketing mix* tools into four broad kinds, which he called *the 4Ps* of marketing: product, price, place and promotion.[42] It is worth noting that the first list had 52 marketing mix elements. The four marketing mix elements were expanded to 7Ps by Boden, which had a more services focus and included process (service process), physical evidence and people (participants). The marketing mix variables under each of the 7Ps are shown in Figure 6.4. A study of European and UK academics highlighted the discontent with the 4Ps of the marketing mix and suggested that the use of the service marketing mix reflected the actual marketing environment.[43]

The marketing manager has a mix of short- and long-term marketing decisions to make once the company has selected the target market. They must also integrate all the marketing mix decisions together so that the distribution suits the product, or that the service process aligns to the pricing strategy and so on. The 7Ps of the marketing mix represent the company's view of the marketing tools available for influencing buyers. From a buyer's point of view, each marketing tool is designed to deliver a customer benefit. Winning companies satisfy customer needs and surpass their expectations economically and conveniently and with effective products or services, priced well, communicated interestingly and distributed in a timely manner or through a process and with people that create the right environment, all leading to a brand that customers support.

Value is a central marketing concept. We can think of marketing as the identification, creation, communication, delivery and monitoring of customer value. **Satisfaction** reflects a person's judgement of a service's or product's perceived performance (or outcome) in relationship to their expectations. If the performance falls short of expectations, the customer is dissatisfied and disappointed. If it matches expectations, the customer is satisfied. If it exceeds them, the customer is delighted.

In practice, marketing follows a logical process. The marketing *planning* process consists of analysing marketing opportunities; selecting target markets; designing positioning strategies; developing marketing mix programmes to reflect a brand that has loyal customers; and managing the marketing effort. After identifying market segments, the marketer then decides which present the greatest opportunity – which are its **target markets**. For each target market, the firm

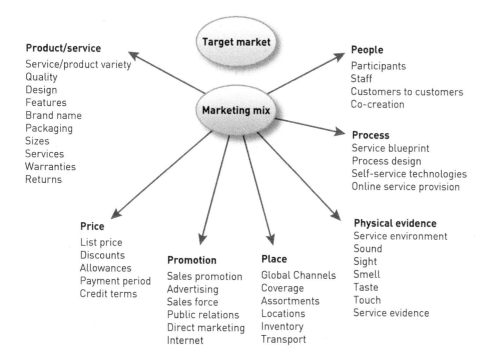

Figure 6.4 The 7Ps components of the marketing mix.

develops a *market* offering that it positions in the minds of the target buyers as delivering some central benefit(s). For example, with the car market we could say that BMW owns 'driving', Mercedes-Benz owns 'prestige', Volvo owns 'safety',[44] as the core positioning for their products in the eyes of the consumer. Companies do best when they choose their target market(s) carefully, choose suitable positioning and then use the full range of the marketing mix variables to develop a brand image and equity.

The challenge is that in highly competitive marketplaces, however, marketing planning and management is fluid and needs to be continually refreshed. Companies must always be moving forward with marketing programmes, innovating products and services, and staying in touch with customer needs, seeking new advantages rather than relying on past strengths. As Steve Jobs of Apple said, 'Innovation distinguishes between a leader and a follower.'

Transactional, relational and network marketing The Contemporary Marketing Practice Framework[45] shows that there are five main marketing practices depending on both the customer and the industry. These are transactional, database, emarketing, interactive and network marketing, encompassing a transactional to relational perspective but with the full range of the marketing mix variables at your disposal for each. (see Table 6.3)

> *Transaction marketing (TM)* is defined as attracting and satisfying potential buyers by managing the elements in the marketing mix, and actively manages communication 'to' buyers in the mass market in order to create discrete, arm's-length transactions.

> **Database marketing (DM)** involves using database technology to create a relationship, thus allowing firms to compete in a manner different from mass transactional marketing. The intent is to retain identified customers, although marketing is still 'to' the customer, rather than 'with' the customer. Relationships per se are not close or interpersonal, and are facilitated and personalised through the use of database technology.

> **Emarketing** (a term no longer in use) was used to describe 'the Internet and other interactive technologies to create and mediate dialogue between the firm and identified customers'.[46] Nowadays there is an extended view of emarketing or information and communication technologies (ICT) in marketing that shows their use across all marketing practices.[47]

> *Interaction marketing (IM)* implies face-to-face interaction between individuals. As such, it is truly 'with' the customer, as both parties in the dyad invest resources to develop a mutually beneficial and interpersonal relationship.

> Similarly, *network marketing (NM)* is 'with' the customer but occurs across and among organisations. In this practice, managers commit resources to develop their firm's position in a network of various firm-level relationships.[48]

Table 6.3 Classifications of marketing practice by relational exchange dimensions

Transactional perspective				Relationship perspective
Transaction marketing	Database marketing	Emarketing	Interaction marketing	Network marketing

Marketing managers usually focus on one main marketing practice but most practise all the different types of marketing. For example Carrefour, the French supermarket chain, has many transactional customers who purchase from it but are not loyal or do not have a relationship with the company. It also has many customers who have developed a relationship with the company either through its loyalty card and database or through interactions in local stores. It also has a range of suppliers who Carrefour are networked to. This reflects the full range of marketing practices that a marketing manager would have to understand for different customer groups. Marketing managers must be aware of which practice suits which aspect of their network, channel members and customers. Some customers would prefer interactions with their bank and want to visit; others would prefer more arm's length contact through ICT or a

Table 6.4 Transaction to relationship marketing

Transaction marketing	Focus ← →	Relationship marketing
One-off exchange, brand management	Focus	Ongoing exchanges, customer management
Short-term focus	Time perspective	Long-term focus
Mass communications	Primary communication	Personal communications
Isolated market research	Customer Feedback Mechanism	Ongoing dialogue
Mass markets or market segments	Market size	Market of one
Market share	Criterion for success	Mind share (share of customer)

Source: Modified from C. Gronroos (1991) The marketing strategy continuum: towards a marketing concept for the 1990s, *Management Decision*, 29(1), 7–13. Emerald Group Publishing Ltd. Copyright © 1991, MCB UP Ltd. Reproduced with permission.

database; while yet others want the bank networked to their organisation and to have a bank member on the board, which is popular in Germany.

Relationship marketing The concept of relationship marketing was developed by the Nordic School from northern Europe and developments from the United States. Relationship marketing in its simplest form is a progression from the dominant and often criticised traditional transactional 4P's focus.[49] It is a move away from the economic origins of marketing based on 'concepts such as exchange, profit maximization, utilities, specializations, the economic man and rationality'.[50] Relational is a focus on building long-term relationships with consumers rather than a focus on new customers as the growth potential. The contrast between transactional and relational marketing can be seen in Table 6.4.

▽ The European marketing environment: company and consumer challenges

The environment in which marketing takes place is crucial. The marketing environment consists of the task environment and the broad environment. The *task environment* includes every company in the network engaged in producing, distributing and promoting the offering. These are the company, suppliers, distributors, dealers, and the target customers. In the supplier group are the material suppliers and service suppliers, such as marketing research agencies, advertising agencies, banking and insurance companies, transportation companies and telecommunications companies. Distributors and dealers include agents, brokers, manufacturing representatives and others who facilitate finding and creating a customer.

The *broad environment* consists of six components: demographic, economic, physical, technological, political–legal and the social-cultural environment. Marketers must pay close attention to the trends and developments in these environments and make timely adjustments to their marketing strategies.

The European environment As a European text it is imperative that the marketing environment in Europe is understood. The contemporary environment is a world of immense complexity, contradiction and change – from global conglomerates to stunning technological development; poverty amidst plenty; ongoing financial crises across the globe; the growth in the European Union to 27 member states, widespread ethnic conflict; and unprecedented stock growth and decline. The continued reign of many European monarchs with the development of the European Union; the post-industrial economies, with high-tech virtual organisational forms and service-dominated sectors; the shift from labour to consumption as the source of identity are some of the many changes.[51]

Externally, the EU has become a model for others to follow, maintaining peace and stability within Europe while pursuing closer political and economic union. From a group of six countries, it has expanded to its present 27. The EU is now the largest single market in the world and the largest player in world trade with a market of over 450 million people. In a book entitled, *The United States of Europe: From the Euro to Eurovision – the superpower nobody talks about*, Reid notes that

> Europe covers just 6 per cent of the Earth's total area and is home to just 12 per cent of the global population; yet Europe has 40 per cent of the world's wealth and accounts for more than half of all global commerce. European countries comprise five of the world's ten richest nations. The continent was the birthplace of 'Western values', the combination of individual rights, democratic governments and free markets that has spread around the world.[52]

A special issue of the *European Journal of Marketing* in 2007 portrayed the diversity of views existing on the complexity of marketing approaches in the enlarged European Union.[53] This is mainly due to the diversity of geography and culture, different levels of economic development, and disposable income.[54] Think of Romania versus France. The diversity in European markets has emerged with new dimensions defying embedded cultural, political, historical and geographical boundaries.[55] Current research suggests that European marketers have to address specific country contexts, issues, industries, cultures and geographic areas. So though the European trading environment is becoming increasingly standardised, national and individual wealth varies across the EU. There is a so-called 'Golden Triangle', a comparatively small area that includes Liverpool and Leeds at the top of the triangle, moving across through Oxford and London to include Paris to the bottom left of the pyramid and Rotterdam, Amsterdam, Dortmund and Dusseldorf to the right of the triangle. This triangle is serviced by a network of new fast trains and the Channel Tunnel, a massive infrastructural investment which clearly points to the fact that Britain and France wanted to move closer together and that Britain wanted to be physically attached to the rest of Europe. It is a much more potent symbol of the EU than the EU flag with its 12 gold stars, which we have been told will never change in number, irrespective of how many nations finally decide to join the EU.[56] Convergence has given rise not only to common consumer behaviour traits but has also created favourable conditions for leveraging marketing expertise across national borders.

There is a dominant position for many EU multinational companies (MNCs) within national and regional markets. For example, three EU MNCs control about 90 per cent of the brewing market in Bulgaria.[57] Many MNCs market global and regional brands at almost no price differential vis-à-vis domestic brands, to ensure market penetration. Similarly, Interbrew, Heineken and SABMiller control about 70 per cent of the Czech beer market and about 95 per cent of the beer market in Hungary. By contrast, the Slovenian brewery Lasko enjoys more than 57 per cent market share in the Slovene market. It exports 35 per cent of its output and has engaged in internationalisation.[58] Confectionery industries in Poland, Bulgaria and the Czech Republic are also dominated by global multinationals.

We can say with some confidence that 'the marketplace isn't what it used to be'. Marketers must attend and respond to a number of significant developments locally, globally and more specifically within the European Union.

Major societal forces

Today the marketplace is radically different as a result of major, and sometimes interlinking, societal forces that have created new behaviours, new opportunities and new challenges:

- **Heightened competition:** Companies are facing more intense competition from domestic and foreign brands, resulting in rising marketing costs and shrinking profit margins. Many strong brands are extending into related product or service categories. EasyJet now has over 17 easy products or services, including easyMobile, easyCinema and easyHotel. Tesco, the UK retailer, has also entered the mobile phone market; as has Italian fashion designer Prada – see the image on the next page. These are all entrants into an already competitive market. Another Italian fashion designer, Armani, has expanded into chocolates and a hotel!

- **Globalisation:** The increase in world trade, an increasing integration of the world's major economies, and the onward march of globalisation means that marketing will continue to have a more global orientation. This, coupled with technological advances in transportation,

Competition has intensified across most industries. The launch of a Prada mobile phone shows just how widespread is the competition.
Source: Luis Gene/AFP/ Getty Images

shipping and communication have made it easier for companies to market and easier for consumers to buy products and services from all over the world. We now consider it normal to ship kiwi fruit from New Zealand and oranges from South Africa, and in the services area we find it normal to access money from ATMs all over the world and to phone home from anywhere without any difficulty. In light of the oil and financial crises in 2008 these options may have to be reconsidered.

- **Increased range of information and communication technologies (ICT):** The marketplace has more ICT then ever before. Companies can communicate and connect globally in minutes and real time online information is becoming normal. The range of ICTs within the marketing domain is extensive – from internets to databases, from kiosks to planning software, from mobile phones to self-service technologies. Marketing managers need to have the skills to understand and embrace a current range of ICTs both internally and externally and with an eye to new technologies ICT and a service perspective.

- **Industry convergence:** Industry boundaries are blurring at an incredible rate as companies are recognising that new opportunities lie at the intersection of two or more industries. The computing and consumer electronics industries are converging as the giants of the computer world release a stream of entertainment devices – from iPods and MP3 players to plasma TVs and camcorders. Nike and iPod have succeeded with a sports and music industry convergence. Nike has teamed with Apple iPod to offer a Nike-Apple workout experience. A sensor is placed in the runner or sports shoe and a receiver is attached to an iPod Nano. During training, the iPod will select music either in tune with the pace of the running or Nike 'sports music', while also recording the statistics of the run. Your iPod can record your running performance, and can coach you, encourage you, give you feedback on your performance and use your favourite music to motivate you.

- **Retail transformation:** Retailing in Europe has been transformed in four ways:

  1 **The growth of own brands:** Within the consumer goods sector powerful retailers now control limited shelf space and are putting out their own store brands in competition with national brands. By offering their own brand labels they can reap higher profit margins and, with the huge quantities they purchase, can bargain hard with their suppliers.

2 **Retail internationalisation:** This has occurred on a significant scale. The French chain Carrefour remains the continent's biggest food retailer, nearly twice the size of its nearest rivals, but Tesco has overtaken the other French retailer, Intermarche, to move into second place. European players dominate retail landscapes across other world regions, for example Carrefour dominates in Latin America.

3 **The retail market in Europe is still very fragmented:** Traditionally the European market has many small retailers but most areas are succumbing to the growing power of giant retailers and 'category killers'.

4 **Competition forces:** Competition from an explosion of retail outlets, out of town shopping centres and the Internet has all caused changes in retailing. In response, entrepreneurial retailers are building entertainment into their shops with bookshop–café combinations, lectures, demonstrations and in-store performances, marketing an 'experience' rather than a product assortment.

▽ MAC Cosmetics, Inc.

A division of French cosmetics giant Estée Lauder, MAC (which stands for Make Up Artist and Customer) Cosmetics is considered a significant reason for Lauder's 13 per cent net make-up sales increase. Yet MAC's 1000 stores worldwide don't simply sell Small Eye Shadow, Studio Fix, Lustreglass and Pro Longwear Lipcolour. Instead, they rely on highly paid 'artists' to bond with each customer during a free make-up consultation and application lesson. While this service process strategy is hardly new in the world of retail make-up, what is unique is that MAC's artists are not out there to bump up their commissions and load customers down with more products. Rather, they're trained to collaborate with customers so they'll leave the store with €50 or more of MAC products *and* the feeling, 'I can definitely do this at home.' The goal, says Matthew Waitesmith, MAC's head of 'artist training and development', is for each customer to feel she's had an authentically artistic experience 'that hopefully means they'll return to the place that makes them feel like an artist'.[59]

- **Disintermediation:** The amazing success of early online dot-coms such as Amazon, Yahoo! and eBay, and dozens of others created *disintermediation* in the delivery of products and services by intervening between the traditional flow of products and services through distribution channels. These so called 'pure-click' companies struck terror into the hearts of many established manufacturers and retailers. In response, many traditional companies engaged in *reintermediation* and became 'brick-and-click' retailers, adding online services to their existing offerings. Many brick-and-click competitors became stronger contenders than pure-click companies, since they had a larger pool of resources to work with and well-established brand names. Companies such as Ryanair and easyJet changed the intermediary model, completely bypassing the traditional travel agent and only allowing online bookings.

New consumer capabilities

Contemporary consumers and consumption patterns are changing.

- **Consumer sophistication:** The customer has become a more sophisticated consumer and marketers have to understand how to market to the marketing-savvy consumer. In some cases consumers have become more cynical about marketing efforts in general, are inundated with hundreds of advertising pitches a day, and are increasingly suspicious of expertise in a world where so many experts disagree.[60] Professor Stephen Brown from the University of Ulster, Northern Ireland, suggests that '*Today's* consumers *were trademarked at* *birth and brought up on branding* {author's italics}'.[61] Children as young as three can recognise brand logos, and the average child in the United Kingdom sees between 20,000 and 40,000 commercials a year.[62]

Consider what consumers have today that they didn't have in yesteryear:

- **A greater variety of available products and services:** As mentioned earlier the range of choice for consumers has grown. RaboBank, a Dutch bank founded over 100 years ago, now offers banking services in 34 countries that span all continents.

- **A great amount of information about practically anything:** People can read almost any newspaper in any language from anywhere in the world. They can access online encyclopedias, dictionaries, medical information, film ratings, consumer reports, and countless other information sources. Google runs the world's largest search engine, handling more than 100 million searches per day. Google Earth allows customers to zoom in on streets and even houses all over the world.

- **Greater ease in interacting and placing and receiving orders:** Today's buyers can place orders from home, office or mobile phone 24 hours a day, seven days a week, and quickly receive services and products at their home or office. Customers can also track and monitor their orders worldwide. DHL provides a tracking service online so that the customer knows where their parcel is at any time.

- **Tech savvy consumers:** Are you online, connected, iGeneration? Across Europe, around 60 per cent of Germans and Britons are online. More than seven in ten Dutch, Swedish and Danish households have a personal computer.[63] Many customers are now technology savvy, interactive, mouse clicking, engaged and intelligent consumers. We live in an era where many consumers are 'tech savvy' – technologically sophisticated, using technology in ways that marketers are only beginning to understand.

  Twenty years ago if you asked someone, 'Do you have a spare needle for my turntable?' most people would have understood. Many people nowadays would have no understanding of what that means. A more suitable sentence for our current level of technology assimilation would be, 'I downloaded a few podcasts to my iPod to share with you'!

  The Internet generation are people who have grown up with computer technology as a commonplace. They usually have no memory of (or nostalgia for) pre-Internet history. The iGeneration (a jocular allusion to the popular iPod boom, experienced by the Internet generation) takes the Internet for granted, accepting the utility of services such as Internet forums, email, Wikipedia, search engines, MySpace, Facebook, imageboards and YouTube. The term 'Generation Now' has been used as well, to reflect the urge for instant gratification that technology has imparted. This is the most wired or connected generation ever with several countries, including the United Kingdom, having more mobile phones than people.

- **Self-expression and interaction:** Rather than companies providing information to customers – what can be called top down – the Internet generation wants to discover new things for themselves and then share their discoveries. The 'me-to-we' generation wants to connect and share and has created an online world that operates beyond traditional boundaries. User-generated content allows customers to express themselves. YouTube or social networking sites such as Bebo and MyFace bring together people with a common interest but also allow consumers to share information. MySpace has had a dramatic impact on the way marketers have to define and interact with their customers. Young adults are moving away from other mediums to social networking. This has been driven by broadband penetration and also ubiquitous digital cameras and camera phones. Social networking sites within Germany reach 45 per cent of the country's online population with 14.8 million unique visitors, with MySpace as the most popular attracting 3.7 million and German site StudiVZals with strong traffic of 3.1 million.[64] These sites allow self-expression, discovery and interplay within a rich interactive environment, thus providing a close-knit neighbourhood and a truly global community. More that 162 million global profiles are registered on MySpace and the site has nearly 100 million unique monthly visits. Marketers need to interpose themselves into the dialogue and engage with customers on their terms.

Table 6.5 European usage of social networking sites – selected countries

	Ranked by total unique visitors		Age 15+ August 2007*		
Territory	Total unique visitors (000)	% reach of country's total online population	Average hours per user	Average pages per user	Average visits per user
Europe	127,297	56.4	3.0	523	15.8
UK	24,857	77.9	5.8	839	23.3
Germany	15,475	46.9	3.1	423	13.8
France	13,332	49.6	2.0	476	16.8
Spain	8,828	61.5	1.8	251	14.9
Italy	8,736	49.3	1.8	346	12.6

*Age 15+, home and work locations; excludes traffic from public computers such as Internet cafés or access from mobile phones or PDAs.
Source: From comScore (2007) U.K. social networking site usage highest in Europe, comScore World Metrix, July (www.comscore.com/press/release.asp?press=1801). Reproduced with permission.

- **A substantial increase in buying power. An ability to compare notes on products and services:** The Internet and other technologies, such as mobile phones and palm pilots, fuel personal connections and user-generated content through social network sites such as MySpace, Wikipedia and YouTube.[65,66] Marketers are eyeing the success of these sites, given that 35 per cent of young, first-time car buyers consider the Internet their most important shopping tool.[67] Buyers are only a click away from comparing competitor prices and product and service attributes on the Internet. They can even name their price for a hotel room, airline ticket or mortgage. Business buyers can run a reverse auction in which sellers compete to capture their business. They can readily join with others to aggregate their purchases and achieve deeper volume discounts.
- **An amplified voice to influence peer and public opinion:** The Internet can be used as a vehicle to influence companies. In late 2004 Kryptonite, a company that makes high-priced bicycle locks, found itself in an awkward position when several blogs showed how the firm's U-shaped locks could be easily picked using only a Bic pen.[68] Many consumers were able to open the iPhone to any network despite the desire of the company to use one network in each European country, with the instructions posted to the web.
- **Co-creation:** Much of consumer experience with brands and companies now involves co-creation, where the consumer shapes their experience of the product or service. Volkswagen-UK now allows you to choose everything from colours, designs and specifications of your new Beetle.

  This also links to **customisation:** traditionally products and services were designed by companies, but now customers have an input into the design role, customising the product or service to suit themselves. Companies can produce individually differentiated products or services, whether they're ordered in person, on the phone or online, thanks to advances in factory customisation technology and the increased sophistication of databases, computers and the Internet. For a price, customers can buy M&M sweets with personalised messages on them and Heinz tomato ketchup bottles with customised messages.[69] BMW's technology now allows buyers to design their own models from among 350 variations, with 500 options, 90 exterior colours, and 170 trims. BMW says that 80 per cent of the cars bought by individuals in Europe are customised.
- **Self-service technologies:** More and more companies are choosing to provide self-service technology options for their customers. Self-service checkouts at supermarkets, self-check-ins at airports, and cinema ticket collection and online investment trading have all proliferated recently. Self-service should be a choice for customers rather than a cost-saving excerise by the company. Many self-service technologies have been designed without

any marketing input. Take the ATM – what would it look like if it had been designed and managed by marketing rather than technologists?

▽ Understanding the philosophy of marketing

The marketing philosophy or concept is one of the most simple ideas but it is also one of the most important, and one that is often difficult for a company to embrace. At its very core is the customer and his or her satisfaction. The marketing concept and philosophy states that the organisation should strive to satisfy its customers' wants and needs while meeting the organisation's profit and other goals. In simple terms, 'the customer is king'. This marketing philosophy needs to be adopted by the whole company. From top management to the lowest levels and across all departments of the organisation, it is a philosophy or way of doing business. The customers' needs, wants and satisfaction should always be foremost in every manager's and employee's mind.[70]

Many companies have not progressed to a marketing philosophy but are challenged to move from the old-fashioned product or sales concept.

The production philosophy

The production concept is one of the oldest concepts in business and looks only to the product or service that the company has or wants to make or provide, rather than to a customer need. It is the idea of a product looking for a market. Managers of production-oriented businesses concentrate on achieving high production efficiency, low costs and mass distribution. The thinking is aligned to the product concept, which proposes that consumers prefer products that offer the most quality, performance or innovative features. Managers in these organisations focus on making superior products or services and improving them over time. However, these managers are sometimes caught up in a love affair with their products or services. They might commit the 'better mousetrap' fallacy, believing that a better mousetrap will lead people to beat a path to their door. A new or improved product or service will not necessarily be successful unless it is aligned to customer needs and then produced, priced, distributed, communicated and managed throughout its life. With this focus you often have a product looking for customers or a product that is way above what the customer wants.

The selling philosophy

The selling concept is a focus on making sales rather than really understanding the customers. The selling concept suggests businesses have to persuade or force customers to buy the organisation's products or services. The organisation must, therefore, undertake an aggressive selling and promotion effort.

Traditionally the selling concept was practised most aggressively with unsought products or services that buyers normally do not think of buying, such as insurance. Some companies also practise the selling concept when they have overcapacity. Their aim is to sell what they make, rather than make what the market wants. Company success based on hard selling carries high risks. It assumes that customers who are coaxed into buying a product or service will like it, and that if they don't, they will not return it or bad-mouth the company or complain to consumer organisations, but that they might even buy it again. The films *Tin Man* and *Glengarry Glen Ross* are very good examples of this concept within the windows and auctioneering areas where the characters put pressure on customers to order products they do not want or need in order to keep their own ugly jobs. These films and their hard-sell antics show clearly the dangers of an over focus on sales.

The marketing philosophy

The marketing philosophy emerged in the mid-1950s.[71] Instead of a product-centred and sales-oriented 'make-and-sell' philosophy, business shifted to a customer-centred, 'sense-and-respond' philosophy. The marketing task is not to find the right customers for your products or services, but to design the right services and products for your customers. Dell Computers doesn't prepare a perfect computer for its target market. Rather, it provides product platforms on which each person customises the features they desire in their computer.

The marketing concept holds that the key to achieving organisational goals is being more effective than competitors in creating, managing, delivering and communicating superior customer value to your chosen target markets.

Theodore Levitt of Harvard Business School explored the contrast between the selling and marketing philosophy and noted that:

> Selling focuses on the needs of the seller; marketing on the needs of the buyer. Selling is preoccupied with the seller's need to convert his product into cash; marketing with the idea of satisfying the needs of the customer by means of the product or service and the whole cluster of things associated with creating, delivering and finally consuming it.[72]

To learn how mid-life companies such as Wal-Mart might benefit from a holistic marketing concept to combat stagnating growth, visit www.prenhall.com/kotler

Today's best marketers recognise the need to have a more complete, cohesive approach to marketing that moves beyond the production or selling approaches to business and really embraces the marketing philosophy. 'Marketing memo: Marketing right and wrong' suggests where companies go wrong – and how they can get it right – in their marketing.

Marketing memo

Marketing right and wrong

The ten deadly sins of marketing

1 The company is not sufficiently market focused and customer driven.

2 The company does not fully understand its target customers.

3 The company needs to better define and monitor its competitors.

4 The company has not properly managed its relationships with its stakeholders.

5 The company is not good at finding new opportunities.

6 The company's marketing plans and planning process are deficient.

7 The company's product and service policies need tightening.

8 The company's brand building and communications skills are weak.

9 The company is not well organised to carry on effective and efficient marketing.

10 The company has not made maximum use of technology.

The ten commandments of marketing

1 The company segments the market, chooses the best segments, and develops a strong position in each chosen segment.

2 The company maps its customers' needs, perceptions, preferences and behaviour and motivates its stakeholders to obsess about serving and satisfying the customers.

3 The company knows its major competitors and their strengths and weaknesses.

4 The company builds partners out of its stakeholders and generously rewards them.

5 The company develops systems for identifying opportunities, ranking them, and choosing the best ones.

6 The company manages a marketing planning system that leads to insightful long-term and short-term plans.

7 The company exercises strong control over its product and service elements.

8 The company builds strong brands by using the most relevant communication and promotion tools and techniques and other mix elements.

9 The company builds marketing leadership and a team spirit among its various departments.

10 The company constantly adds technology that gives it a competitive advantage in the marketplace.

Marketing in a postmodern world and retro marketing

Postmodern marketing forces us to look at marketing and question some of our marketing beliefs. Postmodern consumption patterns are described as culturally diverse, fragmented, increasingly market-mediated, and performative. Whereas in modernity, the focus is on the individual, the market becomes the centre of all meaningful social activity in the post-modern era.[73] Postmodern marketing suggests that we critique or challenge some of the basic understandings of marketing. Professor Steven Brown, in an article entitled 'Torment your customer (they'll love it)', suggests that

> . . . everyone in business today seems to take it as a God-given truth that companies were put on this earth for one purpose alone: to pander to customers. Marketers spend all their time slavishly tracking the needs of buyers, then meticulously crafting products and pitches to satisfy them.'[74]

Brown further suggests that marketers need to tease, torment, tempt and tantalise the customer. The Spanish retailer Zara exemplifies this postmodernism. They do tempt, tease and tantalise the customer. Fashions arrive fast and leave the shop as quickly. If you don't buy now they will be gone. Some customers even monitor the delivery dates for stores and race in to be the first to buy. Average visits per store for fashion outlets are 3 to 4 a year yet Zara averages 14 a year as the consumer is enticed in to see what is there today and will be gone tomorrow. This relates to the customers' demand for high fashion, to the challenge of getting something great in the shop and engaging with the company in this marketing game. Zara really understands its customers and its customers understand the Zara system. According to *Marie Claire* magazine editor Marie O'Riordan, the formula works: 'With other high-street retailers, the risk in buying something is that you'll bump into somebody wearing the same thing, and it spoils the effect,' she says. 'With Zara, because the stock turnover is so fast, you have to get there on day one. It tends to sell out two days later so you have a real chance of being a little bit exclusive, which is quite unusual for a high street shop.'[75]

Postmodernism invites a unique perspective of how to manage marketing and how to understand the consumer. Postmodernism says that social experiences are an interplay of myths which produce regimes of truth and that much of what we understand or believe about the individual, self, freedom, structure and so on is arbitrary and short-lived, fleeting rather than essential and fixed. We need to change our views as the customer changes. Dove is a product that forces us to reconsider what we consider as beautiful and is a good example of a company changing perceptions. The Dove Campaign for Real Beauty is a global effort that is intended to serve as a starting point for societal change. The focus for Dove was on real women celebrating their very real body types, including fuller figures not typically portrayed in advertising. Six ordinary women were recruited off the street and chosen for their confidence and spark – baring all in their underwear without having been airbrushed or retouched in any way. The YouTube video of the Dove Evolution was popular because it challenged consumer thinking and by May 2008 had been viewed over 6 million times.

The main conditions of postmodern marketing are hyperreality, fragmentation, reversals of production and consumption, decentring of the subject, paradoxical juxtapositions (of opposites) and loss of commitment.[76]

- **Hyperreality:** Exemplified by the virtual worlds of cyberspace and the psuedo worlds of theme parks, hotels and heritage centres, hyperreality involves the creation of consumption sites and marketing phenomena that are 'more real then real'. Here the distinction between reality and fantasy is momentarily blurred.
- **Fragmentation:** Marketing in postmodernity is unfailingly fast, furious, frenetic, frenzied, fleeting and hyperactive.
- **Reversals of production and consumption:** Postmodern consumers are active in the production of meaning, of marketing, of consumption. They do rather than have 'done' to them.

- **Decentring of the subject:** Centredness is where individuals are defined by their occupation, social class, demographics, postcode, personalities and so on. Postmodernism suggests that this is not so, and that the harder marketers try to pin down the decentred consuming subject the less successful they will be. In the immortal words of Douglas Coupland, 'I am not a target market.' It is so much harder to market to consumers who cannot be classified.

- **Paradoxical juxtapositions (of opposites):** We have examples of the mixing and matching of opposites and the combination of contradictory styles in the world-famous Irish dance show – Riverdance or Lord of the Rings. The Riverdance show proved to be a huge success with its mixture of Irish, Scottish, Spanish and Russian dance, US tap, square dance, ballet and even break dancing. The musical grossed over €1 billion from performances in 32 countries.

- **Loss of commitment:** Growing disillusionment with the delivery of promises and the willingness to try different experiences has resulted in a *loss of commitment*. The postmodern consumer takes on multiple, sometimes even contradictory projects, to which s/he is marginally and momentarily committed. This is observed in all walks of life: in relationships, in professions, and consumption. Marketing managers experience this when consumer loyalties to brands (which they took for granted) change.

Table 6.6 explores the difference between the postmodern knowledge society and the modern industrial society. Many of these issues will be explored throughout the text but it is clear that markets and marketing practice is moving towards the right side of the table.

An over-focus on the customer can create problems when 'The truth is, customers don't know what they want. They never have. They never will. The wretches don't even know what they *don't* want!' Professor Brown suggests that, 'It's time to get back to an earlier era, to the time when marketers ruled the world with creativity and style. . . . It's time for retromarketing'[77] **Retromarketing** is based on tricksterism, exclusivity, amplification, secrecy and entertainment – TEASE:

Tricksterism – A little mischief adds intrigue and mystery.

Exclusivity – 'Retromarketing eschews the "here it is, come and get it, there's plenty for everyone" proposition – the modern marketing proposition – by deliberately holding back supplies and delaying gratification. You want it? Can't have it. Try again later, pal.' Minimise inventory. Customers as select few. The famous Beanie Babies were marketed as exclusive and only a certain number of each one was manufactured to create interest and demand. This is similar to the current Webkin craze with children logging on and registering their animals for points online.

Table 6.6 Contrasting the modern versus the postmodern marketing environment

Modern industrial society	Postmodern knowledge society
Mass markets, production and mass distribution and homogeneity and standardisation	Market fragmentation; services and ICT; pluralism and freedom of choice
Consumer as consumer; economic systems; value-creating production	Consumer as co-producer; symbolic system; value-creating consumption
Functional divisions; semi-qualified workforce; routine work	Cross-functional teams/projects; knowledge-based competences; learning, tacit processes
Authoritarian hierarchies, vertical communications; controlled ownership	Network, alliances and virtual organisations; horizontal communications; outsourcing

Source: A. O'Driscoll (2007) Advances in marketing theory: the post-modern perspective. Guest Lecture at Trinity College Dublin and A. O'Driscoll (1999) The postmodern condition, Samuel Beckett and marketing malady, Proceedings of the Marketing Paradiso Conclave, St Clement's, Belfast, September, pp. 96–103.

Amplify – 'Ensure that the ticket or cool item is talked about and, more important, that the talking is talked about.' WHO? Affrontery. Outrage. Surprise. Calvin Klein, Citroën Picasso.

Secrecy – Marketing (torment) of *Harry Potter*, where the books were delayed and then released at midnight to cause queues and demand and to create interest. Classic 'secret' recipes of many companies, such as the formula for Coca-Cola and the contents of the figroll.

Entertain – 'Marketing must divert. It must amuse. It must engage.' Imaginative quiz or competition. Marketing is fun.[78]

▽ Overview of marketing management

This section provides an overview and of marketing management that the flowchart in Figure 6.5 highlights.

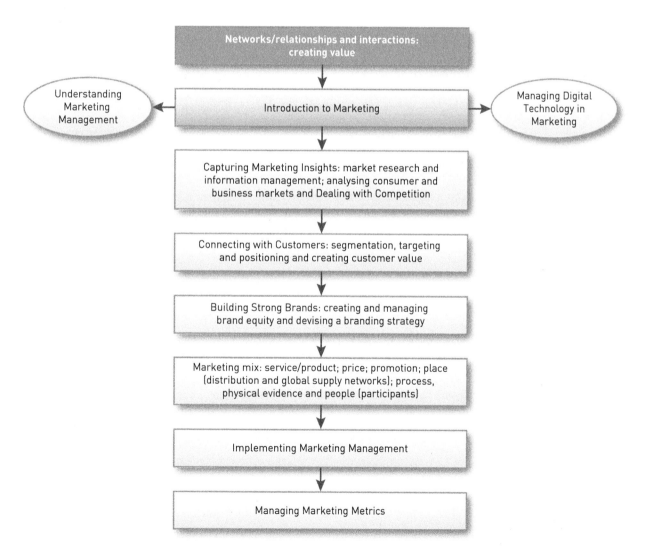

Figure 6.5 An overview of marketing management activities

The following case study provides a brief overview and the main elements of marketing management.

Zeus, Inc. (name disguised), operates in several industries, including cameras, film and chemicals. The company is organised into strategic business units (SBUs). Corporate management is considering what to do with its Atlas camera division, which produces a range of 35 mm and digital cameras. Although Zeus has a sizeable market share and is producing good revenue, the 35 mm market itself is rapidly declining and Zeus's market share is slipping. In the faster-growing digital camera segment, Zeus faces strong competition and has been slow to gain sales. Zeus's corporate management wants Atlas's marketing management to produce a strong turnaround marketing plan for the division.

Understanding marketing management

The marketing strategy should take into account changing global opportunities and challenges, changing customer perspectives and a variety of new challenges and marketing realities. To understand marketing is to understand management and the marketing team must understand the integrated marketing they will need to use throughout the organisation. Marketing management skills will be needed to change the direction of the organisation and to manage both an internally and externally challenging environment.

Developing marketing strategies and plans

The first task facing Atlas is to identify its potential long-run opportunities, given its market experience and core competences. Atlas needs to find the customer need and then it can design its cameras with better features. It can make a line of video cameras, or it can use its core competency in optics to design a line of binoculars and telescopes. Whichever direction it chooses, it must develop concrete marketing plans that specify the marketing strategy and tactics going forward.

Managing digital technology in marketing

Atlas needs to review the full range of information and communication technologies within their organisation and any they may need to acquire for their marketing task. It also needs to review the technological environment for its product in relation to other technologies and also the level of technology know-how its customers have. Other camera manufacturers are embracing technology at the customer interface and have a range of self service devices both in shops and at home for customers. Digital picture frames that play rotating pictures are also becoming very popular. Depending on the target market, more of the communication spend could be linked to technologies, the Internet or digital channels and Atlas needs to understand how to use them innovatively.

Capturing marketing insights

Atlas needs a reliable marketing information system to closely monitor its marketing environment and also needs to understand their internal database information.

Atlas also needs a dependable marketing research system. To transform marketing strategy into marketing programmes, marketing managers must measure market potential, forecast demand, and make basic decisions about marketing expenditures, marketing activities and marketing allocation. Atlas must clearly understand its customers and to do so needs to understand consumer markets. Who buys cameras, and why do they buy? What are they looking for in the way of features and prices, and where do they shop? Atlas also sells cameras to business markets, including large corporations, professional firms, retailers and government agencies, where purchasing agents or buying committees make the decisions. Atlas needs to gain a full understanding of how organisational buyers buy. Atlas must also pay close attention to competitors, anticipating its competitors' moves and knowing how to react quickly and decisively. It may want to initiate some surprise moves, in which case it needs to anticipate how its competitors will respond.

Connecting with customers: segementation, targeting and positioning

Atlas must reconsider the segmentation in the market and how best to create value for its chosen target markets. It must decide how to position in the market. Suppose Atlas decides to focus on the consumer market and to develop a positioning strategy. Should it position itself as the 'Mercedes' brand, offering superior cameras at a premium price with excellent service and strong advertising – such as British Airways in the airline business? Should it build a simple, low-priced camera aimed at more price-conscious consumers such as those who travel on Ryanair or easyJet? Or something in between? It must look to develop strong, profitable, long-term relationships with customers.

Building strong brands

Atlas has a range of marketing mix elements that it must integrate and use to create and maintain its brand in the eyes of its consumers. Atlas must understand the strengths and weaknesses of the Zeus brand as customers see it. A **brand** is an offering from a known source. A brand name such as Virgin carries many associations in people's minds that make up the brand image. In the case of Virgin it could reflect fun and irreverence. For Nokia it could be modern and great phones. Atlas will have to build a strong, favourable and unique brand image within the mind of the consumer through the use of the marketing mix variables. It also has to manage this brand across many European markets and ultimately globally.

Shaping the market offerings

Once the target market and positioning have been selected the marketing managers now have the full range of the marketing mix to match to consumer needs. Aligned to its positioning and at the heart of the marketing programme is the product and service – the tangible offering to the market, which includes all the unique features of managing and marketing a service and also the product quality, design, features and packaging . Introducing new services and products regularly is a core marketing requirement covered in.

A critical marketing decision relates to price. Atlas has to decide on wholesale and retail prices, discounts, allowances and credit terms. Its price should match well with the offer's perceived value or positioning; otherwise, buyers will turn to competitors' products or services.

Delivering value

Atlas must also determine how to manage all aspects of product and service delivery properly in order to deliver to the target market the value embodied in its products and services. Nowadays companies are part of networks and channels making the product and aligned services accessible and available to target customers. Atlas must identify, recruit and link various intermediaries to supply its products and services efficiently to the target market. It must understand the various types of retailers, wholesalers and physical distribution firms and how they make their decisions as well as online Internet channels and other technology-based self-service or distribution systems. Atlas needs to understand the service process the customer will go through, any physical evidence they receive and also the impact of people during the customer–company encounter.

Communicating value

Atlas must also adequately communicate to the target market the value embodied by its products and services. It will need an integrated marketing communication programme that maximises the individual and collective contributions of all communication activities. Atlas needs to set up a communication plan that could consist of advertising, sales promotion, events and public relations and has to plan personal communications, in the form of direct and interactive marketing, as well as hire, train and motivate salespeople.

Implementing marketing management

Finally, Atlas must build a marketing organisation that is capable of implementing the marketing plan. Because surprises and disappointments can occur as marketing plans unfold, Atlas will need feedback and control mechanisms to understand the efficiency and effectiveness of its marketing activities and how it can improve them. Atlas also needs to report back to the corporate board, which will have allocated a budget to this marketing endeavour and will need to see the returns and measure the effectiveness of the marketing strategy and tactics.

Marketing focuses on understanding the customer and honing in on their current (and more importantly their future) needs so that the total company effort is towards customer satisfaction at a profit. Marketing is all organised efforts, activities and expenditure designed to first acquire a customer and second to maintain and grow a customer at a profit.

▽ SUMMARY

1   Marketing is crucial for business success, focusing on understanding customers or 'meeting needs profitably'.

2   Marketing management is *the art and science of choosing target markets and getting, keeping and increasing customers through creating, managing, communicating and delivering superior customer value.*

3   Marketing can be used for services, products, events, experiences, persons, places and ideas.

4   There are many key markets, including consumer, business, global and non-profit, voluntary and government markets. Much of marketing takes place in a network of firms and customers. Marketing no longer competes against one company but against a network of companies.

5   Marketing has five main practices, including transactional, database, emarketing, interaction and network, each of which is used depending on the customer and the industry, but there is usually a dominant marketing practice. These reflect a transactional to relational perspective to marketing.

6   The European marketing environment presents some challenges for marketers. From a company perspective there is heightened competition, globalisation, increased ICT, industry convergence, disintermediation and retailer transformation. From a consumer perspective there is increased consumer sophistication and particularly a technology savvy customer who has greater choice, greater information and greater access to products and services 24/7.

7 Though a simple idea, the philosophy of marketing, which is customer focused, can be hard for companies to embrace. Many companies are stuck in a production or selling philosophy that overlooks the core needs of their customers. The marketing philosophy achieves organisational goals by being more effective than the competiton in creating, managing, delivering and communicating superior customer value to their choosen target market.

8 Postmodern marketing suggests that we should challenge marketing assumptions and tease, torment, tempt and tantilise customers. The move to postmodern marketing is reflective of a move to a more knowledge society where the customer understands tricksterism, exclusivity, amplifications, secrecy and entertainment as core creative needs of marketing mix programmes.

9 The overview of marketing management sets out the core marketing tasks necessary for success to include developing marketing strategies and plans, capturing marketing insights, choosing target markets and positioning, creating long-term growth through building strong brands, and then using the marketing mix to connect with customers, shaping the market offerings, delivering and communicating value, implementing the marketing plan and managing marketing metrics.

▽ APPLICATIONS

Marketing debate

What is marketing? You have been asked by your managing director to justify an increased marketing budget. Explain the role of marketing within the organisation and discuss why an increased spend could benefit the company.

Take a position: Consumers are changing and so too must marketing. Discuss.

Marketing discussion

Select a low-cost airline (such as Ryanair, which was used in the introductory example to this chapter) and then choose a full service airline (e.g. Air France or Lufthansa). Compare and contrast the different marketing activities, from their choice of target markets through to all the variables in the marketing mix.

▽ REFERENCES

[1] Adapted from *The Financial Times*, 21 June 2003, p. 16.

[2] The Conference Board (2007) The CEO challenge 2007 – top ten challenges, Research Report R-1380-05-RR (www.conference-board.org/UTILITIES/pressDetail.cfm?press_ID=3224).

[3] BusinessWeek/Interbrand (2008) Annual ranking of the 100 best global brands.

[4] K. Floor (2006) *Branding a Store: How to Build Successful Retail Brands in a Changing Marketplace*. London: Kogan Page.

[5] See www.allbusiness.com/marketing-advertising/branding-brand-development/4673704-1.html.

[6] S. Meichtry (2007) Benetton picks up the fashion pace: tracking trends with fast deliveries – the Italian brand makes a comeback, *Wall Street Journal* (eastern edition) 10 April, B1.

[7] J. C. Levinson (2007) *Guerrilla Marketing: Easy and Inexpensive Strategies for Making Big Profits from Your Small Business*, 4th edn, Boston, MA: Houghton Mifflin.

[8] E. Gummesson (2007) Exit services marketing: enter service marketing, *Journal of Consumer Behavior*, 6(2), 113–41.

[9] Ibid.

[10] C. Gronroos (2006) On defining marketing: finding a new roadmap for marketing, *Marketing Theory*, 6, 395–417.

[11] Ibid.

[12] J. Bakan (2004) *The Corporation*, London: Constable; N. Klein (2001) *No Logo*, London: Flamingo; G. Ritzer (2000) *The McDonaldization of Society*, Thousands Oaks, CA: California: Pine Forge Press.

[13] R. Gordon, G. Hastings, L. McDermott, and P. Suiquier (2007) The critical role of social marketing, in M. Saren, P. Maclaran, C. Goulding, R. Elliot, A. Shankar and M. Catterall (eds) *Critical Marketing: Defining the Field*, London: Butterworth-Heinemann, pp. 159–73 (at p. 164).

[14] P. Drucker (1973) *Management: Tasks, Responsibilities, Practices*, New York: Harper and Row, pp. 64–5.

[15] S. Vargo and R. Lusch (2004) The four services marketing myths, *Journal of Service Research*, 6(4), 324–35.

[16] H. Winklhofer, R. Palmer and R. Brodie (2007) Researching the service dominant logic: normative perspective versus practice, *Australasian Marketing Journal*, 15(1), 76–83.

[17] C. Gronroos (1991) The marketing strategy continuum: towards a marketing concept for the 1990s, *Management Decision*, 29(1), 7–13.

[18] P. Kotler (1984) Dream vacations: the booming market for designed experiences, *The Futurist*, October, 7–13; B. J. Pine, II and J. Gilmore (1999) *The Experience Economy*, Boston, MA: Harvard Business School Press; B. Schmitt (1999) *Experience Marketing*, New York: Free Press.

[19] From Celebrity magazines, *The Economist*, 28 April 2005.

[20] See www.dailymail.co.uk/pages/live/articles/news/news.html?in_article_id=489645&in_page_id=1770.

[21]P. Kotler, I. J. Rein and D. Haider (1993) *Marketing Places: Attracting Investment, Industry, and Tourism to Cities, States, and Nations*, New York: Free Press; and P. Kotler, C. Asplund, I. Rein and D. H. Haider (1999) *Marketing Places in Europe: Attracting Investments, Industries, Residents and Visitors to European Cities, Communities, Regions, and Nations*, London: Financial Times Prentice-Hall.

[22]See http://ec.europa.eu/enterprise/services/tourism/index_en.htm.

[23]See http://drinkaware.co.uk/.

[24]R. Achrol and P. Kotler (1999) Marketing in the network economy, *Journal of Marketing* (special issue), 146–63.

[25]See www.prb.org.

[26]See www.english.mb-research.de/content/view/15/32/.

[27]C. Bremner (2008) Champagne region expanded to meet world demand, *The Times*, 14 March 2008 (http://www.timesonline.co.uk/tol/life_and_style/food_and_drink/wine/article3548465.ece).

[28]M. Moynagh and R. Worsley (2002) Tomorrow's consumer: the shifting balance of power, *Journal of Consumer Behavior*, 1(3), 293–301 (at 213).

[29]Ibid.

[30]Aquafresh varieties (online image) available at www.aquafresh.com/default.aspx?startPage=varieties, accessed on 5 March 2008.

[31]W. Nelson (2002) All power to the consumer? Complexity and choice in consumers' lives, *Journal of Consumer Behavior*, 2(2), 185–95.

[32]D. Hoffman and T. Novak (2000) How to acquire customers on the web, *Harvard Business Review*, May–June, 21–7.

[33]See http://en.wikipedia.org/wiki/ITunes.

[34]Y. (J.) Wind (2006) Blurring the lines: is there a need to rethink industrial marketing? *The Journal of Business & Industrial Marketing*, 21(7), 474–81.

[35]T. M. Begley and D. P. Boyd (2003) The need for a corporate global mind-set, *MIT Sloan Management Review*, 44(2), 25–32.

[36]Ibid.

[37]C. Vitzthum (2005) Real Madrid needs a new goal, *BusinessWeek*, 25 June (www.businessweek.com/magazine/content/05_26/b3939423.htm).

[38]J. Rayport and J. Sviokla (1994) Managing in the marketspace, *Harvard Business Review*, November–December, 141–50. Also see J. Rayport and J. Sviokla (1995) Exploring the virtual value chain, *Harvard Business Review*, November–December, 75–85.

[39]Ibid and W. Chan Kim and R. Mauborgne (1999) Creating new market space, *Harvard Business Review*, January–February, 1–14.

[40]M. Sawhney (2001) *Seven Steps to Nirvana*, New York: McGraw-Hill.

[41]N. H. Borden (1964) The concept of the marketing mix, *Journal of Advertising Research*, 4, 2–7. For another framework, see G. S. Day (1994) The capabilities of market-driven organizations, *Journal of Marketing*, 58(4), 37–52.

[42]E. J. McCarthy and W. D. Perreault (2002) *Basic Marketing: A Global-Managerial Approach*, 14th edn, Homewood, IL: McGraw-Hill/Irwin.

[43]M. Rafiq and P. K. Ahmed (1995) Using the 7Ps as a generic marketing mix: an exploratory survey of UK and European marketing academics, *Marketing Intelligence & Planning*, 13(9), 4–16.

[44]A. Ries (2006) Is it the end of the ultimate advertising slogan? *Advertising Age*, August (www.ries.com/iframes/articles-read.php?id=9).

[45]N. Coviello, R. Brodie and P. Danaher (2002) How firms relate to their markets: an empirical examination of contemporary marketing practices, *Journal of Marketing*, 66(3), 33–46.

[46]Ibid.

[47]M. Brady, M. Saren and N. Tzokas (2002) Integrating information technology into marketing practice: the IT reality of contemporary marketing practice, *Journal of Marketing Management*, 18(5-6), 555–77.

[48]Coviello et al. (2002) op. cit.

[49]C. Gronroos (1997) Keynote paper: from marketing mix to relationship marketing – towards a paradigm shift in marketing, *Management Decision*, 35, 322–39; E. Gummesson (1998) Implementation requires a relationship marketing paradigm, *Journal of the Academy of Marketing Science*, 26(3), 242–9; A. Payne, M. Christopher, M. Clark and H. Peck (1995) *Relationship Marketing for Competitive Advantage*, London: Butterworth-Heinemann; G. Day and D. Montgomery (1999) Charting new directions for marketing, *Journal of Marketing*, 63 (special issue), 3–13; M. Baker (2000) The future of marketing, in M. Baker (ed.) *Marketing Theory: A Student's Text*, Australia: Business Press Thomson Publishing.

[50]R. Heeler and E. Chung (2000) The economics basis of marketing? in M. Baker (ed.) *Marketing Theory: A Student's Text*, Australia: Business Press Thomson Publishing.

[51]L. Penaloza (2000) Consuming people: from political economy to theaters of consumption – a review, *Journal of Marketing*, 64(1), 106–111; A. Fuat Firat and N. Dholakia (1998) *Consuming People: From Political Economy to Theaters of Consumption*, London and New York: Routledge.

[52]T. Reid (2004) *The United States of Europe*, London: Penguin, p. 245.

[53]L. V. Kurylo and S. J. Maffei (2007) Understanding the legal status of the world's largest business market: the European Union, *Review of Business*, 27(3), 56–62.

[54]E. Kaynak and F. Jallat (2004) *Marketing in Western Europe: A Monolith or Multidimensional Market*, London: Hawthorne Press.

[55]R. Savitt (1998) This thing I call Europe, *International Marketing Review*, 15(6), 444–6.

[56]S. Paliwoda and S. Marinova (2007) The marketing challenges within the enlarged single European market, *European Journal of Marketing*, 41(3/4), 233–44.

[57]M. A. Marinov and S. Marinova (2002) Foreign direct investment in emerging markets of Central and Eastern Europe, *Journal of East-West Business*, 9(3/4), 27–52.

[58]J. Larimo, M. Marinov and S. Marinova (2006) The Central and Eastern European brewing industry since 1990, *British Food Journal*, 108(5), 371–84.

[59]D. Sacks (2006) MAC Cosmetics Inc., *Fast Company*, September, p. 62.

[60]Moynagh and Worsley (2001) op. cit.

[61]S. Brown (2003) Marketing to Generation®, Forethought, *Harvard Business Review*, June, 81(6), 2–3.

[62]M. Lindstrom (2003) Branding is no longer child's play! *The Journal of Consumer Marketing*, 21(213), 175–82.

[63]See http://russiatoday.ru/business/news/6776.

[64]J. Gavin (2008) German social networking community reaches 14.8 million, ComScore, Inc., (www.comscore.com/press/release.asp?press=1737).

[65]A. Kamenetz (2006) The network unbound, *Fast Company*, June, 69–73; see also M. Barrett (2007) The rise of social networking and the lessons for brands, content and all media business, Accenture Global Forum (www.accenture.com/global/services/by_industry/communications/acces_newsletter/articles_index/gcf07_barrett.html).

[66]See www.bikeforums.net/video/1.mov.

[67]D. Kiley (2006) Advertisers, start your engines, *BusinessWeek*, 6 March, p. 26.

[68]The blogs in the corporate machine, *The Economist*, 11 February 2006, 55–6.

[69]B. Horovitz (2006) In trend toward vanity food: it's getting personal, *USA Today*, 9 August.

[70]See www.enotes.com/management-encyclopedia/marketing-concept-philosophy.

[71]J. B. McKitterick (1957) What is the marketing management concept?, in F. M. Bass (ed.) *The Frontiers of Marketing Thought and Action*, Chicago: American Marketing Association, pp. 71–82; F. J. Borch (1957) The marketing philosophy as a way of business life, in *The Marketing Concept: Its Meaning to Management* (Marketing Series, No. 99), New York: American Management Association, pp. 3–5; R. J. Keith (1960) The marketing revolution, *Journal of Marketing*, January, 35–8.

[72]T. Levitt (1960) Marketing myopia, *Harvard Business Review*, July–August, 50–65.

[73]L. Penaloza (2000) op. cit.; A. Fuat Firat and N. Dholakia (1998) op. cit.

[74]S. Brown (2001) Torment your customers (they'll love it), *Harvard Business Review*, September–October, 82–91.

[75]See www.fashionunited.co.uk/news/archive/inditex1.htm.

[76]A. Fuat Firat, N. Dholakia and A. Venkatesh (1995) Marketing in a postmodern world, *European Journal of Marketing*, 29(1), 40–56.

[77]Brown (2001) op. cit., p. 84.

[78]A. O'Driscoll (1999) The postmodern condition, Samuel Beckett and marketing malady, Proceedings of the Marketing Paradiso Conclave, St Clement's, Belfast, September, pp. 96–103.

## Chapter 7

Managing marketing metrics

IN THIS CHAPTER, WE WILL ADDRESS THE FOLLOWING QUESTIONS:

1 What are marketing metrics?
2 What is the need for marketing metrics?
3 What are useful marketing metrics?
4 What are the key marketing metrics?
5 What metrics do companies use?
6 What is a marketing dashboard?

To stay in business a company needs positive cash flows, which in turn are generated from the company's ability to create value. Since value is defined by customers, marketing makes a fundamental contribution to long-term business success. Recognising that evaluating marketing performance is a key task for management, marketing metrics are concerned with calculating the value of marketing activity in a company.

What you can't measure, you can't manage – this is the true marketing metrics philosophy.
Source: Curt Pickens/iStockphoto

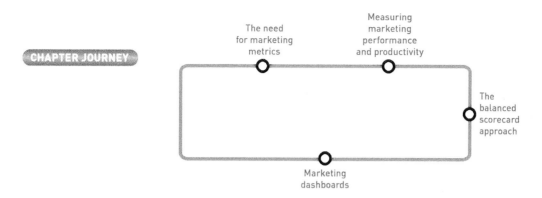

Brands spend large amounts of marketing money and the brand owners and their agencies need to be accountable for this money, and how it is spent. There is a constant need to create growth and thus prioritise spend behind campaigns, and media that are more effective, to get a 'bigger bang for our buck'. But you only know what is more effective if you measure and monitor the effect properly. BrandScience – a specialist unit within OmnicomMediaGroup – is a global network of econometric and marketing analysis experts specialising in delivering state-of-the-art, 100 per cent tailor-made brand, business and communication evaluation by quantifying and measuring properly what matters to businesses. Advanced statistical modelling methods are employed on hard data on the brand's sales, marketing and communications history, competitors and economic context in order to identify significant drivers of the businesses, separate the effects of different drivers and isolate and quantify the contribution from marketing both on a short-, medium- and long-term basis.[1]

Marketing managers are increasingly being held accountable for their investments and must be able to justify marketing expenditures to senior management.[2] Marketing metrics provide valuable data points against which the marketing organisation can track its progress, demonstrate accountability and allow marketers to better know, act upon and align efforts.[3] This chapter explores how companies can measure and improve their marketing performance by applying marketing metrics.

▽ The need for marketing metrics

In the modern business environment, companies to an increasing degree derive substantial and sustained competitive advantage from intangible assets such as brand equity, knowledge, networks and innovative capability. Measuring the return on both tangible (fixed assets, e.g., land, buildings and machinery) and intangible (assets that have no physical substance, e.g., brand names, copyrights and patents, strong channel relationships, etc.) assets has therefore now become imperative for managers.[4] Without metrics to track performance, marketing and business plans are ineffective.

Marketing metrics are the set of measures that help firms to quantify, compare and interpret their marketing performance. In 2005 the American Marketing Association (AMA) established the following definition of marketing accountability: 'The responsibility for the systematic management of marketing resources and processes to achieve measurable gains in return on marketing investment and increased marketing efficiency, while maintaining quality and increasing the value of corporation.' A number of factors have elevated the importance of measuring marketing performance:[5]

- **Corporate trend for greater accountability of value added**: Companies that want to measure the return on marketing need to treat marketing expenditures as an investment instead of just a short-term expense. The investment perspective allows managers to compare marketing to other assets and thus enables companies to be financially accountable. Being financially accountable is also necessary when a company wants to be cost effective and/or wants to reduce costs. Moreover, marketing is generating a stream of revenue (through sales), and therefore it should be possible to pay for marketing activities by their results.[6]
- **Discontent with traditional metrics**: Conventional methods (e.g., balance sheets, income statements, gross margins) of productivity and return are often historical and say little about the future long-term performance of a company. In a competitive and highly dynamic company environment, past performance is a poor and almost useless predictor of future performance. In compliance with treating marketing as an investment, marketing metrics should be forward looking and should also involve a long-term performance perspective.
- **Availability of ICT and Internet infrastructure**: The development of ICT and the Internet has facilitated the development of new methods for marketing metrics. In addition, the prevalence of enterprise resource planning software, supply chain management software and customer relationship management software enable the use of more advanced and forward looking marketing metrics.

Unfortunately, however, while many companies may be aware of the opportunities associated with marketing metrics, the reality is that many still rely on traditional historic metrics[7] such as balance sheets, gross margins, and so on.

What marketing metrics should do

More than ever, marketers are being pressured to deliver hard data on how their efforts increased the company's bottom line. This trend seems to be global.[8] A focus on metrics can mean the difference between a marketing department that is considered highly valuable and one on the brink of extinction. For example, research giant IDC surveyed senior marketing executives in IT companies to determine their priorities for the coming year. Measuring and justifying their efforts and steering marketing initiatives towards tangible results were at the top of their lists.[9]

To find out more about how the Stockholm based Ericsson Group, a world-leading telecommunications company, utilises a portfolio of metrics to monitor both operating efficiency and market effectiveness of their marketing activities, go to www.pearsoned.co.uk/marketingmanagementeurope

Recently, researchers Seggie, Cavusgil and Phelan[10] have formulated seven themes, or dimensions, that together define the capabilities of the 'ideal marketing metrics' – and at the same time also provide guidelines on how existing marketing metrics may be improved.

1   Marketing metrics should be financial. By speaking the same financial language as the rest of the company, senior management can obtain a greater understanding of marketing initiatives, intervene when necessary and take appropriate remedial action.

2 You cannot drive a car, or a company, by looking in the rearview mirror. Companies wanting to survive intense competition have to be at the forefront of environmental development and also need to be able to forecast the future results of actions taken today. In order to be forward, rather than backward looking, metrics should not just be projecting past results inflated by an uplift (an adjustment) factor.

3 Marketing actions may have both short- and long-term effects. By regarding marketing as an expense, the short-term perspective has been emphasised at the expense of the long-term perspective. However, the view of marketing as an investment introduces the long-term perspective necessary for the purpose of comparing the real benefits of marketing activities.

4 Looking only at aggregated, or average, tendencies among customers may mask important shifts among customer segments or even individual customers. Sufficient marketing metrics should therefore be capable of transforming data at the macrolevel into microlevel data.

5 Independent metrics should be moved from separate measures to causal chains, thereby facilitating the direct measure of marketing activities as evaluated by their effect on the bottom line. Intermediate variables such as consumer attitudes and market share should be taken into account.

6 No company exists in a vacuum and value is most often reached in competition with company rivals. Reflecting this, marketing metrics should also be relative – not just absolute – to allow managers to contrast performance with that of the company's competitors.

7 Marketing metrics should be able to deliver objective data, which can be used for comparisons with other companies and with other company activities – and that can facilitate accountability.

Marketing researchers Rust, Ambler, Carpenter, Kumar and Srivastava[11] propose that there are three challenges to the measurement of marketing productivity. The first challenge is relating marketing activities to long-term effects. The second is the separation of individual marketing activities from other actions. Third, the use of purely financial methods has proved inadequate for justifying marketing investments.

Non-financial metrics are needed, for example metrics that relate to innovations or employees. Since the late 1990s the economy has increasingly recognised that intangible (market-based) assets are the drivers of value.[12] A company's tangible or balance sheet assets (e.g., factories, raw materials, financial assets) have traditionally been seen as its most vital resource. However, in the modern market economy investors increasingly view intangible assets (e.g., brands, company knowledge, reputation, skills) as the key to superior business processes.[13]

London Business School's Tim Ambler suggests that if companies think they are already measuring marketing performance adequately they should ask themselves five questions:[14]

1 Do you routinely research consumer behaviour (retention, acquisition, usage) and why consumers behave that way (awareness, satisfaction, perceived quality)?

2 Do you routinely report the results of this research to the board in a format integrated with financial marketing metrics?

3 In those reports, do you compare the results with the levels previously forecast in the business plans?

4 Do you also compare them with the levels achieved by your key competitor using the same indicators?

5 Do you adjust short-term performance according to the change in your marketing-based asset(s)?

Ambler believes firms must give priority to measuring and reporting marketing performance through marketing metrics. He believes evaluation can be split into two parts: (1) short-term results; and (2) changes in brand equity. Short-term results often reflect profit-and-loss

Table 7.1 Sample marketing metrics

1 External	2 Internal
Awareness	Awareness of goals
Market share (volume or value)	Commitment to goals
Relative price (market share value/volume)	Active innovation support
Number of complaints (level of dissatisfaction)	Resource adequacy
Consumer satisfaction	Staffing/skill levels
Distribution/availability	Desire to learn
Total number of customers	Willingness to change
Perceived quality/esteem	Freedom to fail
Loyalty/retention	Autonomy
Relative perceived quality	Relative employee satisfaction

Source: T. Ambler (2001) What does marketing success look like?, *Marketing Management*, Spring, 13–18. Reproduced with permission.

concerns as shown by sales turnover, shareholder value, or some combination of the two. Brand-equity measures could include customer awareness, attitudes and behaviours; market share; relative price premium; number of complaints; distribution and availability; total number of customers; perceived quality; and loyalty and retention.[15] DoubleClick, Inc., which places roughly 200 billion ads a month for clients, offers 50 different types of metrics, such as pauses, restarts, average view times and full screen views for video ads, to monitor campaigns.[16]

Companies can also monitor an extensive set of metrics internal to the company, such as innovation; for example, 3M tracks the proportion of sales resulting from its recent innovations. Ambler also recommends developing employee measures and metrics, arguing that 'end users are the ultimate customers, but your own staff are your first; you need to measure the health of the internal market'. Table 7.1 summarises a list of popular internal and external marketing metrics from Ambler's survey in the United Kingdom.[17]

To date, marketing metrics results have been largely internal to the firm, although it has been argued that they should also be communicated to shareholders, subject to commercial confidentiality.[18]

The chain of marketing productivity

Regarding marketing as investment implies that the marketing assets in which the company invests should be identified. Also, it should be understood that these assets contribute to profits in the short run and provide potential for growth and sustained profits in the long run. Emphasis is not on underlying products, pricing or customer relationships but on marketing expenditures such as marketing communications, promotions and other activities, and how these expenditures influence marketplace performance.[19] Marketing expenditures may influence, for example, customers' beliefs, attitudes, feelings and behaviour, which in turn may impact on the financial performance of the company, such as profit and shareholder value. Marketing actions both create and leverage market-based assets; for example, an advertising effort may improve, or build, brand equity. Brand equity may in turn be leveraged to improve short-term productivity – advertising in combination with stronger brands is usually more productive. Figure 7.1 illustrates 'the chain of marketing productivity'.[20]

The chain of marketing productivity is concerned with marketing activities that require expenditures. Companies' strategies might include promotion strategy, product strategy, or any

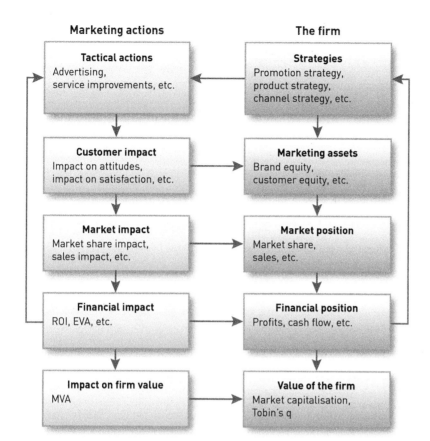

Marketing actions

Tactical actions
Advertising,
service improvements, etc.

Customer impact
Impact on attitudes,
impact on satisfaction, etc.

Market impact
Market share impact,
sales impact, etc.

Financial impact
ROI, EVA, etc.

Impact on firm value
MVA

The firm

Strategies
Promotion strategy,
product strategy,
channel strategy, etc.

Marketing assets
Brand equity,
customer equity, etc.

Market position
Market share,
sales, etc.

Financial position
Profits, cash flow, etc.

Value of the firm
Market capitalisation,
Tobin's q

Figure 7.1 The chain of marketing productivity

Source: Adapted from R. T. Rust, T. Ambler, G. S. Carpenter, V. Kumar and R. K. Srivastava (2004) Measuring marketing productivity: current knowledge and future directions, *Journal of Marketing*, 68, October, 77. Copyright © 2004 American Marketing Association. Reproduced with permission.

other marketing or company strategy. These strategies lead to tactical marketing actions taken by the firm, such as advertising campaigns, service improvement efforts, branding initiatives, loyalty programmes, or other specific initiatives designed to have a marketing impact. The tactical actions in turn impact customer satisfaction and attitude, and other customer-centred elements. Such customer-centred elements represent marketing assets to a company such as brand equity and customer equity. Customer behaviour influences may change market share and sales and thereby the market position of a company. The changes in market share, sales, etc., may have financial impact in terms of, for example, return on investment and economic value added (EVA), that is, net operating profit after taxes less the money cost of capital. Net operating profit after taxes (NOPAT) and cost of capital are considered in subsequent sections of this chapter. Return on investment (ROI) and EVA in turn influence the financial position of the company. The financial impacts have consequences for firm value in terms of MVA (market value added), which together with the financial position of the firm influences the value of the firm. 'Marketing insight: What metrics do companies use?' provides some insight on what metrics are used by companies.

Effectiveness versus efficiency

The company should distinguish between the 'effectiveness' and the 'efficiency' of marketing actions.[21] For example, price cuts can be efficient in that they deliver short-term revenues and cash flows. However, to the extent that they invite competitive actions and destroy long-term profitability and brand equity, they may not be effective. Businesses also need to know which success factors require measuring, and they must understand the differences between measurements (the raw outcomes of quantification), metrics (ideal standards for measurement) and benchmarks (the standards by which all others are measured).[22]

Marketing insight

What metrics do companies use?

Marketing metrics include all internal and external measurements related to marketing and market position, which are believed to be linked to short- and long-term financial performance.[23] Barwise and Farley[24] have recently studied adoption of six metrics in the top five global markets: the United States, Japan, Germany, the United Kingdom and France. The six metrics were market share, perceived product or service quality, customer loyalty or retention, customer or segment profitability, relative price and actual or potential customer/segment lifetime value.

Most businesses in these five countries said that they now report one or more of the six metrics to the board, with market share (79 per cent) and perceived product/service quality (77 per cent) the most used. Least used (40 per cent) was customer/segment lifetime value. Germany was above average for all six metrics, especially market share (97 per cent) and relative price (84 per cent). Japan was below average on all metrics. The US and UK samples were fairly close to average, while France was high on both market share and customer/segment lifetime value. No significant differences related to industry use of metrics were found. Some systematic firm-related differences were found in that multinational subsidiaries and larger firms tended to use more metrics.

Source: Based on P. Barwise and J. U. Farley (2004) Marketing metrics: status of six metrics in five countries, *European Management Journal*, 22(3), 257–62.

▽ Measuring marketing performance and productivity

Marketing performance and productivity is multidimensional and therefore different metrics should be seen as complements rather than substitutes.[25] Marketing has the main responsibility for achieving profitable revenue growth and this is done by finding, keeping and growing the value of profitable customers.[26] Taking this perspective, marketing metrics must relate to finding customers (customer acquisition), keeping customers (consumer retention) and growing customer value (monetisation). This approach[27] connects marketing to essential business outcomes, customer acquisition to market share, customer retention to lifetime value and monetisation to customer/brand equity and shareholder value. We divide these marketing metrics into three dimensions: (1) counting-based (or activity) metrics; (2) accounting-based (or operational) metrics; and (3) outcome metrics. All three dimensions may comprise both external and internal company metrics.

Counting-based metrics

Counting-based metrics include, for example, number of complaints, sales, headcounts, number of customers, number of orders and new hires. In principle, any internal and external factor that can be counted may serve as a counting-based metric.

Accounting-based metrics

ROI and ROA

Most marketing research on company performance has relied on accounting-based ratio measures, such as return of investment and return on assets (ROA).[28] The formula for calculating ROI is:

$$\text{ROI\%} = \frac{\text{Net income before tax} \times 100}{\text{investment}}$$

ROI is usually calculated for a specific activity or campaign at a specific point in time. Consider a company that invests €1,500,000 on marketing a new product where the company expects to earn a net profit of €200,000 the first year. ROI% can then be calculated as:

$$\text{ROI\%} = \frac{€200,000 \times 100}{€1,500,000} = 13.3\%$$

The investment profitability rate of 13.3 per cent is here reported before taxes – but sometimes it is reported after taxes in comparing geographical areas where taxes vary substantially.[29]

The formula for calculating ROA is:

$$\text{ROA\%} = \frac{\text{Net income before tax} \times 100}{\text{total assets}}$$

Total assets are the invested capital in the company, comprising both debt and equity. The major disadvantage of ROA is that the invested assets have multiple ways of being measured, including historical costs, book values, appraisal value, market value, and so on.[30] ROA tells how effectively the company converts invested capital into net income, usually before taxes. Thus if net income is €1,500,000 and assets are €10,000,000, the ROA% is 15 per cent. ROA can vary substantially across industries.

The ROI and ROA measures are both limited by two deficiencies.[31] First, the cost of capital is not considered. The company needs to set a standard for acceptable performance at a level above the company's cost of capital. If the cost of capital is 10 per cent, the estimated ROI or ROA must be higher to make the investment. Second, the measures may lead to potential dysfunctional decision making by unit managers. Some marketing managers acting in self-interest may choose to estimate ROI on the high side to get money for the project or on the low side to discourage undertaking a project.

Another limitation is that ROI and ROA do not fully measure impact. Studies by the advertising agency Young & Rubicam suggest that only one-third of a brand's impact is realised in current sales and operating earnings, while two-thirds of its influence is obtained via future financial performance. Thus, while ROI analyses may provide some insight into the short-term financial performance of marketing activities they may capture only one-third of the total value creation of the marketing programme. Net present value (NPV) is a method that explicitly deals with the expected future cash flows as a result of company marketing activity.

NPV

Having €1000 in your hand today is better than having €1000 in five years from now. The reason is that over five years that €1000 that you have today would have a chance to grow by investing it. To calculate the net present value we discount the anticipated cash inflows with an acceptable discount rate.[32] NPV is the sum of all such discounted cash flows associated with a project.[33] NPV is calculated as:[34]

$$\text{NPV} = \sum_{t=0}^{n} \frac{C_t}{(1 + i)^t}$$

where

t = the time of the cash flow

n = the total time of the project

i = the discount rate

C_t = the net cash flow at time t.

The discount rate is usually arrived at as a weighted average cost of capital. The company may also choose to use variable discount rates, for example by using higher discount rates for riskier projects. Using an appropriate discount rate assures that the company only accepts projects where the expected cash flows add value to the company.

Outcome metrics

Marketing accountability also means that marketers must more precisely estimate the effects of different marketing investments. *Marketing-mix models* analyse data from a variety of sources, such as retailer scanner data, company shipment data, pricing, media, and promotion spending data, to understand more precisely the effects of specific marketing activities.[35] To deepen understanding, marketers can conduct multivariate analyses to sort through how each marketing element influences marketing outcomes such as brand sales or market share.[36]

Figure 7.2 Sales decomposition – obtained through advanced econometric modelling

Source: Sales modelling carried out by BrandScience. Copyright © Omnicom Media Group Reproduced with permission.

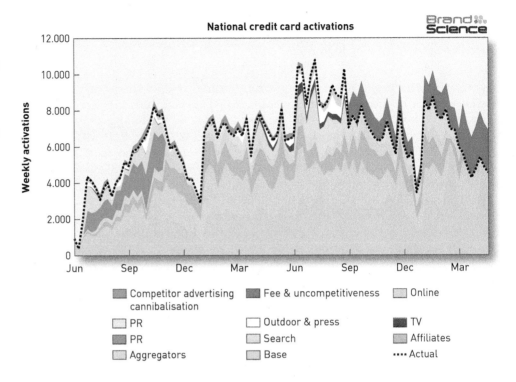

Advanced econometric modelling methods enable BrandScience to separate the effects of the different drivers and to isolate and quantify the contribution from marketing. Figure 7.2 shows a sales decomposition conducted for a European financial services brand, where the weekly number of credit card activations has been modelled and the significant drivers and their changing influence over time identified.

The blue dotted line represents the actual number of activations that has been decomposed via econometric modelling. The light blue base is the 'worst case sales' if all marketing activities had not occurred. In the base the following effects have been aggregated in order to show the impact from marketing more clearly: the base line, seasonality, internal structural changes and increased brand awareness. At the end of the period the uncompetitiveness (lack of competiveness) has prevented the company from realising the actual sales potential illustrated with the untapped dark blue area above the blue dotted *actual* line.

Four outcome metrics – shareholder value, customer lifetime value, brand equity measures and balanced scorecard are described and discussed.

Marketing metrics and shareholder value

Metric researcher Peter Doyle maintains that 'the real objective of marketing in the business enterprise is to develop and implement customer-led strategies that create shareholder value'.[37] **Shareholder value** is the value of the firm minus the future claims (future claims are also known as debts):

$$\text{Shareholder value} = \text{company value} - \text{debts}$$

where

$$\text{company value} = (\text{present value of all future cash flows} + \text{value of non-operating assets})$$

Non-operating assets are assets that are not essential to the ongoing operations of a business, but may still generate income or provide a return on investment – for example, a company may own some property that generates a yearly income.[38] While the shareholder value can be used to estimate the value of the shareholders' stake in a company or business unit, it can also be used to formulate and evaluate marketing decisions.[39] Consider the illustration opposite.

▽ Launching an advertising campaign for a French women's fragrance: the impact on shareholder value

The marketing department of a French producer of exclusive women's fragrances considers launching a €5 million advertising campaign in upmarket women's magazines such as *Elle* and *Vogue* in order to further promote its already popular series of fragrances.

The advertising campaign will run for five years with €1 million invested each year; the marketing department estimates that sales will increase by 5 per cent each year as a result. The company wants to estimate how the advertising campaign might affect the company's shareholder value. The calculations are shown in Table 7.2.

We assume an operating margin of 10 per cent. **Operating margin** is the ratio of operating profit divided by net sales. In year 1 the operating margin is obtained as: 10.5 (operating profits)/105 (sales) = 0.10. Since operating margin is 10 per cent this means that operating costs are 90 per cent of sales – for example in year 1: 94.5/105 = 0.90. Also, we assume that taxes are 25 per cent. Taxes are paid out of operating profits.

In Table 7.2 NOPAT is a company's after-tax operating profit. It is defined as follows:

$$\text{NOPAT} = \text{Operating profits} \times (1 - \text{tax rate})$$

Following this definition year 2 NOPAT is obtained as NOPAT = $11.0 \times (1 - 0.25) = 8.25$, which we round off to €8.3 million.

The opportunity cost of capital is the return the capital could obtain if it was invested elsewhere in projects/activities of similar risk.[40] We estimate the opportunity cost of

How will an advertising campaign for a women's fragrance impact on shareholder value?

Source: The Advertising Archives

Table 7.2 Advertising campaign: calculating cash flow and shareholder value (€ million)

	Year					
	0	1	2	3	4	5
Sales	100.0	105.0	110.3	115.8	121.6	127.6
Operating costs	90.0	94.5	99.2	104.2	109.4	114.9
Operating profits	10.0	10.5	11.0	11.6	12.2	12.8
Tax (25%)	2.5	2.6	2.8	2.9	3.0	3.2
NOPAT	7.5	7.9	8.3	8.7	9.1	9.6
Advertising campaign		1.0	1.0	1.0	1.0	1.0
Cash flow		6.9	7.3	7.7	8.1	8.6
Discount factor (10%)		0.909	0.826	0.751	0.683	0.621
Net present value of cash flow		6.3	6.0	5.8	5.5	5.3
Cumulative net present value		6.3	12.3	18.1	23.6	28.9
Net present of value of cash flows after planning horizon						59.6
Value of company operation (including advertising campaign)						88.5
Initial shareholder value (before advertising campaign)						75.0
Shareholder value added from advertising campaign						13.5

capital (the discount factor), i, to be 10 per cent. The *annual* discount factor is calculated as:

$$\text{Annual discount factor} = 1/(1 + i)^t \text{ where } t = 1, 2, \ldots \text{ is the year}$$

For example, the annual discount factor for year 3 ($t = 3$) is:

$$\text{Annual discount factor, year 3} = 1/(1 + 0.10)^3 = 0.751$$

By multiplying the year 3 cash flow, which is €7.7 million, with the year 3 annual discount factor, which is 0.751, we get €5.8 million (the net present value of cash flow in year 3). Similar calculations can be carried for years 1, 2, 4 and 5. NPV of cash flows during planning horizon is now obtained as the cumulative present value in year 5: €6.3 + €6.0 + €5.8 + €5.5 + €5.3 = €28.9 million.

In principle, cash flows for all future years beyond the planning period (year 6, year 7, year 8, etc.) should be estimated in a similar way in order for the value of the advertising campaign to be accurately determined. However, a short-cut approach is often used in practice.[41] Here the NPV of cash flows after the planning horizon is calculated by the standard perpetuity model, which is the year 5 NOPAT/i multiplied by the year 5 discount factor (= 0.621). Thus, the perpetuity method simply assumes that beyond the five-year planning period competition will drive down profits to a level such that new investments just earn the company's cost of capital.[42] The year 5 NOPAT is €9.6 million (Table 7.2) and the discount factor, i, is 10 per cent. Thus we can now calculate NPV of cash flows after planning horizon as 9.6/0.10 × 0.621 = €59.6 million.

Future cash flows have thus been divided into two time periods: those that occur during the planning horizon, and those that occur after the planning horizon. We add the cash flows from these two time periods and get the value of company operation: €28.9 + €59.6 = €88.5 million

The perpetuity method can also be used for calculating the initial shareholder value of the company. The company's initial shareholder value before the advertising campaign is €75 million. This is estimated by dividing the year 0 NOPAT (= €7.5 million) by the cost of capital: €7.5/0.10 = €75 million. The expected shareholder value added from the advertising campaign is then the 'value of company operation' (including advertising campaign) less the 'company's initial shareholder value': €88.5 − €75 = €13.5 million.

Taking a shareholder perspective may enhance the opportunity of making marketing recognised as a significant corporate value driver. Lukas, Whitwell and Doyle have emphasised five contributions of a shareholder value approach to marketing:[43]

1 **A shareholder value approach helps marketing properly define its objective**: To the extent that the governing business objective of a company is to maximise shareholder value, marketing should focus on contributing to this objective.

2 **A shareholder value approach provides the language for integrating marketing more effectively with the other functions of the company**: Shareholder value analysis is rooted in the discipline of finance, which is also the most common language in the boardroom. Unless marketing learns to speak this language its influence will be limited.

3 **A shareholder value approach allows marketing to demonstrate the importance of its assets**: Many marketing assets are intangible (e.g., brand equity, customer loyalty). By relating these assets to shareholder value marketing has the potential to increase its strategic influence in the company.

4 **A shareholder value approach protects marketing budgets from profit-maximisation policies**: Taking a shareholder value approach may prevent cuts in marketing budgets. Fundamentally a shareholder approach is long term, with an explicit disdain for short-term solutions. Moreover, the shareholder approach emphasises that marketing assets should be considered as investments, which in turn emphasises that short-term, profit-driven marketing budgets may destroy rather than build company value.

5 **A shareholder value approach puts marketing in a pivotal role in the strategy formulation process**: Creating shareholder value is essential for creating a competitive advantage. Marketing provides the tools for creating such a competitive advantage.

The shareholder perspective should not be confused with the stakeholder perspective. The stakeholder perspective regards the purpose of a company to create value for all involved parties. Advocates say that this is even more likely to produce higher profits for the shareholders because the other parties will be more productive and better rewarded.

Customer lifetime value

As modern economies become predominantly service based, companies increasingly derive revenue from the creation and sustenance of long-term relationships with their customers. In such an environment marketing serves the purpose of maximising customer lifetime value. The case for maximising long-term customer profitability is captured in the concept of customer lifetime value.[44] Customer lifetime value is rapidly gaining acceptance as a metric to acquire, grow and retain the 'right' customers in customer relationship management.[45]

The CLV approach assumes that customers who stay with a company for a long period generate more profits as compared with customers who only stay for a short period. It is more cost effective to deal with established customers whose needs and wants are known, and satisfied customers are also more likely to increase their purchases and to recommend the company to other customers. CLV can be seen as the series of transactions between a company and a customer over the period of time that the customer remains with the company.[46] CLV can be measured as the present value of the future net cash flows that are expected to be received over the lifetime of a customer, consisting of the revenue obtained from the customer less the cost of attracting, serving and satisfying the customer.[47] A key decision is what time horizon to use for estimating CLV. Typically, three to five years is reasonable.

The formula for estimating customer lifetime value is:

$$\text{CLV} = \sum_{t=0}^{T^*} \frac{(p_t - c_t)}{(1 + i)^t} - \text{AC},$$

where

p_t = price paid by a consumer at time t
c_t = direct cost of servicing the customer at time t
i = discount rate
t = expected lifetime of a customer
AC = acquisition cost

The formula can be applied for an individual customer and for segments of customers. CLV is a suitable metric for both business and consumer markets.

For example, a company may invest €10,000 in attracting a business customer. This acquisition cost (AC) consists of the costs associated with convincing a consumer to buy your product or service, including marketing, advertising costs, negotiating expenses in terms of human resources and travelling, conducting research and preparing various analyses on how to serve the customer in the best way, and so on. The customer stays with the company for three years, each year generating a €5000 NOPAT to the company. The company estimates the opportunity cost of capital, i, to be 10 per cent. The annual discount factor for year 1 is calculated to be 0.909, for year 2 it is calculated to be 0.826, and for year 3 it is calculated to be 0.751. The lifetime value of the customer can now be calculated as CLV $= -10,000 + 5000/1.10 + 5000/1.10^2 + 5000/1.10^3 = $ €2434.

We find the lifetime value of this customer to be €2434. Since the lifetime value is larger than zero, this customer is expected to contribute positively to the value of the company.

It is useful for a company to find out what types of customers are the most profitable, how much it should spend on them and what product offerings should be made. The service and repair company Midas uses customer lifetime value as a tool for its direct marketing effort in several European countries. Midas tracks cars based on vehicle mileage and contacts customers to remind them of service and brake opportunities over the life of their vehicle.[48]

By comparing CLV with different types of customers, service activities and product offerings, the company can obtain highly useful knowledge and may also estimate **customer equity**. Customer equity (CE) is defined as the lifetime value of current and future customers.[49] CLV and CE focus on the long-term rather than the short-term profit or marketshare. Therefore, maximising CLV, and hence CE, is effectively maximising the long-term profitability and financial health of a company.[50]

▽ Variations in customer lifetime value

Customers may vary dramatically in their overall value to a company. Niraj, Gupta and Narasimhan[51] recently studied the drivers of current customer profitability in a supply chain for a large distributor with a heterogeneous client base. They found that a small percentage of customers contributes to a large percentage of total profits, and that a substantial percentage (32 per cent of total) of customers is unprofitable.

An important question relating to CLV is whether shareholder value would benefit from changing the level of marketing investment in a certain customer. Spending too much on an individual customer, or a segment of customers, can have a damaging impact on shareholder value. Some bankers are known for lavish dinners or rounds of golf with VIPs, long-term customers who are probably unlikely to switch to another bank. On the other hand, insufficient spending can also decrease shareholder value because an underserved customer may defect to a competitor or reduce spending volume.[52]

Companies wanting to take advantage of the CLV measurement should build individual-level customer databases. Without such data true longitudinal data analysis of customers' behavioural responses to marketing actions – and related costs – cannot be implemented.[53]

Brand equity and financial performance

Brand equity is probably the most prized measure for many companies of the value of the marketing asset.[54] Brand equity we conceptualise as 'the added value endowed to products and services' by the brand name. This value may be reflected in how consumers think, feel and act with respect to the brand. Brand equity is an important intangible asset that has psychological and financial value to the company. Positive equity is likely to be associated with behaviour that benefits the brand through purchase frequency, brand loyalty, price insensitivity and willingness to recommend.[55]

There are two primary perspectives related to brand equity, one based on financial outcomes for the company and the other on softer, consumer-based perceptions of company performance. Most studies have focused on the consumer-based perspective. Also, much of the data necessary to test the financially based brand equity perspective are confidential and not available to marketing researchers.[56]

In the consumer-based brand equity (CBBE) perspective, the power of a brand lies in what customers have learned, thought, felt, seen and heard about the brand as a result of their experiences over time.[57]

There is a direct and an indirect approach to measure CBBE. The indirect approach requires measuring potential sources of brand equity by identifying and tracking consumer brand knowledge structures. The direct approach requires experiments in which one group of customers responds to an element in the marketing programme when it is attributed to the brand, and another group of customers responds to the same element when it is attributed to a fictitiously named or unnamed version of the product or service. 'Blind tests' constitute an example of the direct approach.[58] The indirect approach is concerned with detecting the causes of brand equity, whereas the direct approach is concerned with assessing the added value of the brand.

Examples of operationalising direct measures include price premiums for brand switching and purchase intention, while examples of indirect measures include unaided and aided recall (awareness), familiarity, brand image favourability and rating of beliefs of associations (brand image strength). No single concept or dimension can be applied for measuring CBBE since it is a multi-dimensional construct.

One view suggests that brand equity arises from the strength and favourability of the two components of consumer-based brand knowledge structures: brand awareness and brand image. Brand awareness relates to the strength of a brand in memory, and the likelihood and ease with which the brand will be recognised or recalled under various conditions. Brand image is defined as 'perceptions about the brand as reflected by the brand associations held in consumer memory'.[59] Netemeyer and his colleagues[60] found that in the fast food industry the dimensions 'perceived brand quality' and 'perceived brand value for the cost' (these dimensions were collapsed into one dimension) and brand uniqueness are highly relevant in predicting customer-based brand equity.

Brand equity was operationalised (measured) as the willingness to pay a price premium for a brand. This operationalisation included four measurement items:

1　The price of (brand name) would have to go up quite a bit before I would switch to another brand of (product).

2　I am willing to pay a higher price for the (brand name) brand of (product) than for other brands of (product).

3　I am willing to pay X per cent more for the (brand name) brand over other brands of (product): 0 per cent, 5 per cent, 10 per cent, 15 per cent, 20 per cent, 25 per cent, 30 per cent, or more.

4　I am willing to pay a lot more for the (brand name) than for other brands of (product category).

Items were measured on seven-point 'strongly disagree' to 'strongly agree' scales.

Higher levels of brand awareness and positive brand image are thought to increase the probability of brand choice, as well as produce greater customer loyalty and decrease vulnerability to marketing actions.[61] Some researchers have suggested that brand equity measures should also rely on market-based, objective measures because consumer attitude and preference measures are inherently subjective. Silverman, Sprott and Pascal[62] have explored the relationship between customer-based and financial/market-based brand equity measurements. They found only small, but positive, relationships between brand awareness – assessed by familiarity, usage and favourability – and market-based outcomes of brand value – measured by annual sales and Financial World brand ratings (see www.financialworld.co.uk).

Advertising agency Young & Rubicam has developed a model of brand equity called brand asset valuator, which can be accessed on its website – http://www.yrbav.com/. BAV measures brand value by applying four broad factors:[63] (1) differentiation (the ability of a brand to stand apart from its competitors); (2) relevance (consumers' actual and perceived importance of the brand); (3) esteem (consumers' perceived brand quality together with their assessment of the popularity of the brand); and (4) knowledge (consumers' brand awareness together with their understanding of the brand's identity).

Recently Young & Rubicam[64] has investigated to what extent BAV contributes to a company's financial performance.[65] Using unanticipated change in stock price as the dependent variable (i.e., financial measure), the relative contribution of individual brand components to changes in stock price was explored. The results revealed that energised brand strength (a combination of energy, differentiation and relevance) demonstrates a significant relationship with market value. BAV's energised brand strength was found to be 81 per cent as effective as sales growth in explaining changes in market value.

▽ The balanced scorecard approach

Kaplan and Norton developed and advocated a balanced scorecard approach (BSC) on the grounds that purely financial metrics may tell the wrong story about a company. Consider the following racing car metaphor offered by Andra Gumbus.[66]

▽ The need for both financial and non-financial metrics

Organisations that focus solely on financial measures can be compared to a racing car driver who only monitors his or her speed during a race. Suppose you are a driver in Formula 1 and are monitoring your car by looking at the RPM (revolutions [of the engine] per minute) gauge on your dashboard. You are not noticing the MPG (miles per gallon of fuel), nor the MPH (miles per hour, or speed your car is travelling), nor the temperature gauge. You might win the race, but you are putting yourself and your car at risk by not monitoring *all* the gauges while focusing exclusively on the RPM dial. You might run out of fuel, overheat the engine, crash into another car and make other errors in navigating the course.

Installing BSC in a company requires active participation from top management and sustaining the practice over time.[67] BSC provides a systematic tool that combines financial and non-financial performance metrics in one coherent measurement system. Metrics are constructed according to a predefined strategy, and the company's processes are aligned towards this strategy. BSC systematically measures the company in four areas:[68]

1 The *financial perspective* uses traditional accounting measures in order to evaluate a firm's short-term financial results. Metrics include ROI, cash flow analyses and return on equity.

2 The *customer perspective* measures relate to customer satisfaction of identified target groups and is generally marketing focused. Metrics include delivery performance to customers, customer satisfaction rate and customer retention.

3 The *internal business process perspective* is based on the concept of the (firm-internal) value chain, including the process (or steps) needed to realise the intended product or service. Metrics include opportunity success rates, number of activities and defect rates.

4 The final dimension comprises the *innovation and learning perspective* that is inherent in a company by measuring various human resources-focused effects as well as learning systems support effectiveness. Metrics include illness rate, internal promotions in per cent and employee turnover.

By combining these four measures, Kaplan and Norton establish the BSC as a representation of a company's shared vision (see Figure 7.3).

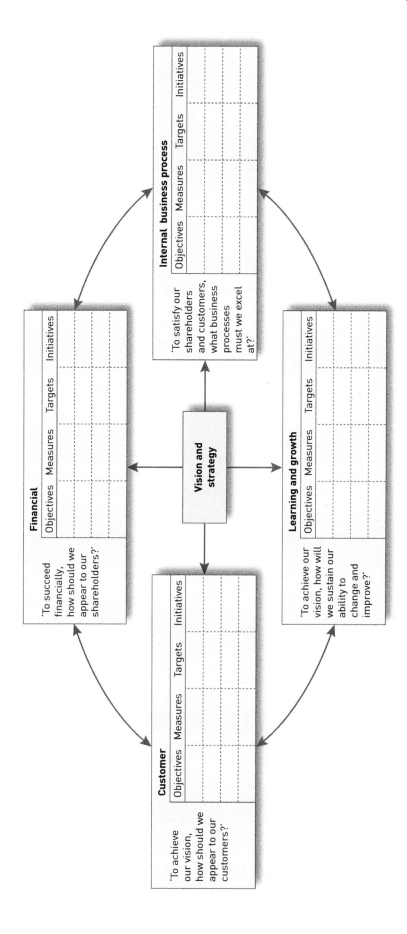

Figure 7.3 Translating vision and strategy: four perspectives

Figure 7.4 Managing
strategy: four
processes

Source: Adapted from R. S.
Kaplan and D. P. Norton
(2007) Using the balanced
scorecard as a strategic
management system,
Harvard Business Review,
July–August, 150–61.
Copyright © 2007 by the
President and Fellows of
Harvard College. All rights
reserved. Reproduced with
permission.

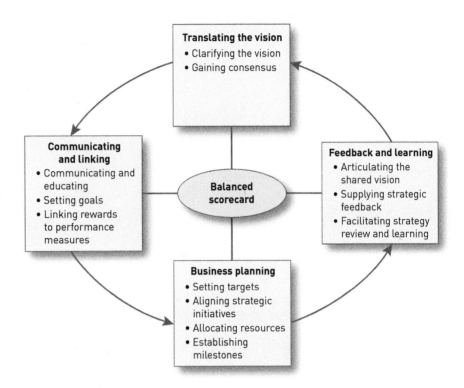

BSC is not only a tool for measurement, but also a tool for strategic management.[69] BSC has not been developed to serve strategy formulation, but to implement strategy. BSC can be regarded as a tool for translating a company's strategy into measurable goals, actions and performance measures. According to Kaplan and Norton the set of measures gives top managers a fast but comprehensive view of the business. Kaplan and Norton[70] have developed four management processes that contribute to linking long-term strategic objectives with short-term actions (see Figure 7.4).

- **The first process**: *translating the vision* – assists managers to build a consensus around the company's vision and strategy. For example, a top management vision that the company wants to be the 'number one supplier' offers by itself little guidance on how to operationalise that vision.
- **The second process**: *communicating and linking* – assists managers to communicate their strategy up and down the organisation and link it to objectives at the departmental and individual level, for example by linking rewards to performance measures.
- **The third process**: *business planning* – assists companies to integrate their business and financial plans, for example by setting targets and allocating sufficient resources.
- **The fourth process**: *feedback and learning* – enables companies to achieve strategic learning. The feedback and learning process facilitates feedback on all four perspectives (financial performance, customers, internal business processes, and learning and growth).

Accounting professor Erkki K. Laitinen argues that it is difficult to identify the relative importance of and the trade-offs between the suggested four perspectives of the approach.[71] Moreover, it is also difficult to identify the links between financial and non-financial performance measures. Kaplan and Norton acknowledge this criticism to a certain degree when stating that 'accumulating sufficient data to document significant correlations and causation among balanced scorecard measures can take a long time – months or years'.[72] Such data may enable a company to establish correlations between the various measures from the four perspectives.

▽ Marketing dashboards

Firms can assemble a summary set of relevant internal and external measures in a *marketing dashboard* for synthesis and interpretation. Marketing dashboards are like the instrument panel in a car or plane, visually displaying real-time indicators to ensure proper functioning. They are only as good as the information on which they are based, but sophisticated visualisation tools are helping bring data alive to improve understanding and analysis.[73]

Some companies are also appointing marketing controllers to review budget items and expenses. Increasingly, these controllers are using business intelligence software to create digital versions of marketing dashboards that aggregate data from disparate internal and external sources.

As input to the marketing dashboard, companies should include two key market-based scorecards that reflect performance and provide possible early warning signals.

1 A **customer-performance scorecard** records how well the company is doing year after year on such customer-based measures as those shown in Table 7.3. Management should set norms for each measure and take action when results get out of bounds.

2 A **stakeholder-performance scorecard** tracks the satisfaction of various constituencies who have a critical interest in and impact on the company's performance: employees, suppliers, banks, distributors, retailers and stockholders. Again, management should take action when one or more groups register increased or above-norm levels of dissatisfaction.[74]

Some executives worry that they'll miss the big picture if they focus too much on a set of numbers on a dashboard. Others are concerned about privacy and the pressure the technique places on employees. But most experts feel the rewards offset the risks.[75] 'Marketing insight: Marketing dashboards to improve effectiveness and efficiency' provides practical advice about the development of these marketing tools.

Table 7.3 Sample customer-performance scorecard measures

- percentage of new customers to average number of customers;
- percentage of lost customers to average number of customers;
- percentage of win-back customers to average number of customers;
- percentage of customers falling into very dissatisfied, dissatisfied, neutral, satisfied, and very satisfied categories;
- percentage of customers who say they would repurchase the product;
- percentage of customers who say they would recommend the product to others;
- percentage of target market customers who have brand awareness or recall;
- percentage of customers who say that the company's product is the most preferred in its category;
- percentage of customers who correctly identify the brand's intended positioning and differentiation;
- average perception of company's product quality relative to chief competitor;
- average perception of company's service quality relative to chief competitor.

Marketing insight

Marketing dashboards to improve effectiveness and efficiency

Marketing consultant Pat LaPointe sees marketing dashboards as providing all the up-to-the-minute information necessary to run the business operations for a company – such as sales versus forecast, distribution channel effectiveness, brand equity evolution and human capital development. According to LaPointe, an effective dashboard will focus thinking, improve internal communications and reveal where marketing investments are paying off and where they aren't.

LaPointe observes four common measurement 'pathways' marketers are pursuing today (see Figure 7.5).

- The *customer metrics pathway* looks at how prospects become customers, from awareness to preference to trial to repeat purchase. Many companies track progression through a 'hierarchy of effects' model to follow the evolution of broad market potential to specific revenue opportunities.

- The *unit metrics pathway* reflects what marketers know about sales of product/service units – how much is sold by product line and/or by geography; the marketing cost per unit sold as an efficiency yardstick; and where and how margin is optimised in terms of characteristics of the product line or distribution channel.

- The *cash-flow metrics pathway* focuses on how well marketing expenditures are achieving short-term returns. Programme and campaign ROI models measure the immediate impact or net present value of profits expected from a given investment.

- The *brand metrics pathway* tracks the development of the longer-term impact of marketing through brand equity measures that assess both the perceptual health of the brand from customer and prospective customer perspectives as well as the overall financial health of the brand.

LaPointe emphasises that a marketing dashboard can present insights from all the pathways in a graphically related view that helps management see subtle links between them. A well-constructed dashboard can have a series of 'tabs' that allow the user to toggle easily between different 'families' of metrics

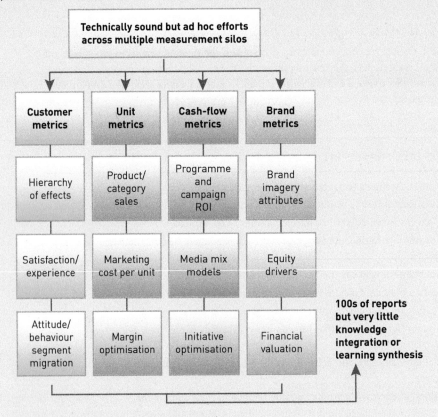

Figure 7.5   Marketing measurement pathways

Source: Adapted from D. Schultz (2005) Chapter 13 in P. Kotler and A. Tybout (ed.) *Kellogg on Branding: The Marketing Faculty of the Kellogg School of Management*, New York: John Wiley & Sons. Copyright © 2005 John Wiley & Sons, Inc. Reproduced with permission.

▶ **Marketing insight** *(continued)*

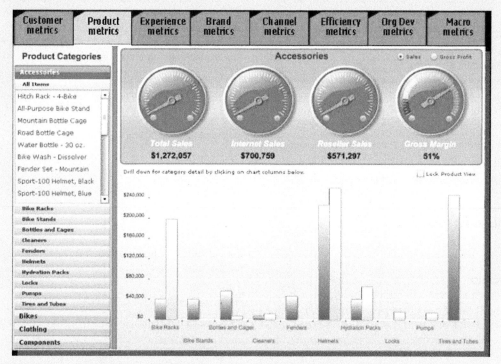

Figure 7.6 The marketing dashboard

Source: Adapted from P. LaPointe (2005) *Marketing by the Dashboard Light – How to Get More Insight, Foresight, and Accountability from Your Marketing Investments.* Copyright © 2005 Patrick LaPointe. Reproduced with permission.

organised by customer, product, brand, experience, channels, efficiency, organisational development or macroenvironmental factors. Each tab presents the three or four most insightful metrics, with data filtered by business unit, geography or customer segment based upon the users' needs (see Figure 7.6 for an example).

Ideally, the number of metrics presented in the marketing dashboard would be reduced to a handful of key drivers over time. Importantly, the process of developing and refining the marketing dashboard will undoubtedly raise and resolve many key questions about the business.

▽ SUMMARY

1 Marketers must be able to justify marketing expenditures to company management. Marketing metrics is the set of measures that helps firms to quantify, compare and interpret their marketing performance.

2 Good marketing metrics are financial, forward-looking and capture both short-term and long-term effects.

3 Marketing performance and productivity is multidimensional and therefore different metrics should be seen as complements rather than substitutes. Marketing has the main responsibility for achieving profitable revenue growth and this is done by finding, keeping and growing the value of profitable customers.

4 Marketing metrics are divided into three dimensions: (1) counting-based (or activity) metrics;

(2) accounting-based (or operational) metrics; and (3) outcome metrics. All three dimensions comprise both external and internal metrics.

5 While ROI analyses may provide some insight into the financial performance of marketing activities, they may at the same time capture only one-third of the total value creation of the marketing programme. Net present value is a method that explicitly deals with the expected future cash flows as a result of company marketing activity.

6 Marketing should develop and implement customer-led strategies that create shareholder value. Taking a shareholder perspective enhances the opportunity of making marketing recognised as a significant corporate value driver.

7   Customer lifetime value is the net profit or loss to a company from a customer flowing from the lifetime of that customer's transactions with the company. CLV assumes that customers who stay with a company for a long period of time generate more profits as compared to customers who stay for only a short period of time.

8   There are two primary perspectives related to brand equity, one based on financial outcomes for the company and one based on softer, consumer-based perceptions of company performance. Marketing performance during a period will be judged by whether brand equity has risen, is static, or has declined.

9   The balanced scorecard approach provides a systematic tool that combines financial and non-financial performance metrics in one coherent measurement system. Metrics are constructed according to a predefined strategy, and the company's processes are aligned towards this strategy. BSC systematically measures the company from four perspectives: the financial perspective, the customer perspective, the internal business process perspective, and the innovation and learning perspective.

10   A marketing dashboard provides up-to-the-minute information necessary to run the business operations for a company – such as sales versus forecast, distribution channel effectiveness, brand equity evolution and human capital development.

▽ APPLICATIONS

Marketing debate

Take a position: For any marketing activity there should be an established link between the activity and its measurement in terms of cash flow, ROI, effect on shareholder value, and so on. Otherwise that activity should not be carried out *versus* Marketing activities are often based on feelings, experiences, and so on, which are difficult to quantify. Therefore the outcome of a marketing activity need not be measurable for the marketing activity to be carried out.

Marketing discussion

What marketing activities need to be measured? Why? Which ones do not? What metrics should be used in relation to what companies and in relation to what activities?

▽ REFERENCES

[1]Based on dialogue with BrandScience; www.brandsciencenetwork.com.

[2]J. McManus (2004) Stumbling into intelligence, *American Demographics*, April, 22–5.

[3]L. Patterson (2007) MP 'classic truths': if you don't measure, you can't manage – the best metrics for managing marketing performance, *MarketingProfs*, 23 October.

[4]S. H. Seggie, E. Cavusgil and S. E. Phelan (2007) Measurement of return on marketing investment: a conceptual framework and the future of marketing metrics, *Industrial Marketing Management*, 36, 834–41.

[5]Ibid.

[6]M. Uncles (2005) Marketing metrics: a can of worms or the path to enlightenment?, editorial to *Brand Management*, 12(6), 412–18.

[7]T. Ambler, F. Kokkinaki and S. Puntoni (2004) Assessing marketing performance: reasons for metric selection, *Journal of Marketing Management*, 29(3/4), 475–98; P. Barwise and J. U. Farley (2004) Marketing metrics: status of six metrics in five countries, *European Management Journal*, 22(3), 257–62; Seggie et al. (2007) op. cit.

[8]Barwise and Farley (2004) op. cit.

[9]Marketing metrics: where to get them? Which ones work?, *Advertising & Marketing Review*, http://www.ad-mkt-review.com/public_html/docs/fs059.html, accessed December 2007.

[10]Seggie et al. (2007) op. cit.

[11]R. T. Rust, T. Ambler, G. S. Carpenter, V. Kumar and R. K. Srivastava (2004) Measuring marketing productivity: current knowledge and future directions, *Journal of Marketing*, 68 (October), 76–89.

[12]AMI (2004) 'What value marketing? A position paper on marketing metrics in Australia', Australian Marketing Institute, Sydney, 1, available at http://www.ami.org.au.

[13]P. Doyle (2001) Shareholder-value-based brand strategies, *Brand Management*, 9(1), 20–30.

[14]T. Ambler (2003) *Marketing and the Bottom Line: The New Methods of Corporate Wealth*, 2nd edn, Harlow, England: Pearson Education.

[15]K. L. Ailawadi, D. R. Lehmann and S. A. Neslin (2003) Revenue premium as an outcome measure of brand equity, *Journal of Marketing*, 67 (October), 1–17.

[16]S. Baker (2006) Wiser about the Web, *BusinessWeek*, 27 March, 53–7.

[17]Ambler (2003) op. cit.

[18]T. Ambler, P. Barwise and C. Higson (2001) *Market Metrics: What Should We Tell the Shareholders?*, Institute of Chartered Accountants in England and Wales, Centre for Business Performance, London; Barwise U. Farley (2004) op. cit.

[19]T. Rust et al. (2004) op. cit.

[20]Ibid.

[21]Ibid.

[22]Patterson (2007) op. cit.

[23]Ambler (2003) op. cit.

[24]Barwise and Farley (2004) op. cit.

[25]Ibid.

[26]P. Kotler (1999) *Kotler on Marketing: How to Create, Win, and Dominate Markets*, New York: Free Press.

[27]L. Patterson (2007) Case study: taking on the metrics challenge, *Journal of Targeting, Measurement and Analysis for Marketing*, 15(4), 270–6.

[28]E. W. Anderson, C. Fornell and S. K. Mazvancheryl (2004) Customer satisfaction and shareholder value, *Journal of Marketing*, 68, 172–85.

[29]http://en.wikipedia.org/wiki/Return_on_investment.

[30]R. D. Dillon and J. E. Owers (1997) EVA® as a financial metric: attributes, utilization, and relationship to NPV, *Financial Practice and Education*, Spring/Summer, 32–40.

[31]Ibid.

[32]http://moneyterms.co.uk/discount-rate/.

[33]http://www.smartcapitalist.com/blog_36.shtml.

[34]http://en.wikipedia.org/wiki/Net_present_value.

[35]G. J. Tellis (2006) Modeling marketing mix, in R. Grover and M. Vriens (eds) *Handbook of Marketing Research*, Thousand Oaks, CA: Sage.

[36]J. Neff (2004) P&G, Clorox rediscover modeling, *Advertising Age*, 29 March, 10.

[37]P. Doyle (2000) Valuing marketing's contribution, *European Management Journal*, 18(3), 233–45.

[38]http://www.investopedia.com/terms/n/nonoperatingasset.asp.

[39]S. Cooper and M. Davies (2004) Measuring shareholder value: the metrics in *Maximising Shareholder Value Achieving Clarity in Decision-making, CIMA Technical Report*, London: The Chartered Institute of Management Accountants, November, 10–15.

[40]Doyle (2000) op. cit.

[41]Cooper and Davies (2004) op. cit.

[42]Doyle (2000) op. cit.

[43]B. A. Lukas, G. J. Whitwell and P. Doyle (2005) How can a shareholder value approach improve marketing's strategic influence?, *Journal of Business Research*, 58(4), 414–22.

[44]S. Gupta, D. Hanssens, B. Hardie, W. Kahn, V. Kumar, N. Lin and N.R.S. Srinam (2006) Modeling Customer Lifetime Value, *Journal of Service Research*, 19(2), 139–55.

[45]R. Venkatesan and V. Kumar (2004) A customer lifetime value framework for customer selection and resource allocation strategy, *Journal of Marketing*, 68, 106–25.

[46]D. Jain and S. S. Singh (2002) Customer lifetime value research in marketing: a review and future directions, *Journal of Interactive Research*, 16(4), 34–46.

[47]R. H. Chenhall and K. Langfield-Smith (2007) Multiple perspectives of performance measures, *European Management Journal*, 25(4), 266–82.

[48]R. Baran, C. Zerres and M. Zerres Customer relationship management, free-learning summary in cooperation with www.ventus.dk; www.midas.com.

[49]S. Gupta and V. Zeithaml (2006) Customer metrics and their impact on financial performance, *Marketing Science*, 25(6), 718–39.

[50]Ibid.

[51]R. Niraj, M. Gupta and C. Narasimhan (2001) Customer profitability in a supply chain, *Journal of Marketing*, 65, July, 1–16.

[52]G. Cokins (2006) Measuring customer value: how BPM supports better marketing decisions, *Business Performance Management*, February, 13–18.

[53]Rust et al. (2004) op. cit.

[54]T. Ambler and Wang Xiucun (2003) Measures of marketing success: a comparison between China and the United Kingdom, *Asia Pacific Journal of Management*, 20, 267–81.

[55]T. J. Reynolds and C. B. Phillips (2005) In search of true brand equity metrics: all market share ain't created equal, *Journal of Advertising Research*, June, 171–86.

[56]S. A. Taylor, G. L. Hunter and D. L. Lindberg (2007) Understanding (customer-based) brand equity in financial services, *Journal of Services Marketing*, 21(4), 241–52; K. L. Keller (1993) Conceptualizing, measuring, and managing customer-based brand equity, *Journal of Marketing*, 57(1), 1–23.

[57]K. L. Keller (2003) *Strategic Brand Management: Building, Measuring and Managing Brand Equity*, 2nd edn, Englewood Cliffs, NJ: 2003 Prentice-Hall, E. Atilgan, S. Aksoy and S. Akinci (2005) Determinants of the brand equity: a verification approach in the beverage industry in Turkey, *Marketing Intelligence & Planning*, 23(3) 237–48.

[58]Keller (1993) op. cit.; Hong-bumm Kim, Woo Gon Kim and Jeong A. An (2003) The effect of consumer-based brand equity on firms' financial performance, *Journal of Consumer Marketing*, 20(4), 335–51.

[59]Keller (1993) op. cit.

[60]R. G. Netemeyer, B. Krishnan, C. Pullig, G. Wang, M. Yagci, D. Dean, J. Ricks and F. Wirth (2004) Developing and validating measures of facets of customer-based brand equity, *Journal of Business Research*, 57, 209–24.

[61]Keller (1993) op. cit.

[62]S. N. Silverman, D. E. Sprott and V. J. Pascal (1999) Relating consumer-based sources of brand equity to market outcomes, *Advances in Consumer Research*, 26, 352–8.

[63]http://www.valuebasedmanagement.net/methods_brand_asset_valuator.html.

[64]In collaboration with Robert Jacobson from the University of Washington School of Business and Natalie Mizik from the Columbia Graduate School of Business.

[65]J. Gerzema (Young & Rubicam Brands), E. Lebar (BrandAsset® Valuator, Worldwide), M. Sussman (Y&R, North America) and J. Gaikowski (Young & Rubicam Brands) (2007) Energy: igniting brands to drive enterprise value, *International Journal of Market Research*, 49(1), 25–45.

[66]A. Gambus (2005) Introducing the balanced scorecard: creating metrics to measure performance, *Journal of Management Education*, 29(4), 617–30.

[67]Ibid.

[68]S. C. Voelpel, M. Leibold, R. A. Eckhoff (2006) The tyranny of the balanced scorecard in the innovation economy, *Journal of Intellectual Capital*, 7(1), 43–60; R. S. Kaplan and D. P. Norton (1992) The balanced scorecard: measures that drive performance, *Harvard Business Review*, 70(1), 71–85.

[69]Voelpel et al. (2006) op. cit.

[70]R. S. Kaplan and D. P. Norton (2007) Using the balanced scorecard as a strategic management system, *Harvard Business Review*, July–August, 150–61.

[71]E. K. Laitinen (2006) A constant growth model of the firm: empirical analysis of the balanced scorecard, *Review of Accounting and Finance*, 5(2), 140–73.

[72]Citation from Kaplan and Norton (2007) op. cit., 160.

[73]J. Zabin (2006) Marketing dashboards: the visual display of marketing data, *Chief Marketer* 26 June.

[74]R. S. Kaplan and D. P. Norton (1996) *The Balanced Scorecard*, Boston, MA: Harvard Business School Press.

[75]S. Ante (2006) Giving the boss the big picture, *BusinessWeek*, 13 February, 48–50.

Part 4 Human Resource Management

Chapter 8

Performance management

Julia Pointon

Objectives

- To explain the distinction between performance measurement and performance management.
- To present an overview of performance appraisal including reference to some of the limitations of appraisal.
- To review the links between performance management and human resource management.
- To consider how organisations manage performance in relation to collaborative working, a diverse workforce, an ageing workforce and a volunteer workforce.

Introduction

It is fair to say that in the past there has been a tendency for the term performance measurement, and specifically the term performance appraisal, to become synonymous with, and sometimes used interchangeably with, the term performance management, but that is slightly misleading and obscures the subtle but important differences between the two concepts. In this chapter we review approaches to performance measurement, in particular appraisal, and make a clear distinction between it and the broader concept of performance management. We consider the extent to which there has been a significant shift away from equating performance measurement with 'individual employee' effort and achievement towards a conceptualisation of performance management that encompasses and involves, the 'whole organisation'.

This shift in focus has been stimulated by changes in the marketplace. As business has become more global and aggressive, organisations have sought to survive by achieving and sustaining a distinct competitive advantage. They are increasingly aware of value for money along with the need to make cost reductions and efficiency savings. They are experiencing increasing demands from customers and external stakeholders for a more rapid service of ever higher quality with increasingly competitive pricing. As a consequence, organisations are demanding even higher levels of performance from their employees. In short, employer's expectations about employee competence, organisational commitment and performance contribution are escalating.

This reconfiguration of the competition and performance agenda has extended what was once a relatively straightforward process of assessing an individual's performance against predefined criteria, into a more integrated, holistic and developmental exercise spanning the entire organisation. In so doing, attention has been placed on the contribution human resource management (HRM) makes to the management of performance.

This chapter starts by providing an overview of the more traditional approaches to measuring performance, in particular performance appraisal and the growth of 360-degree feedback. We consider what performance appraisal is and how it is used in organisations. We will also reflect on some of the associated limitations of appraisal, in particular from a Foucoudian perspective. We then extend the focus to consider the wider and more sophisticated application of performance management. In this context, we review the association between HRM and performance management and again consider some of the associated limitations. Finally, the chapter reviews some of the specifics of managing performance in different organisational contexts, for example in collaborating organisations and in relation to specific groups of employees, for example a diverse workforce, an ageing work force and volunteer workers.

The history of performance measurement?

Many of the roots of performance measurement can be traced back to Taylor's 'time and motion' studies. More recently, measurement has been influenced by the development of other business systems, for example, programming and budgeting, zero-based budgeting (ZBB) and in the UK in particular, 'management by objectives' (MBO). This approach, advocated by Drucker (1999), gained much popularity because it encouraged management to set individual objectives for employees at the commencement of the defined time period and to review progress at the end of the period. It provided a relatively easy and clear indication of the extent to which the employee had performed and achieved their predefined targets. In the late 1990s and early 2000 performance measurement became more extensive and, arguably, more intensive, to the point where some authors (see Adair *et al.* 2003, Harris *et al.,* 2007; Hyde *et al.,* 2006 and Bourgon, 2008) considered that performance measurement became one of the most striking features of the business agenda and, in particular, a central feature of the public sector reform agenda.

Workplace Employment Relations Survey (WERS) data for 2004 suggest that appraisals constitute one of the main tools used in measuring performance. The use of performance appraisals has increased since 1998. In 2004, 78 per cent of managers in workplaces reported that performance appraisals were undertaken compared with 73 per cent in 1998. However,

| Box 8.1 | **Defining performance measurement** |

In the context of performance measurement, performance appraisal represents just one tool in the toolkit. It is a way of eliciting information about the performance of one or more employees against certain predefined criteria or dimensions.

DeNisi (2000: 121) defines performance appraisal as 'the system whereby an organization assigns some "score" to indicate the level of performance of a target person or group'.

Fletcher (2001: 473) defines performance appraisal more broadly as 'activities through which organisations seek to assess employees and develop their competence, enhance performance and distribute rewards'. The focus was on performance ratings and other such limited and measurement-focused issues, but more recently has broadened and currently addresses social and motivational aspects of appraisal. Fletcher's definition reflects this shift in focus.

Mondy *et al.* (2002: 58) define performance appraisal as a system of review and evaluation of an individual's (or team's) performance and the process of appraising performance (who appraises and how is it done) within organisations. The emphasis on the organisations signals a further evolution in the nature of performance appraisal.

Table 8.1 Performance appraisal in UK workplaces

Private 1998	Public 1998	All 1998	Private 2004	Public 2004	All 2004
72	79	73	75	91	78

Base: All workplaces with 10 or more employees.

Figures are weighted and based on responses from 2191 managers in 1998 and 2024 managers in 2004.

Source: WERS 2004 (Kersley *et al.*, 2006).

performance appraisals were not always conducted on a regular basis or used for all employees. Two-thirds (65 per cent) of all workplaces conducted regular appraisals for most (60 per cent or more) non-managerial employees. This represented an increase since 1998, when the equivalent figure was 48 per cent.

The growth in the use of performance appraisal has been linked to a raise in performance-related pay schemes (PRP), but as Bach (2005) comments, this is not really the full picture as there is in fact, 'little evidence to suggest that performance appraisal was introduced to support individual performance pay' (2005: 297). Rather, Bach (2005) suggests, the increased use is more closely associated with the commitment of successive Conservative and, more recently, Labour governments to introduce private sector 'best practice' into the public sector in response to the need to increase efficiency and enhance managerial authority noted above. A further stimulus to organisations to review the performance of their employees came in the mid to late 1990s with the expansion of interest in gaining externally accredited recognition awards, for example Investors in People (IiP) and BSO 5750, ISO 9000. The need to evidence that training and development needs were regularly reviewed against organisational aims and objectives was a central feature of IiP and could be demonstrated through the use of a formal appraisal scheme.

This however, is only one purpose for appraisals, in 2003a, the Industrial Relations Services (IRS) found that approximately 15 per cent of respondents considered one of the main purposes for introducing appraisals was to help identify and deal with poor or underperformance.

Other reported purposes of performance appraisal were:

- promotion, separation and transfer decisions;
- feedback to the employee regarding how the organisation viewed the employee's performance;
- evaluations of relative contributions made by individuals and entire departments in achieving higher level organisation goals;
- criteria for evaluating the effectiveness of selection and placement decisions, including the relevance of the information used in the decisions within the organisation;
- reward decisions, including merit increases, promotions and other rewards
- ascertaining and diagnosing training and development decisions;
- criteria for evaluating the success of training and development decisions;
- information upon which work scheduling plans, budgeting and human resources planning can be used.

In many instances the actual appraisal is undertaken via a face-to-face discussion, but it is important to note that this may be changing as the use of information technology and software packages such as 'Performance Pro' means that appraisals can easily be undertaken on line (see Case study).

The case of TRW

TRW Inc., is a global automotive, aeronautics, electronics and information-systems company with 100,000 employees, based in 36 countries on five continents and with four core businesses. It was originally called 'Thompson Ramo Wooldridge Inc.', but was shortened to TRW Inc. in 1965.

In 2001, the company had a heavy debt load following a large acquisition in the automotive sector and in the face of current adverse market conditions, TRW was challenged to become more competitive and performance-driven and to provide greater value to shareholders. To reach those goals, the senior management committee instituted dramatic change throughout the company. Business units were empowered to operate more autonomously than they had in the past, and the corporate headquarters itself was renamed the 'Business Support Centre.'

To guide the creation of a new and energised work culture, a new set of company-wide TRW 'Behaviours' was developed and communicated throughout the company. The aim was to organise and operate a performance-appraisal, professional-development and succession-management system that not only attempted to create a more performance-driven, customer-oriented organisation, but also command respect and workers acceptence. The solution was to select a team of IT experts and key HR people from each of the businesses. Each member was faced with the task of allowing their own particular business's way of doing things (some were used to working with two-page appraisal forms, others had ten) to be incorporated into a single system. The employee performance and development process they came up with, although common to the entire organisation, was allowed to flow within particular units as was felt best, both standardisation and flexibility being recognised as essentials.

To position TRW competitively for the twenty-first century, the company stands committed to excellence and quality, exploring new markets, and satisfying its customers, shareholders and employees. To meet those commitments, TRW has created a set of six behaviours that distinguishes it in the marketplace through performance and technology.

The six behaviours that guide performance management are:

1 **Create trust:**
   - create an open and constructive environment;
   - deal with reality;
   - communicate with candour and honesty;
   - honour commitments;
   - take personal accountability for results.

2 **Energise people**   :
   - rigorously select, empower and grow people who demand the best of themselves and others;
   - reward performance and initiative.

3 **Performance driven**
   - deliver profitable growth;
   - develop and achieve demanding goals . . . short and long term;
   - continuously improve productivity and quality;
   - execute with facts, urgency and decisiveness;
   - create energy that doesn't tolerate bureaucracy.

4 **Embrace change**
   - passion for innovation;
   - a thirst for new ideas;

- be adaptable and flexible;
- know your markets . . . lead your competitors.

5 Customer-oriented
- understand our customers;
- relentlessly focus on their needs;
- develop lasting relationships.

6 Build teamwork
- share information and best practices;
- speak up;
- encourage diverse views;
- get the facts . . . make decisions;
- ACT!
- support it.

Note: The TRW behaviours were instituted in 2001 to guide the culture of the company (Neary, 2002).

Approaches to performance appraisal

The scope and method for reviewing performance varies between organisations, but in general, appraisal takes a 'free text' form, in which the appraiser and the appraisee review performance in general, although the problem with such qualitative forms of appraisal is that they have the potential to ignore important areas that would benefit from being appraised, thereby making them highly selective and highly subjective.

An alternative is to undertake a straight ranking of performance against predefined criteria or traits. On the basis of an assessment against the dimensions, employees are given the final rankings. Any approach using predetermined criteria has limitations, especially if the same criteria are employed across a wide range of job roles, as not each criterion may be relevant. Traits such as resourcefulness, loyalty or enthusiasm may be open to different interpretations by different appraisers and the appraisee, leaving them open to bias and prejudice. Finally, the criteria may become obsolete, for example in the banking sector the use of creativity, innovation and imagination may not be as desirable in the first half of the twenty-first century as it was in the latter half of the twentieth century.

A critical incident method is one in which the appraiser rates the employee on the basis of critical events and how the employee behaved during those incidents. It includes both negative and positive points. The drawback of this method is that the appraiser has to note down the critical incidents and the employee behaviour as and when they occur.

A checklist approach is one in which the appraiser is given a list of statements or descriptions of the desired knowledge, skills competences and behaviours of the employees. The list may be drawn from key aspects of the role or directly from the job description. Often the appraisee and appraiser indicate which description most closely reflects the job performance of the employee. This is often undertaken independently of each other at the start of the process, but later, during a formal discussion, the appraiser and appraisee seek to reach agreement as to which description is most appropriate. This approach is referred to as 'Behaviourally anchored rating scales (BARS)' or 'behaviourally observed rating scales (BOS)', and is a reasonably equitable method, as the possibility of personal bias is reduced, especially if there is a requirement to reach a consensus decision.

Another approach, and one that seeks to make the process even more equitable, establishes job objectives or goals, and each year reviews the extent to which they have been met to a satisfactory level. In this style of appraisal, the CIPD suggest the following points should be considered:

- What they have achieved during the review period, with examples and evidence.
- Any examples of objectives not achieved with explanations.
- What they most enjoy about the job and how they might want to develop the role.
- Any aspect of the work in which improvement is required and how this might be achieved.
- Employee learning and development needs with arguments to support their case for specific training.
- What level of support and guidance employees require from their manager.
- Employees aspirations for the future, both in the current role and in possible future roles.
- Objectives for the next review period (CIPD, 2009a).

Have you ever been appraised? How did you find the experience? How could the experience have been improved?

The extent to which the appraisee is involved in establishing performance goals varies between organisations, but motivational theory suggests goals are most effective in terms of motivating performance when the employee has been directly involved in setting them (see Box 8.2). A variation on this theme is to use a competency based framework as the basis against which performance is appraised. Many schemes use a combination of competency assessment, objectives and role accountabilities.

Performance may also be measured by gathering raw data (see Box 8.3). It is frequently used, for example to monitor activity rates of computer operators, call handling speed and ability of operators in call or throughput rates for staff in fast food restaurants. Performance measurement or employee monitoring can also be conducted in other ways that were not possible until very recently. For example, some cellular telephones have built-in global positioning systems that enable employers to track the physical location of employees at all times. Employers can then track every physical and electronic move an employee makes. Furthermore, employers can now

Box 8.2   Goal setting theory and performance management

Goal setting theory was established by Latham and Locke in 1984 in which he argued that goals pursued by employees can play an important part in motivating improved performance. In striving to achieve the goals employees reflect upon their behaviour and performance, and if they surmise that their goals may not be realised they will modify their behaviour. Heslin *et al.* (2009) suggest a prime axiom of goal setting theory is that specific, difficult goals lead to higher performance than when people strive to simply 'do their best' (Locke, 1966; Locke and Latham, 1990). The performance benefits of challenging, specific goals have been demonstrated in laboratory and field studies (Locke and Latham, 1990, 2002). Specific challenging goals do not, however, necessarily lead to such desirable personal and organisational outcomes. Rather, contribution goal setting can make to effective performance management depend on issues pertaining to goal commitment, task complexity, goal framing, team goals and feedback. For goals to be motivating they need to:

- be specific rather than vague;
- be demanding but attainable and realistic;
- generate feedback that is timely and meaningful;
- be accepted by the employees as desirable.

Box 8.3   **Wireless real-time production and employee performance measurement**

The system is referred to as 20/20 Data Collection/Monitoring & Management System and is used in any production or manufacturing context, from assembling computers, to answering telephone calls in a call centre, to packing chocolate biscuits. It is a wireless real-time shop floor data collection and management system that is designed to enhance the production management to a higher level thereby allowing productivity gains. It works by constantly monitoring the work rate of the operators to show if specific operators or assembly stations are constraining overall production throughput. Performance and line balancing reports rank the bottleneck operators and stations according to their constraint on system output. With real-time data access, managers are able to make well-informed decisions, such as reprioritising a job or reallocating staffing. Productivity analysis allows managers to measure individual employee performance and analyse labour costs by employee, department or work assembly station. In terms of performance management real time measurement data enables managers to:

- improve productivity by leveraging production monitoring and motivating the workers to meet the standards;
- access detailed analysis allowing managers to monitor performance and labour costs in terms of each employee;
- indicate and monitor individual operator efficiency and output;
- use the reported information to determine the precise cause of any defect and the action necessary to resolve the issue;
- identify poor operator performance before it causes a problem;
- use the data as part of a continuous total quality improvement programme.

conduct their own private investigations into employment applicants, partly because of the reluctance of former employers to give references. So, instead, employers may collect information about prospective employees from driving records, vehicle registration records, bankruptcy proceedings. Social Security records, property ownership records, military records, sex offender lists, incarceration records, drug testing records, professional licensing records, workers' compensation records and credit reports. In performance measurement, electronic monitoring and surveillance of employees has grown, especially the monitoring of email and web browsing (Sipor and Ward, 1995; Stanton, 2000). The ethical implications of such an approach will be discussed later when we consider some of the limitations of performance appraisal.

What, if any, are the ethical implications of wireless real-time production and employee performance measurement?

The CIPD suggest there are five key elements of the performance appraisal:

- *Measurement*: assessing performance against agreed targets and objectives.
- *Feedback*: providing information to the individual on their performance and progress.
- *Positive reinforcement*: emphasising what has been done well and making only constructive criticism about what might be improved.
- *Exchange of views*: a frank exchange of views about what has happened, how appraisees can improve their performance, the support they need from their managers to achieve this and their aspirations for their future career.
- *Agreement*: jointly coming to an understanding by all parties about what needs to be done to improve performance generally and overcome any issues raised in the course of the discussion (CIPD, 2009a).

Box 8.4	**Performance appraisal at Tata Sons**

Mr Satish Pradhan, Executive Vice President – HR at Tata Sons, based in Mumbai, and with over 20 years of international and national experience in human resource management, explained how performance appraisal at Tata Sons was built on two principles:

- no surprises;
- reward for performance.

Mr Pradhan took time to explain that effective performance appraisal was all about trust and development. He stated: 'If our employees trust that we have their best interests at heart and that we genuinely want them to succeed in their careers at Tata Sons, then their commitment to us and performance for us; will excel.' He said that at no stage in the performance appraisal process should an employee be told anything they were not already aware of or had not had sufficient time to reflect upon. He was also keen to demonstrate that while financial incentives were part of the reward for performance, money was not the whole story. For Tata Sons, non-financial rewards, for example being chosen to represent the company on the platform of an international convention, are held in as much, if not more esteem among the employees, than a salary increase.

How far do you agree with Mr Satish Pradhan, Executive Vice President – HR at Tata Sons, that there should be 'no surprises' in a performance appraisal?

Why do you think he is so keen to emphasise that non-financial rewards are also part of the system of performance recognition?

Limitations of performance measurement

Over recent years, there has been a growing discomfort with measuring performance through the use of appraisal indicators and targets. Callahan (2007) provides a clear steer to all managers involved in measuring performance through such traditional indices, to start to think outside the performance box. He suggests that performance measurement is inadequate because it fails to recognise the key concepts of accountability and citizen participation and fails to emphasise the critical importance of their relationship. In other words, performance appraisals are compromised because they are used for a range of often conflicting purposes. In addition, they are undertaken by stakeholders who themselves have a range of roles and responsibilities – which, again, may be conflicting (Wilson, 2002). To illustrate, the appraiser can be placed in the position, described by McGregor (1957) as being required to 'play God'. Appraisers invariably judge and rate the performance of their staff member. This role sits at odds with their responsibility to motivate and develop the same staff member, and may sit in opposition to their role as employee counsellor. Newton and Findlay (1996) make the point that employees are less likely to confide their limitations, development needs or anxieties about job competence to their appraiser because it could adversely affect their rating at the next performance review and may affect reward levels if performance is linked to remuneration.

Appraisers may equally be reluctant to give their staff a poor review because it might prove demotivating, could create conflict and might suggest they lacked the necessary management skills to elicit high performance. Additional limitations relate to what is known as the 'halo effect', which, as the name implies, causes managers to see only an 'angel' in an employee and blinds them into ignoring smaller problem areas that require growth and development. The 'comparing employees effect', in which a manager evaluates one employee against another without considering the different tasks they are required to perform, and the 'recency effect', when managers rate employees on the basis of their most recent encounter with them or on their most recent knowledge of their performance, and the 'central tendency' effect, when managers are reluctant to be overly lenient or harsh – so they opt for the safe midway or central point, may all reduce the effectiveness of appraisal. Research undertaken by Geddes and Konrad (2003) and Thornton and Rupp (2007) indicate that appraisal ratings are also influenced by gender, ethnic origins and physical attractiveness.

According to Bach (2005: 304), one of the most common responses to rater bias is to 'redouble training efforts to ensure managers are trained in conducting appraisals, and be aware of some of the potential limitations'. Another response has been to seek multiple sources of data from multiple stakeholders. One such example is the use of the 'balanced scorecard' (Kaplan and Norton, 1992, 1996). The balanced scorecard is a performance management approach to monitor progress toward an organisation's strategic goals. Each major unit throughout the organisation is tasked with establishing its own scorecard which, in turn, is integrated with the scorecards of other units to achieve the scorecard of the overall organisation. It focuses on various overall performance indicators, often including:

● financial perspective;

● customer perspective;

● internal process perspective; and

● innovation and learning perspective.

360-degree appraisal

A second approach to performance appraisal is the use of 360-degree feedback, or 'multi-rater feedback'. This approach was first developed and used by General Electric in the USA in 1992, and despite Newbold's (2008) suggestion that it went out of fashion for a while, it is now back in vogue with many organisations using it. Aswathappa (2005: 234) lists GE (India) Reliance Industries, Godrej soaps, Wipro, Infosys, Thermex and Thomas Cook as examples of organisations currently using the 360-degree system of performance appraisal. It is an approach in which performance data is sought from peers, subordinates, superiors and nominated significant others who may be internal or external to the organisation.

Self-assessment is an indispensable part of 360-degree appraisals; they therefore have high employee involvement and also have the strongest impact on behaviour and performance. As it provides a '360-degree review' of the employees' performance, it is often considered to be one of the most credible performance appraisal methods. The 360-degree appraisal is also a powerful developmental tool because, when conducted at regular intervals, it helps monitor changes in the perceptions of others' about particular employee's performance, and so hold greater surface validity.

STOP and think

What might be the advantages and limitations of 360-degree appraisal?

The points noted above relate to limitations in the design and operational implementation of performance appraisal. Another level of critical commentary has emerged which draws attention to the ethical and philosophical limitations of performance appraisal and the fact that appraisal can be seen as a means of manufacturing consent among employees. These accounts reject the unitary assumptions and managerialist prerogatives that underpin traditional approaches to performance appraisal and replace them with a radical ideology that questions managerial objectives, their power to control, manipulate and direct employee behaviour and the extent to which they have a right to engage in the covert surveillance of employees. Bach (2005) provides an excellent summary of this proposition, in which he suggests that those influenced by the work of French philosopher Michel Foucault view trends in appraisal as part of a more sinister management regime to control all aspects of employee behaviour and eliminate any scope for employee resistance or misbehaviour.

Understanding Foucault

Foucault's work involves reference to Bentham's panopticon. Bentham was a utilitarian theorist, believing human beings are intrinsically bound to seek pleasure and avoid pain, wherever possible, and that 'good' and 'bad' are defined by what is pleasurable and painful. The object of legislation therefore, according to Bentham, should be to secure the greatest happiness for the greatest number of people; consequently, the pain of punishment should be proportional to the happiness that it secured. As a part of his vision of rational social control, Bentham devised an architectural device he called the 'Panopticon', which is Greek for 'all seeing'. The panopticon was based on the design for a Russian factory that minimised the number of supervisors required, it was proposed by Bentham for the design of prisons, workhouses, mental asylums and schools. The supervisors were able to view and monitor the inmates, but the inmates could not see the supervisors. The underlying principle is that the total and constant surveillance of inmates or workers would encourage them to conform to all the desired behaviours and beliefs and eventually each individual would themselves become an overseer of others. The strong illusion of a powerful, controlling and all-seeing eye would become an inner reality of self-policing. Bentham believed this approach could be successfully adopted in any environment, including work organisations, which involved any level of supervision – i.e. of employees. (**http://www.mdx.ac.uk/www/study/ybenfou.htm**).

The same principles about power, control and observation were enshrined in much of Foucault's (1977) thinking about the role of managers controlling the behaviour and thoughts of their employees. In the example we saw earlier of the 20/20 data collection used as a wireless real-time production and employee performance measurement system, it is easy to appreciate how this distant but all embracing surveillance of the action, speed of work quality and production can be regarded as an example of why Foucault exhibited concern over the extent to which employees were being manipulated, controlled and monitored by others and saw appraisal as epitomising a desire for observation in order to make every employee a knowable, calculable and administrative object (Miller and Rose, 1990: 5). Foucault, like Townley (1993b) and Grey (1994) in their work on appraisals and career management, questioned the ethics of such close and consistent intrusion into an employees working life and saw such involvement as a negative feature of performance appraisal. However, to leave the story at that junction would be to tell only half of it as others, in particular Findlay and Newton (1998), use their discussion of performance appraisal to highlight Foucault's apparent neglect of human agency (Newton, 1994) and to suggest that to see all aspects of intervention as a negative use of power is to ignore the mutuality of interests that characterise many aspects of the modern labour process.

To what extent do you share the view of Townley (1993a, 1993b, 1994, 1997) and Grey (1994) about the 'negative' aspects of performance appraisal?

Performance management

As the limitations of performance measurement and some aspects of appraisal became more apparent, and as the role of HRM became more accepted and respected, the agenda shifted to embrace a more strategic, systematic, integrated and organisationally focused approach to the management (rather than measurement) of performance. As an area of academic study and research, performance management dates back to the late 1980s with commentators such as Johnson and Kaplan, 1987; Lynch and Cross, 1991; Eccles, 1991; Kaplan and Norton, 1992; and Thorpe, 2004, setting the scene. Den-Hartog *et al.* (2004: 556) describe performance management as being concerned with the:

> challenges organizations face in defining, measuring, and stimulating employee performance with the ultimate goal of improving overall organisational performance. Performance management involves multiple levels of analysis and is clearly linked to the topics studied in strategic human resource management (HRM).

Armstrong and Baron (2005: 15) define performance management as a process rather than an event, and so it operates in a continuous cycle. It 'contributes to the effective management of individuals and teams in order to achieve high levels of organizational performance'. They go on to stress that it is 'a strategy which relates to every activity of the organization set in the context of its human resource policies, culture, style and communications systems. The nature of the strategy depends on the organizational context and can vary from organization to organization' (Armstrong and Baron, 2005: 16). Armstrong and Baron argue the principle value of performance management is to:

- communicate a shared vision of the purpose of the organisation;
- define expectations of what must be delivered and how;
- ensure employees are aware of what high performance means and how they can achieve it; and
- to enhance levels of motivation and enable employees to monitor their own performance and understand what needs to be done to improve their overall level of performance.

To quote from the CIPD *Fact Sheet on Performance Management* (2009b), it should be:

> - *strategic*: it is about broader issues and longer-term goals;
> - *integrated*: it should link various aspects of the business, people management and individuals and teams.
>
> And incorporate:
>
> - *performance improvement*: throughout the organization, for individual, team and organizational effectiveness;
> - *development*: unless there is continuous development of individuals and teams, performance will not improve;
> - *managing behaviour*: ensuring that individuals are encouraged to behave in a way that allows and fosters better working relationships.

Armstrong and Baron (2004) stress that, at its best, performance management is a tool to ensure that managers manage effectively; that they ensure the people or teams they manage:

- know and understand what is expected of them;
- have the skills and ability to deliver on these expectations;
- are supported by the organisation to develop the capacity to meet these expectations are given feedback on their performance; and
- have the opportunity to discuss and contribute to individual and team aims and objectives.

Human resource management and performance management

Human resource management, and in particular strategic HRM (SHRM), has developed since the early 1980s and provides us with a framework to understand the contribution HR practices can make – directly or indirectly – to individual and organisational performance. We have already read about the different approaches to HRM, but to recap there are essentially three major perspectives that emerge from the existing literature:

1 Universalistic
2 Contingency
3 Configuration.

The universalistic or 'best practice' perspective posits there are certain policies and procedures which, if followed, will always result in higher performance. The aim of HR practitioners is to identify precisely what these are. Although there is no undisputed list of high involvement/performance/commitment HRM practices, it has been claimed that rigorous recruitment and selection processes, performance-contingent compensation systems, extensive development and training activities and commitment to employee involvement are generally considered key to 'best practice'

The contingency, or 'external fit', perspective suggests that different HR policies and practices are required to ensure high performance depending on the type and nature of the organisation in which they are being operated. In other words, perspective emphasises the 'fit' between business strategy and HRM practices, implying that business strategies are followed by HRM practices in determining business performance.

The configurational perspective posits a simultaneous internal and external fit between a firm's external environment, business strategy and HRM strategy, implying that business strategies and HRM practices interact according to organisational context in determining business performance.

At its most basic, HRM is about aligning the management of people with the needs of the business. This, according to Roberts (2001), involves the organisation being clear about its mission, its values, its strategic direction and its goals. It involves establishing and articulating specific organisational, departmental, team and individual objectives designed to meet the stated goals and translating those into a meaningful set of targets for every individual involved. This can involve a panoply of specific actions and processes: performance appraisal, strategic approaches to reward, training and development, sophisticated communication and feedback mechanisms, coaching and individual career planning, mechanisms for monitoring the effectiveness of performance management systems and interventions, and even cultural management techniques.

So far our discussion has focused on the performance of the individual; we now move on to consider the links between individual performance and that of the organisation as a whole. The relationship between performance management and human resource management practices is longstanding, if not always evidence-based or consistent. In fact, since the concept of HRM first emerged in the early 1980s, two basic paths of research have developed. The first approach assumes there is a 'direct' relationship between individual HRM practices and organisational performance (see Schuler and Jackson, 1987, 1999). The second is based on the assumption that there is no quantifiable direct link, but there is an 'indirect' relationship between individual HRM practices and organisational performance (see Ferris *et al.*, 1998; Edwards and Wright, 2001).

To illustrate this difference in opinion, international authors such as Boselie *et al.* (2001) from the Netherlands, argue there is an obvious and direct link between HRM and performance management, in particular in relation to employee involvement and internal regulation. Seeking to confirm or refute the link, Boselie *et al.* (2005) analysed 104 referred journal articles between 1994 and 2005. They concluded that there were a number of hidden assumptions in most of the conceptual models developed in the research; and that in most of the studies there was empirical evidence to confirm that human resource management does affect organisational performance. However, they also pointed out that the variety of methods used in the research made it impossible to compare results and concluded overall that there is no consistent picture of what human resource management is or what it does. Björkman and Budhwar (2007) were similarly interested in exploring whether the proposed effects of HRM were universalistic or contingent on the national context of the organisation. Based on an analysis of companies in India, they concluded the key message for practitioners is that HRM systems do improve organisational performance in the Indian subsidiaries of foreign firms, but that an emphasis on the localisation of HRM practices can further contribute in this regard. In a further research study undertaken in India, Chand and Katou (2007) sought to demonstrate the operational link between HRM and performance and concluded that the financial and commercial success of hotels in India is positively related to their HRM systems of recruitment, selection, HR planning, job design, training and development, quality circles and pay systems. Other commentators, notably Legge (1995) and more recently Hall (2004) from the UK, are less convinced. While we are, therefore, advised to treat clear proclamations of cause and effect with a degree of caution, the general consensus developed among researchers is that HRM practices and/or HRM systems do not influence business performance directly (Budhwar et al., 2006; Katou and Budhwar, 2007). Rather, they influence firm resources, such as human capital, or employee behaviours, and it is these resources and behaviours that ultimately lead to performance. This implicit model assumes that there are variables that mediate a link between HRM practices and business performance, although only a few researchers (Huselid, 1995; MacDuffie, 1995) have measured these mediators and addresses their importance.

Critique of links between HRM and performance

Links between HRM and performance management have a natural logic about them: good HRM practices can improve employee commitment; higher levels of commitment can positively affect employee performance, which in turn impacts on the organisation's financial performance and ultimately competitive advantage and success. The central concerns are ability, motivation and opportunity to participate and practice or AMO for short. The successful organisation not only has to have better than average human capital, through recruitment (where organis-ational reputation is important), selection and development and then appropriate job design, motivation, communication and involvement systems, but also better processes or capabil-ities. These combine human and non-human resources together in ways highly appropriate for end-users and markets and in ways which other firms find hard to copy. In terms of managing performance Purcell, in a paper from Bath University refers to ability, motivation and opportunity as the prime building blocks of HR architecture if employees, individually and collectively are to engage in the sort of discretionary behaviour that is beneficial to the organisation. Purcell states that effective performance management must recognise and make provision for three conditions of AMO:

- There must be enough employees with the necessary ability (skills, experience, knowledge) to do current, and perhaps future, jobs.
- There must be adequate motivation for them to apply their abilities. These motivation factors may be financial but will almost certainly include social rewards (and sanctions) and recognition of contribution as applied by co-workers and immediate bosses.
- There must be an opportunity to engage in discretionary behaviour (thus the importance of job cycle time). Opportunity is the invitation to participate and take part, or get involved. This occurs both within the job itself in terms of how the job can best be done (known as 'online participation') and outside the job as a member of a team or work area, and a 'citizen' of the organisation (offline participation). This is where opportunities may

exist, and certainly can be created, which provide space for wider participation and involvement, so employees contribute knowledge and ideas on how things should be done and how to respond to the change. AMO is therefore considered to be at the heart of effective performance management and strategic human resource management.

This intricate relationship between the individual and the organisation epitomises that espoused by Guest (2000) and embodies the essential elements in his earlier, more detailed model developed in 1997. It too has an innate appeal.

However, authors Richardson and Thompson (1999) and, in particular Hall (2004) identify a number of problems with research which claims to demonstrate a significant relationship between 'progressive' HR practices and internal and external performance outcomes. First, Hall notes that the way HR practices are assessed lacks reliability, consistency, depth and breadth; in particular, the line manager's and the employee's perspectives are excluded and the samples inadequate. The assessment of performance outcomes are also criticised in terms of relevance, unhelpfully narrow limits, short-termism and manipulability. She also suggest that while some significant relationships have been found between HR practices and performance outcomes, these are variable and suggests the relationships should be treated with caution. Hall (2004) also advises caution is needed as the statistics do not provide any evidence of a causal relationship. This leads her to conclude that progressive HR practices may lead to higher performance outcomes or higher performance outcomes may lead to investment in more progressive HR practices, or these factors may both be influenced by something else which has yet to be identified and measured.

The set of assumptions underpinning the body of research also warrants caution. Studies are carried out with an implicit or explicit assumption that 'best practice' can be revealed and then used to guide other companies in their choices; such an unquestioned universalist perspective is contested (see Legge, 1995) as is the unitarist assumption – and as employee views were not sought in the majority of the research examples, this raises questions about their validity. Looking at the internal measure of employee performance from a completely different perspective, Patterson et al. (1997) found that the greatest influence on employee performance was not HR practices per se, but rather the culture of the organisation – a factor not reported on in some studies, although it was discussed by Guest (1997). Patterson et al. (1997) also found that welfare provision of all HR policies had the greatest influence on employee performance.

Finally, Hall (2004) identifies a further difficulty in making a definitive and direct link between the impact of HR practices and performance, namely that the majority of research was collected without the use of a theoretical framework, and in particular with no regard to the intervening mechanism which mediates HR practices and performance outcomes. This, she concludes, leaves the existing research with no explanatory power.

Collaborative performance management

So far in this chapter we have focused on the measurement and management of performance within an organisation. We have noted that in order for organisations to make the most effective use of performance measurement outcomes they must be able to make the transition from simply *measuring* performance to actually *managing* performance and be able to anticipate needed changes in the strategic direction of the organisation and have a methodology in place for effecting strategic change. To put it another way, effective performance management provides organisations with the opportunity to refine and improve their development activities. In this next section we consider some of what Waggoner et al. (1999: 52) call the 'various forces that shape organisational performance management systems'. In particular, we will consider the challenges of managing performance in a diverse workforce, an ageing workforce and whether managing the performance of a volunteer is in any respect different from managing the performance of salaried employees.

The fact that today's marketplace is more fiercely competitive than ever before is indeed widely acknowledged (Fawcett and Magnan 2002; Patterson *et al.* 2003). Globalisation, technological change and demanding customers constantly push the performance bar upward. In response to this new global economic order Bititci *et al.* (2004) suggest that over the past decade or so, businesses have been forced to become more responsive and adapt to a continuously changing business environment, to be more agile and persistently restructure themselves and find new ways of continuously improving processes, systems and performance. Longnecker and Fink (2001) and Longnecker *et al.* (1999) suggest that in response to both recognising the potential limitations of performance measurement and responding to the demands inherent in a new global business world, organisational processes and delivery systems are being re-engineered and streamlined so that cycle-times are reduced and efficiencies are improved. Relationships with both customers and suppliers are being redefined so that 'strategic partnerships' may be forged and leveraged. Workforce effectiveness and productivity initiatives are being developed to improve employee performance. Total quality and customer service are no longer viewed as individual programmes but rather are being integrated into organisational cultures and operating practices as 'simply a way of life'. In addition, technology is 'exploding' in most industries and must be properly integrated and implemented if it is to be leveraged to provide competitive advantage. Enlightened approaches to human resource management are also being used as a vehicle to leverage human capital in the emerging global workplace.

Burgess *et al.* (1997) cited in Busi and Bititci (2006: 10) summarised the impact of this new territory by suggesting that in order 'to cope with today's increasing competitive marketplace, companies have, and should, become more collaborative' and to form a network that boasts as a whole all those resources and competencies needed to satisfy the end-customer. In short, to survive and meet new demands, organisations will struggle to go it alone; collaboration and networking have been earmarked as key themes of success. The collaborative model is based on breaking down traditional physical boundaries and getting the partners to behave as a single unit. Integrating different organisations implies forming teams of different people with different cultures, policies and routines (Holmberg, 2000). Managing multidisciplinary teams poses a number of challenges related to communication, the psychological contract, trust and behaviour.

Amaratunga and Baldry (2002) argue that in order for organisations to achieve the level of collaboration and competitive advantage they seek, they will need to move away from an approach to performance management that seeks to optimise internal activities and applied within the tight organisational boundaries of a specific firm, towards an approach that recognises their relationship with other stakeholders and their respective performance. As Busi and Bititci (2006) suggest, the move toward more collaborative types of networks calls for new processes, new strategy, new measures and new way of managing performance. In the collaborative enterprise, companies will be closer than ever and, unlike in the past, the performance of an enterprise will depend as much on the performance of its partners in the value chain as on its own performance. Collaborative performance measurement and management means that customers and suppliers get access to performance information beyond their own firm and give access to performance information to the other partners in the network. By sharing performance data with partners, firms can identify bottlenecks and 'weak links' (2006: 11).

In other words, collaborative organisations will need to move away from an isolated, internally focused 'performance measurement' to 'performance management'. Armstrong and Baron (1998) see performance management as a continuous process involving performance reviews focusing on the future rather than the past. They emphasise the strategic and integrated nature of performance management, which in their view focuses on: 'increasing the effectiveness of organisations by improving the performance of the people who work in them and by developing the capabilities of teams and individual contributors' (1998: 38–39). The definition offered by Busi and Bititci (2006) retains a strong sense of measurement, while nonetheless acknowledging the strategic goal-orientation of the process:

> the use of performance measurement information to effect positive change in organizational culture, systems and processes, by helping to set agreed-upon performance goals, allocating and prioritising resources, informing managers to either confirm or change current policy or programme directions to meet those goals, and sharing results of performance in pursuing those goals.
> (Busi and Bititci, 2006: 11)

In determining the manner in which a collaborative/networked organisation should approach performance management Longnecker and Fink (2001) suggest HR practitioners should ask the following critical questions, the answers to which will greatly influence the quality of performance management:

- Do all of our managers have a clear and unambiguous understanding of their role in our changing organisation?
- Do we provide all of our managers with ongoing and balanced performance feedback?
- Do we have a systematic approach to helping our managers 'learn by doing'?
- Is management development truly a management priority at our organisation?
- Do we take active steps to ensure that our management development efforts are designed to meet the actual needs of our managers?

Busi and Bititci (2006) build on this foundation and characterise a network-wide collaborative approach to performance management as focusing on:

- managing extended processes within and beyond the single company's boundaries;
- managing the collaborative enterprise performance, rather than only measuring it;
- creating and managing cross-organisational multidisciplinary teams;
- deploying integrated ICT across organisations;
- creating and sharing knowledge.

As Busi and Bititci (2006) summarise, the supporting collaborative performance management system would include the following key elements:

- a structured methodology to design the performance measurement system;
- a structured management process for using performance measurement information to help make decisions, set performance goals, allocate resources, inform management, and report success (see also Amaratunga and Baldry, 2002);
- a set of requirements specifications of the necessary electronic tools for data gathering, processing and analysis (see also Waggoner *et al.* 1999);

Box 8.5 | **The aims of collaborative performance management**

- Translate organisational vision into clear measurable outcomes that define success, and which are shared throughout the organisation and with customers and stakeholders.
- Provide a tool for assessing, managing and improving the overall health and success of performance management systems.
- Continue to shift from prescriptive, audit and compliance-based oversight to an ongoing, forward-looking strategic partnership.
- Include measures of quality, cost, speed, customer service and employee alignment, motivation and skills to provide an in-depth, predictive performance management system.
- Replace existing assessment models with a consistent approach to performance management.

Source: Adapted from Procurement Executives' Association (1999).

- theoretical guidelines on how to manage through measures. (As Adair *et al.,* 2003) point out, performance management systems are used to apply the information and knowledge arising from performance measurement systems);

- a review process to ensure that measures are constantly updated to reflect changes in strategy and/or market conditions (see also Waggoner *et al.,* 1999).

As we have seen, the traditional focus of performance measurement has been on process operations within the organisational boundaries of one particular firm. With changes in the structure and economy of the global business world, collaboration became a necessary business development, capable of rendering single-business and internally focused performance measurement systems inappropriate. However, the difficulty of developing a collaborative culture and the difficulty of developing appropriate cross-cultural and translational performance indices have been identified as major barriers to the successful implementation of collaborative performance management systems.

Busi and Bititci (2006) advise that various studies that analyse the issue of local versus overall performance measures conclude that collaborative performance measurement systems should evaluate both local measures and business network-wide measures in order to maintain relevance and effectiveness in the collaborative enterprise business model. As the collaborative enterprise business model is based on breaking down traditional physical boundaries and getting the partners to behave as a single unit, integrating different organisations implies forming teams of different people with different cultures, policies and routines. Managing such multidisciplinary teams poses a number of ongoing challenges, indicating that future research should continue to investigate collaboration performance management in more detail.

Managing performance in a diverse workforce

As the composition of the workforce continues to become more inclusive and diverse, understanding how this dimension affects performance has become an increasingly significant issue for HRM, and a number of organisations across different sectors have begun efforts to understand workforce diversity in relation to performance. Both scholars and practitioners have begun to explore the consequences of increased diversity on work-related outcomes. Indeed, emphasis on diversity and its management has become a primary theme in the public management research literature, with inquiry devoted to diversity management programmes (Kellough and Naff, 2004; Naff and Kellough, 2003), the impact of diversity on performance outcomes (Pitts and Wise, 2004; Pitts, 2005; Wise and Tschirhart, 2000), the status of minority groups in public employment (Lewis and Smithey, 1998), and the role of diversity in public administration education (Pitts and Wise, 2004; Tschirhart and Wise, 2002).

In the USA, for example, Pitts (2009) suggested that almost 90 per cent of federal agencies reported they were actively managing diversity but, despite this high level of interest, there remained little empirical research to test the relationships between diversity management, job satisfaction and work group performance. To address this deficit Pitts (2009) conducted a study among 140,000 federal government employees. His findings indicated that diversity management was positively and significantly related to job satisfaction. The most satisfied employees worked in units where they reported diversity management was strong. His work provides evidence for the argument that it is poor diversity management that is leading some segments of the workforce to be less satisfied with their jobs, rather than the jobs themselves.

The practical implications of his study are clear and direct: diversity management matters. At the organisational level, it means that resources should be devoted to diversity management programmes and training opportunities. Diversity should be viewed as a core competency for all employees, particularly managers. At the suborganisational level, it means that managers who are concerned with the effective management of performance should put time and energy into understanding the different perspectives of employee groups. The managers who are likely to be most successful are those who effectively acknowledge and manage the diversity present in their groups. As a field, this means that HR practitioners must view diversity management as a core tool in the toolkit of performance management and should strive to include diversity-related competencies and raise levels of understanding and awareness across the entire organisation.

What features distinguish a diverse workforce and how, if at all, might they affect an organisations approach to managing performance?

Managing performance in an ageing workforce

As we have seen above, effective performance management demands that organisations confront many of the demographic changes occurring in the workforce, such as increasing racial and ethnic diversity, along with greater numbers of women workers. Calo (2008) identifies a further aspect of performance management in the context of diversity, which involves recognising that in many developed economies, the workforce is steadily ageing, a reflection of declining birth rates and the greying of the baby boom generation. Most HR practitioners are vaguely aware that a major demographic shift is about to transform their societies and their companies. The statistics are compelling. For example, in the US the percentage of the workforce between the ages of 55 and 64 is growing faster than any other age group. The situation is described by Strack *et al.* (2008), as being particularly acute in certain industries. In the US energy sector, more than a third of the workforce is already over 50 years old, and that age group is expected to grow by more than 25 per cent by 2020. In Japan, the number of workers over the age of 50 in the financial services sector is projected to rise by 61 per cent between now and then. Indeed, even in an emerging economy like China's, the number of manufacturing workers aged 50 or older will more than double by 2025.

An ageing workforce can also create a mismatch between labour supply and demand, for example, Germany currently faces an immediate shortage of qualified engineering graduates. Experienced engineers are retiring and because engineering ceased to be an attractive career option in the late 1980s, there is a massive shortage of new recruits. In 2006 the country had a deficit of approximately 48,000 engineers and that figure is expected to grow significantly in coming years. At the same time, the country has too many unskilled workers: the unemployment rate of unskilled labour is more than six times higher than that of university graduates and many industrialised countries face similar situations.

In terms of performance management, an ageing workforce has two important HR implications, namely: organisations must ensure the transfer of the valuable knowledge that older workers possess before they retire; and second, organisations must address the issue of how to maintain efficient levels of performance among the older workers while they remain in the organisation.

As the workforce driving the knowledge economy ages, new challenges arise, particularly the risk of a significant loss of valuable knowledge as older workers retire from the workforce. Researchers and practitioners have discussed the importance of knowledge transfer to an organisation's success, and knowledge has become recognised as the most strategically significant resource of organisations. When Drucker (1993) originally alerted organisational leaders to the rise of the knowledge society, he described the radical change in the meaning of knowledge and how knowledge had assumed even greater importance than either capital or labour for nations. O'Dell and Grayson (1998: 6) referred to knowledge management as a broad concept, defining it as 'a conscious strategy of getting the right knowledge to the right people at the right time' and as a way of putting knowledge into action to improve organisational performance. How to transfer knowledge from one person to others or to the broader organisational knowledge base is a challenging aspect of the performance management process because knowledge transfer does not occur spontaneously or naturally. While it is difficult to calculate accurately the financial consequences of losing critical knowledge, the risks certainly include lost productivity, increased errors, and diminished creativity. The essential point, argues Calo (2008), is that organisational leaders need to recognise that once knowledge and expertise have left their organisation, they are difficult to recover, so difficult as to make their recovery unlikely. Knowledgeable older workers will be leaving organisations in record numbers over the coming decade, so before they leave it is imperative that organisations take steps to retain their knowledge. Calo (2008) suggests that conducting a knowledge risk assessment is one such strategy. It would involve all managers within the organisation being tasked with the responsibility of first identifying the at-risk positions, and then of developing a plan to identify a successor, of having an accelerated learning plan for the identified successor, and of facilitating the transfer of knowledge from the incumbent workers to successors. This approach would serve to emphasise the overall institutional commitment to a knowledge transfer process.

As noted above, Calo (2008) has drawn our attention to many of the concerns that have been expressed regarding the risk of the ageing workforce involved in the loss of knowledge from the retirement of the baby boomers and the potential shortage of workers to fill the gaps left by exits from the workforce. A distinct, but related, concern is highlighted here and must be addressed: how to make the best use of older workers who remain in the workforce. Today, the workforce of most organisations has a higher overall age than at any time in history. While many older workers are members of the first wave of baby boomers, the 50–54 age group is the fastest growing segment of the population, and the 45–49 age group is the second fastest growing. The concerns, then, should not be only about the imminent retirement of the first wave of the baby boomers, but that organisations will need to confront many new performance issues as a result of having a larger number of older workers on their payrolls. As Cappelli (2008) advised, managing an ageing workforce is going to be an ongoing and integral component part of an organisation's approach to performance management.

Strack *et al.* (2008) suggest that initiatives that focus on performance management of older workers can help address the implications an ageing workforce has for productivity. They advise that conducting a systematic review of current HR policies and processes could alert the organisation to possible adjustments in a variety of areas to turn age-related challenges into competitive opportunities. The most obvious involves training programmes that help older workers update their skills and leverage their performance. However, in training older workers it is important to remember that one-age-fits-all courses are not necessarily geared to the particular needs, knowledge and strengths of older workers. For example, older manufacturing employees' lack of familiarity with the internet may make typical web-based or blended training programmes unappealing to them.

Another obvious area for performance enhancement is healthcare management. On average, older employees don't become ill more often than younger employees, they just are ill for longer periods. Proactive measures, designed to prevent sickness and injury, can reduce the problem significantly. Such measures should be targeted at employees with a high risk of health problems and tailored to the jobs they do. Strack *et al.* (2008) reviewed RWE's strategy for managing older workers. RWE Power is a German electric power and natural gas public utility based in Essen and is the second largest electricity producer in Germany. Strack *et al.* report that in 2006, RWE Power found that an older workforce reduced performance in production-related job families. To counter this trend it is managing the performance of older workers through personalised work schedules in which shift lengths are tailored to employees' abilities. It is also exploring the possibility of 'lifetime working programmes,' in which employees accumulate credit for overtime hours that can be used to reduce work hours when they are older.

The performance of older workers can also be enhanced through the development of creative performance incentives. For example, Strack *et al.* (2008) suggest older workers might serve as mentors to new workers, which can increase motivation and performance.

Employees with critical knowledge might be offered the chance to return to the company and work on special projects on a freelance basis after they have retired. This latter approach has demonstrated multiple benefits: reducing capacity shortfalls in a crucial job category and keeping valuable knowledge in the company, as well as motivating employees near retirement to perform well so that they will be considered for this post-retirement opportunity.

In summary, performance management of a diverse and ageing workforce is not a passing fad. It is a pressing and competitive priority for all organisations in this era of rapid demographic and social change.

What features distinguish an ageing workforce and how, if at all, might these affect an organisation's approach to managing performance?

Managing performance in a volunteer workforce

Volunteers are the lifeblood of many non-profit organisations. Non-profit organisations have traditionally relied on volunteers to perform crucial agency functions. As staffing costs continue to rise, and as job seekers continue to look for valuable experience, non-profits will continue to rely more heavily on volunteers and other unpaid staff than do their for-profit counterparts. To put this into context, Cilenti *et al.* (2007) estimate that in the United States in 2000, adult volunteers devoted 15.5 billion hours of time to non-profit organisations throughout the nation, representing a total dollar value of $239 billion in volunteer time. Between September 2004 and September 2005, more than 65 million people did some kind of volunteer work, up from 59.8 million people in 2002.

The author of this article contends that well-managed non-profits have become expert at several crucial components of running a successful organisation, and can serve as examples to the for-profit sector. In short, non-profits often have well-defined, unwavering missions; they make wise use of their board of directors as a resource; and they seem to know a lot about managing paid employees and volunteers. Geber (1991) suggests that because volunteers often come from the ranks of the employees it is vital to give them meaningful work that suits their level of expertise. This involves matching the volunteer's skills to an available position, preparing detailed job or project descriptions to facilitate a fast, thorough orientation, giving them high-quality but streamlined on-the-job training, and providing formal performance appraisals, while also offering less formal forms of feedback and recognition. Although these approaches may not sound much different from those that should be used with any paid employee, the importance of keeping volunteers satisfied and fulfilled with their assigned work, the necessity of expediency in their orientation and training, and the significance of giving recognition to their contribution accentuate the importance of these elements.

Performance Managing Volunteers at the CIPD

The Chartered Institute of Personnel and Development (CIPD), the professional lead body for all HRM practitioners, relies extensively on the use of volunteers to maintain the branch network and to operate as directors on the National Executive Board. In June 2008, under the Executive Leadership of Robin Jordan, the CIPD developed a series of competencies required at board level for all directors. In line with best performance management practice the competencies are regularly reviewed and currently comprise:

- *Strategic direction*: the ability to contribute to setting the vision, values and purpose for CIPD, and ensure CIPD has the resources – people and financial – to achieve its goals. A person with the ability to think and plan ahead strategically.

- *Business judgement*: the ability to weigh evidence and analyse ideas before reaching an independent and objective conclusion, including an understanding of financial information at a complex business level; also the ability to assimilate information quickly and effectively.

- *Governance*: the ability to ensure that the CIPD is managed with integrity and probity, and bring those qualities and independence of mind to the role.

- *Relationships*: the ability to work supportively and build team cohesiveness with fellow board members and executive management colleagues, while at the same time, constructively probing, challenging and adding value to the strategic direction, decision making and performance of CIPD.

The unique aspect of how the CIPD manage their volunteers at director level is that each volunteer board director has a 'conversation with purpose'. This is essentially a structured performance appraisal with the Chair. Whilst acknowledging the voluntary nature of Board appointments, the principles associated with good governance suggest that this 'conversation with a purpose' involves:

- The opportunity for at least an annual meeting between the Chair and each director. (Opting out of the annual meeting is possible, except where the director indicates an intention to seek re-election.)

- The meeting is a two-way conversation, with opportunity to discuss the contribution of the director and the Chair.

- Three areas should be covered: constructive feedback; aspirations for other roles or re-election; development needs:

  (i) *Constructive feedback*
    - consider examples to illustrate contributions made and behaviours apparent;
    - demonstrates appropriate preparation, attendance and commitment;
    - provides valuable input to board meetings;
    - asks demanding questions of the executive team;
    - challenges others constructively within the board;
    - contributes to strategy and policy discussion;
    - involved in promoting the work of the CIPD outside board meetings;
    - additional inputs in relation to feedback to the Chair may include management of board agendas;
    - encouragement and participation of board members.

  (ii) *Aspirations for other roles*
    - What aspirations or potential have you considered for another role on the board or its subcommittees?
    - Are you considering a second term (if applicable)? If so how do you meet the current requirements for non-executive directors?

  (iii) *Development needs*
    - What personal development would be appropriate and how might it be achieved?
    - How might the board's development be addressed?

- A record of the meeting is held by both the director and the Chair, to be used in subsequent discussions and within the context of succession and development planning.

The 'conversations with a purpose' have aided effective performance management by clearly establishing the requirements of the role the volunteer is committing to. The conversations have the benefit of providing a formal opportunity for the volunteer board director to discuss with the Chair their performance and contribution, needs and aspirations and development plans. This serves to ensure the volunteer is aware of their role and is able to fulfil the requirements satisfactorily. In this respect Robin Jordan, the retiring Chair suggested managing volunteers is no different from managing salaried staff, there is a role to be performed and there is an expectation about the way in which it will be undertaken. He said: 'There are roles and responsibilities and volunteers have a duty to undertake the performance of their work as effectively as possible.' In the approach to managing the performance of volunteers adopted by the CIPD, the level of support available from the host organisation is the same for volunteers and their needs and career aspiration are taken just as seriously as those of paid staff.

Managing the performance of volunteers is a vital part of managing organisational performance. The innovative, creative and responsive approach adopted by the CIPD is a role model for many organisations who will increasingly rely on the contributions and effort of non-paid associates.

In summary, the following points are advised when managing volunteers:

- Understand individuals' motivations;
- Find the right fit;
- Manage the relationship with full-time staff;
- Match roles to talents;
- Implement best practices;
- Keep volunteers in the loop.

STOP and think

To what extent do you agree with Robin Jordan, the retiring Chair of the National Executive of the CIPD, that managing volunteers is the same as managing paid staff?

Conclusion

This chapter has focused on performance management. It has demonstrated how our understanding and appreciation of the difference between performance measurement and performance management has evolved over the years. It has demonstrated that despite a growing understanding of the limitations of performance appraisal, it remains one of the most widely employed approaches in the contemporary management of employees. The critique related to operational limitations – referring to manifestations such as rater bias, the recency effect and the tendency for raters to award grades in the middle of the scale to avoid overt conflict with the appraisee or to mitigate potential accusations concerning their own poor management techniques – a poor employee indicates a poor manager. The critiques also reflected the multiple and often conflicting applications to which appraisals are applied – and highlighted the inherent tensions of using essentially the same process to achieve different outcomes, for example, some are related to pay and development while others are related just to development. However, the growing awareness of possible limitations has hastened the search for alternatives, and the advent of 360-degree appraisal is possibly one such solution.

The application of technology is likely to hasten the evolution still further. The ability of organisations to undertake covert surveillance of workers by monitoring how long they take to process a particular piece of work or complete a call in a call centre leaves a hollow and cautious 'Big Brother' feel to some of the approaches to measurement techniques currently being developed. Concerns over the ethical probity of monitoring the work of employees so closely and of managers being in a position of such authenticated power left some commentators feeling rather nervous and just a little sceptical about the motivations behind performance appraisal to control human behaviour, thoughts and actions. While such fears may have some justification, there is a danger of underestimating employees' ability to influence the appraisal process and casting the manager as despot and villain – almost without trial.

Caution is needed here, because if we truly subscribe to the idea that effective HRM can lead to a genuine level of employee engagement and commitment, the desires, aims and objectives of the managers and the workers and their employment relationship ceases to be one characterised by antagonistic objectives, underpinned by adversarial and conflicting tensions and becomes one in which mutuality, trust and respect prevail. In such circumstances, any power held by the manager would be used to further consolidate the effectiveness of the working relationship – rather than jeopardise it by trying to subvert the worker or manipulate them through covert surveillance techniques. Performance appraisal does have the potential to be misused, but it also has the potential to help the development and career opportunities of many employees. In many respects it appears that the jury is still out, with the culture of the organisation perhaps being the single biggest factor to influence the direction of the path followed.

The chapter observed a trend in the extension of performance management from that concerned solely with individual employees to an approach that embraced the whole organisation. In this context, attention was drawn to the way in which organisational structures and operating boundaries are shifting, and bring new demands and a need for new ways of approaching performance management. Working across cultures and between collaborating organisations requires the effective management of knowledge and the ability to translate organisational visions into clear measurable outcomes that define success, and are shared throughout the organisation with customers and stakeholders. This emerging perspective on performance management continues the shift from prescriptive, audit- and compliance-based oversight to an ongoing, forward-looking strategic partnership. Managing the performance of older workers and the performance of volunteers were reviewed in the chapter and served to demonstrate the extent to which the management of performance will increasingly become an organisation focused rather than an individual-focused activity. For further evidence of this trend one only needs to review the press and observe the extent to which organisations are increasingly concerned with the effective management of their performance within society and within the community. The ability to demonstrate an active engagement with the corporate social responsibility agenda is growing rapidly. Perhaps therefore, in the future, performance management will be less about quantifying the output of individual employees and more about the effective performance of the organisation in society.

Summary

- There are differences between performance measurement and performance appraisal.
- Approaches to performance measurement are typically represented in a performance appraisal process.
- Performance appraisal has limitations which result in part resulting from the many competing aims it seeks to achieve.
- The ethics of probity of performance appraisal has been questioned and represented as a management tool which enables managers to monitor and engage in constant surveillance of their employees.
- Information and communication technology will change the nature and scope of performance management.

- Effective performance management will need to address changes in organisational structure and composition, in particular in relation to an increasingly global and competitive market, a diverse and ageing workforce and to manage a rising number of volunteer workers.
- In the future, performance management will be less about individual performance and more about the performance of the organisation as a world player and social partner with a conscience.

Questions

1 What are the organisational advantages and limitations of performance measurement?

2 For what reason has performance appraisal has been so severely critiqued?

3 What role do you envisage for ICT in the management of performance, are there any associated risks?

4 What are the theoretical links between HRM and performance appraisal?

5 What new challenges will organisations face in managing performance in the years to come?

6 What factors would you take into account if you were designing an approach to performance management?

Case study

Performance-based reward at DIY Stores

DIY Stores (DIYS) is a chain of large warehouse-style stores selling DIY equipment, self assembly furniture, plumbing appliances and garden tools. It is a wholly-owned subsidiary of a larger retail group and is ranked in the top five in terms of its UK market share. Its annual turnover exceeds £50 million and its annual profits are around £1million. DIYS currently runs 250 stores across the country, serves over a million customers a week and employs 12,000 people.

In response to a slight fall in market share over the past year, the board of directors has recently produced a new company mission statement. High on the list of core aims for the coming two years is the desire to substantially improve efficiency and performance levels. Ambitious targets have been set, and statements issued about the need to create a more dynamic, performance-focused corporate culture. Reform of the existing approach to performance management in DIYS is now very much on the agenda.

The present approach is well established and clearly understood by all DIYS employees. It is distinguished by the emphasis it places on the role of the store manager (i.e. the general managers responsible for running each of the 250 stores). Store managers are rewarded with a standard package of terms and conditions which is noticeably more generous than that offered to other managers and staff. In addition to the basic salary they enjoy a range of benefits (including private health care and additional holiday), the right to purchase share options and substantial discounts on products sold by DIYS and its parent company. In addition, they each receive an annual, individual, performance-related pay (PRP) award dependent on the extent to which their stores meet pre-agreed targets.

Performance objectives are all specific and measurable, being made up of targets in five categories:

- target increase in total store takings (e.g. 5% over the year)
- target reduction in stock loss (e.g. 7% over the year)
- target increase in average spend per customer (e.g. £3.00)
- target improvement in product availability (e.g. to 97%)
- target increase in customer care (e.g. by 10%).

This last measure is determined by the scores awarded to each store by 'mystery shoppers' employed by the company to visit stores incognito.

Other members of staff, including managers below store manager level, receive a considerably less generous reward package and no performance-based reward. Managers are expected to raise performance levels and achieve their targets through effective supervision, 'pats on the back' and, where necessary, the application of disciplinary measures. For senior staff, the expectation of promotion into a store manager role has for long been used as the main method of motivation.

A number of criticisms have been made of existing performance management arrangements. The most important are:

1 Managers working below store manager level can improve their financial position only through promotion. Those who are performing very effectively in their present roles and have no interest in promotion are not properly rewarded for their efforts. This leads to dissatisfaction and avoidable staff turnover. There is also a failure to maximise performance among this group.

2 Store managers are limited in the range of performance-management techniques available to them to apply within their stores. No financial incentives can be given, beyond a few pounds in the form of 'employee of the month' prizes and small gifts at Christmas. This means that managers have to rely on close supervision and the use of disciplinary approaches in order to achieve their targets. The result is de-motivated staff, high employee turnover and a low-trust employee relations culture.

3 Store managers themselves, because of the way the PRP system works, are encouraged to focus wholly on the performance of their own stores. Overall corporate performance is of less interest to them, as is the performance of their regional divisions. Indeed, there is huge competition between store managers in each locality, leading to situations in which they fail to co-operate with one another. Ideas are rarely shared and there is resistance to transferring staff from one store to another to cover sickness and holidays. More damaging is the tendency to hold on to stock, even when other stores have run short due to unexpected high demand.

Source: from CIPD case study site, with the permission of the publisher, the Chartered Institute of Personnel and Development, London (www.cipd.co.uk).

Your task

What changes would you suggest should be made to the established performance management and reward procedures? How would you justify the changes you have recommended if asked to do so at a presentation to the board of directors?

References and further reading

Adair, C., Simpson, L., Birdsell, J., Omelchuk, K., Casebeer, A., Gardiner, H., Newman, S., Beckjie, A. and Clelland, S. (2003) *Performance Measurement Systems in Health Care Services: Models, Practices and Effectiveness*. Alberta: The Alberta Heritage Foundation for Medical Research.

Amaratunga, D. and Baldry, D. (2002) 'Moving from performance measurement to performance management', *Facilities*, 20: 217–23.

Armstrong, M. and Baron, A. (1998) *Performance Management: The New Realistic*. London: IPD.

Armstrong, M. and Baron, A. (2004) *Managing Performance: Performance Management in Action*. London: CIPD.

Armstrong, M. and Baron, A. (2005) *Managing Performance: Performance Management in Action* London: CIPD.

Aswathappa, K. (2005) *Human Resource and Personal Management: Text and Cases*, 4th edn. Delhi: Tata McGraw-Hill.

Bach, S. (2005) *Managing Human Resources: Personnel Management in Transition*, 4th edn. Oxford: Blackwell.

Bentham, J. (1995) *The Panopticon Writings*, (ed. M Bozovic). London: Verso.

Bititci, U., Martinez, V., Albores, P. and Parung, J. (2004) 'Creating and maintaining value in collaborative networks', *International Journal of Physical Distribution and Logistics Management*, 34: 251–68.

Björkman, I. and Budhwar, P. (2007) 'When in Rome ...?', *Employee Relations*, 29: 595–610.

Boselie, P., Dietz, G. and Boon, C. (2005) 'Commonalities and contradictions in HRM and performance research', *Human Resource Management Journal*, 15: 67–94.

Boselie, P., Paauwe, J. and Jansen, P. (2001) 'Human resource management and performance: lessons from the Netherlands', *International Journal of Human Resource Management*, 12: 1107–25.

Boxall, P. and Purcell, J. (2008) *Strategy and Human Resource Management*. Basingstoke: Palgrave Macmillan.

Bourgon, J. (2008) 'Performance management: it's the results that count', *Asian Pacific Journal of Public Administration*, 30, 1: 41–58.

Budhwar, P., Varma, A., Singh, V. and Dhar, R. (2006) 'HRM systems of Indian call centers in India: an exploratory study', *International Journal of Human Resource Management*, 17, 5: 881–97.

Burgess, T., Gules, H. and Tekin, M. (1997) 'Supply chain collaboration and success in technology implementation', *Integrated Manufacturing Systems*, 8: 323–32.

Busi, M. and Bititci, U. (2006) 'Collaborative performance management: present gaps and future research', *International Journal of Productivity and Performance Management*, 55: 7–25.

Callahan, K. (2007) *Elements of Effective Governance: Measurement, Accountability and Participation* New York: CRC Press: Taylor Francis.

Calo, T. (2008). 'Talent management in the era of the aging workforce: the critical role of knowledge transfer', *Public Personnel Management*, 37, 4: 403–41.

Cappelli, R. (2008) 'Talent management for the twenty-first century', *Harvard Business Review*, 86: 74–81

Chand, M. and Katou, A. (2007) 'Human resource management: organisational performance; Hotel and Catering Industry, India', *Employee Relations*, 29: 576–94.

Cilenti, M., Guggenheimer, E. and Kramnick, R. (2007) *The Volunteer Workforce: Legal Issues and Best Practices for Nonprofits*. New York: Lawyers Alliance for New York.

CIPD (2009a) *Fact Sheet on Performance Appraisal*. Wimbledon: CIPD.

CIPD (2009b) *Fact Sheet on Performance Management*. Wimbledon: CIPD.

Den-Hartog, D., Boselie, P. and Paauwe, J. (2004) 'Performance management: a model and research agenda', *Applied Psychology: An International Review*, 53: 556–69.

DeNisi, A. (ed.) (2000) *Performance Appraisal and Performance Management: A Multilevel Analysis*. San Francisco, CA: Jossey-Bass.

Drucker, P. (1999) *The Practice of Management*, Oxford: Butterworth-Heinemann.

Drucker, R. (1993) 'The rise of the knowledge society', *Wilson Quarterly*, 17: 52–69.

Eccles, R. (1991) 'The performance measurement manifesto', *Harvard Business Review*, 69, 1: 131–37.

Edwards, P. and Wright, M. (2001) High-involvement work systems and performance outcomes: the strength of variable, contingent and context-bound relationships', *International Journal of Human Resource Management*, 12, 4: 568–85

Fawcett, S. and Magnan, G. (2002) 'The rhetoric and reality of supply chain integration', *International Journal of Physical Distribution and Logistics Management*, 32: 339–61.

Ferris, G., Arthur, M., Berkson, H., Kaplan, D., Harell-Cook, G. and Frink, D. (1998) 'Toward a social context theory of the human resource management–organization effectiveness relationship', *Human Resource Management Review*, 8: 235–64.

Findlay, P. and Newton, T. (1998) 'Re-framing Foucault: the case of performance appraisal', in P. Findlay and T. Newton (eds) *Foucault, Management and Organization Theory*. London: Sage.

Fletcher, C, (2001) 'Performance appraisal and management: the developing research agenda', *Journal of Occupational and Organisational Psychology*, 74: 473–88.

Foucault, M. (1977) *Discipline & Punish: The Birth of the Prison*. London: Penguin Books.

Geber, B. (1991) 'Managing Volunteers', *Training*, 28: 21–26.

Geddes, D. and Konrad, A. (2003) 'Demographic differences and reactions to performance feedback', *Human Relations*, 56: 1485–514.

Grey, C. (1994) 'Career as a project of the self and labour process discipline', *Sociology*, 28: 479–97.

Guest, D. (1997) 'Human resource management and performance: a review and research agenda', *Journal of Human Resource Management*, 8: 263–76.

Guest, D. (2000) 'Human resource management, employee well-being and organizational performance', in D. Guest (ed.) *CIPD Professional Standards Conference 11th July*. Keelle: Keele University.

Hall, L. (2004) 'HRM practices and employee and organizational performance: a critique of the research and guest's model', Department of Business and Management discussion paper No. 5. Manchester: Manchester Metropolitan University.

Harris, C. Cortvriend, P. and Hyde, P. (2007) 'Human resource management and performance in healthcare organizations', *Journal of Health and Organization Management*, 21: 448–59.

Heslin, P. Carson, J. and VandeWalle, D. (2009) 'Practical applications of goal setting theory to performance management', in J.W. Smither *Performance Management: Putting Research into Practice*. San Francisco, CA: Jossey Bass, pp. 89–114.

Holmberg, S. (2000) 'A system perspective on supply chain management', *International Journal of Physical Distribution and Logistics Management*, 30: 847–68.

Huselid, M. (1995) 'The impact of human resource management practices on turnover, productivity and corporate financial performance. *Academy of Management Journal*, 38: 635–70.

Hyde, P., Boaden, R. Cortvriend, P. Harris, C., Marchington, M., Sparrow, P. and Sibbald, B. (2006) *Improving Health Through Human Resource Management*. London: CIPD.

Industrial RS (2003a) 'Time to talk – how and why employers conduct appraisals', *Employment Trends*, 769: 8–14.

Johnson, H. and Kaplan, R. (1987) *Relevance Lost: The Rise and Fall of Management Accounting*. Boston, MA: Harvard Business School Press.

Kaplan, R. and Norton, D. (1992) 'The balanced scorecard – measures that drive performance', *Harvard Business Review*, 70, 1: 79–80.

Kaplan, R. and Norton, D. (1996) 'Using the balanced scorecard as a strategic management system', *Harvard Business Review*, January/February: 75–85.

Katou, A. and Budhwar, P. (2006) 'Human resource management systems and organisational performance: a test of a mediating model in the Greek manufacturing context', *The International Journal of Human Resource Management*, 17: 1223–53.

Katou, A. and Budhwar, P. (2007) 'The effect of human resource management policies on organizational performance in Greek manufacturing firms', *Thunderbird International Business Review*, 49: 1–35.

Kellough, J. and Naff, K. (2004) 'Responding to a wake-up call: an examination of Federal Agency diversity management programs', *Administration & Society*, 36: 62–90.

Kersley, B., Alpin, C., Bewley, H., Dix, G. and Oxenbridge, S. (2006) *Inside the Workplace: Findings from the 2004 Workplace Employment Relations Survey*. London: Routledge.

Latham, G. and Locke, E. (1984) *Goal Setting: A Motivational Technique that Works*. Englewood Cliffs, NJ: Prentice-Hall.

Legge, K. (1995) *Human Resource Management Rhetorics and Realities*. Basingstoke Macmillan.

Lewis, G. Smithey, P. (1998) 'Gender, race, and training in the Federal Civil Service', *Public Administration Quarterly*, 22: 204–08.

Locke, E. (1966) 'The relationship of intentions to level of performance' *Journal of Applied Psychology*, 50: 60–88.

Locke, E. and Latham, G. (1990) 'Work motivation and satisfaction: light at the end of the tunnel', *Psychological Science*, 1: 240–6.

Locke, E. and Latham, G. (2002) 'Building a practically useful theory of goal setting and task motivation: a 35-year odyssey', *American Psychologist*, 57: 705–17.

Longenecker, C. and Fink, L. (1997) 'Keys to designing and running an effective performance appraisal system: lessons learned', *Journal of Compensation and Benefits*, 13: 28–35.

Longnecker, C. and Fink, L. (2001) 'Improving management performance in rapidly changing organisations', *Journal of Management Development*, 20, 1: 7–18.

Longnecker, C. Simonetti, J. and Sharkey, T. (1999) 'Why organizations fail: the view from the front line', *Management Decision*, 15: 503–13.

Lynch, R. and Cross, K. (1991) *Measure Up! Yardstick for Continuous Improvement*. Cambridge, MA: Blackwell Business.

MacDuffie, J. (1995) 'Human resource bundles and manufacturing performance: flexible production systems in the world auto industry', *Industrial Relations and Labour Review*, 48: 197–221.

McGregor, D. (1957) 'An uneasy look at performance appraisals', *Harvard Business Review*, 5: 89–95.

Miller, P. and Rose, N. (1990) 'Governing economic life', *Economy and Society*, 19: 1–31.

Mondy, R., Noe, R. and Premeaux, S. (2002) *Human Resource Management*, 8th edn. Upper Saddle River, NJ: Prentice-Hall.

Naff, K. and Kellough, E. (2003) 'Ensuring employment equity: are federal programs making a difference?', *International Journal of Public Administration*, 26: 1307–36.

Neary, D.B. (2002) 'Creating a company-wide, on-line, performance management system', *Human Resource Management*, 41: 491–98.

Newbold, C. (2008) '360-degree appraisals are now a classic', *Human Resource Management International Digest*, 16: 38–40.

Newton, T. and Findley, P. (1996) 'Playing God: the performance of appraisal', *Human Resource Management Journal*, 6: 42–58.

Newton, T. (1994) 'Discourse and agency: the example of personnel psychology and assessment centers', *Organization Studies*, 15: 879–902.

O'Dell, C. and Grayson, C. (1998) *If Only We Knew What We Know*. New York: Free Press.

Patterson, K., Grimm, C. and Thomas, M. (2003) 'Adopting new technologies for supply chain management', *Transportation Research Part E*, 39: 95–121.

Patterson, M., West, M., Lawthom, R. and Nickell, S. (1997) *The Impact of People Management on Business Performance*. London: IPD.

Pitts, D. (2005) 'Diversity, representation, and performance: evidence about race and ethnicity in public organizations', *Journal of Public Administration Research and Theory*, 15: 615–31.

Pitts, D. (2009) 'Diversity management, job satisfaction, and performance: evidence from U.S. federal agencies', *Public Administration Review*, 69: 328–39.

Pitts, D. and Wise, L. (2004) 'Diversity in professional schools: a case study of public affairs and law', *Journal of Public Affairs Education*, 10: 142–60.

Procurement Executives Association (1999) *Guide to a Balanced Scorecard Performance Management Methodology*. Procurement Executives' Association. Available at **http://management. energy.gov/documents/BalancedScorecardsPerfAndMeth.pdf**.

Purcell, J. 'Sustaining the HR and performance link in difficult times', University of Bath. **http://www.bath.ac.uk/werc/ pdf/toughCIPD_8_02.pdf**, accessed 3 June 2009.

Richardson, R. and Thompson, M. (1999) 'The impact of people management practices on business performance: a literature review', in CIPD *Issues in People Management*. London: CIPD.

Roberts, I. (2001) 'Reward and performance management', in I. Beardwell and L. Holden (eds) *Human Resource Management: A Contemporary Approach*, Harlow: FT/Prentice-Hall, pp 506–58.

Schuler, R. and Jackson, S. (1987) 'Linking competitive strategies with human resource management practices', *Academy of Management Executive*, 1: 207–19.

Schuler, R. and Jackson, S. (1999) *Strategic Human Resource Management: A Reader*. London: Blackwell.

Sipor, J. and Ward, B. (1995) 'The ethical and legal quandary of email privacy', *Communications of the Association for Computing Machinery*, 38: 8–54.

Stanton, J. (2000) 'Reactions to employee performance monitoring: framework, review and research directions', *Human Performance*, 13, 1: 85–113.

Strack, R., Baier, J. and Fahlander, A. (2008) 'Managing demographic risk', *Harvard Business Review*, 86: 119–28.

Taylor, F. (1911) *The Principles of Scientific Management*. New York, NY: W.W. Norton. Published in Norton Library 1967 by arrangement with Harper & Row, Publishers, Inc.

Thornton III G. and Rupp, D. (2007) *Assessment Centers in Human Resource Management: Strategies for Prediction, Diagnosis and Development*. London: Taylor & Francis.

Thorpe, R. (2004) 'The characteristics of performance management research, implication and challenges', *International Journal of Productivity and Performance Management*, 53: 334–44.

Townley, B. (1993a) 'Foucault, power/knowledge and its relevance for HRM', *Academy of Management Review*, 18: 518–45.

Townley, B. (1993b) 'Performance appraisal and the emergence of management', *Journal of Management Studies*, 36: 287–306.

Townley, B. (1994) *Reframing Human Resources Management: Power, Ethics and the Subject at Work*. London: Sage.

Townley, B. (1997) 'The institutional logic of performance appraisal', *Organization Studies* 18: 261–85.

Tschirhart, M. and Wise, L. (2002) 'Responding to a diverse class: insights from seeing a course as an organization', *Journal of Public Affairs Education*, 8: 165–77.

Waggoner, D., Neely, A. and Kennerley, M. (1999) 'The forces that shape organizational performance measurement systems: an interdisciplinary review', *International Journal of Production Economics*, 60: 53–60.

Wilson, F. (2002) 'Dilemmas of appraisal', *European Management Journal*, 20: 620–29.

Wise, L. and Tschirhart, M. (2000) 'Examining empirical evidence on diversity effects: how useful is diversity research for public sector managers?', *Public Administration Review*, 60: 286–395.

For multiple-choice questions, exercises and annotated weblinks related to this topic, visit **www.pearsoned.co.uk/mymanagementlab**.

## Chapter 9

Employee reward

Amanda Thompson and Alan J. Ryan

Objectives

- To present the historical and theoretical foundations underpinning contemporary employee reward practice.
- To define employee reward and identify the key components of reward.
- To explore the concept of reward management and the benefits and difficulties associated with introducing a strategic approach to reward.
- To consider key employee reward choices facing organisations.
- To explore the economic and legal context for reward and the implications for employee reward practice.
- To identify the internal/organisational factors affecting organisational approaches to reward and the influence of sector.
- To consider key choices and emergent trends in terms of establishing pay levels, designing pay structures and determining criteria for pay progression.

Introduction

This chapter identifies and discusses developments in employee reward and considers the practical ways in which reward management can be used, as part of a suite of human resource practices, to elicit employee engagement and drive individual and organisational performance. The chapter traces the historical path of reward, focusing initially on the nature of the wage–effort bargain and previous, somewhat limited approaches to reward, revolving principally around the key construct of pay. The chapter then moves to identify and explore the meaning of reward in the contemporary setting, focusing upon reward as a potential strategic lever which can be used by organisations to orient individuals and teams in the direction of business goals and values. The overarching themes of the remainder of the chapter concern the economic and legal environment for reward and the challenges associated with designing a reward strategy that is affordable, equitable and relevant. Embedded within these themes, emphasis is placed on pragmatic reward choices and dilemmas experienced by organisations in the twenty-first century, including decisions about the relative importance of internal equity and external pay comparability, the role of job evaluation, the factors which tend to be influential in shaping the reward 'mix', where to pitch pay and how to design pay structures and manage pay progression.

The historical and theoretical foundations of employee reward

We now outline and examine the extent to which human resource management (HRM) has developed current practical and theoretical issues surrounding the management of reward systems within modern organisations. A critical element of these discussions is the management of structures and strategies. This chapter introduces the notion of reward(s) as a central function in the development of a strategic role for HR functionaries and offers some explanation of the objectives of current reward management structures, strategies and systems.

'There's only one reason we come here – the money' has not been an unusual comment heard from employees in all organisations since the period of industrialisation. Such comments echo the nature of the employment relationship as a reward/effort bargain. Whether openly, covertly, personally or collectively, we all become involved in the resolution of this bargain at some time during our working life. This chapter discusses how management have resolved and continue to resolve their problem of converting the labour potential, obtained by their transactions in the labour market, into the labour performance they desire; simply securing the required effort levels without rewarding at levels detrimental to the generation of sufficient profit. In this sense we view reward as a core function for HR managers and rewards as composed of more than the mere 'notes' in the pay packet. Terms such as 'pay', 'compensation' and 'remuneration' are all recognisable expressions, but as we argue below 'reward' is something qualitatively different in that the issues covered encompass both financial and non-financial benefits.

The development of reward systems

As a distinctive concern for managerial functionaries, the topic of reward is a recent addition, indeed it is fair to say that reward management has often been viewed as the 'poor relation'. Within the early labour management literature, it was discussed in terms of the management of figures and procedures (Urwick, 1958; Yates, 1937). Such discussions clearly view 'reward' as solely a matter of financial benefits (wage/effort) rather than including consideration of the non-financial benefits. We can argue from this initial analysis that during the development of a 'factory-based' system, in the late nineteenth/early twentieth centuries, it appears wage, rather than effort, was the central concern. Further that this period was accompanied by a system within which owners frequently found difficulty in securing consistent levels of control of the effort side of the bargain (Hinton, 1986; Lovell, 1977; Zeitlin, 1983). Employees, who were until that time self-controlled and in many respects driven by subsistence needs, had worked in small 'cottage' industries within which the product of labour was owned by the producers (workers themselves; notably in regard to the skilled artisans) and they worked only as hard as necessary in order to meet their subsistence needs. As Anthony suggests, 'A great deal of the ideology of work is directed at getting men [sic] to take work seriously when they know that it is a joke' (1977: 5).

Owners found that getting workers to keep regular hours and to commit the effort owners considered to constitute 'a fair day's work' was problematic. In response to this dilemma they employed the 'butty' system of wage management. Under this system, owners committed a specific level of investment to a selected group of workers (normally skilled artisans) who then hired labour on 'spot contracts' by the day. The major problem for the owners with this system was that these 'subcontractors' had control over the effort/reward bargain and were able to enrich themselves at the expense of the owners. The owners enjoyed little or no control over the process of production so the system was economically inefficient and failed to deliver the returns (rents/profits) required or more importantly the returns that were possible from the process of industrialisation.

From this group of 'favoured' workers, along with the introduction of some university graduates there grew a new management cadre. This was a slow process, Gospel notes that generally, in UK industry, this group (management, technical and clerical) amounted to only 8.6 per cent of the workforce in most manufacturing organisations by the start of the First World War (1992: 17). It can be further argued that even within these organisations the development of a dedicated, specialised managerial function was uneven and patchy. These changes did little to address the problems associated with the wage/effort bargain, meaning productivity was below optimum levels. A key component in these problems was that they were underpinned by the actuality that 'the managers' brain was still under the workers' cap', or more precisely that these new managers rarely possessed the skills or knowledge of the production process held by the workers. This led to lower than optimum levels of production and reduced profits, a system F.W. Taylor described as 'systematic soldiering'. This activity was engaged in by workers, according to Taylor, 'with the deliberate object of keeping their employers ignorant of how fast work can be done' (Taylor, 1964: 74). From his observations Taylor took the view that workers acting in this manner were merely behaving as 'economically rational actors' desiring their own best interests. It was clear therefore that management needed to take the reins of the production process and reclaim their right to determine the outcome of the wage/effort bargain.

Taylor, as the so-called 'father of scientific management', developed a system of measuring work, which assisted the process of reclaiming managerial rights. Jobs were broken down into specific elements which could then be timed and rated, whilst in the process, returning the determination of the speed of work to management and allowing for the development of pay systems which reflected, however crudely, performance. This scientific system devised by Taylor became the basis of countless pay systems operating effectively alongside the routinisation and deskilling of work which is often associated with scientific management within the literature (see, for example, Braverman, 1974; Burawoy, 1985; Hill, 1981; Littler, 1982, 1985; Thompson, 1983; Wood, 1982). Whilst this allowed management to reassert their control over the level of outputs, to relocate the managers' brain under their own hats and hence the determination of the wage/effort bargain, it did generate problems in relation to managerial attempts to convince workers to take work seriously. In straightforward terms we can suggest that the 'measured-work' techniques advocated by adherents of Taylorism further separated conception from execution and led to feelings of alienation. Alienation can be defined as 'various social or psychological evils which are characterized by a harmful separation, disruption or fragmentation which sunders things that properly belong together' (Wood, 2000: 24); in our terms that means the separation of workers from that which they produce. Blauner (1964) argued that such an objective state is created as an offshoot of the subjective feelings of separation which workers experience under modern production systems. These feelings and their outcomes can be briefly outlined in the following manner:

- *Powerlessness*: the inability to exert control over work processes.
- *Meaninglessness*: the lack of a sense of purpose as employees only concentrated on a narrowly defined and repetitive task and therefore could not relate their role to the overall production process and end product.
- *'Self-estrangement'*: the failure to become involved in work as a mode of self-expression.
- *Isolation*: the lack of sense of belonging (adapted from Blauner, 1964).

Although scientific management originated at the beginning of the twentieth century, its legacy has lived on in many areas. Similar experiences have been reported in the design of work in service industries and call centres (Ritzer, 1997, 2000; Taylor and Bain, 1999; Taylor and Bain, 2001; Callaghan and Thompson, 2001). The solution to this problem has been sought, following Taylor's notion of man as an economic actor, by the introduction of various reward systems and mechanisms, the core objectives of which were originally to operationalise effective control over the wage/effort bargain and later with current systems to alleviate the feelings of alienation and generate commitment to organisational goals.

In this regard it is possible to argue that such reward systems are not designed in the 'perfect world' that some commentators have imagined. Rather they are controlled by various external and internal stimuli and operate within a complex landscape. These incentives or pressures can be broken down and identified in simple terms which highlight some of the more complex debates we address within this chapter. In no particular order, we can see that they include the ability of the organisation to pay, which in the current times of financial restraint and turbulence is greatly reduced. To this we can add the bargaining strength – both internally and more widely – of trades unions. Whilst the decline in trade union membership alongside the rise in non-union forms of representation (Dundon and Rollinson, 2004; Gollan 2007), and the increased importance of small firms (Marlow *et al.*, 2005) especially within the private sector, may have weakened such power there are still sectors within the economy where organisations have to make a judgement about the residual power available to trade unions. Such residual power is also a dynamic force behind moves to maintain differentials in line with existing custom and practice. A further element in this consideration is the wider increase in the 'cost of living' which places strains on both the employer and the employees. This is not ameliorated by the recent period of rapid technological change which has influenced labour markets and available skills patterns. Whilst organisational and technological change may have increased productivity, and hence arguably created increased profits, employers must decide what percentage of such increases can be used to develop wage systems which reflect current effort (see the discussion below on new pay). These pressures have been crystallised into three main features which affect the quantity given:

- labour market pressures – supply and demand;
- product markets – competition and demand;
- organisational factors – sector, technology and size (Milkovitch and Newman, 1996).

These consideration lead to a discussion of the extent to which employers can develop, design, and control reward systems in an ever-changing (some would say globalised) economy.

Design and debates

Whilst this chapter often discusses reward systems in a manner which appears to offer a chronological explanation, we would note that the development of a 'new' system does not indicate the total removal of other older mechanisms. Evidence suggests that in many modern organisations we continue to find both 'old' and 'new' pay systems operating in tandem, delivering control on different levels for various groups of workers (Armstrong and Brown, 2006; Armstrong and Stephens, 2005).

In terms of the types of reward mechanism applied, we can note the application of a number of different mechanisms based on 'time worked'. Time rates are mechanisms whereby reward is related to the number of hours worked and are often applied to manual workers in the form of hourly rates and non-manual workers by the application of monthly or annual salaries. In the past, these rates were set in a number of ways which relied on the power of employers to unilaterally lay down the appropriate amount, by statutory enactment, or by collective bargaining. Employer discretion has been limited in a number of ways by the introduction of statutory rules and regulations ranging from the Truck Acts, enacted in the mid nineteenth century which required payment in cash – an attempt to prevent the misuse by employers of 'factory shop vouchers' – to the 1891 Fair Wages Resolution which obliged employers on local or national government projects to pay the standard/recognised rate for a job. Both of these measures, along with the Wage Councils, which were first established in 1909, were modified or repealed in the 1980s – with the Agricultural Wages Board, due in part to employer support, being the only survivor. More recently the government has put in place the National Minimum Wage Act (1999) which sets hourly rates across the whole economy for various groups of workers – primarily manual workers. These rates were set following meetings of the Low Pay Commission and graduated according to the age of the worker concerned.

A criticism of time-based mechanisms is that they are often related to historic rather than current value, and can result in discrimination, demarcation disputes and a sense of injustice. Such time-related mechanisms are often based on the notion of a pay hierarchy in which groups of jobs/skills are banded. Although widely applied basic versions of these instruments are poor in terms of relating wage to current effort; often rewarding effort which has been applied externally (gaining a recognised skill) and is inappropriate to current tasks. The advantages of these systems are that management can control wage costs by

(a) limiting the access to various grades in the hierarchy;

(b) by limiting the range of the grade (say 4 per cent top to bottom); and

(c) demonstrating they are fair in relation to agreed procedures.

The problems created are not necessarily with the pay hierarchy system per se but with the manner in which skills relating to specific grades are defined; solutions must then address the structure, strategy and rationale of the reward system rather than the application of such mechanisms.

Bowey and Lupton (1973) developed a scheme for highlighting the manner in which such hierarchies are built and sustained. They argued that five factors are in play when selecting, deciding the location of each job within the hierarchy. These were:

- skill;
- responsibility;
- mental effort;
- physical effort; and
- working conditions (Bowey and Lupton 1973).

Using these factors it is possible to identify similarities between jobs rather, than is the case with standard job evaluation schemes, differences. Following the identification of these similarities it is possible to locate various jobs within the pay hierarchy. What is more difficult is to translate this identification into a pay structure due to the various allocation or availability of the elements which make up an individual pay packet. Most conspicuous are the differences in the elements which are included in the individual pay packet at each level. So, for example, elements such as overtime, shift premium, individual bonus payments and other special allowances, lead to increased earnings for some groups but not others. It is possible, in part, to explain the gender differences in earnings by reference to these elements. Hellerstein and Newmark (2006) argue that the difference in directly observable reward maybe be founded on either productivity differences or pure (taste-based) discrimination. In adopting this residual wage approach to wage discrimination they suggest it is possible to estimate the true level of taste-based wage difference – whether looking at ethnicity, gender, age, disability or other forms of discrimination. (See discussion on equal pay below.)

Conboy (1976) noted that the key advantage of these time-based instruments is that both parties have a clear idea of the 'wage' element of the bargain. For management the problem is that these mechanisms do not give any clear indication of the 'effort' element of the bargain. This has led to time rate instruments being complicated by the addition of 'performance' elements, often in the form of 'piece-rates' or other complex 'bonus' calculations in an attempt to determine acceptable effort levels (e.g. predetermined motion time systems and measured-day-work). The traditional form of such schemes can be demonstrated using the diagram shown in Figure 9.1.

Figure 9.1 The traditional form of time rate instruments

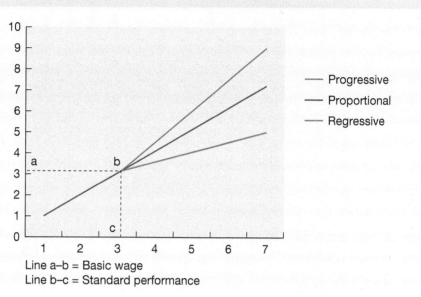

Line a–b = Basic wage
Line b–c = Standard performance

Many schemes give guaranteed basic earnings which are then supplemented in ways which we can class as proportional (wages increase in direct relationship to output), progressive (wages increase more than output) or regressive (wages increase at a slower rate than output).

An important element in this discussion regards the manner in which the 'base' element is decided. We have become familiar with the notion of a National Minimum Wage, which sets the minimum rate for specified groups; outwith this scheme, organisations need some mechanisms by which to assign values to various roles within the organisation. Traditional mechanisms (and in a slightly modified manner 'new pay' systems) have related to hierarchy calculations or simplistic forms of job evaluation scheme. A job evaluation scheme operates by allocating values to each of a series of elements (e.g. skill or responsibility) and then measuring each 'job' in order to arrive at an agreed 'score'. The scores are then placed on the pay spine in relation to accepted criteria. These criteria will be formed by the interaction of two sets of relativities. Scores will need to reflect 'external relativities', by which we mean the situation that appears to hold in relation to external markets and environmental conditions, and 'internal relativities', meaning an appearance of fairness in relation to other jobs/roles within the organisation. In the basic form, these schemes introduce us to the notion of reward packages under which different elements can be rewarded in various ways. However, these schemes fell out of favour in some respects because they are seen to 'pay-the-job' rather than 'pay-the-worker', and as such were difficult to relate to individual performance (see the discussion below).

Time-based pay is clearly the simplest form of wage payment system, easily understood by both parties; it allows the development of 'overtime' payments for work completed in addition to the contracted hours in any given period and formed the basis of the creation of systems classed as payment by results (PBR). Early PBR schemes were time based in that they used the time accumulated by the pace of work as a percentage of the time allowed to form a foundation for the calculation of performance payments. So, in a simple form, if a task is timed to take 8 minutes but is completed in 6 then there is a saving of 25 per cent, but the increase in performance is 33⅓ per cent in that if the job is completed in 6 minutes then the 2 minutes left is equal to a third of the new job time. From the employers point of view therefore paying a 25 per cent bonus leaves a surplus per piece of 8⅓ per cent. This adds to the perceived advantages of this style of PBR linked to hierarchical reward systems by providing increased worker effort because they see the resultant higher pay within weeks and higher output.

During the twentieth century such structures/systems were widely used within British industry in an attempt to increase productivity. However, they are associated with a number of detrimental effects and disadvantages. Often the rates were negotiated following a work-measurement exercise which led to discontent and disillusionment. Too often operators can find easy ways around the rate in order to secure high earnings without the expected higher performance; these routes around the scheme often resulted in a reduced level of quality – in part because workers felt under pressure to produce and in part because quality and speed do not always combine. Further, by leaving the production levels in the hands of the workers it undermines managerial attempts to secure control and, indeed, may even be said to have resulted in both a loss of managerial prerogative and the abrogation of managerial roles. As these rates were often set within tightly defined employer/trade union collective agreements they encouraged the increased – notably during the 1950s–1970s – of local shop agreements which resulted in considerable 'wage drift' during a period of economic restraint. Many of these problems are to some extent mirrored in the bonus schemes within the financial sector in the twenty-first century.

We can conclude then that such payment by results systems, whilst originally crude, developed alongside the more extensive division of labour achieved by the increasing use and application of technology, ergonomics (pseudo-scientific work measurement) and mechanical production methods. These early techniques can be easily applied to such divided work because of four basic characteristics of such work:

- short job cycles;
- high manual content (which, using sophisticated ergonomic processes, can be measured);
- batch production (with repeated orders/processes);
- no marked fluctuations in required outputs (adapted from Conboy, 1976).

The simplistic assumptions underlying these and other PBR systems are twofold. First, workers are motivated to increase performance (work harder) by money, and second, any increases in output will result in equivalent increases in wages. The schemes are intended to be self-financing and designed to reduce 'wasteful activity' in that they can be used to redesign the labour process. Whilst such schemes now enjoy less popularity than they have in previous decades, there is still evidence that they are used in relation to specific groups of workers.

Hierarchy schemes in general continue to find favour especially amongst salaried staff. A key element of such schemes is the practice of incremental progression. Such schemes operate on the simple premise that advancing years of service result in additional reward because of loyalty or greater experience. Whilst they have recently been challenged – on the basis that they discriminate on the grounds of age – they continue to form a foundation for the solution of the labour problem for many organisations.

To what extent do you think the solutions to the labour problem suggested so far reflect management's inability to clearly determine the 'effort' side of the bargain?

Having set out the basic framework within which the wage/effort bargain can be viewed, we now move on to consider developments that are more recent. In the discussion that follows we move from an analysis of solutions to the labour problem founded on the cash nexus to a series of arguments which indicate more complex and considered solutions.

Employee reward

The subject of reward is vast and continually evolving, in short it has been described as a 'bundle of returns offered in exchange for a cluster of employee contributions' (Bloom and Milkovich, 1996: 25). This is a rather loose definition and sheds little light on what form 'returns' might take or what contribution employees might make to reap such returns. Usefully, the definition does, however, capture the multiplicity of returns and possible employee contributions, suggesting that reward comprises a blend of offerings and that employees' contributions can be numerous and eclectic.

The notion of a *range* of different forms of return in exchange for employee contributions of various types signals a departure from a narrow focus upon wages and effort. Wages or monetary return for the effort expended by employees, as charted in the opening part of this chapter, remain central to the employment relationship; however, the advent of the concept of reward, and more pointedly reward management, prompts organisations to consider the differing ways in which employees positively impact the organisation via a range of contributions (not restricted to effort) and how best to signify organisational appreciation. The practice of reward veers away from a single dimensional focus on wages and instead encompasses a plethora of financial and non-financial returns employees might potentially receive in exchange for favourable contributions to the organisation. In terms of employee contributions to the organisation, effort becomes but one input amongst many potential offerings, indeed its value to the organisation may well be considered less important and less attractive than other employee behaviours, for example, measureable *outcome-related* contributions. It is clear thus that reward is a more inclusive term than wages or payment and that it is used to denote a diverse range of devices at the organisation's disposal to recognise the role individuals and teams play in the operation of, and ultimate success of the business. Reward steps beyond the perimeters of compensation, remuneration and benefits terminology where emphasis is placed on pay and other settlements which carry a monetary value to a new plane in which almost anything could be construed as a return to employees for exhibiting desirable behaviour, from a cash bonus or health care benefit to employee involvement in decision making, increased role responsibility, autonomy, access to more interesting work and other factors relating to the nature of the work itself and the environment in which it is carried out.

Components of reward

As indicated above, reward comprises several elements, extending beyond base pay thus presenting employers with a number of complex decisions. The first of these is which components to include in the reward package and the associated rationale for inclusion or rejection. Further decisions entail whether to permit employees a degree of choice in the reward 'mix' so that they can, for example, sacrifice salary in exchange for benefits or indeed choose from a menu of benefits to a defined value or cash limit. In addition, employers have fundamental decisions to make concerning whether the reward offering will be standardised and universal (applied to all employees) or tailored and status/seniority related (Marchington and Wilkinson, 2008). Such decisions will be influenced by the nature of the external operating environment, the behaviour of competitors and a range of internal organisational factors; these key determinants of the features of organisational reward systems will be explored later within the chapter.

For all workers, base pay forms the starting point in the reward package. The term is used to denote the hourly rate, wage or annual salary employees are paid for the work they do based either upon some measure of job size or some aspect of the person, for example, qualifications, skill set or demonstrable competencies. Base pay is a critical component as it is used as the anchor rate for calculating redundancy payment entitlement, sick pay, pension level in a final salary scheme, overtime rates, as applicable, and other such employee rights. Base pay might be set deliberately low if, for example, commissions can be earned in excess and the organisation is keen to incentivise sales activity, base pay might also be suppressed where benefits are generous and so the overall worth of the reward bundle is considered to be commensurate with market rates. As is detailed later, however, the introduction of the National Minimum Wage (NMW) in April 1999 imposed minimum limits on base pay in an attempt to curb the problem of low pay in the economy, as a result employers are now obliged to adhere to minimum rates and review pay in accordance with changes in the NMW rates. The level of base pay awarded to employees and movement in base pay can be individually negotiated between managers and employees, unilaterally determined by owners/management, the subject of collective bargaining with relevant trades unions recognised within the industry and /or organisation or as occurs in some cases, set by National Pay Review Bodies.

Over and above base pay, further decisions may be made concerning supplementary payments attributable to skill or performance, for example, and other additions such as overtime, danger or dirt money, shift premium, bonuses or commissions. Dominant reward terminology refers to supplementary payments which are consolidated into base pay as forms of contingent pay and those that are non-consolidated as elements of variable pay (Armstrong, 2002). In practice, both forms of pay described are event- and/or behaviour-dependent and therefore not an assured, regular form of payment. Variable pay in particular is sometimes described as 'at risk' pay by being non-consolidated employees are compelled to repeat activities and behaviours to trigger variable pay in each subsequent business period and so secure a consistent level of reward. In addition, employees are disadvantaged in the sense that base pay, the driver of other entitlements, remains unaffected by variable pay, regardless of how frequently variable pay is awarded or what portion of total salary variable pay comprises. The combination of base pay plus variable pay and/or contingent pay represents total earnings and is reflected in the employee pay advice slip, yet entitlement to employee benefits enables the employee to accumulate additional remuneration. Employee benefits, sometimes called 'perks' (perquisites) or fringe benefits carry a financial value or afford the recipient tax advantages which result in a net financial gain, however in contrast to earnings, benefits are often presented in non-cash form. Where benefits are particularly generous and constitute a substantial component of the reward package they tend to be identified in job advertisements to indicate the total financial value of the role to potential applicants (see Box 9.1).

Benefits can be classified as *immediate, deferred or contingent*. Employees derive value from immediate benefits instantaneously, such benefits might include the provision of a company car, a laptop computer, discounts, expensed mobile phone or subsidised meals. Where benefits are deferred their value accrues and has a future rather than present value to the employee, a clear example of such a benefit is a pension plan or share scheme. Contingent benefits are

---

Box 9.1

West Midlands Fire Service

HR Officer (Employee Relations)

Salary: £25,146–£26,706 per annum + relocation + benefits

Royal Mail

HR Business Partners

South East/South West and Home Counties
Salary up to £60,000 per annum + benefits to include car allowance and bonus

Trafford College

Director of Human Resources

£54k plus contributory pension scheme

Source: People Management, 15, 2, January 2009.

those that are triggered in certain circumstances, for example sick pay schemes, paternity and maternity pay and leave arrangements. Rather than deferring to the aforementioned classification, Wright (2004: 182) prefers to consider benefits in four distinct groupings:

- *Personal, security and health benefits*: for example, pension, company sick pay scheme, life cover, medical insurance, loans.
- *Job-, status- or seniority-related benefits*: for example, company car, holiday leave beyond statutory minimum, sabbaticals.
- *Family friendly benefits*: for example, childcare or eldercare facilities, nursery vouchers, enhanced maternity/paternity/parental leave arrangements.
- *Social or 'goodwill' or lifestyle benefits*: for example, subsidised canteen, gym/sports facilities, discounts, ironing collection/dry cleaning.

Benefits can be voluntary, affording employees the choice whether to 'opt in' and use them according to their personal needs and financial position. Should employees elect to purchase benefits such as childcare vouchers, cycle-to-work scheme loan, life cover or pension contributions, arrangements tend to be set up for deductions to occur at source, this can attract tax advantages for the employee, for example, where childcare assistance is purchased. The 'Advantages' benefits package operated by DHL Logistics is typical of voluntary benefit schemes. It incorporates the company's Voyager pension scheme, childcare savings via the 'Care-4' scheme, Denplan dental care, AXA PPP healthcare and a range of leisure, health, motoring and financial discounts and offers. Details of the scheme are presented in a booklet distributed to all employees and staff take up is encouraged. To promote the scheme, further value illustrations are available to demonstrate to individual employees the total worth of the benefits should they choose to make use of 'Advantages'. A recent CIPD survey reports that voluntary benefit schemes are in use in 27 per cent of organisations (CIPD, 2008a). In other organisations benefits are universal, in other words provided to all and regarded as 'perks' of the job. This is in direct contrast to status or seniority-related benefits, which employees only qualify for if they have accrued the requisite number of year's service or are employed at or beyond a prescribed grade or level. Flexible benefit schemes or 'cafeteria benefits', so named because of the choices presented to employees, have been around for a number of years in some organisations, however, data depicting the prevalence of such schemes would suggest a degree of employer reticence. Of all the organisations surveyed by the CIPD (2008a) just 13 per cent operated flexible benefits and a further 12 per cent indicated plans to introduce such a scheme. Flexible schemes were present in 22 per cent of organisations with over 5000 staff, possibly indicating that larger workplaces are more likely to be able to resource a system of flexible benefits, both financially and logistically. Earlier data (Employee Benefits, 2003) estimated adoption of flexible benefits in around 8 per cent of organisations, again suggesting that this mode of providing employee benefits enjoys relatively narrow appeal. The basic premise of a flexible or cafeteria benefits scheme is that employees can spend up to a points limit or cash total, purchasing benefits from a defined menu. Cafeteria schemes may comprise fixed (inflexible, core) benefits and flexible ones (a so-called 'core plus' scheme) or offer complete freedom of choice to the maximum cash value/points value. In other schemes pre-packaged sets of benefits may be on offer to employees; these schemes are referred to as modularised benefits (Wright, 2004: 207).

It is difficult to generalise the provision of benefits as part of the overall reward package and predict the types of benefits any one organisation will deem appropriate to adopt. The impetus for providing benefits can be viewed from a number of perspectives:

- Do organisations see benefits as a way of compensating for lower pay or do higher pay and generous benefits tend to co-exist as part of a deliberate strategy aimed at attracting and retaining staff?
- Do employers select benefits in the belief that they will motivate employees and instil a greater sense of loyalty and commitment?

- Is benefit provision enhanced by employers where trade unions lobby successfully to expand the reward package on behalf of their members?
- Are benefits a mechanism for employer branding, the costs of which some organisations are prepared to bear? (Wright, 2009.)

The answers to these questions are intricate and beyond the scope of this chapter. We do know, however, that whilst employee benefits in themselves are a fairly steadfast feature of reward in the UK, recent years have witnessed some shifts in the types of benefits more commonly provided by employers. Wright (2009: 175) detects 'cutbacks in the most costly benefits and at the same time a growth in low-cost lifestyle and voluntary benefits'. She attributes such trends to the dual influences of the changing composition of the labour force (particularly the influx of mothers) and the need for employers to be economically prudent and focus on value for money as competition intensifies. These trends would seem to be reflected to some extent in the benefits top-ten (see Table 9.1), particularly in the list of benefits most commonly provided to all employees.

Non-financial reward

Whilst the components of reward identified and discussed so far have a financial basis, reward can also be non-financial, or relational (Brown and Armstrong, 1999), for example praise, thanks, opportunities to develop skills and recognition awards such as 'employee of

Table 9.1 Top ten employer-provided benefits by provision

Provided to all employees	Provision dependent on grade/seniority	Part of a flexible benefit scheme only
Training and career development (71%)	Mobile phone (business use) (58%)	Dental insurance (9%)
25 days' or more paid leave (67%)*	Car allowance (50%)	Childcare vouchers (6%)
Tea/coffee/cold drinks (free) (62%)	Company car (49%)	Critical illness insurance (5%)
Christmas party/lunch (free) (62%)	Private medical insurance (32%)	Cycle-to-work scheme loan (5%)
On-site car parking (60%)	Relocation assistance (25%)	Health screening (5%)
Childcare vouchers (56%)	Fuel allowance (21%)	Private medical insurance (5%)
Life assurance (51%)	25 days' or more paid leave (20%)*	Healthcare cash plans (4%)
Eyecare vouchers (46%)	On-site car parking (14%)	Permanent health insurance (3%)
Enhanced maternity/paternity leave (43%)	Permanent health insurance (13%)	Life assurance (3%)
Employee assistance programmes (42%)	Health screening (12%)	Gym (on-site or membership) (2%)

Percentage of respondents in brackets.
*Excludes statutory leave.

Source: from *Reward Management: A CIPD Survey*, CIPD (2009) p. 13, with the permission of the publisher, the Chartered Institute of Personnel and Development, London (www.cipd.co.uk).

the month', 'going the extra mile' and service awards. Awards are often publicly acknowledged in ceremonies and/or in company newsletters and notice boards thus communicating to the wider workforce the employee behaviours the organisation values and is prepared to reward. Non-financial rewards also include the general quality of working life (QWL), for example the work environment, flexibility, work-life balance, managerial style/attitude, job-role autonomy and responsibility plus opportunities for employee involvement and employee voice; collectively these factors might be termed the work 'experience'. Definitions of non-financial rewards are bound up with the concept of total reward described below, emphasising the potential benefits to be derived from considering reward in the broadest of senses. As Perkins and White conclude (2008: 315),

> definitions of non-financial reward are multi-faceted and often complex, requiring dissection of the elements to facilitate detailed cost–benefit analysis while simultaneously seeking to promote 'holistic employment experience' value greater than the sum of the parts.

Total reward

In recent years there has been interest in the notion of managing rewards such that the various components are carefully crafted together to support one another and so maximise the satisfaction employees experience in the course of, and as a result of their employment. This approach is the essence of a total rewards process (Armstrong and Murlis, 1998). Worldat-Work (2000) loosely describe total rewards as all of the employer's available tools that may be used to attract, retain, motivate and satisfy employees, encompassing every single investment that an organisation makes in its people, and everything employees value in the employment relationship. The components of total rewards are succinctly presented in the model shown in Figure 9.2.

Figure 9.2 Model of total rewards

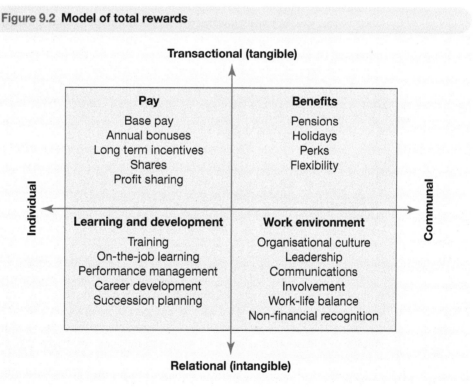

Source: Brown and Armstrong (1999: 81).

Thompson and Milsome (2001) insist that the concept of total rewards is necessarily holistic and integrative, it should also provide an approach to reward in the organisation which augurs well with the business objectives and desired organisational culture and as such is conflated with strategic approaches to reward. In addition, it is people centred, customised, distinctive (offering support to a unique employer brand) and it is evolutionary, in the sense that it is developed incrementally as opposed to the product of drastic, sudden change. A total rewards approach is reputed to offer potential for organisations striving to reduce costs, heighten visibility in a tight labour market, recruit and retain successfully, increase flexibility and improve productivity (Armstrong, 2002: 10) and so would certainly seem to 'tick the boxes' for contemporary organisations. In practice however, the latest CIPD Reward Survey (CIPD, 2009a) reports that only one fifth of organisations claim to have implemented total rewards while a further 22 per cent plan to introduce it during 2009. It could perhaps be deduced from these findings that a total rewards approach is somewhat elusive and difficult for employers to establish.

Reward management and the emergence of strategic approaches to reward

The term 'reward management' was first used in 1988 by Armstrong and Murlis to denote the development of a new field or collective set of activities to emerge within the arena of HRM. The new term recognised that static techniques, principally concerned with salary administration, were fast giving way to a more dynamic approach emphasising the use of pay (and other rewards) in a flexible and innovative way with the aim of improving individual, team and organisational performance. The activity 'reward management', has been described as encompassing not only the development, maintenance, communication, and evaluation of reward processes, but also concerned with the development of appropriate organisational cultures, underpinning core values and increasing the commitment and motivation of employees (Armstrong and Murlis, 1998).

It is, however, widely considered that the most effective approaches to reward are based upon careful consideration of an underlying philosophy and strategy that corresponds to overall business strategy (Taylor, 2008; Storey, 1992; Lawler, 1990). In accordance with this belief, the mantra follows that organisations should seek to ensure that the philosophy behind their approach to reward is in keeping with the organisation's values and beliefs and that reward strategy supports the achievement of wider corporate objectives; indeed this is part of the total rewards approach referred to earlier and strongly conveyed in the rhetoric of 'new pay' or 'strategic pay' purported by American writers Lawler (1990, 1995, 2000) and Schuster and Zingheim (1992). The precise function reward has to play in advancing organisational objectives, however, is unclear. Early models of strategic HRM such as the Harvard model (Beer et al., 1984) placed reward centrally as an integral HR activity and Storey (1992) identified reward as a 'key strategic lever'. Resource-based models too suggest pay acts as an important lever and can support a firm in achieving sustained competitive advantage. Kessler (2001), however, still needs to be convinced that there is sound evidence based upon credible methodologies that reward contributes to business performance and leads to sustained competitive advantage. There must also be a degree of reservation about the ease with which reward strategy can be matched seamlessly with business strategy and the extent to which employees will respond as intended to reward mechanisms designed to elicit certain desired behavioural patterns (Lewis, 2006).

Despite these doubts it appears to have become established orthodoxy that a strategic approach to reward can be used to leverage the kinds of employee behaviours that contribute to business goals (Marchington and Wilkinson, 2008). Proponents of strategic reward suggest it is possible for reward strategies, intentionally or otherwise, to signal what the organisation considers important and what it clearly does not value. For example, reward strategies that rest on service-related salary increments are likely to convey messages that the organisation values loyalty and long tenure above all else whereas the use of competence-related pay would suggest a need for employees to develop and demonstrate core competences and job-specific competences. Table 9.2 seeks to demonstrate a number of aligned relationships between the key thrust of business strategy and the direction of reward strategy.

Table 9.2 Examples of alignment: reward strategy and business strategy

Business strategy	Reward strategy
Achieve value added by improving employee motivation and commitment	Introduce or improve performance pay plans – individual, team, gain sharing
Achieve added value by improving performance/productivity	Introduce or improve performance pay plans and performance management processes
Achieve competitive advantage by developing and making best use of distinctive core competencies	Introduce competence-related pay
Achieve competitive advantage by technological development	Introduce competence-related or skills-based pay
Achieve competitive advantage by delivering better value and quality to customers	Recognise and reward individuals and teams for meeting/exceeding customer service and quality standards/targets
Achieve competitive advantage by developing the capacity of the business to respond quickly and flexibly to new opportunities	Provide rewards for multi-skilling and job flexibility. Develop more flexible pay structures (eg. broad-banding)
Achieve competitive advantage by attracting, developing and retaining high-quality employees	Ensure rates of pay are competitive. Reward people for developing their competencies and careers (for example, using the scope made possible in a broad-banded grading structure)

Source: from *Reward srategy: How to develop a reward strategy. A CIPD Practical Tool*, CIPD (CIPD 2005) http://www.cipd.co.uk/subjects/pay/general/tools.htm?IsSrchRes=1, with the permission of the publisher, the Chartered Institute of Personnel and Development, London (www.cipd.co.uk).

*What messages does the reward strategy in your own organisation convey? Are these the messages that the organisation **intends** to convey?*

Reward strategy in practice

Latest CIPD survey information (CIPD, 2009a) illustrates that 26 per cent of the sample acknowledges the existence of a reward strategy within their organisations while a further 24 per cent plan to adopt one in 2009. These figures seem to show a retraction when compared with the same survey a year and indeed two years earlier (CIPD, 2007, 2008a). In 2008, 33 per cent of respondents claimed to have a reward strategy, in 2007 the corresponding figure was 35 per cent with a further 40 per cent of respondents planning to introduce one in the course of 2007, the 2008 findings would suggest that this was not something they did in fact manage to do! The 2009 survey ponders whether the falling portion of respondents claiming to have a reward strategy could be attributed to some organisations perhaps questioning whether they had a reward strategy in the first place, a kind of crisis of confidence, or whether some employers did have a strategy but have recently had to relinquish it due to the fragility of the economic climate (CIPD, 2009a: 6). Of those organisations claiming to have a reward strategy, 85 per cent maintain that implementing their reward strategy has been difficult at times. The survey shows that overall the main inhibitors to the effective operation of the reward strategy are budgetary constraints/pressures, line managers' skills and abilities, line management attitudes and staff attitudes, although respondents from different sectors report notably different barriers to success.

Concerns over the ability of organisations to mount strategic approaches to reward are not new. In research conducted by the Institute for Employment Studies, Bevan (2000: 2) commented that having a reward strategy sounded like a 'tall order'. To be successful, he argues, reward strategy is supposed to be downstream from business strategy and reinforce business goals, drive performance improvements within the business, deliver cultural and behavioural change, integrate horizontally with other HR practices and keep pay budgets under control, so 'little wonder that so many employers under-perform in the design and delivery of a truly strategic approach to reward – if such a thing exists' (2000: 2). The same IES research (Bevan, 2000) detected ten common mistakes responsible for contributing to the under achievement of many reward strategies. The errors revolve around design or delivery and are summarised in Table 9.3.

Table 9.3 Reward strategy: ten common mistakes (Bevan, 2000)

1 Starting at the end	Trying to emulate the reward system used by competitors without recognising unique organisational drivers and what the business strategy requires
2 Having no success criteria	Failing to think through the underpinning reward philosophy and objectives and what success might look like so little idea whether the reward strategy is performing
3 Trusting the business strategy	Problems with the business strategy, for example failure to articulate it clearly and the chance that business strategy changes faster than reward is able to follow
4 Equating complexity with flexibility	Trying to build over-elaborate reward systems in an attempt to appeal to a diverse workforce, this can have the effect of confusing employees such that they fail to see a clear line of sight between performance and reward
5 Confusing speed with haste	Trying to rush in new reward systems, potentially damaging employee relations and harming the culture of the organisation
6 Focus on excellence	Focusing reward on excellence in the minority as opposed to encouraging performance improvements among the majority
7 Ignoring pay architecture	Getting weighed down in detail, for example wrangles over performance markings, rather than paying proper attention to pay structures and frameworks used to facilitate reward decisions
8 Failing to get real 'buy-in'	Failing to get full commitment from senior managers and line managers
9 Having too much faith in line managers	Relying on the skills and abilities of line managers to make difficult reward decisions without the necessary training and support
10 Failing to integrate reward with other strands of HR	Lack of logic between reward processes and systems and other HR practices, this can be due to a variety of reasons including conflicting process goals, process ownership issues and timing

Source: Bevan (2000: 3)

STOP and think

Do you recognise any of the above mistakes in your own organisation's efforts to design and implement a reward strategy capable of supporting and reinforcing strategic business objectives?

Which mistakes have occurred and how might they be rectified?

Key reward choices

Whilst accepting the notion of aligning reward to business strategy to optimise the utility of reward mechanisms a number of key, value-laden choices must be made in the process. Marchington and Wilkinson (2008: 464) suggest that there are five essential reward decisions an organisation needs to draw consensus on:

- what to pay for, job size, time, performance, skills/qualifications or some other person-centred attribute or behaviour;
- whether to place primary focus on internal equity when determining pay or be more concerned with external benchmarks;
- whether to operate a centralised or decentralised approach to reward or a hybrid with some central control and a degree of localised latitude;
- whether to build hierarchy into the reward system such that there are seniority or status related rewards or to devise a harmonised, single-status approach;
- the precise nature of the reward 'mix'.

Getting these decisions right is critical if reward is to reinforce the strategic direction of the organisation. Similarly, the decisions made need to be ones most likely to motivate individuals to orient their actions and behaviours towards business goals. This is demanding for any organisation given that motivation is individualised and complex. Thought needs to be invested in considering the extent to which different rewards are capable of motivating employees, the value of intrinsic and extrinsic motivation to employees, the role of pay in motivating people and the importance of equity in reward systems and reward management practices.

Motivation theory offers useful insight and can help guide the design and management of reward processes. Notably amongst the many theories of motivation, Herzberg's 'Two-Factor Theory' (Herzberg, 1966) suggests that pay is a *hygiene* factor rather than a motivator and so in itself it is unlikely to motivate. Herzberg contends that pay needs to be adequate to prevent dissatisfaction but other factors induce a motivational state such as responsibility and autonomy. This is, indeed, a salutary message particularly to those organisations that attempt to use pay or the prospect of financial rewards as an incentive for greater output, better quality or other outcomes they determine to be desirable.

Process theories of motivation such as 'Expectancy Theory' (Vroom, 1982) attempt to explain the internal thought processes that instil a motivational state. Expectancy theory offers us the insight that employee motivation is the result of a complex set of decisions and assumptions made by the individual. For an employee to be motivated and therefore to expend effort, the rewards on offer have to be something that the individual values (hold 'valence'), hence the importance of the reward 'mix. In addition, the individual must have belief that the rewards are achievable. An appreciation of expectancy theory encourages organisations to construct a clear 'line of sight' so that employees are in no doubt what it is they need to do in order to gain the rewards offered. If there is ambiguity or partiality disturbing the line of sight individuals are likely to be de-motivated, even if the potential rewards hold personal valence.

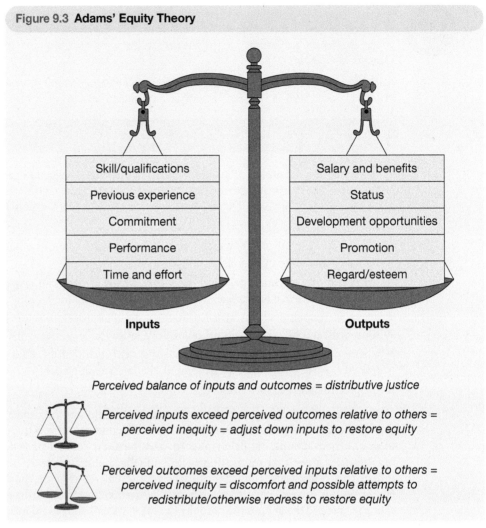

Figure 9.3 Adams' Equity Theory

Inputs	Outputs
Skill/qualifications	Salary and benefits
Previous experience	Status
Commitment	Development opportunities
Performance	Promotion
Time and effort	Regard/esteem

Perceived balance of inputs and outcomes = distributive justice

Perceived inputs exceed perceived outcomes relative to others = perceived inequity = adjust down inputs to restore equity

Perceived outcomes exceed perceived inputs relative to others = perceived inequity = discomfort and possible attempts to redistribute/otherwise redress to restore equity

Source: Adams (1965)

Finally, Adams' 'Equity Theory' (Adams, 1965) prompts organisations to consider the perceived fairness of rewards and their application. Adams suggests that employees will compare the rewards they receive (outputs) in return for their effort, skill, qualifications, time and other contributions (inputs). Employees will be motivated where they perceive 'distributive justice' and de-motivated where they perceive inequity. Employees may seek to adjust their inputs when they perceive inequity. Using the subliminal messages inherent in Adams' theory, organisations would be advised to take steps to ensure that their reward systems are fair, consistently applied and sufficiently transparent so that employees can see for themselves how reward decisions are determined (see Figure 9.3).

Factors influencing organisational approaches to reward practice and pay determination

An organisation's approach to reward generally, and to pay determination, will be shaped both by factors in the external environment within which it operates and an array of internal firm-specific characteristics, namely the nature of the business, the size of operation, organisational structure and culture, types of employees, jobs and technology, management and ownership and so forth. Each of the reward choices Marchington and Wilkinson (2008) posit in the segment above cascade a range of further ancillary choices thus creating the potential for multiple models of reward practice. Because of this it is difficult to generalise about approaches to reward and impossible to be prescriptive. More safely, an organisation's approach to developing a reward strategy ought to start from the standpoint 'what makes sense for this organisation?' (Wright, 2004: 8) whilst subsuming relevant knowledge relating to the internal and external factors influencing choice. In this segment of the chapter we briefly discuss the key factors in the external and internal environment that shape and influence organisational approaches to reward.

The economic climate

This chapter has already alluded to some of the ways in which the economic environment might influence reward, notably the way in which employers are likely to switch to less costly benefits in tougher economic conditions, and the way in which employers can reduce risk and financial burden by making more extensive use of variable pay. The economic context is an important determinant of pay levels and a barometer for future trends. In setting pay levels, employers cannot help but be influenced by the market rates for jobs. As Kessler (2007: 167) remarks 'organisations cannot survive if they fail to pay competitive labour market rates to attract employees with the skills needed to provide a service or manufacture a product'. Of course, there is no such thing as a single market rate for a job, rather several rates or a zone of discretion, the spread of which is influenced by the supply of and demand of labour, geographical factors and the actions of employers competing for labour. In tight labour markets, where competition for resources is intensive and supply is low, market rates are driven higher, affecting the price employers have to pay to attract adequate resources. Economic activity rates and unemployment indicators are thus key factors influencing pay levels. In addition, for most organisations the rate of growth in the economy is a critical benchmark for the salary review process and impacts upon organisations' ability to pay. According to the IRS (2008) employers use various measures of inflation to guide pay increases, of these the Retail Prices Index (RPI) is the most popular measure with more than eight in ten employers (81.7 per cent) saying they would refer to this measure during forthcoming pay reviews. In an economic downturn there is evidence to suggest that employers tighten their belts where pay is concerned and look to minimise or avoid pay increases. Cotton (2009) suggests that in the current climate of an economy in recession and mounting insolvencies, workers are not optimistic that they will receive a pay rise during 2009.

The legal context for reward

Since the rise of industrialisation there have been numerous legal interventions into the realm of reward management. These have ranged from the Truck Acts of the nineteenth century, which were designed to ensure skilled workers were paid in cash, through to more recent interventions in terms of minimum wage regulation. These demonstrate the ways in which legal regulation can be seen to shape reward practices. Statutory regulation has been in place in the United Kingdom for some 30 years which was intended to ensure pay equity in gender terms. More recently, legislation has been implemented to regulate pay at the lower extreme of the labour market, to impose minimum holiday entitlement and a restraint on working hours. Here we briefly discuss in turn the ways in which the Equal Pay Act 1970, The National Minimum Wage Regulations 1999 and the Working Time Directive 1998 constrain and influence employee reward practices.

The Equal Pay Act 1970 (EqPA)

> Labor market discrimination occurs when groups of workers with equal average productivity are paid different average wages.
>
> (Baldwin and Johnson 2006: 122)

Equal Pay regulations have a history founded in the Convention on Equal Pay approved by the International Labour Organisation in 1950–51, a regulation that had antecedents within the Treaty of Versailles in 1919, if not before (Jamieson, 1999). In the UK the EqPA was enacted as part of the move towards membership of the European Economic Community (now the EU) in the early 1970s. Employers were allowed five years' 'grace' to voluntarily adjust and to permit them to get their reward structures in order before the legislation came into force in 1975. Broadly, the legislation is designed to grant everyone the right to equal terms and conditions of employment in situations where they do the same work as a colleague of the opposite sex. Over the ensuing period this has been widened by the application of European Law to the extent that the UK has modified its laws (see the Employment Act 2002 s 42 for example) to include in this group colleagues of the opposite sex who do work that has been rated as equivalent under a job evaluation scheme or where it can be proved by other mechanisms that the work is of equal value. The manner in which this is achieved is to imply into all contracts of employment an 'equality clause', which has the consequence of requiring the employer not to treat persons of different genders less favourably simply on the basis of gender. In spite of this legislation, there still exist very significant inconsistencies between men's and women's pay. It does not matter whether wages are measured hourly or weekly, women currently receive approximately 83 per cent of the full-time male average, whilst in part-time work 'almost 50 per cent of women who work part-time earn nearer 60 per cent' of their average for their male counterparts (McColgan, 2008: 401). As McColgan (2008) notes, bringing equal pay claims is a sluggish, unwieldy and costly process, especially as the government refuses to go along with the development of class actions and shows even less willingness to implement legislation which places a positive obligation on employers to eliminate pay discrimination.

In spite of this lack of legislative backing to pursue equal pay, some employers seek to address such inequality within their reward structures. This can be achieved by the introduction of a number of reward polices and practices such as:

- ensuring employees reach the top of a given scale within a reasonable timescale;
- setting targets for all staff to reach pay points within a specific timescale;
- setting competency *and* experience criteria for each pay point;
- shortening the scales;
- reducing the number and range of performance measures (Equality and Human Rights Commission, 2009).

As Fredman (2008) suggests, the fact that the current difference in gender-related pay is down to 12.6 per cent when measured using the median figure (rather than the usual mean which rates it at 17.2 per cent) following 34 years of equal pay legislation gives no reason for satisfaction. Indeed, the change in the mechanisms for calculation merely masks the continuing inability of some groups to secure equality of treatment especially where 'the median part-time gender pay gap was a scandalous 39.1% in 2007' (Fredman 2008: 193). The continuing gap indicates the need for a more complex response which addresses both government and employer unwillingness and the narrow coverage of the current legislation.

Whilst some inroads have been made, to what extent do you think the continued reliance upon the three requirements for equal pay claims (same or equivalent establishment, same employer and equal work) continue to limit the progress towards equal pay?

Consider an organisation of which you are aware and indicate mechanisms they could institute in order to address inequalities in terms and conditions.

National Minimum Wage Regulations 1999

The regulation of wages is a central debate within the realm of 'worker protection, globalization, development and poverty reduction' (Evain, 2008: 20). These were put in place in order to develop the dual goals of fairness and efficiency. As the report of the Low Pay Commission suggested it can be argued that low wages lead to a malevolent cluster which comprises low morale, low performance and low productivity. The introduction of a national minimum wage is said to have benefited some 1.3 million workers (Low Pay Commission, 2001). Many of those affected worked in organisations where pay setting was inexact and did not recognise the need for formal systems, further the new wage levels benefited women more than men due to inequality and the extent of part-time work amongst women. The UK currently has three rates covering those over compulsory school age but under 18, those aged between 18 and 21 and those aged 22 and above. The rates are changed in October each year and from 2008 they were £3.53, £4.77 and £5.73 respectively. As with the Wage Council rates before them these rates are poorly policed and many small employers, especially those in the service sector, avoid enforcement (Arrowsmith and Gilman, 2005). Arrowsmith and Gilman argue that in such small firms 'Pay levels reflect not only economic, product and labour market factors but also the informality of internal pay structures' (2005: 169). As we note below, such indeterminacy and informality support existing pay bias, as it is often based on pre-determined skill patterns, time worked and length of service.

The level within the UK is set at above the equivalent of US$1,000 per month (in the period 2006–07) which locates the UK within the top 18 per cent of countries where such a minimum is set (Evain, 2008) and within a group of industrialised countries where the rate is set other than by government alone. Evain (2008) notes more than 100 countries in membership of the International Labour Organisation (ILO), which have ratified the Minimum Wage Fixing Convention 1970 (No 131), either enact minimum wage legislation, set such rates following the recommendation of a specialised body, or through collective bargaining. World-wide, the average range of minimum rates vary from US$30 in Africa, US$75 in many Asian countries, US$480 in Eastern Europe and Latin America to the US$1,000 or above in the majority of industrialised countries. These rates reflect national, regional, sectored and/or global imperatives and satisfy many competitive pressures. By removing wage calculation out of competition organisations can, in domestic and global settings, strive for alternative means of differentiation in terms of product or service. The issue then becomes the enforcement mechanism, Eyraud and Saget (2005) suggest that these regulations are often poorly enforced leading to a continued decline in working conditions across the globe. The extent to which the legislation in the UK is enforced, and the individualised mechanisms for enforcement, tend to support the view that whilst the existence of such regulation is designed to ensure a high level of protection, the continued avoidance of such rules as indicated by Arrowsmith and Gilman (2005) is wide spread.

Minimum wage legislation is said to advance a wide range of policy goals.

What do you think such goals might be and how effectively does the current UK regulation achieve these goals?

Working Time Regulations 1998

Placing limits on working hours is an essential activity in the quest for worker protection and ensuring the health and safety of those at work. In the current climate it has also become a touchstone of the movement towards securing a sustainable work-life balance. In terms of the latter, there are two discourses which each have a separate focus. These uses of the concept cover the *personal control of time* on the one hand and the notion of *workplace flexibility* on the other (see Humbert and Lewis, 2008). In terms of the reward agenda, we concentrate primarily on the latter in that we are seeking solutions to the question of providing options for people with a work place focus who also enjoy non-work (chiefly family) commitments. In that respect the Working Time Regulations (1998) [WTR] offer some attempt to balance the demands of the employer with the needs of family life by placing limits on a range of working time issues. At a glance the key provisions are:

- maximum 48-hour working week for many groups;
- An average eight-hour shift in each 24-hour period for night workers;
- A rest break after six consecutive hours' work;
- Rest periods of 11 continuous hours daily and 35 continuous hours weekly; and
- A minimum of 5.6 weeks' leave per annum.

The UK regulations have their basis in the EU Directive (93/104/EC), which is said to have introduced the new principle of 'humanisation' into EU social regulations, under which employers should be required to take into account the general principle of adapting work and wage in order to alleviate monotonous work and work at a pre-determined rate. The fact that the UK has implemented the directive subject to a number of derogations does not alter the fact that reward managers need to consider the effects of the regulations. That the Employment Appeals Tribunal (EAT) could in a recent case (*Corps of Commissionaires Management Ltd* v *Hughes* [2008] EAT|196|08) hold that the rest break is only triggered after six hours and not multiples thereof, is a simple indication of the minimalist approach of the UK government and the reluctance of management to extend the protection within the UK. During 2009 elements of the EU Directive relating to the definition of 'working time' – notably in relation to 'on-call' time and junior doctors – will come into force and change the options for UK reward managers. The development of 24/7 production and 'rolling shifts' has not been unduly limited by the daily or weekly rest periods due to the availability of opt-outs, however, as these opt-outs are withdrawn it will present fresh challenges for reward managers in the UK.

World-wide most members of the ILO have some form of regulation on working time. In a recent survey (Evain, 2008), attention is drawn to the fact that working time regulation was the subject of the very first ILO convention (Convention 1: 1919) and that the topic has been a major regulatory concern since that date. The general rule, where a normal hourly figure is placed on the working week, is that the figure of 40 or less is applied. In the UK we have no universal normal working limit because the WTR exclude 'professional workers' and/or workers who are not paid in relation to time. The latter group includes many clerical workers, most managers and almost all professional workers. This limitation is not unique to the UK as it can be found in some 24 per cent of industrialised countries. A key result of such exceptions has been the development of 'extreme work' hours most of which are unpaid. It is reported that managers in the UK work the longest hours in Europe, with 42 per cent working in excess of 60 hours a week; this phenomenon runs alongside evidence that work has also intensified (Burke and Cooper, 2008). Hewlett and Luce (2006) describe the amalgamation of these two factors, in the work of 'high earners', as the basis for the creation of 'extreme work'. Such work is portrayed as combining elements such as:

- unpredictable workflow;
- fast pace under tight deadlines;
- scope of responsibility that amounts to more than one job;

- work-related events outside regular working hours;
- availability to clients and/or more senior managers 24/7;
- large amounts of travel;
- large (and increasing) number of direct reports;
- physical presence at the workplace on average at least 10 hours a day (adapted from Hewlett and Luce, 2006).

For reward managers, these elements present few problems because they tend to either describe the role chosen and adopted by the individual or take place within the terms of the existing contract of employment. As such, they are rewarded by existing reward structures including PBR or other personalised reward agreements. In their survey of US business managers and professionals, Hewlett and Luce found that 91 per cent cited unpredictability as a key pressure point whilst 86 per cent also included increased pace within tight deadlines, 66% included work-related events outside normal hours and 61 per cent 24/7 client demands (2006: 54). Perhaps the words of the eighteenth-century washer-woman Mary Collier better fit modern managers and professionals both male and female;

> Our toil and labour daily so extreme,
> that we have hardly ever the time to dream.
>
> (Quoted in Thompson 1991: 81)

From this discussion we can begin to see that legislative activity, whilst a key source for elements which influence reward structures, are not the only, nor perhaps the most important, influences.

Internal/organisational factors and the influence of sector

In addition to reflecting factors in the external environment, organisations' chosen approach to reward will be shaped by the idiosyncratic nature of the firm and sector-specific factors. There are no hard and fast rules, so the full plethora of reward choices is theoretically at the disposal of the organisation. As far as its capabilities stretch, the organisation must develop an approach to reward that is compliant, cost-effective and capable of attracting, retaining and motivating employees commensurate with the needs of the business. It is beyond the boundaries of this chapter to discuss in detail the complex configurations of reward and corresponding internal drivers that are likely to be significant in each case. Instead, a more general stance is adopted, which notes some of the discernable differences between reward practices according to workplace characteristics such as ownership/sector, unionisation and workplace size. We return to these themes in the final part of the chapter, where contemporary trends in pay and reward practices are discussed against rhetoric of heightened strategic use of reward.

Large-scale surveys such as the Workplace Employment Relations Survey (WERS) (Kersley *et al.*, 2006) and the CIPD Annual Reward Survey allow changes and trends in employee reward practice to be tracked over time; they also provide a snapshot of employee reward practices at the time of the survey. CIPD research provides analysis by firm size (number of employees), firm sector (manufacturing and production, private sector services, voluntary sector and public services) and by occupation (senior management, middle/first-line management, technical/professional and clerical/manual), whilst WERS provides further industry breakdown and in addition, considers the variance between reward practices in unionised and non-unionised workplaces and foreign-owned and UK-owned workplaces. A sample of observations is drawn from WERS 2004 (Kersley *et al.*, 2006) and the latest CIPD survey (2009a) and shown in Table 9.4.

Table 9.4 Trends in reward practice

Reward strategy	• The incidence of reward strategy shows little variance by sector but does appear to be more closely correlated to workplace size – 48 per cent of respondents in workplaces of 5000+ employees reported the existence of reward strategy compared with 20 per cent of repondents where there were between 50 and 249 employees
Pay structures	• In the public sector and to a lesser extent in the voluntary sector, employers are far more likely to us pay spines • The most common approach to pay structures taking all sectors into account is the use of individual pay rates/ranges and spot salaries although there are variations by sector and by occupation • Broad-banding is most prevalent in manufacturing and production • Most senior managers are paid according to individual pay rates/ranges/spot salaries as are most clerical and manual workers
Pay progression	• The CIPD report that the most common approach to pay progression is to use a combination of factors (combined approach) in contrast to a single factor such as length of service, skills or individual performance • Combination approaches are more common in manufacturing and production and private sector services than they are in the voluntary sector and public services • Where combination approaches are used, the most common combination in the public sector is individual performance and length of service, individual performance is the most popular factor across all sectors, market rates feature strongly in the private sector and competency is more typical in the voluntary sector
Pay/salary determination	• Market rates are shown to be more important in determining salaries in private sector firms • In the public sector collective bargaining was the dominant form of pay setting • In the private sector, the percentage of employees with pay set through collective bargaining was much higher in foreign-owned workplaces than in UK-owned workplaces • Clerical and manual staff are more likely to be covered by collective bargaining arrangements than managerial staff • The views of the owner/managing director are more likely to be a factor in setting salary levels in small firms than in large organisations (CIPD, 2009a) • Pay set by management where this is the sole method of pay determination is a growing phenomenon in private sector workplaces (43 per cent of private sector workplaces in 2004 compared with 32 per cent in 1998) (Kersley et al., 2006) • Job evaluation processes are more likely to underscore salary determination in the public sector and voluntary sectors than in the private sector • Job evaluation is more likely to be used by large employers than small employers • Public sector organisations are far more likely to have conducted an equal pay reviews (EPR) to audit internal pay equity than private sector employers

Pay determination – internal or external focus?

As the final segment of Table 9.4 demonstrates, a key decision when setting levels of pay is whether to place emphasis on comparability with the external market or internal equity. The lure of the external market would appear to be more compelling for private sector organisations, whereas the greater use of tools such as job evaluation and the Equal Pay Review process in the public sector suggests internal equity is more paramount here. Ultimately, however, any approach must try and reconcile the need to keep pace with external market rates with due concern for internal equity.

Job evaluation has come in for criticism in recent years for being excessively paperwork-driven and costly and too rigid to be of value to organisations trying to be adaptable and flexible in the face of intensive competitive pressures. The notion of conceiving tightly defined job descriptions, of the kind needed for traditional job evaluation schemes is also heralded in some quarters as incompatible with flatter organisational structures and associated desire to create flexible ways of rewarding employees. Job evaluation consequently is supposed to have withered away, at least from mainstream use. On the contrary, IDS (2000) suggest that much of the criticism directed at job evaluation is unsupported by hard empirical evidence and that in practice organisations are showing signs of using it to complement broad-banding and in conjunction with role profiling and competencies. Brown and Dive (2009: 29) would appear to agree,

> By evolving to meet the needs of organisations for more fluid structures, more market- and person-driven pay and more talented leaders – as well as performing its traditional function as a foundation for fair pay management – job evaluation seems to be securing its place in the HR professional's toolkit for the foreseeable future.

Typically, job evaluation schemes attempt to fairly address issues of internal comparability in terms of pay. Job evaluation is defined as 'the process of assessing the relative size of jobs within an organisation' (Armstrong and Murlis, 1998: 81). The term 'size' in this context means the value of the job to the organisation.

Armstrong and Murlis identify the defining characteristics of job evaluation (JE) as:

- *A judgemental process*: always (to some extent) reliant on the exercise of judgement in interpreting facts and situations and applying these to decisions about the relative 'size' of jobs.
- *An analytical process*: it is about making informed judgements based upon an analytical process of gathering facts about jobs (based on job analysis techniques).
- *A structured process*: a framework is provided to help evaluators make consistent and rational decisions.
- *A job-centred process*: JE focuses on jobs, not on the people doing them and/or how well they do them. This aspect has clearly raised questions about the value of JE to organisations that adopt a person-based approach as opposed to job-based approach to reward.

Job evaluation is therefore, not a 'perfect' determinant of job relativities. As we can see, it relies to some extent on subjective judgements and it may present some challenges in contemporary workplaces where there is likely to be greater fluidity in job roles.

Devising pay structures

Whether or not organisations engage systematically with the process of job evaluation or take a stronger lead from benchmarking salaries in the external market without recourse to job evaluation techniques, most would agree with Armstrong (2002: 204), that 'pay structures are needed to provide a logically-designed framework within which equitable, fair and consistent reward policies can be implemented'. Perkins and White (2008: 98) argue that grading structures are 'the core building blocks of any organisation's human resource management system, not just for pay but often for conditions of service and career development as well'. The degree of sophistication characterising the design of pay structures in organisations can vary considerably according to firm size, sector and occupational group. For example, smaller firms are generally less likely to operate formal pay structures especially during the formative stages of the business, relying perhaps instead on management discretion to set individual rates of pay for employees (Perkins and White, 2008). However, research in small and medium-sized organisations (SMEs) would indicate that as small firms grow, an informal approach to HRM becomes less tenable (Barrett and Mayson, 2007; Barrett *et al.*, 2008; Mazzarol, 2003); it is at this point that SMEs are likely to begin to inject greater levels of formalisation across a range of human resource practices, including reward. Further, the 2009 CIPD Reward Survey points to sectoral differences and occupational differences.

Responses indicate that pay spines with fixed incremental points are common at all levels in the public sector, while individual pay rates or ranges, which allow for greater flexibility, are more prevalent in the private sector. By occupation, senior managers are most likely to be subject to individual pay rates or ranges.

According to Armstrong (2002: 203) a pay structure:

- defines the different levels of pay for jobs or groups of jobs by reference to their relative internal value as established by job evaluation, to external relativities as established by market rate surveys and, where appropriate, to negotiated rates for the job;
- except in the case of 'spot rates', provides scope for pay progression in accordance with performance, skill, contribution or service;
- contains an organisation's pay ranges for jobs grouped into grades, individual jobs or job families; or pay scales for jobs slotted into a pay spine; or the spot rates for individual jobs where there is no scope for progression.

In essence, a pay structure defines the rate, or range of the payment rate, for jobs within the organisational structure. Whilst this might sound a relatively simple task, there are a number of design choices to be made:

- Should the organisation establish spot rates for individual jobs or devise a more complex structure or series of pay structures?
- How many pay structures are necessary?
- What types of pay structures are suitable?
- If a grading structure is deemed appropriate, how many grades should there be; how wide should each grade or band be; and how close should grade differentials be?

Further decisions must subsequently be made about 'whether, or on what basis, employees will progress through the pay structure' (Perkins and White, 2008: 152).

General design features

As a rule, pay structures need to be flexible enough to accommodate change in the organisation or in the external market and sufficiently clear for individuals to understand where in the structure they are placed and how pay progression is achieved. Spot rates, as referred to in Armstrong's definition above, are set rates of base pay for individual jobs, independent to one another and not tied to a scale or range. Where there is a spot rate for a job, all employees incumbent in the role are paid the same base rate for the job; this may be supplemented by forms of variable pay such as overtime and shift premium or attendance bonus. Spot rates tend to preside in manufacturing and warehouse/distribution centres and in other forms of manual work (Armstrong, 2002). It is difficult to regard a series of spot rates as a pay structure per se, however, spot rates can be customised to personify typical features of a pay structure, for example a mini-series of spot rates (generally referred to as an individual pay range) could be assigned to a role such that there is scope to pay a lesser training or learning rate to individuals new to the role, a target spot rate for a fully competent employee and a further (higher) rate to recognise superior skill, experience or performance. In other circumstances, organisations may elect to manage spot rates in such a way as to incentivise consistently high levels of output, this might be attempted in a somewhat punitive fashion, by dropping lower performing employees to a less favourable spot rate until such a time as higher productivity is resumed.

Whilst, as illustrated, a degree of tailoring is possible, spot rates do not readily offer scope for pay progression; rather they supply a series of detached job rates. Such an approach may be eminently suitable where jobs are fairly static in nature and career development opportunities and expectations are limited. In contrast grading, pay spines and job families, more aptly fit the description of a framework for the enactment of pay policy, in addition, they offer options for pay progression, through the spine, grade or family of jobs based upon length of service or other criterion best suited to the organisation's strategic business objectives.

A single structure or several structures?

An organisation may be able to design and implement a single pay structure to incorporate the entire range of jobs (or the vast majority of jobs) across the organisation, alternatively two or more structures may be in place to assimilate different groups of roles represented within the organisation (for example, a manual pay scale and an office and managerial salary structure). In recent years, both the National Health Service (NHS) and the Higher Education (HE) sector have untaken extensive pay reform, underpinned by job evaluation to develop single pay structures. The NHS scheme, 'Agenda for Change', succeeded in introducing a single national pay scale for NHS hospital employees (with the exception of doctors and consultants), similarly the National Framework Agreement in Higher Education has created a single pay spine for support staff and academic staff in HE institutions.

What benefits do you think hospitals and universities are likely to derive from the formulation of single pay structures in their respective organisations?

Pay spines

A pay spine is a series of fixed incremental salary points reflecting all jobs from the highest paid through to the lowest paid incorporated in the structure. Incremental points may increase at an evenly distributed rate throughout the spine, for example each increment might be set 2.5 per cent above the next from the bottom to the top of the structure. Alternatively, increments might be wider at higher levels in the organisation (Armstrong, 2002). Pay spines are common in the public services sector including education, health, local government and the police service (Perkins and White, 2008). In these work environments, pay grades are superimposed upon the pay spine to form a structure in which a series of increments apply within each grade. Employees' annual salaries are typically automatically raised to the next incremental point on the basis of length of service, this either occurs on an individual basis, triggered by the anniversary of the employee joining the organisation or collectively at a fixed date in the calendar. Except in extreme cases of poor performance, where an increment might be withheld or where progression 'gateways' have to be crossed, employees continue to receive automatic annual increments (and possibly accelerated increments awarded according to performance criteria) until such a time as they reach the top point in the grade. Pay progression thereafter, in the form of increments, is contingent on the employee gaining promotion to a higher grade. In some organisations further additional discretionary points may be available beyond the upper limit of the grade boundary, reserved for those employees who have performed exceptionally throughout the year or those who have made a special contribution. In public services, where pay spines are prevalent, uplift to the pay spine is the subject of national pay bargaining between trade unions and employers; where a cost of living percentage increase in pay is agreed the incremental scale is adjusted upwards accordingly. Pay spines offer employees a degree of pay progression certainty and give employers certainty in terms of total salary expenditure, but may be perceived as bureaucratic and excessively rigid.

Try to think of other potential benefits and disadvantages associated with pay spines.

Graded pay structures

Aside from the use of a central pay spine, organisations opting for a formal pay structure are likely to use some form of grading. The general principles of a pay-grading structure are that jobs are grouped together into grades or bands, often according to some measure of job size. Graded structures require firms to determine how many grades or bands to build into the structure, the width of each grade ('bandwidth'), the degree of overlap to configure between grades and the size of grade differentials to apply throughout the structure. Jobs should be grouped together such that a distinction can be made between the characteristics of the jobs in different grades and the grade hierarchy should broadly take account of the organisational hierarchy. Additionally, there should be a significant step in demands on job holders in the next highest grade such that salary differentials can be suitably justified (www.e-reward.co.uk, January 2007).

Narrow-graded pay structures

Narrow-graded pay structures, or 'traditional' graded structures as they are sometimes referred to, comprise a large number of grades, typically ten or more with jobs of broadly equivalent worth slotted into each of the grades (Armstrong, 2002). As the name would suggest, the width of each grade within the structure ('bandwidth') is narrow, perhaps amounting to a range where the upper salary limit of the grade is anywhere between 20 per cent and 50 per cent higher than the lower salary limit (www.e-reward.co.uk, January 2007). Salary differentials between pay ranges are invariably around 20 per cent (Armstrong, 2002), calculated with reference to the grade mid-point. There is usually an overlap between ranges, which can be as high as 50 per cent (www.e-reward.co.uk, January 2007). The purpose of an overlap is to provide the employer with the scope to recognise and reward a highly experienced and/or qualified employee at the top of a grade more generously than someone who is still in the learning curve zone of the next higher grade (see Figure 9.4). Ultimately, however, the individual placed in the higher grade has greater scope for salary progression. He/she will be able to move closer towards, and eventually, beyond the target rate for a fully competent employee within the grade, contingent upon on satisfying the criteria for pay progression used by the organisation.

For illustrative purposes Figure 9.5 shows a single narrow grade with a bandwidth of 40 per cent, while Figure 9.6 shows an extract of a narrow graded pay structure where the bandwidth is 40 per cent throughout the structure, a grade overlap of 20 per cent is applied and the differential between grades is set at 20 per cent.

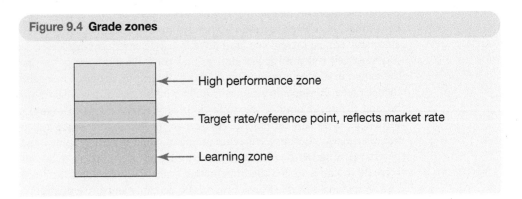

Figure 9.4 **Grade zones**

High performance zone

Target rate/reference point, reflects market rate

Learning zone

Figure 9.5 Narrow salary grade (40 per cent bandwidth)

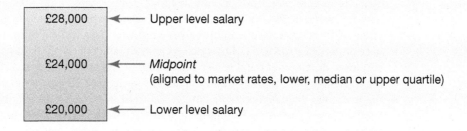

Figure 9.6 Extract of narrow-graded pay structure

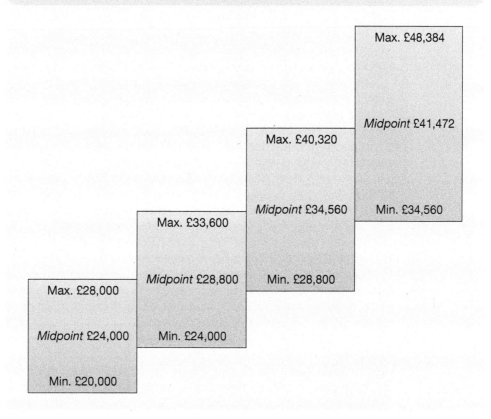

It is practice to identify a reference point or target rate in each grade which is the rate for a fully competent individual who is completely qualified and experienced to execute the job to the required standard. This target rate is frequently, but not always, the *midpoint* in the range, aligned to market rates for similar jobs and set in accordance with the organisation's pay stance (upper, median or lower quartile), (www.e-reward.co.uk, January 2007). Analysis seems to show that among private sector service employers, the target rate does tend to be the mid-point in the range, whereas in the public sector the target rate is close to the top of the range. In the manufacturing and production sectors and across the voluntary sector employers are broadly divided as to whether the target salary is at the mid-point or towards the top end of the pay band (CIPD, 2009b).

252 Business Performance Management

Broad-banded pay structures

In contrast to a narrow-graded pay structure, a broad-banded structure involves the use of a small number of pay bands, usually just four or five (Armstrong, 2002), each with a band-width of between 70 and 100 per cent (Perkins and White, 2008). The broader salary range attached to bands in the structure gives employers greater flexibility than is possible in a narrow-graded structure and is arguably more suitable for use in flatter organisations where employee development and career progression is not inextricably linked to vertical movement through the hierarchy. Flatter organisations tend to develop a more flexible outlook as far as careers are concerned, promoting lateral career development and 'zig-zag' careers. Whilst narrow grades might inhibit such moves, broad bands allow employers to recognise and reward non-vertical career movement and role growth. For this reason broad-banded pay structures are sometimes labelled career-based structures (CIPD, 2000). The CIPD (2000) is keen to point out, however, that some organisations claiming to have made the transition to a broad-banded structure have simply collapsed several narrow grades into fewer wider grades and crucially failed to re-position their own and their workforce's perceptions in terms of career development and salary progression. The CIPD suggests pay structures of this type ought to be called broad-*graded* because of their attachment to the vertical progression mentality more closely associated with narrow-grading structures, the CIPD also offers the less flattering term 'fat-graded' to describe such structures.

A further feature of true broad-banded pay structures is that they afford employers greater latitude in establishing starting salaries and so the opportunity to pay more to attract suitably qualified and experienced staff to 'hard to fill' positions. Whilst this facility might be perceived useful, especially in tight labour markets, the opportunity to place an employee on a salary anywhere within the wide range between the band minimum and maximum gives managers the discretion to apply individual differentiation and therein license to cloud any notion of transparency (IDS, 2006). Where this is the case, broad-banding would appear to heighten the risk of an equal pay claim whilst simultaneously loosening the employer's rein on the pay budget, potentially leading to higher reward costs. So can pay levels be managed fairly and cost-consciously within a broad-banded pay structure?

Managing pay within a broad-banded pay structure

Perkins and White (2008) suggest employers have indeed been anxious about the potential for untrammelled pay progression as a result of wide pay bands. In an effort to curb costs and manage pay more systematically within a broad-banded structure, some organisations have sought to mark out zones within bands to indicate the expected salary range for particular roles. The salary level reflected in the zone is likely be arrived at by benchmarking with comparators in the external market. Similarly, a series of target rates for particular jobs in the band could be identified and superimposed upon the band to denote the market rate for a fully competent individual performing in the job. Further, a series of bars or gateways can be etched into the band to serve as thresholds. To cross a threshold and thereby access the higher salary zone beyond the bar, job holders might be required to demonstrate defined competency levels or reach particular standards of performance. These methods of managing pay within a broad-banded pay structure would appear to improve transparency and provide a surer basis for ensuring equal pay for work of equal value. The role for job evaluation in establishing a hierarchy of jobs within a broad-banded structure is also more apparent where zones or target rates for roles are incorporated.

STOP
and
think

- *Is there a grading structure within your organisation?*
- *How many grades/bands exist within your own organisation?*

Number of bands	Senior executives	Managerial/professional	Staff /manual
3 or less	☐	☐	☐
4–5	☐	☐	☐
6–9	☐	☐	☐
10+	☐	☐	☐

- *Would you classify your own organisation's pay structure as* **broad-graded**, **broad-banded** *or* **traditional (narrow-graded)**?
- *What advantages and disadvantages are associated with the pay structure in place within your own organisation?*

Job families

Finally, pay structures can be characterised wholly or partially by the use of job family structures, or labour market structures as they are sometimes called. Armstrong (2002: 206) maintains that

> a job family structure consists of separate grade or pay structures for jobs which are related through the activities carried out and the basic skills used, but are differentiated by the level of responsibility, skill or competence required.

There may be six to eight levels within each job family, representing the range of jobs in the family from lower ranking jobs through to higher ranking posts (CIPD, 2008b). In essence, this approach to devising pay structures treats different occupations or functions separately and results in a series of pay ladders for different sets of jobs. Alternatively, a single job family structure could co-exist with a main stream pay structure in an organisation where the family of jobs concerned cannot easily be assimilated in the mainstream structure without giving rise to anomalies. In practice, job family pay structures are beneficial where an organisation needs to recruit to job roles within a particular occupational group and there is fierce competition in the labour market forcing the price of wages up. A job family pay structure allows the organisation to align to the external market more closely and so improve its chances of attracting and retaining adequate resources (CIPD, 2008b).

Pay progression

As Wright (2004: 78) argues 'there is little point in organisations having elaborate pay structures unless they are offering employees some progression opportunities for their pay *within* the pay structure' (original emphasis). A number of means are at the organisation's disposal to manage employees' movement within the salary structure, indeed, the way in which this is done in different types of organisations tends to vary far more than actual levels of wages and salaries (Perkins and White, 2008). *How* organisations pay portrays their stance on reward and is in many ways a more strategic decision than *how much* to pay. Where a strategic approach to reward is manifest, methods of pay progression will be informed by a clear notion of the organisation's values and strategic imperatives such that the 'right' individuals are recognised and rewarded for the 'right' behaviours. As was suggested earlier in this chapter, strategic approaches to reward are not universally applied, and even where they are, weaknesses and difficulties often mire best efforts. Where pay progression is concerned sometimes pragmatic decisions, underscored by the lack of resources and expertise to design and manage more elaborate pay progression mechanisms, drive organisations to apply blanket solutions such as automatic annual increments linked to employee service and across-the-board percentage pay increases. Indeed, for some organisations, and the stakeholders involved in the particular employment relationship, annual service-related increments and unified pay awards may signify equity, parity and transparency and therefore be viewed more positively than other means of salary progression.

However, whilst service-related pay progression rewards the build-up of expertise in the job and may help employers with retention, it risks signalling to employees that longevity of service is more important than the quality and/or quality of the work undertaken and the manner in which work is conducted. Similarly, universal pay increases, resulting in the same pay award to everyone regardless of their contribution, fail to take into account other factors that might justifiably be used to determine the speed and scale of individual salary progression. Service-related increments are a traditional method of pay progression in the public sector, but they are less frequently used by private sector employers who tend to prefer mechanisms that reward other factors such as performance, competence and skill (CIPD, 2008c). Similarly the 2009 CIPD Reward Survey shows that the use of collective bargaining, resulting in the same percentage pay increase for represented groups of employees, is far more prevalent in the public sector than it is in private sector and voluntary sector organisations.

In contrast, a number of alternative means of managing salary progression are available including:

Individual performance-related pay (PRP)

PRP links individual pay progression with employee performance. The basic notion of individual PRP is that the promise of rewards contingent on performance will incentivise employees to perform optimally thus raising individual performance and leading to improved levels of organisational performance. Within a PRP scheme, employee performance is typically assessed against pre-set targets or pre-agreed objectives often at appraisal time, although a separate pay review meeting could be used to determine a PRP increase. PRP payments may be consolidated into base pay or paid as a bonus (variable pay). PRP schemes ebb and flow in popularity and have been the subject of much controversial debate in the reward literature. In particular the supposed causal link between PRP and performance or productivity has been heavily questioned (Thompson, 1992; Marsden and Richardson, 1994; Kessler and Purcell, 1992). Indeed, rather than glowing accolades heralding the benefits of PRP, much attention has been drawn to the potential negative ramifications associated with using it. Reservations tend to revolve around the following issues:

- PRP schemes operate on the basis that employees will be motivated by money whereas motivational theories suggest money is not the only motivator, or even necessarily an effective motivator.
- The size of the 'pay pot' and how to divide this appropriately commensurate with individual performance achievements.
- Problems associated with measuring performance in a fair and objective manner.
- The ability of managers to manage the award of PRP; to make, communicate and justify difficult and potentially divisive reward decisions.
- Potential for pay discrimination/bias.
- Potential harm to efforts to engender team-work as individual PRP encourages employees to focus on their own performance targets or objectives without concern for the greater good of the team, department or wider organisation.
- Focus on output/outcomes, but not the means used to accomplish performance outcomes.

Further, Kessler and Purcell (1992) argue that linking assessments of performance to pay can induce tunnel vision whereby employees concentrate on those aspects of their job that trigger pay increases and ignore other parts of their job role. They also suggest that the limitations of the pay pot may mean that even employees with positive appraisal ratings only receive relatively small pay-outs that fail to measure up to the 'felt-fair' principle. In view of the criticisms individual PRP has attracted, the CIPD (2008c) indicates that some employers are moving towards a broader concept of contribution-related pay which not only measures outcomes but takes into account how employees achieved the performance outcome. Pay schemes related to contribution propose a more holistic view of individual performance taking into account processes and behaviour.

Contribution-related pay

As indicated above, interest in contribution-related pay is partly prompted by concern that individual performance-related pay takes too narrow an interpretation of performance by focusing upon outcomes in isolation. Organisations expressing a preference for contribution-related pay signal an interest in how the results are achieved as well as the results themselves. Indeed, the way in which employees conduct their work and the attitudes and behaviours they display may have been identified by such organisations as a critical factor in securing competitive advantage, so to try to match pay to softer measures of behaviours as well as harder results data would seem to indicate an attempt to design a pay progression mechanism that places due emphasis on strategic fit. Armstrong (2002: 309) defines contribution-related pay as 'a process for making pay decisions which are based on assessments of both the outcomes of the work carried out by individuals and the level of skill and competence which have influenced these outcomes'. It is thus an attempt at a mixed, blended or hybrid method incorporating the ethos of performance-related pay and competence based pay. It means paying for results (outcomes) and competence, for past performance and potential for future success (see Figure 9.7).

The mechanisms used to pay for contribution can vary considerably. Recognising that contribution-related pay incorporates multi-dimensional measures, some organisations reward the acquisition and display of required competencies in base pay, and reward results achieved with an unconsolidated bonus (variable pay) whilst others arrive at a composite increase in base pay taking into account both competence and results pay-outs (Brown and Armstrong, 1999).

Competence-related pay

Competence-related pay, used alone as means of pay progression, adopts a relatively narrow focus akin to the use of individual performance-related pay, however, emphasis is placed on employees' input to the job, rather than performance or output. The aim of competence-related pay is to encourage and reward the development of particular competencies desired by the organisation; it amounts to a method of paying employees for *the ability to* perform as opposed to paying *for* performance (Armstrong, 2002). Perkins and White (2008: 176) comment that 'whereas individual performance related pay can appear to be simply a punitive system to

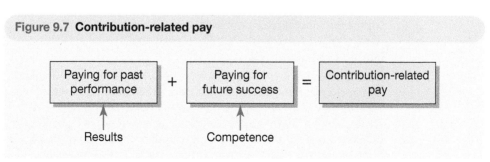

Figure 9.7 **Contribution-related pay**

Source: Adapted from Brown and Armstrong (1999: 137).

Table 9.5 The advantages and disadvantages of competence-related pay

Advantages	Disadvantages
• Encourages competence development	• Relies on appropriate, relevant and agreed competence profiles
• Fits de-layered organisations by facilitating lateral career moves	• Assessment of competence levels may be difficult
• Helps to integrate role and organisational core competencies	• Might pay for irrelevant competencies
• Forms part of an integrated, competence-based approach to people management	• Links to pay may be arbitrary
• Delivers message that competence is important	• Costs may escalate if inappropriate or unused competencies are rewarded

Source: from *Employee Reward*, 3rd ed., CIPD (Armstrong, M. 2002) p. 306, with the permission of the publisher, the Chartered Institute of Personnel and Development, London (www.cipd.co.uk).

penalise workers, competency-based systems can in contrast appear positive for employees' own career development'. The introduction of competence-based pay requires a competency framework to be in place and means for measuring individual competence levels to be agreed and understood by managers and employees alike. Table 9.5 summarises the advantages and disadvantages of competence-related pay.

> Skills based pay provides employees with a direct link between their pay progression and the skills they have required and can use effectively.   (Armstrong, 2002: 314)

Skills-based pay

Skills-based pay is sometimes referred to as 'pay for knowledge' or 'knowledge-based pay' (Perkins and White, 2008: 181). The aim of skills-based pay is to encourage employees to acquire additional skills, units of skill or specific qualifications that are deemed important to meet business needs. Skills-based pay might be closely tied to NVQs (National Vocational Qualifications) and the units and levels of qualifications set out in modular qualification frameworks of this type, alternatively the organisation may identify discernable skills or blocks of skills and arrange these in a hierarchy to indicate progressive skill levels. Marchington and Wilkinson (2008) identify both constraints and benefits in the use of skills-based pay. They argue that in order for skills-based pay to aid the efficiency and effectiveness of the organisation, thorough skills-needs analysis needs to be conducted to ensure only those skills critical to business success are encouraged and rewarded. Further, the organisation must pledge a clear commitment to training to underpin the scheme. Finally, whilst skills-based pay is likely to encourage a desire for upward mobility and thirst for skills acquisition amongst workers, care must be taken to ensure that only skills used are paid for, otherwise costs will escalate and the organisation will fail to profit. In addition to costs concerns, Armstrong (2002) suggests employees may become frustrated and de-motivated once they exhaust the skills hierarchy and pay progression grinds to a halt.

Team-based pay

Team rewards involve linking pay increases or a portion of individuals' pay increase to an assessment of performance at team rather than at an individual level. Team-based pay is essentially a variant of individual performance-related pay, designed to reinforce collaborative working and team results. Pay for the achievement of team objectives or targets can be distributed as a fixed sum to all team members or can be calculated as a percentage of base salary (Armstrong, 2002). Armstrong and Murlis (1998: 395) contest that 'the case for team pay looks good in theory but there are some formidable disadvantages':

- its effectiveness relies on the existence of well-defined and mature teams;
- distinguishing individual team members' contributions to the team could be problematic;
- it can be difficult to develop fair and objective methods for measuring team outcomes;
- team rivalry may develop;
- organisational flexibility may be hampered in the sense that employees in high-performing, well-rewarded teams might be unwilling to change roles;
- high performers in low-achieving teams may feel unduly penalised and dissatisfied.

Pay progression based on measures of organisational performance

Finally, there are a three main ways in which individuals' pay can be linked to organisational performance, namely gain-sharing, profit-related pay and share-ownership schemes. The general premise of all three schemes is that by linking pay to organisational performance, employees will be encouraged to focus on value-added activities and will identify more closely with the goals of the organisation. Where the organisation is successful as a result of employees' efforts and contributions, due rewards are passed to employees either in the form of a consolidated payment, a cash one-off payment (unconsolidated, variable pay) or the issue of company shares, and hence a financial stake in the organisation, where the preferred method of linking pay to organisational performance is a share-ownership scheme. Briefly, gain-sharing schemes apply a formula to award individuals a share of the financial gains made by the organisation as a result of improvements in quality, productivity enhancements or cost reduction strategies assisted by employees. Profit-related pay or profit-sharing, on the other hand, typically rewards employees with a slice of the company profits generated over and above a pre-specified profit target or level. The level of payouts varies between 2 and 3 per cent of salary and 10 per cent and more (Armstrong 2002: 356). CIPD data (2009a) would suggest that pay progression based on organisational performance is used as part of the pay progression criterion in around a half of all private sector organisations but that its use in the voluntary sector and in the public sector is limited.

Trends in reward practice – towards a strategic approach or more traditionalism?

Since the early 1990s 'new pay' enthusiasts (Lawler, 1990, 1995, 2000; Schuster and Zingheim, 1992) have consistently promoted the efficacy of transforming pay and reward such that it serves as a more effective driver of organisational performance. In essence, 'new pay' or 'dynamic pay' (Flannery *et al.*, 1996) advocate a far more managerialist view of the design and application of reward tools, resonating with the acclaimed superiority of strategic approaches to reward and the notion of 'total rewards'. Its key ingredients include a greater helping of variable pay, a move away from rigid payment structures to fluid and flexible ones, pay centred on the person not on the job, pay progression dependent on performance, competence, skills, contribution or some other form of contingent pay and a shift away from collectivism to individualism in reward. Such practices are considered to offer the organisation greater agility to reward individual employees commensurate with the impact they make upon critical business objectives and greater control over the pay budget. In this final part of the chapter, we discuss the extent to which organisations in the UK appear to echo the new pay rhetoric by marking out the support of business goals as the supreme priority governing reward objectives and throwing out traditional pay practices in favour of the new.

As we have learned throughout this chapter, there are a multitude of ways to do reward. At the same time, there is a strong tide running through business text books, the HR practitioner press and the professional body, persuading organisations that the right way to do reward is to align it with business strategy. Much of the evidence would suggest that despite the pressure to make the link to business strategy few have grasped the nettle firmly. Indeed, the 2009 CIPD Reward Survey indicates a smaller proportion of respondents with a reward strategy in place than the year before and no more enthusiasm to devise one in the year ahead. The CIPD attributes the drop to the current economic turmoil but their reward adviser, Charles Cotton, considers this foolhardy, 'I believe that during these difficult times it becomes even more important for practitioners to determine whether their reward practices support the objectives of the business' (2009a: 35).

Whilst there might be loose attachment to fully fledged reward strategy, there is evidence that elements of 'new pay' are permeating reward practices, particularly in the private sector. Here we see greater use of broad-banded pay structures, greater reference to market rates when determining salary levels and a higher propensity to use more varied and individualised methods of pay progression, 'Only in the public sector and the not for profit sector is seniority-based pay still the most common form of progression' (Perkins and White, 2008: 193). The decline of collective bargaining in the private sector and the rise in performance-related pay would also seem to indicate that a managerial agenda of individualism and greater use of contingent pay in place of uniform rates for jobs is winning through (Kersley *et al.*, 2006). In contrast, much of the public sector, at least in non-managerial roles, remains riddled with traditionalism.

Summary

This chapter began by outlining seven key objectives and these are revisited here.

- Historically, the area of HRM that we now recognise and understand as employee reward, majorly concerned wages and payment systems and the ways in which these could be used to exert control over both sides of the wage/effort bargain, enlarge the area of managerial control and so maximise organisational profitability.

- Contemporaneously, employee reward is defined more broadly to include base pay, variable pay, benefits and non-financial rewards.

- Reward is now recognised by many employers as a key strategic lever which can be used to mould and direct employee behaviour such that it supports and reinforces business goals. Strategic approaches to reward emphasise the importance of matching reward systems and practices to corporate strategy and integrating reward such that it complements other HR policies and practices. Debates persist, however, as to the precise contribution reward can make to business performance and doubts are cast on the ability of employers to design and implement reward strategy effectively.

- There are no right and wrong approaches to employee reward, rather, a myriad of choices are available to organisations. Key choices entail whether to pay for the person or pay for the job, whether to centralise or decentralise reward decision making, whether to place primary focus on internal equity when determining pay or be more concerned with external benchmarks, whether to build hierarchy into the reward system such that there are seniority or status related rewards or to devise a harmonised, single-status approach and how to determine the precise nature of the reward 'mix'.

- Reward decisions are influenced by a range of factors in the external operating environment. In particular, the economic climate affects employers' ability to pay and it guides organisations in determining salary levels/size of the pay review. The legal framework surrounding reward is designed to protect the low paid, set standards for hours of work and holiday entitlement and to ensure equal pay for work of equal value.

- In practice, approaches to reward are influenced by the size and nature of the organisation, the presence of trade unions, ownership/sector and types of workers employed
- Notable differences emerge between the public sector and private sector in terms of favoured methods for establishing pay levels, the design of pay structures and the criteria for pay progression.
- Despite the rhetoric of 'new pay' and the resounding case for strategic approaches to reward, traditionalism remains pervasive alongside experimentation with the new.

Case study

Changes to reward and recognition at KCLSU

King's College London Students' Union (KCLSU) is an independent, voluntary-sector organisation, affiliated to the National Union of Students (NUS). It enjoys a close relationship with King's College London (KCL), the organisation's current regulator and principal source of funding. KCLSU's purpose is to represent the voice of students at KCL and provide services and facilities to both support and enrich students' lives. KCLSU employs a number of permanent staff in a range of managerial and support roles, in addition, four students are elected annually by the student body to serve a sabbatical year as officers of the union. Elected officers join the payroll of KCLSU during their period of office. This case study captures the process of reviewing reward at KCLSU and poses two alternatives for the future direction of reward strategy within the organisation.

Background

Pay structures and reward strategy at KCLSU need to be reviewed for three main reasons:

- KCLSU currently uses the pay structure in place at King's College London (KCL), an arrangement that has persisted for many years. Along with much of the higher education sector, KCL is currently undergoing a process of modernisation within its pay structures and the current structure is in the process of being phased out. KCLSU is unsure whether the new KCL pay framework will be appropriate for adoption in the students' union. Also, a reconsideration of the logic of KCLSU sharing the KCL pay structure is timely as the organisation is on the brink of becoming regulated by the Charity Commission, rather than the college, and subject to more diversified funding.
- The recognition that there is a need for a modern pay structure to reflect the values of KCLSU, such as contribution and development, and the fact that KCLSU is a modern, forward thinking organisation

- KCLSU needs to be a competitive employer within the voluntary sector, this is essential for staff recruitment and retention purposes

Current system

As indicated above, KCLSU currently utilises the pay scales and process in operation at KCL. The current pay structure is based on the following criteria:

- Several pay spines exist for different grades of staff within the college. KCLSU currently uses two of the existing KCL pay spines: 'Academic and related', which is used primarily for the senior management team and 'Clerical and related' for all other staff.
- The pay spines are divided into overlapping grades; each grade has up to nine increments including discretionary increments at the top of each of grade.
- Individual salary progression is via automatic annual increment to the top of a grade.
- A cost of living increase is awarded annually in August (usually in the region of 3 per cent).
- Discretionary increments are subject to authorisation by a staff member's line manager, historically these have been awarded without question and there is an expectation in place that they will be granted.
- Once a staff member has reached the top of their grade, a proposal for progression to the next grade can be submitted to the HR Committee, who will make a decision as to whether progression will be authorised or not. Currently, the President, Chief Executive and Human Resources Manager sit on the HR Committee.
- If progression to the next grade is not authorised, the staff member will stay at the top of their current grade. The HR Committee will automatically review their salary annually.
- Salaries for new staff members are determined through comparison with existing roles.

This system has a number of inherent problems.

Case study continued

Issues with the current system

There are a number of significant issues with the current pay structure:

- *Progression*: currently, progression through the grades and the award of annual increments is primarily automatic and based on length of service rather than individual contribution. Several staff members will reach the upper limit of their current grade or scale within the next 12–18 months.
- *CEO remuneration*: the KCL pay scales have historically proved unsuitable for the remuneration of the KCLSU Chief Executive due to their upper limits. Therefore KCLSU has developed its own scale for this post and advises the KCL payroll for pay-processing purposes.
- *Benchmarking*: historically benchmarking has only taken place within the students' union sector and not against charity, not-for-profit or public sector equivalents. Increasingly, staff are being attracted to public sector/charity roles as opposed to staying with the students' union world. A recent salary benchmarking exercise drawing information from *Charity Rewards 2005/2006: A Comprehensive National Survey of Pay and Benefits in the Voluntary Sector*[1] has highlighted that current KCLSU salaries may be uncompetitive within the voluntary sector, especially at junior and middle management level i.e. 42 per cent of staff. In fact, the current upper limits of the salary ranges for KCLSU middle and junior managers are below the lower quartile for the charity sector. Taking a wider view, all the upper limits of the current salary ranges are below the median for the charity sector with the exception of the Skilled Manual and Specialist Clerical roles, where the upper limit of the salary range sits £617 above the median. All the lower limits of the current salary ranges are below the lower quartile for the sector, except that for Skilled Manual and Specialist Clerical roles. Elected officer remuneration is typically below that of graduate entrants.
- *Pay and performance*: the KCL pay scales have no latitude for relating pay to performance; there is no reward for good performance other than discretionary rises; there is no organisational imperative added to personal performance. The pay structure has no 'bonus' mechanism.

Observations and developments

KCL pay and modernisation programme

The pay and modernisation programme is KCL's response to the National Framework Agreement (NFA), which focuses on modernising pay within the Higher Education sector. The guiding principles of the programme are those of equal pay for work of equal value and consistency of grading.

- The programme also aims to harmonise terms and conditions of employment for all job roles within the college.
- The new pay structure will focus on rewarding individual contribution; progression will be linked to satisfactory performance and tied into a new appraisal scheme.
- Individual contribution will be measured by both performance (outputs) and competence (inputs).
- The new pay structure will provide the ability to make annual additional payments for rewarding outstanding individual performance.
- The new pay structure will use a single set of pay grades for all staff. Position of a role on the pay spine is to be determined by a single job evaluation scheme. The scheme in use is HERA (Higher Education Role Analysis).
- There are five job families of associated job roles, which are designed to aid job evaluation and underpin career paths.

Considerations – stay with KCL or 'go it alone'?

KCL has indicated that KCLSU is welcome to assimilate to the new KCL pay structure and continue to use college payroll services, however, KCLSU is unsure whether continuing to mirror KCL's pay structures and philosophy will adequately reflect and support the competencies and values KCLSU is striving to embed. KCLSU is also concerned that the issues it currently experiences as a result of adopting KCL's reward framework will prevail with the new, modernised version.

KCLSU want to adopt a reward strategy capable of harnessing the skills and enthusiasm of KCLSU staff to provide a fantastic service to students at KCL, through a clear and sustainable link between reward and achievement. In particular they are keen to ensure that the new approach will:

- provide the flexibility to respond to different demands in a way that is simple, clear and free from bureaucracy, recognising that different parts of the business have different needs;
- provide predictable or guaranteed earnings that give financial certainty, but with the opportunity to reflect upon business success, and reward people for the passion or creativity that contributes to that success;

Case study continued

- value people for what they do and how they do it, so that KCLSU delivers on its promises and makes a difference to the quality of student life at KCL;
- act as an effective magnet to attract good people, recognising the need for a steady influx of fresh thinking and new approaches, alongside the development of existing talent;
- support KCLSU values and reward employees for living KCLSU values (see Table).

KCLSU values

Value	Examples of how this might be demonstrated
Making sure every person in the organisation matters	• Communicates openly and honestly, always giving consideration to the views and feelings of others • Listens to others, questions when unclear to ensure mutual understanding and allows for discussion • Gives and receive feedback sensitively creating an environment where issues can be discussed constructively • Acts as a team player, actively supports team and organisation objectives • Demonstrates cross-organisational understanding • Shows respect and consideration for the needs of others, and the context within which they work • Demonstrates an understanding of the value of diversity, and the strengths and skills of others
Focusing on our students	• Has a clear understanding of role, and how it relates to the team's and KCLSU's objectives • Demonstrates dedication and enthusiasm towards students • Represents KCLSU positively to students • Seeks and acts upon feedback from both students and internal/external sources.
Continually striving to improve	• Is focused on meeting and exceeding objectives • Is prepared to ask for support from colleagues/line manager when required, to help meet objectives • Sets challenging targets that encourage personal development • Committed to innovation, developing new ideas and solutions • Demonstrates adaptability, flexibility, and a willingness to experiment • When required is entrepreneurial and willing to take appropriate risks
Not being complacent, overcoming unnecessary bureaucracy	• Actively seeks and shares information for the benefit of themselves, team and KCLSU • Seeks to develop effective and efficient ways of working at individual, team and organisational level • Sees mistakes as an opportunity to learn and encourages others to think in the same way
Being confident of our role	• Promotes positive understanding of the aims of KCLSU • Acts as a role model inspiring, supporting, motivating and encouraging others • Raises awareness and understanding of issues affecting students • Values the contribution of others, and recognises and celebrates others' achievements
Managing people well	• Articulates a clear vision for staff; establishes clear aims and objectives for individuals and teams • Ensures that every team member has a clear understanding of their role and how it relates to KCLSU's objectives • Manages individuals and teams consistently, objectively and fairly • Carries out constructive performance reviews with team members • Encourages colleagues to continue their professional development • Listens to feedback and forms recommendations to improve service, develop ideas and deal with issues • Helps develop a culture in which people are valued and able to reach their full potential

1. Croner Reward 2005.

Source: KCLSU

Case study continued

Questions

1 Critically assess the degree to which KCL's pay and modernisation programme is likely to address the issues and concerns KCLSU currently experiences as a result of using the KCL pay framework

2 Consider the benefits and risks associated with KCLSU 'going it alone'.

3 Identify the immediate and on-going/longer-term resource implications for KCLSU if the organisation decides to break away from the KCL pay framework and supporting infrastructure.

4 Using your knowledge and understanding of reward options identify and justify a set of preliminary proposals for a KCLSU 'tailor-made' reward strategy.

References and further reading

Adams, J. (1965) 'Inequity and social exchange' in L. Berkowitz (ed.) *Advances in Experimental Social Psychology 2*, New York: Academic Press, pp. 267–96.

Anthony, P.D. (1977) *The Ideology of Work*. London: Tavistock Publications.

Armstrong, M. (2002) *Employee Reward*, 3rd edn. London: CIPD.

Armstrong, M. and Brown, D. (2006) *Strategic Reward*. London: Kogan Page.

Armstrong, M. and Murlis, H. (1998) *Reward Management; A Handbook of Remuneration Strategy and Practice*. London: Kogan Page.

Armstrong, M. and Stephens, T. (2005) *A Handbook of Employee Reward Management and Practice*. London: Kogan Page.

Armstrong, M., Cummins, A., Hastings, S. and Wood, W. (2003) *Job Evaluation: A Guide to Achieving Equal Pay*. London: Kogan Page.

Arrowsmith, J. and Gilman, M. (2005) 'Small firms and the national minimum wage' in S. Marlow, D. Patton and M. Ram (eds) *Managing Labour in Small Firms*. London: Routledge, pp. 159–77.

Baldwin, M. and Johnson, W. (2006) 'A critical review of studies of discrimination against workers with disabilities' in W. Rodgers III (ed.) *Handbook on the Economics of Discrimination*. Gloucester: Edward Elgar, pp. 119–60.

Barrett, R. and Mayson, S. (2007) 'Human resource management in growing small firms', *Journal of Small Business and Enterprise Development*, 14, 2, 307–20.

Barrett, R., Mayson, S. and Warriner, M. (2008) 'The relationship between small firm growth and HRM practices' in R. Barrett and S. Mayson (eds) *International Handbook of Entrepreneurship and HRM*. Cheltenham: Edward Elgar, pp. 186–204.

Beer, M. (1984) *Managing Human Assets*. New York: Free Press.

Beer, M., Spector, B., Lawrence, P., Mills, D. and Walton, R. (1984) *Human Resource Management; A General Manager's Perspective*. New York: Free Press.

Bevan, S. (2000) *Reward Strategy: 10 Common Mistakes*. London: Institute for Employment Studies.

Blauner, R. (1964) *Alienation and Freedom: The Factory Worker and his Industry*. Chicago, IL: University of Chicago Press.

Bloom, M.C. and Milkovich, G. (1996) 'Issues in managerial compensation research' in C.L. Cooper and D.M. Rousseau (eds) *Trends in Organizational Behavior*, Vol. 3. Chichester: John Wiley, pp. 23–47.

Bowey, A. and Lupton, T. (1973) *Job and Pay Comparisons*. Aldershot: Gower.

Braverman, H. (1974) *Labour and Monopoly Capital: The Degradation of Work in the Twentieth Century*. London: Monthly Review Press.

Brown, D. and Armstrong, M. (1999) *Paying for Contribution; Real Performance-Related Pay Strategies*. London: Kogan Page.

Brown, D. and Dive, B. (2009) 'Level-pegging'. *People Management*, 15 January: 26–29.

Burawoy, M. (1985) *The Politics of Production*. London: Verso.

Burke, R. and Cooper, C. (2008) *The Long Work Hours Culture: Causes, Consequences and Choices*. Bingley: Emerald.

Callaghan, G. and Thompson, P. (2001) 'Edwards revisited; technical control and call centres' 22 *Economic and Industrial Democracy*, 22: 13–40.

CIPD (2000) *A Study of Broad-banded and Job Family Pay Structures*. CIPD Report. London: CIPD.

CIPD (2003) *Total Reward*. Research Summary. London: CIPD.

CIPD (2005) *Reward Strategy: How to Develop a Reward Strategy*. A CIPD Practical Tool. London: CIPD.

CIPD (2007) *Reward Management*. A CIPD Survey. London: CIPD.

CIPD (2008a) *Reward Management*. A CIPD Survey. London: CIPD.

CIPD (2008b) *Market Pricing; Approaches and Considerations*. CIPD Factsheet. London: CIPD.

CIPD (2008c) *Pay Progression*. CIPD Factsheet. London: CIPD.

CIPD (2009a) *Reward Management*. CIPD Survey. London: CIPD.

CIPD (2009b) *Pay and Reward: An Overview*. CIPD Factsheet. London: CIPD.

Conboy, B. (1976) *Pay at Work*. London: Arrow Books.

Cotton, C. (2009) 'Workers gloomy about their pay prospects', *Impact: Quarterly update on CIPD Policy and Research*, 26: 18–19.

Druker, J. and White, G. (2009) 'Introduction' in G. White and J. Druker (eds) *Reward Management: A Critical Text*. Abingdon: Routledge, pp. 1–22.

Dundon T. and Rollinson, D. (2004) *Employment Relations in Small Firms*. London: Routledge.

Employee Benefits/MX Financial Solutions (2003) 'Flexible Benefits Research 2003', *Employee Benefits*, April: 4–9.

Equality and Human Rights Commission (2009) www.equalityandhumanrights.org.

e-Reward (2007) *Graded Pay Structures*, factsheet. www.e-reward.co.uk.

Evain, E. (2008) *Working Conditions Laws 2006–2007*. Geneva: ILO.

Eyraud, F. and Saget, C. (2005) *The Fundamentals of Minimum Wage Fixing*. Geneva: ILO.

Flannery, T.P., Hafrichter, D.A. and Platten, P.E. (1996) *People, Performance and Pay*. New York: The Free Press.

Fredman, S. (2008) 'Reforming equal pay laws', 37 *Industrial Law Journal 193*.

Fudge, J. and Owens, R. (2006) *Precarious Work, Women and the New Economy*. Oxford: Hart Publishing.

Gollan, P. (2007) *Employee Representation in Non-Union Firms*. London: Sage.

Gospel, H. (1992) *Markets, Firms and the Management of Labour in Modern Britain*. Cambridge: Cambridge University Press.

Heery, E. (2000) 'The new pay: risk and representation at work' in D. Winstanley and J. Woodall (eds) *Ethical Issues in Contemporary Human Resource Management*. Basingstoke: Palgrave, pp. 172–88.

Hellerstein, J. and Newmark, D. (2006) 'Using matched employer-employee data to study labor market discrimination' in W. Rodgers III (ed.) *Handbook on the Economics of Discrimination*. Gloucester: Edward Elgar, pp. 29–60.

Herzberg, F. (1966) *Work and the Nature of Man*. Cleveland, OH: World Publishing.

Hewlett, S. and Luce, C. (2006) 'Extreme jobs: the dangerous allure of the 70-hour work week', *Harvard Business Review*, (December): 49.

Hill, S. (1981) *Competition and Control at Work*. London: Heinemann.

Hinton, J. (1986) *Labour and Socialism*. London: Wheatsheaf Books.

Humbert A.L. and Lewis, S. (2008) 'I have no life other than work – long working hours, blurred boundaries and family life' in R. Burke and C. Cooper *The Long Work Hours Culture: Causes, Consequences and Choices*. Bingley: Emerald, pp. 159–82.

IDS (2000) 'Job evaluation', *Incomes Data Services StudyPlus*; Autumn.

IDS (2002) 'Kingsmill recommends a package of measures to address the gender pay gap', *Incomes Data Services Report 848*, January: 4–5.

IDS (2006) *Developments in Occupational Pay Differentiation. A Research Report of the Office for Manpower Economics*, October 2006. London: Incomes Data Services.

IRS (2003) 'Employers value job evaluation', *IRS Employment Review 790 /Employment Trends*, 19 December: 9–16.

IRS (2008) 'Survey of pay prospects'.

Jamieson, S. (1999) 'Equal Pay' in A. Morris and T. O'Donnell (eds) *Feminist Perspectives on Employment Law*. London: Cavendish, pp. 223–40.

Kersley, B., Alpin, C., Forth, J., Bryson, A., Bewley, H., Dix, G. and Oxenbridge, S. (2006) *Inside the Workplace: Findings from the 2004 Workplace Employment Relations Survey*. Abingdon: Routledge.

Kessler, I. (2001) 'Reward system choices' in J. Storey (ed.) *Human Resource Management: A Critical Text*, 2nd edn. London: Thomson Learning, pp. 206–31.

Kessler, I. (2007) 'Reward choices: strategy and equity' in J. Storey, (ed.) *Human Resource Management: A Critical Text*, 3rd edn. London: Thomson Learning, pp. 159–76.

Kessler, I. and Purcell, J. (1992) 'Performance related pay; objectives and application'. *Human Resource Management Journal*, 2, 3, Spring: 16–33.

Kohn, A. (1993) 'Why incentive plans cannot work', *Harvard Business Review*, September–October: 54–62.

Lawler, E. (1990) *Strategic Pay*. San Francisco, CA: Jossey-Bass.

Lawler, E. (1995). 'The new pay; a strategic approach', *Compensation and Benefits Review*, July/August: 46–54.

Lawler, E. (2000) 'Pay and strategy; new thinking for the new millennium', *Compensation and Benefits Review*, January/February: 7–12.

Lewis, P. (2006) 'Reward management' in T. Redman and A. Wilkinson (eds) *Contemporary Human Resource Management*, 2nd edn. London: FT/Pearson, pp. 126–52.

Littler, C. (1982) *The Development of the Labour Process in Capitalist Societies*. London: Heinemann.

Littler, C. (ed.) (1985) *The Experience of Work*. Aldershot: Gower.

Lovell, J. (1977) *British Trade Unions 1875–1933*. London: MacMillan.

Low Pay Commision (2001) *1st Report of the Low Pay Commission*. London: HMSO.

Marchington, M. and Wilkinson, A. (2008) *HRM at Work; People Management and Development*, 4th edn. London: CIPD.

Marlow, S., Patton, D. and Ram, M. (2005) *Managing Labour in Small Firms*. London: Routledge.

Marsden, D. and Richardson, R. (1994) 'Performing for pay? The effects of "merit pay" in a public service', *British Journal of Industrial Relations*, June: 243–61.

Mazzarol, T. (2003) 'A model of small business HR growth management', *International Journal of Entrepreneurial Behaviour and Research*, 9: 27–49.

McCann, D. (2005) *Working Time Laws: A Global Perspective*. Geneva: ILO.

McColgan, A. (2008) 'Equal pay' in P. Cane and J. Conaghan, *The New Oxford Companion to Law*. Oxford: Oxford University Press, pp. 401–02.

Milkovitch, G. and Newman, J. (1996) *Compensation*, 5th edn. Burr Ridge: Irwin.

Murlis, H. (2004) 'Managing rewards' in D. Rees and G. McBain (eds) *People Management: Challenges and Opportunities*. Basingstoke: Palgrave, pp. 152–70.

Perkins, S.J. and White, G. (2008) *Employee Reward: Alternatives, Consequences and Contexts*. London: CIPD.

Pfeffer, J. (1998) 'Six dangerous myths about pay', *Harvard Business Review*, May–June: 108–21.

Ritzer, G. (1997) *The McDonaldization Theory*. London: Sage.

Ritzer, G. (2000) *The McDonaldization of Society*. London: Sage.

Schuster, J. and Zingheim, P. (1992) *The New Pay: Linking Employee and Organisational Performance*. New York: Lexington Books.

Storey, J. (1992) *Developments in the Management of Human Resources*. Oxford: Blackwell.

Taylor, F.W. (1964) *Scientific Management*. New York: Harper & Row.

Taylor, P. and Bain, P. (1999) 'An assembly line in the head' *Industrial Relations Journal*, 30: 101–17.

Taylor, P. and Bain, P. (2001) 'Trade unions, workers rights and the frontier of control in UK call centres', *Economic and Industrial Democracy*, 22: 29–41.

Taylor, S (2008) *People Resourcing*, 4th edn. London: CIPD.

Thompson E.P. (1991) 'Time, work-discipline and Industrial Capitalism' in E.P. Thompson *Customs in Common*. Harmondsworth: Penguin, pp. 68–92.

Thompson, M. (1992) 'Pay and performance; the employer experience', *Institute of Manpower Studies*. Report No. 218, London.

Thompson, M. (2009) 'Salary progression systems' in G. White and J. Druker (eds) *Reward Management; A Critical Text*. Abingdon: Routledge, pp. 120–47.

Thompson, P. (1983) *The Nature of Work*. London: Macmillian.

Thompson, P. and Milsome. S. (2001) *Reward Determination in the UK*. Research Report, London: CIPD.

Urwick, L. (1958) *Personnel Management in Perspective*. Oxford: Oxford University Press.

Vroom, V. (1982) *Work and Motivation*. New York: John Wiley.

White, G. (2009) 'Determining pay' in G. White and J. Druker (eds) *Reward Management: A Critical Text*. Abingdon: Routledge, pp. 23–48.

Wood, A.W. (2000) 'Alienation' in *Concise Routledge Encyclopedia of Philosophy*. London: Routledge, p. 24.

Wood, S. (ed.) (1982) *The Degradation of Work?* London: Hutchinson.

WorldatWork (2000) *Total Rewards: From Strategy To Implementations*. Scottsdale, AZ: WorldatWork.

Wright, A. (2004) *Employee Reward in Context*. London: CIPD.

Wright, A. (2009) 'Benefits' in G. White and J. Druker (eds) *Reward Management: A Critical Text*. Abingdon: Routledge, pp. 174–91.

Yates, M.L. (1937) *Wages and Labour Conditions in British Engineering*. Cambridge.

Zeitlin, J. (1983) 'The labour strategies of British engineering employers 1890–1922' in H. Gospel and C. Littler, *Managerial Strategies & Industrial Relations*. Aldershot: Gower, pp. 25–54.

 For multiple-choice questions, exercises and annotated weblinks related to this topic, visit **www.pearsoned.co.uk/mymanagementlab**.

Part 5 Logistics and Supply Chain Management

Chapter 10

Operations strategy

Key questions

➤ What is strategy and what is operations strategy?

➤ What is the difference between a 'top-down' and a 'bottom-up' view of operations strategy?

➤ What is the difference between a 'market requirements' and an 'operations resources' view of operations strategy?

➤ How can an operations strategy be put together?

Introduction

No organization can plan in detail every aspect of its current or future actions, but all organizations need some strategic direction and so can benefit from some idea of where they are heading and how they could get there. Once the operations function has understood its role in the business and after it has articulated its performance objectives, it needs to formulate a set of general principles which will guide its decision-making. This is the operations strategy of the company. Yet the concept of 'strategy' itself is not straightforward; neither is operations strategy. This chapter considers four perspectives, each of which goes partway to illustrating the forces that shape operations strategy. Figure 10.1 shows the position of the ideas described in this chapter in the general model of operations management.

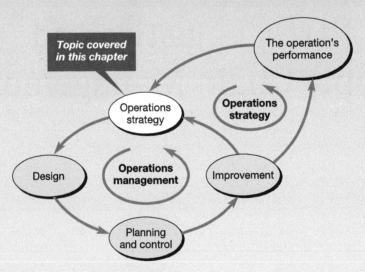

Figure 10.1 This chapter examines operations strategy

Operations in practice Two operations strategies: Flextronics and Ryanair[1]

The two most important attributes of any operations strategy are first that it aligns operations activities with the strategy of the whole organization, and second that it gives clear guidance. Here are two examples of very different businesses and very different strategies which nonetheless meet both criteria.

Ryanair is today Europe's largest low-cost airline (LCAs) and whatever else can be said about its strategy, it does not suffer from any lack of clarity. It has grown by offering low-cost basic services and has devised an operations strategy which is in line with its market position. The efficiency of the airline's operations supports its low-cost market position. Turnaround time at airports is kept to a minimum. This is achieved partly because there are no meals to be loaded onto the aircraft and partly through improved employee productivity. All the aircraft in the fleet are identical, giving savings through standardization of parts, maintenance and servicing. It also means large orders to a single aircraft supplier and therefore the opportunity to negotiate prices down. Also, because the company often uses secondary airports landing and service fees are much lower. Finally, the cost of selling its services is reduced where possible.

Ryanair has developed its own low-cost Internet booking service. In addition, the day-to-day experiences of the company's operations managers can also modify and refine these strategic decisions. For example, Ryanair changed its baggage handling contractors at Stansted airport in the UK after problems with misdirecting customers' luggage. The company's policy on customer service is also clear. *'We patterned Ryanair after Southwest Airlines, the most consistently profitable airline in the US'*, says Michael O'Leary, Ryanair's Chief Executive. *'Southwest founder Herb Kelleher created a formula for success that works by flying only one type of airplane – the 737, using smaller airports, providing no-frills service on-board, selling tickets directly to customers and offering passengers the lowest fares in the market. We have adapted his model for our marketplace and are now setting the low-fare standard for Europe. Our customer service'*, says O'Leary, *'is about the most well defined in the world. We guarantee to give you the lowest air fare. You get a safe flight. You get a normally on-time flight. That's the package. We don't, and won't, give you anything more. Are we going to say sorry for our lack of customer service? Absolutely not. If a plane is cancelled, will we put you up in a hotel overnight? Absolutely not. If a plane is delayed, will we give you a voucher for a restaurant? Absolutely not.'*

Source: Corbis

Flextronics is a global company based in Singapore that lies behind such well-known brand names as Nokia and Dell, which are increasingly using electronic manufacturing services (EMS) companies, such as Flextronics, which specialize in providing the outsourced design, engineering, manufacturing and logistics operations for the big brand names. It is amongst the biggest of those EMS suppliers that offer the broadest worldwide capabilities, from design to end-to-end vertically integrated global supply chain services. Flextronics' operations strategy must balance their customers' need for low costs (electronic goods are often sold in a fiercely competitive market) with their need for responsive and flexible service (electronics markets can also be volatile). The company achieves this in number of ways. First, it has an extensive network of design, manufacturing and logistics facilities in the world's major electronics markets, giving them significant scale and the flexibility to move activities to the most appropriate location to serve customers. Second, Flextronics offers vertical integration capabilities that simplify global product

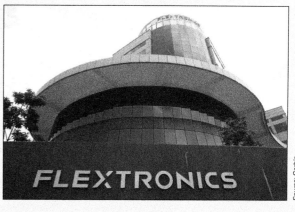

Source: Corbis

development and supply processes, moving a product from its initial design through volume production, test, distribution, and into post-sales service, responsively and efficiently. Finally, Flextronics has developed integrated industrial parks to exploit fully the advantages of their global, large-scale, high-volume capabilities. Positioned in low-cost regions, yet close to all major world markets, Flextronics industrial parks can significantly reduce the cost of production. Locations include Gdansk in Poland, Hungary, Guadalajara in Mexico, Sorocaba in Brazil, Chennai in India and Shanghai in China. Flextronics own suppliers are encouraged to locate within these parks, from which products can be produced on-site and shipped directly from the industrial park to customers, greatly reducing freight costs of incoming components and outgoing products. Products not produced on-site can be obtained from Flextronics' network of regional manufacturing facilities located near the industrial parks. Using this strategy, Flextronics says it can provide cost-effective delivery of finished products within 1–2 days of orders.

What is strategy and what is operations strategy?

Surprisingly, 'strategy' is not particularly easy to define. Linguistically the word derives from the Greek word '*strategos*' meaning 'leading an army'. And although there is no direct historical link between Greek military practice and modern ideas of strategy, the military metaphor is powerful. Both military and business strategy can be described in similar ways, and include some of the following.

- Setting broad objectives that direct an enterprise towards its overall goal.
- Planning the path (in general rather than specific terms) that will achieve these goals.
- Stressing long-term rather than short-term objectives.
- Dealing with the total picture rather than stressing individual activities.
- Being detached from, and above, the confusion and distractions of day-to-day activities.

Strategic decisions

Here, by '**strategic decisions**' we mean those decisions which are widespread in their effect on the organization to which the strategy refers, define the position of the organization relative to its environment, and move the organization closer to its long-term goals. But 'strategy' is more than a single decision; it is the *total pattern of the decisions* and actions that influence the long-term direction of the business. Thinking about strategy in this way helps us to discuss an organization's strategy even when it has not been explicitly stated. Observing the total pattern of decisions gives an indication of the *actual* strategic behaviour.

Operations strategy

Operations strategy concerns the pattern of strategic decisions and actions which set the role, objectives and activities of the operation. The term 'operations strategy' sounds at first like a contradiction. How can 'operations', a subject that is generally concerned with the day-to-day creation and delivery of goods and services, be strategic? 'Strategy' is usually regarded as the opposite of those day-to-day routine activities. But '*operations*' **is not the same as** '*operational*'. 'Operations' are the resources that create products and services. 'Operational' is the opposite of strategic, meaning day-to-day and detailed. So, one can examine both the operational *and* the strategic aspects of operations. It is also conventional to distinguish between the '**content**' **and the** '**process**' of operations strategy. The *content* of operations strategy is the specific decisions and actions which set the operations role, objectives and activities. The *process* of operations strategy is the method that is used to make the specific 'content' decisions.

'Operations' is not the same as 'operational'

The content and process of operations strategy

From implementing to supporting to driving strategy

Most businesses expect their operations strategy to improve operations performance over time. In doing this they should be progressing from a state where they are contributing very little to the competitive success of the business through to the point where they are directly responsible for its competitive success. This means that they should be able to, in turn, master the skills to first 'implement', then 'support', and then 'drive' operations strategy.

Implement strategy

Implementing business strategy. The most basic role of operations is to **implement strategy**. Most companies will have some kind of strategy but it is the operation that puts it into practice. You cannot, after all, touch a strategy; you cannot even see it; all you can see is how the operation behaves in practice. For example, if an insurance company has a strategy of moving to an entirely online service, its operations function will have to supervise the design of all the processes which allow customers to access online information, issue quotations, request further information, check credit details, send out documentation and so on. Without effective implementation even the most original and brilliant strategy will be rendered totally ineffective.

Support strategy

Supporting business strategy. **Support strategy** goes beyond simply implementing strategy. It means developing the capabilities which allow the organization to improve and refine its strategic goals. For example, a mobile phone manufacturer wants to be the first in the market with new product innovations so its operations need to be capable of coping with constant innovation. It must develop processes flexible enough to make novel components, organize its staff to understand the new technologies, develop relationships with its suppliers which help them respond quickly when supplying new parts, and so on. The better the operation is at doing these things, the more support it is giving to the company's strategy.

Drive strategy

Driving business strategy. The third, and most difficult, role of operations is to **drive strategy** by giving it a unique and long-term advantage. For example, a specialist food service company supplies restaurants with frozen fish and fish products. Over the years it has built up close relationships with its customers (chefs) as well as its suppliers around the world (fishing companies and fish farms). In addition it has its own small factory which develops and produces a continual stream of exciting new products. The company has a unique position in the industry because its exceptional customer relationships, supplier relationship and new product development are extremely difficult for competitors to imitate. In fact, the whole company's success is based largely on these unique operations capabilities. The operation drives the company's strategy.

Hayes and Wheelwright's four stages of operations contribution

The ability of any operation to play these roles within the organization can be judged by considering the organizational aims or aspirations of the operations function. Professors Hayes and Wheelwright of Harvard University,[2] developed a **four-stage model** which can be used to evaluate the role and contribution of the operations function. The model traces the progression of the operations function from what is the largely negative role of stage 1 operations to its becoming the central element of competitive strategy in excellent stage 4 operations. Figure 10.2 illustrates the four stages.

The four-stage model of operations contribution

Stage 1: Internal neutrality. This is the very poorest level of contribution by the operations function. It is holding the company back from competing effectively. It is inward-looking and, at best, reactive with very little positive to contribute towards competitive success. Paradoxically, its goal is 'to be ignored' (or 'internally neutral'). At least then it isn't holding the company back in any way. It attempts to improve by 'avoiding making mistakes'.

Stage 2: External neutrality. The first step of breaking out of stage 1 is for the operations function to begin comparing itself with similar companies or organizations in the outside market (being 'externally neutral'). This may not immediately take it to the 'first division' of companies in the market, but at least it is measuring itself against its competitors' performance and trying to implement 'best practice'.

Stage 3: Internally supportive. Stage 3 operations are amongst the best in their market. Yet, stage 3 operations still aspire to be clearly and unambiguously the very best in the market.

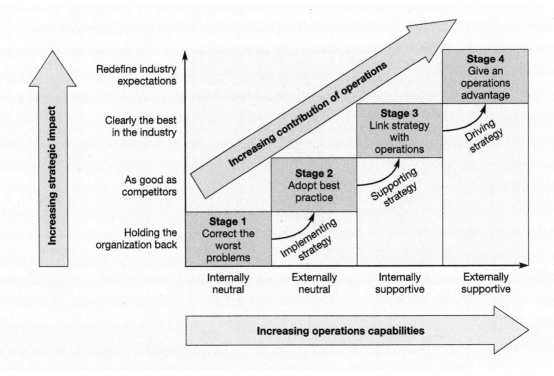

Figure 10.2 The four-stage model of operations contribution

They achieve this by gaining a clear view of the company's competitive or strategic goals and supporting it by developing appropriate operations resources. The operation is trying to be 'internally supportive' by providing a credible operations strategy.

Stage 4: Externally supportive. Yet Hayes and Wheelwright suggest a further stage – stage 4, where the company views the operations function as providing the foundation for its competitive success. Operations looks to the long term. It forecasts likely changes in markets and supply, and it develops the operations-based capabilities which will be required to compete in future market conditions. Stage 4 operations are innovative, creative and proactive and are driving the company's strategy by being 'one step ahead' of competitors – what Hayes and Wheelwright call 'being externally supportive'.

Critical commentary

The idea that operations can have a leading role in determining a company's strategic direction is not universally supported. Both Hayes and Wheelwright's stage 4 of their four-stage model and the concept of operations 'driving' strategy do not only imply that it is possible for operations to take such a leading role, but are explicit in seeing it as a 'good thing'. A more traditional stance taken by some authorities is that the needs of the market will always be pre-eminent in shaping a company's strategy. Therefore, operations should devote all their time to understanding the requirements of the market (as defined by the marketing function within the organization) and devote themselves to their main job of ensuring that operations processes can actually deliver what the market requires. Companies can only be successful, they argue, by positioning themselves in the market (through a combination of price, promotion, product design and managing how products and services are delivered to customers) with operations very much in a 'supporting' role. In effect, they say, Hayes and Wheelwright's four-stage model should stop at stage 3. The issue of an 'operations resource' perspective on operations strategy is discussed later in the chapter.

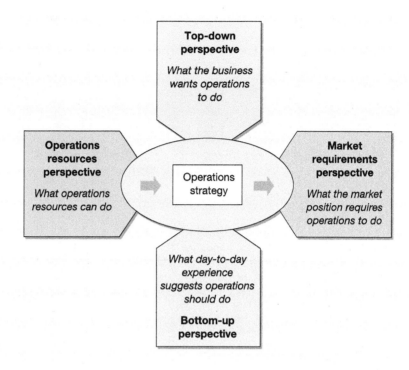

Figure 10.3 The four perspectives on operations strategy

Perspectives on operations strategy

Different authors have slightly different views and definitions of operations strategy. Between them, four 'perspectives' emerge:[3]

Top-down

Bottom-up

Market requirements

Operations resource capabilities

- Operation strategy is a **top-down** reflection of what the whole group or business wants to do.
- Operations strategy is a **bottom-up** activity where operations improvements cumulatively build strategy.
- Operations strategy involves translating **market requirements** into operations decisions.
- Operations strategy involves exploiting the **capabilities of operations resources** in chosen markets.

None of these four perspectives alone gives the full picture of what operations strategy is. But together they provide some idea of the pressures which go to form the content of operations strategy. We will treat each in turn (*see* Figure 10.3).

The 'top-down' and 'bottom-up' perspectives

Top-down strategies

Corporate strategy

Business strategy

A large corporation will need a strategy to position itself in its global, economic, political and social environment. This will consist of decisions about what types of business the group wants to be in, what parts of the world it wants to operate in, how to allocate its cash between its various businesses, and so on. Decisions such as these form the **corporate strategy** of the corporation. Each business unit within the corporate group will also need to put together its own business strategy which sets out its individual mission and objectives. This **business strategy** guides the business in relation to its customers, markets and competitors, and also the

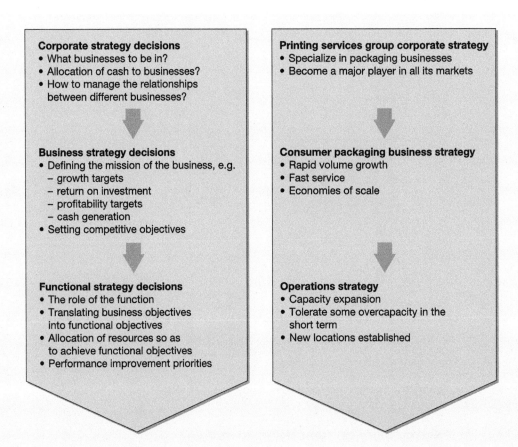

Figure 10.4 The top-down perspective of operations strategy and its application to the printing services group

Functional strategy

strategy of the corporate group of which it is a part. Similarly, within the business, **functional strategies** need to consider what part each function should play in contributing to the strategic objectives of the business. The operations, marketing, product/service development and other functions will all need to consider how best they should organize themselves to support the business's objectives.

So, one perspective on operations strategy is that it should take its place in this hierarchy of strategies. Its main influence, therefore, will be whatever the business sees as its strategic direction. For example, a printing services group has a company which prints packaging for consumer products. The group's management figures that, in the long term, only companies with significant market share will achieve substantial profitability. Its corporate objectives therefore stress market dominance. The consumer packaging company decides to achieve volume growth, even above short-term profitability or return on investment. The implication for operations strategy is that it needs to expand rapidly, investing in extra capacity (factories, equipment and labour) even if it means some excess capacity in some areas. It also needs to establish new factories in all parts of its market to offer relatively fast delivery. The important point here is that different business objectives would probably result in a very different operations strategy. The role of operations is therefore largely one of implementing or 'operationalizing' business strategy. Figure 10.4 illustrates this strategic hierarchy, with some of the decisions at each level and the main influences on the strategic decisions.

'Bottom-up' strategies

The 'top-down' perspective provides an orthodox view of how functional strategies *should* be put together. But in fact the relationship between the levels in the strategy hierarchy is more complex than this. Although it is a convenient way of thinking about strategy, this hierarchical model is not intended to represent the way strategies are always formulated. When any group is reviewing its corporate strategy, it will also take into account the circumstances, experiences and capabilities of the various businesses that form the group. Similarly, businesses, when reviewing their strategies, will consult the individual functions within the business about their constraints and capabilities. They may also incorporate the ideas which come from each function's day-to-day experience. Therefore an alternative view to the top-down perspective is that many strategic ideas emerge over time from operational experience. Sometimes companies move in a particular strategic direction because the ongoing experience of providing products and services to customers at an operational level convinces them that it is the right thing to do. There may be no high-level decisions examining alternative strategic options and choosing the one which provides the best way forward. Instead, a general consensus emerges from the operational level of the organization. The 'high-level' strategic decision-making, if it occurs at all, may confirm the consensus and provide the resources to make it happen effectively.

Suppose the printing services company described previously succeeds in its expansion plans. However, in doing so it finds that having surplus capacity and a distributed network of factories allows it to offer an exceptionally fast service to customers. It also finds that some customers are willing to pay considerably higher prices for such a responsive service. Its experiences lead the company to set up a separate division dedicated to providing fast, high-margin printing services to those customers willing to pay. The strategic objectives of this new division are not concerned with high-volume growth but with high profitability.

Emergent strategies

This idea of strategy being shaped by operational level experience over time is sometimes called the concept of **emergent strategies.**[4] Strategy is gradually shaped over time and based on real-life experience rather than theoretical positioning. Indeed, strategies are often formed in a relatively unstructured and fragmented manner to reflect the fact that the future is at least partially unknown and unpredictable (*see* Figure 10.5). This view of operations strategy is perhaps more descriptive of how things really happen, but at first glance it seems less useful in providing a guide for specific decision-making. Yet while emergent strategies are less easy to categorize, the principle governing a bottom-up perspective is clear: shape the operation's objectives and action, at least partly, by the knowledge it gains from its day-to-day activities. The key virtues required for shaping strategy from the bottom up are an ability to learn from experience and a philosophy of continual and incremental improvement.

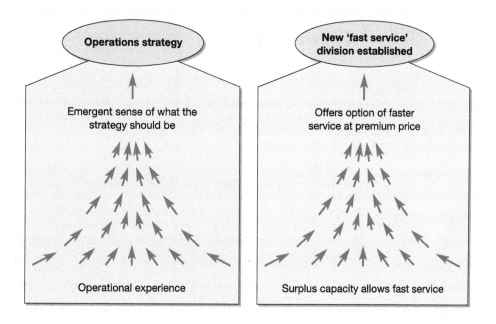

Figure 10.5 The 'bottom-up' perspective of operations strategy and its application to the printing services company

The market requirements and operations resources perspectives

Market-requirements-based strategies

One of the obvious objectives for any organization is to satisfy the requirements of its markets. No operation that continually fails to serve its markets adequately is likely to survive in the long term. And although understanding markets is usually thought of as the domain of the marketing function, it is also of importance to operations management. Without an understanding of what markets require, it is impossible to ensure that operations is achieving the right priority between its performance objectives (quality, speed, dependability, flexibility and cost). For example, the short case Giordano describes a company that designed its operations to fit what it saw as a market that was starting to prioritize quality of service.

Short case
Giordano

With a vision that explicitly states its ambition to be *'the best and the biggest world brand in apparel retailing'*, Giordano is setting its sights high. Yet it is the company that changed the rules of clothes retailing in the fast-growing markets around Hong Kong, China, Malaysia and Singapore, so industry experts take its ambitions seriously. Before Giordano, up-market shops sold high-quality products and gave good service. Cheaper clothes were piled high and sold by sales assistants more concerned with taking the cash than smiling at customers. Jimmy Lai, founder and Chief Executive of Giordano Holdings, changed all that. He saw that unpredictable quality and low levels of service offered an opportunity in the casual clothes market. Why could not value and service, together with low prices, generate better profits? His methods were radical. Overnight he raised the wages of his salespeople by between 30 and 40 per cent, all employees were told they would receive at least 60 hours of training a year and new staff would be allocated a 'big brother' or 'big sister' from among experienced staff to help them develop their service quality skills. Even more startling by the standards of his competitors, Mr Lai brought in a 'no-questions-asked' exchange policy irrespective of how long ago the

Source: Alamy Images

garment had been purchased. Staff were trained to talk to customers and seek their opinion on products and the type of service they would like. This information would be immediately fed back to the company's designers for incorporation into their new products. How Giordano achieved the highest sales per square metre of almost any retailer in the region and its founding operations principles are summarized in its 'QKISS' list.

- Quality – do things right.
- Knowledge – update experience and share knowledge.
- Innovation – think 'outside the box'.
- Simplicity – less is more.
- Service – exceed customers' expectations.

The market influence on performance objectives

Operations seek to satisfy customers through developing their five performance objectives. For example, if customers particularly value low-priced products or services, the operation will place emphasis on its cost performance. Alternatively, a customer emphasis on fast delivery will make speed important to the operation, and so on. These factors which define the customers' requirements are called **competitive factors**.[5] Figure 10.6 shows the relationship between some of the more common competitive factors and the operation's performance objectives. This list is not exhaustive; whatever competitive factors are important to customers should influence the priority of each performance objective. Some organizations put considerable effort into bringing an idea of their customers' needs into the operation.

Competitive factors

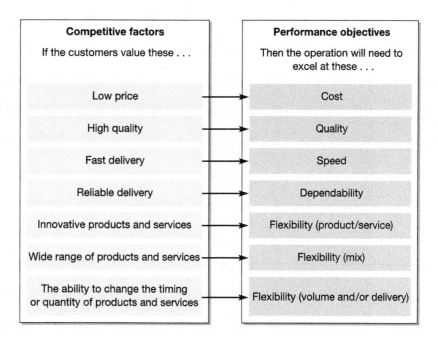

Figure 10.6 Different competitive factors imply different performance objectives

Order-winning and qualifying objectives

Order-winning factors

Qualifying factors

Less important factors

A particularly useful way of determining the relative importance of competitive factors is to distinguish between 'order-winning' and 'qualifying' factors.[6] **Order-winning factors** are those things which directly and significantly contribute to winning business. They are regarded by customers as key reasons for purchasing the product or service. Raising performance in an order-winning factor will either result in more business or improve the chances of gaining more business. **Qualifying factors** may not be the major competitive determinants of success, but are important in another way. They are those aspects of competitiveness where the operation's performance has to be above a particular level just to be considered by the customer. Performance below this 'qualifying' level of performance will possibly disqualify the company from being considered by many customers. But any further improvement above the qualifying level is unlikely to gain the company much competitive benefit. To order-winning and qualifying factors can be added **less important factors** which are neither order-winning nor qualifying. They do not influence customers in any significant way. They are worth mentioning here only because they may be of importance in other parts of the operation's activities.

Figure 10.7 shows the difference between order-winning, qualifying and less important factors in terms of their utility or worth to the competitiveness of the organization. The curves illustrate the relative amount of competitiveness (or attractiveness to customers) as the operation's performance at the factor varies. Order-winning factors show a steady and significant increase in their contribution to competitiveness as the operation gets better at providing them. Qualifying factors are 'givens'; they are expected by customers and can severely disadvantage the competitive position of the operation if it cannot raise its performance above the qualifying level. Less important objectives have little impact on customers no matter how well the operation performs in them.

Different customer needs imply different objectives

If, as is likely, an operation produces goods or services for more than one customer group, it will need to determine the order-winning, qualifying and less important competitive factors for each group. For example, Table 10.1 shows two 'product' groups in the banking indus-

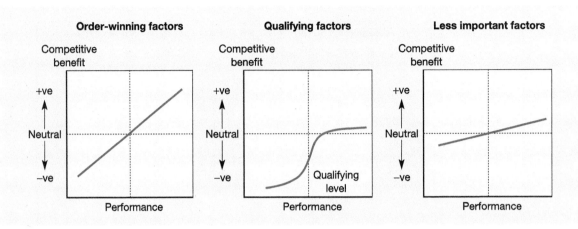

Figure 10.7 Order-winning, qualifying and less important competitive factors

Table 10.1 Different banking services require different performance objectives

	Retail banking	*Corporate banking*
Products	Personal financial services such as loans and credit cards	Special services for corporate customers
Customers	Individuals	Businesses
Product range	Medium but standardized, little need for special terms	Very wide range, many need to be customized
Design changes	Occasional	Continual
Delivery	Fast decisions	Dependable service
Quality	Means error-free transactions	Means close relationships
Volume per service type	Most services are high-volume	Most services are low-volume
Profit margins	Most are low to medium, some high	Medium to high

Competitive factors		
Order winners	Price Accessibility Speed	Customization Quality of service Reliability
Qualifiers	Quality Range	Speed Price
Less important		Accessibility

Internal performance objectives	Cost Speed Quality	Flexibility Quality Dependability

try. Here the distinction is drawn between the customers who are looking for banking services for their private and domestic needs (current accounts, overdraft facilities, savings accounts, mortgage loans, etc.) and those corporate customers who need banking services for their (often large) organizations. These latter services would include such things as letters of credit, cash transfer services and commercial loans.

Worked example

'It is about four years now since we specialized in the small-to-medium firms market. Before that we also used to provide legal services for anyone who walked in the door. So now we have built up our legal skills in many areas of corporate and business law. However, within the firm, I think we could focus our activities even more. There seem to be two types of assignment that we are given. About forty per cent of our work is relatively routine. Typically these assignments are to do with things like property purchase and debt collection. Both these activities involve a relatively standard set of steps which can be automated or carried out by staff without full legal qualifications. Of course, a fully qualified lawyer is needed to make some decisions; however, most work is fairly routine. Customers expect us to be relatively inexpensive and fast in delivering the service. Nor do they expect us to make simple errors in our documentation, in fact if we did this too often we would lose business. Fortunately our customers know that they are buying a standard service and don't expect it to be customized in any way. The problem here is that specialist agencies have been emerging over the last few years and they are starting to undercut us on price. Yet I still feel that we can operate profitably in this market and anyway, we still need these capabilities to serve our other clients. The other sixty per cent of our work is for clients who require far more specialist services, such as assignments involving company merger deals or major company restructuring. These assignments are complex, large, take longer, and require significant legal skill and judgement. It is vital that clients respect and trust the advice we give them across a wide range of legal specialisms. Of course they assume that we will not be slow or unreliable in preparing advice, but mainly it's trust in our legal judgement which is important to the client. This is popular work with our lawyers. It is both interesting and very profitable. But should I create two separate parts to our business, one to deal with routine services and the other to deal with specialist services? And, what aspects of operations performance should each part be aiming to excel at?' (Managing Partner, Branton Legal Services)

Analysis

Table 10.2 has used the information supplied above to identify the order winners, qualifiers and less important competitive factors for the two categories of service. As the Managing Partner suspects, the two types of service are very different. Routine services must be relatively inexpensive and fast, whereas the clients for specialist services must trust the quality of advice and range of legal skills available in the firm. The customers for routine services do not expect errors and those for specialist services assume a basic level of dependability and speed. These are the qualifiers for the two categories of service. Note that qualifiers are not 'unimportant'. On the contrary, failure to be 'up to standard' at them can lose the firm business. However, it is the order winner that attracts new business. Most significantly, the performance objectives which each operations partner should stress are very different. Therefore there does seem to be a case for separating the sets of resources (e.g. lawyers and other staff) and processes (information systems and procedures) that produce each type of service.

Table 10.2 Competitive factors and performance objectives for the legal firm

Service category	Routine services	Specialist services
Examples	Property purchase Debt collection	Company merger deals Company restructuring
Order winner	Price Speed	Quality of service Range of skills
Qualifiers	Quality (conformance)	Dependability Speed
Less important	Customization	Price
Operations partners should stress	Cost Speed Quality	Quality of relationship Legal skills Flexibility

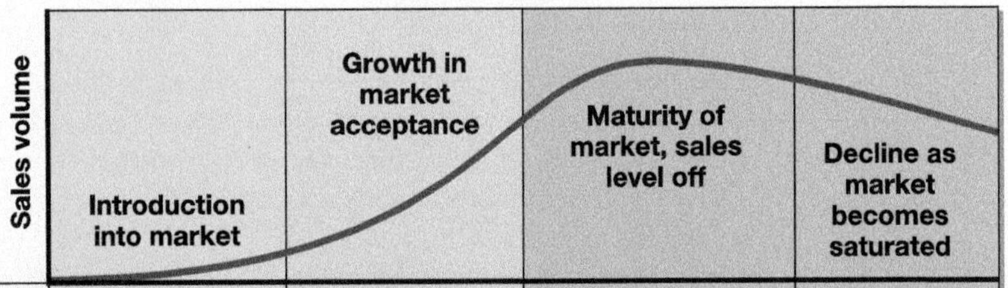

	Introduction into market	Growth in market acceptance	Maturity of market, sales level off	Decline as market becomes saturated
Customers	Innovators	Early adopters	Bulk of market	Laggards
Competitors	Few/none	Increasing numbers	Stable number	Declining number
Likely order winners	Product/service specification	Availability	Low price Dependable supply	Low price
Likely qualifiers	Quality Range	Price Range	Range Quality	Dependable supply
Dominant operations performance objectives	Flexibility Quality	Speed Dependability Quality	Cost Dependability	Cost

Sales volume (vertical axis label)

Figure 10.8 The effects of the product/service life cycle on operations performance objectives

The product/service life cycle influence on performance objectives

One way of generalizing the behaviour of both customers and competitors is to link it to the life cycle of the products or services that the operation is producing. The exact form of **product/service life cycles** will vary, but generally they are shown as the sales volume passing through four stages – introduction, growth, maturity and decline. The important implication of this for operations management is that products and services will require operations strategies in each stage of their life cycle (*see* Figure 10.8).

Introduction stage. When a product or service is first introduced, it is likely to be offering something new in terms of its design or performance, with few competitors offering the same product or service. The needs of customers are unlikely to be well understood, so the operations management needs to develop the flexibility to cope with any changes and be able to give the quality to maintain product/service performance.

Growth stage. As volume grows, competitors may enter the growing market. Keeping up with demand could prove to be the main operations preoccupation. Rapid and dependable response to demand will help to keep demand buoyant, while quality levels must ensure that the company keeps its share of the market as competition starts to increase.

Maturity stage. Demand starts to level off. Some early competitors may have left the market and the industry will probably be dominated by a few larger companies. So operations will be expected to get the costs down in order to maintain profits or to allow price cutting, or both. Because of this, cost and productivity issues, together with dependable supply, are likely to be the operation's main concerns.

Decline stage. After time, sales will decline with more competitors dropping out of the market. There might be a residual market, but unless a shortage of capacity develops the market will continue to be dominated by price competition. Operations objectives continue to be dominated by cost.

Product/service life cycles

The operations resources perspective

Resource-based view

The fourth and final perspective we shall take on operations strategy is based on a particularly influential theory of business strategy – the **resource-based view** (RBV) of the firm.[7] Put simply, the RBV holds that firms with an 'above-average' strategic performance are likely to have gained their sustainable competitive advantage because of the core competences (or capabilities) of their resources. This means that the way an organization inherits, or acquires, or develops its operations resources will, over the long term, have a significant impact on its strategic success. Furthermore, the impact of its 'operations resource' capabilities will be at least as great as, if not greater than, that which it gets from its market position. So understanding and developing the capabilities of operations resources, although often neglected, is a particularly important perspective on operations strategy.

Resource constraints and capabilities

No organization can merely choose which part of the market it wants to be in without considering its ability to produce products and services in a way that will satisfy that market. In other words, the constraints imposed by its operations must be taken into account. For example, a small translation company offers general translation services to a wide range of customers who wish documents such as sales brochures to be translated into another language. A small company, it operates an informal network of part-time translators who enable the company to offer translation into or from most of the major languages in the world. Some of the company's largest customers want to purchase their sales brochures on a 'one-stop shop' basis and have asked the translation company whether it is willing to offer a full service, organizing the design and production, as well as the translation, of export brochures. This is a very profitable market opportunity; however, the company does not have the resources, financial or physical, to take it up. From a market perspective, it is good business; but from an operations resource perspective, it is not feasible.

However, the operations resource perspective is not always so negative. This perspective may identify *constraints* to satisfying some markets but it can also identify *capabilities* which can be exploited in other markets. For example, the same translation company has recently employed two new translators who are particularly skilled at web site development. To exploit this, the company decides to offer a new service whereby customers can transfer documents to the company electronically, which can then be translated quickly. This new service is a 'fast response' service which has been designed specifically to exploit the capabilities within the operations resources. Here the company has chosen to be driven by its resource capabilities rather than the obvious market opportunities.

Intangible resources

Intangible resources

An operations resource perspective must start with an understanding of the resource capabilities and constraints within the operation. It must answer the simple questions, what do we have, and what can we do? An obvious starting point here is to examine the transforming and transformed resource inputs to the operation. These, after all, are the 'building blocks' of the operation. However, merely listing the type of *resources* an operation has does not give a complete picture of what it can do. Trying to understand an operation by listing its resources alone is like trying to understand an automobile by listing its component parts. To describe it more fully, we need to describe how the component parts form the internal mechanisms of the motor car. Within the operation, the equivalent of these mechanisms is its *processes*. Yet, even for an automobile, a technical explanation of its mechanisms still does not convey everything about its style or 'personality'. Something more is needed to describe these. In the same way, an operation is not just the sum of its processes. In addition, the operation has some **intangible resources**. An operation's intangible resources include such things as its relationship with suppliers, the reputation it has with its customers, its knowledge of its process technologies and the way its staff can work together in new product and service development. These intangible resources may not always be obvious within the

Amazon, what exactly is your core competence?[8]

The founder and boss of Amazon, Jeff Bezos, was at a conference speaking about the company's plans. Although Amazon was generally seen as an Internet book retailer and then a more general Internet retailer, Jeff Bezos was actually pushing three of Amazon's 'utility computing' services. These were: a company that provides cheap access to online computer storage, a company that allows program developers to rent computing capacity on Amazon systems, and a service that connects firms with other firms that perform specialist tasks that are difficult to automate. The problem with online retailing, said Bezos, is its seasonality. At peak times, such as Christmas, Amazon has far more computing capacity than it needs for the rest of the year. At low points it may be using as little as 10 per cent of its total capacity. Hiring out that spare capacity is an obvious way to bring in extra revenue. In addition, Amazon had developed a search engine, a video download business, a service (Fulfilment By Amazon) that allowed other companies to use Amazon's logistics capability including the handling of returned items, and a service that provided access to Amazon's 'back-end' technology.

Amazon's apparent redefinition of its strategy was immediately criticized by some observers. 'Why not', they said, 'stick to what you know, focus on your core

Source: Alamy Images

competence of Internet retailing?' Bezos's response was clear. 'We *are* sticking to our core competence; this is what we've been doing for the last 11 years. The only thing that's changed is that we are exposing it for [the benefit of] others.' At least for Jeff Bezos, Amazon is not so much an Internet retailer as a provider of Internet-based technology and logistics services.

operation, but they are important and have real value. It is these intangible resources, as well as its tangible resources, that an operation needs to deploy in order to satisfy its markets. The central issue for operations management, therefore, is to ensure that its pattern of strategic decisions really does develop appropriate capabilities within its resources and processes.

Structural and infrastructural decisions

Structure

Infrastructure

A distinction is often drawn between the strategic decisions which determine an operation's **structure** and those which determine its **infrastructure**. An operation's structural decisions are those which we have classed as primarily influencing design activities, while infrastructural decisions are those which influence the workforce organization and the planning and control, and improvement activities. This distinction in operations strategy has been compared to that between 'hardware' and 'software' in computer systems. The hardware of a computer sets limits to what it can do. In a similar way, investing in advanced technology and building more or better facilities can raise the potential of any type of operation. Within the limits which are imposed by the hardware of a computer, the software governs how effective the computer actually is in practice. The most powerful computer can only work to its full potential if its software is capable of exploiting its potential. The same principle applies with operations. The best and most costly facilities and technology will only be effective if the operation also has an appropriate infrastructure which governs the way it will work on a day-to-day basis. Table 10.3 illustrates both structural and infrastructural decision areas, arranged to correspond approximately to the chapter headings used in this book. The table also shows some typical questions which each strategic decision area should be addressing.

Table 10.3 Structural and infrastructural strategic decision areas

Structural strategic decisions	Typical questions which the strategy should help to answer
New product/service design	How should the operation decide which products or services to develop and how to manage the development process?
Supply network design	Should the operation expand by acquiring its suppliers or its customers? If so, what customers and suppliers should it acquire? How should it develop the capabilities of its customers and suppliers? What capacity should each operation in the network have? What number of geographically separate sites should the operation have and where should they be located? What activities and capacity should be allocated to each plant?
Process technology	What types of process technology should the operation be using? Should it be at the leading edge of technology or wait until the technology is established?
Infrastructural strategic decisions	Typical questions which the strategy should help to answer
Job design and organization	What role should the people who staff the operation play in its management? How should responsibility for the activities of the operations function be allocated between different groups in the operation? What skills should be developed in the staff of the operation?
Planning and control	How should the operation forecast and monitor the demand for its products and services? How should the operation adjust its activity levels in response to demand fluctuations? What systems should the operation use to plan and control its activities? How should the operation decide the resources to be allocated to its various activities?
Inventory	How should the operation decide how much inventory to have and where it is to be located? How should the operation control the size and composition of its inventories?
Supplier development	How should the operation choose its suppliers? How should it develop its relationship with its suppliers? How should it monitor its suppliers' performance?
Improvement	How should the operation's performance be measured? How should the operation decide whether its performance is satisfactory? How should the operation ensure that its performance is reflected in its improvement priorities? Who should be involved in the improvement process? How fast should the operation expect improvement in performance to be? How should the improvement process be managed?
Failure prevention, risk and recovery	How should the operation maintain its resources so as to prevent failure? How should the operation plan to cope with a failure if one occurs?

The process of operations strategy

The process of strategy formulation is concerned with 'how' operations strategies are put together. It is important because, although strategies will vary from organization to organization, they are usually trying to achieve some kind of alignment, or 'fit', between what the market wants, and what the operation can deliver, and how that 'alignment' can be sustained over time. So the process of operations strategy should both satisfy market requirements through appropriate operations resources, *and also* develop those resources in the long term so that they can provide competitive capabilities in the longer term that are sufficiently powerful to achieve sustainable competitive advantage.

There are many 'formulation processes' which are, or can be, used to formulate operations strategies. Most consultancy companies have developed their own frameworks, as have several academics. Typically, these formulation processes include the following elements:

- A process which formally links the total organization strategic objectives (usually a business strategy) to resource-level objectives.
- The use of competitive factors (called various things such as order winners, critical success factors, etc.) as the translation device between business strategy and operations strategy.
- A step which involves judging the relative importance of the various competitive factors in terms of customers' preferences.
- A step which includes assessing current achieved performance, usually as compared against competitor performance levels.
- An emphasis on operations strategy formulation as an iterative process.
- The concept of an 'ideal' or 'greenfield' operation against which to compare current operations. Very often the question asked is: 'If you were starting from scratch on a green-field site, how, ideally, would you design your operation to meet the needs of the market?' This can then be used to identify the differences between current operations and this ideal state.
- A 'gap-based' approach. This is a well-tried approach in all strategy formulation which involves comparing what is required of the operation by the marketplace against the levels of performance the operation is currently achieving.

What should the formulation process be trying to achieve?

So what should any operations strategy be trying to achieve? Clearly, it should provide a set of actions that, with hindsight, have provided the 'best' outcome for the organization. But that really does not help us. What do we mean by 'the best', and what good is a judgement that can only be applied in hindsight? Yet, even if we cannot assess the 'goodness' of a strategy for certain in advance, we can check it out for some attributes that could stop it being a success. First, is the operations strategy comprehensive? Second, is there is internal coherence between the various actions it is proposing? Third, do the actions being proposed as part of the operations strategy correspond to the appropriate priority for each performance objective? Fourth, does the strategy prioritize the most critical activities or decisions?

Comprehensive

The notion of 'comprehensiveness' is a critical first step in seeking to achieve an effective operations strategy. Business history is littered with world-class companies that simply failed to notice the potential impact of, for instance, new process technology or emerging changes in their supply network. Also, many strategies have failed because operations have paid undue attention to only one key decision area.

Coherence

As a comprehensive strategy evolves over time, different tensions will emerge that threaten to pull the overall strategy in different directions. This can result in a loss of coherence. Coherence is when the choices made in each decision area do not pull the operation in different directions. For example, if new flexible technology is introduced which allows products or services to be customized to individual clients' needs, it would be 'incoherent' to devise an organization structure which did not enable the relevant staff to exploit the technology because it would limit the effective flexibility of the operation. For the investment in flexible technology to be effective, it must be accompanied by an organizational structure which deploys the organization's skills appropriately, a performance measurement system which acknowledges that flexibility must be promoted, a new product/service development policy which stresses appropriate types of customization, a supply network strategy which develops suppliers and customers to understand the needs of high-variety customization, a capacity strategy which deploys capacity where the customization is needed, and so on. In other words, all the decision areas complement and reinforce each other in the promotion of that particular performance objective.

Correspondence

Equally, an operation has to achieve a correspondence between the choices made against each of the decision areas and the relative priority attached to each of the performance objectives. In other words, the strategies pursued in each decision area should reflect the true priority of each performance objective. So, for example, if cost reduction is the main organizational objective for an operation, then its process technology investment decisions might err towards the purchase of 'off-the-shelf' equipment from a third-party supplier. This would reduce the capital cost of the technology and may also imply lower maintenance and running costs. Remember, however, that making such a decision will also have an impact on other performance objectives. An off-the-shelf piece of equipment may not, for example, have the flexibility that more 'made-to-order' equipment has. Also, the other decision areas must correspond with the same prioritization of objectives. If low cost is really important then one would expect to see capacity strategies which exploit natural economies of scale, supply network strategies which reduce purchasing costs, performance measurement systems which stress efficiency and productivity, continuous improvement strategies which emphasize continual cost reduction, and so on.

Criticality

In addition to the difficulties of ensuring coherence between decision areas, there is also a need to include financial and competitive priorities. Although all decisions are important and a comprehensive perspective should be maintained, in practical terms some resource or requirement intersections will be more critical than others. The judgement over exactly which intersections are particularly critical is very much a pragmatic one which must be based on the particular circumstances of an individual firm's operations strategy. It is therefore difficult to generalize as to the likelihood of any particular intersections being critical. However, in practice, one can ask revealing questions such as, 'If flexibility is important, of all the decisions we make in terms of our capacity, supply networks, process technology, or development and organization, which will have the most impact on flexibility?' This can be done for all performance objectives, with more emphasis being placed on those having the highest priority. Generally, when presented with a framework such as the operations strategy matrix, executives can identify those intersections which are particularly significant in achieving alignment.

Short case
Sometimes any plan is better than no plan[9]

There is a famous story that illustrates the importance of having some kind of plan, even if hindsight proves it to be the wrong plan. During manoeuvres in the Alps, a detachment of Hungarian soldiers got lost. The weather was severe and the snow was deep. In these freezing conditions, after two days of wandering, the soldiers gave up hope and became reconciled to a frozen death on the mountains. Then, to their delight, one of the soldiers discovered a map in his pocket. Much cheered by this discovery, the soldiers were able to escape from the mountains. When they were safe back at their headquarters, they discovered that the map was not of the Alps at all, but of the Pyrenees. The moral of the story? A plan (or a map) may not be perfect but it gives a sense of purpose and a sense of direction. If the soldiers had waited for the right map they would have frozen to death. Yet their renewed confidence motivated them to get up and create opportunities.

Implementation

A large number of authors, writing about all forms of strategy, have discussed the importance of effective implementation. This reflects an acceptance that no matter how sophisticated the intellectual and analytical underpinnings of a strategy, it remains only a document until it has been implemented. Ken Platts of Cambridge University has written about the nature of the operations strategy formulation process. His generic description of the **process** is referred to as the five Ps.

The five Ps of operations strategy formulation

1 *Purpose*. As with any form of project management, the more clarity that exists around the ultimate goal, the more likely it is that the goal will be achieved. In this context, a shared understanding of the motivation, boundaries and context for developing the operations strategy is crucial.
2 *Point of entry*. Linked with the above point, any analysis, formulation and implementation process is potentially politically sensitive and the support that the process has from within the hierarchy of the organization is central to the implementation success.
3 *Process*. Any formulation process must be explicit. It is important that the managers who are engaged in putting operations strategies together actively think about the process in which they are participating.
4 *Project management*. There is a cost associated with any strategy process. Indeed one of the reasons why operations have traditionally not had explicit strategies relates to the difficulty of releasing sufficient managerial time. The basic disciplines of project management such as resource and time planning, controls, communication mechanisms, reviews and so on, should be in place.
5 *Participation*. Intimately linked with the above points, the selection of staff to participate in the implementation process is also critical. So, for instance, the use of external consultants can provide additional specialist expertise, the use of line managers (and indeed staff) can provide 'real-world' experience and the inclusion of cross-functional managers (and suppliers etc.) can help to integrate the finished strategy.

Critical commentary

The argument has been put forward that strategy does not lend itself to a simple 'stage model' analysis that guides managers in a step-by-step manner through to the eventual 'answer' that is a final strategy. Therefore, the models put forward by consultants and academics are of very limited value. In reality, strategies (even those that are made deliberately, as opposed to those that simply 'emerge') are the result of very complex organizational forces. Even descriptive models such as the five Ps described above can do little more than sensitize managers to some of the key issues that they should be taking into account when devising strategies. In fact, it is argued that articulating the 'content' of operation strategy that is more useful than adhering to some over-simplistic description of a strategy process.

Summary answers to key questions

Check and improve your understanding of this chapter using self assessment questions and a personalised study plan, audio and video downloads, and an eBook – all at www.myomlab.com.

➤ What is strategy and what is operations strategy?

- Strategy is the total pattern of decisions and actions that position the organization in its environment and that are intended to achieve its long-term goals.

- Operations strategy concerns the pattern of strategic decisions and actions which set the role, objectives and activities of the operation.

- Operations strategy has content and process. The content concerns the specific decisions which are taken to achieve specific objectives. The process is the procedure which is used within a business to formulate its strategy.

➤ What is the difference between a 'top-down' and a 'bottom-up' view of operations strategy?

- The 'top-down' perspective views strategic decisions at a number of levels. Corporate strategy sets the objectives for the different businesses which make up a group of businesses. Business strategy sets the objectives for each individual business and how it positions itself in its marketplace. Functional strategies set the objectives for each function's contribution to its business strategy.

- The 'bottom-up' view of operations strategy sees overall strategy as emerging from day-to-day operational experience.

➤ What is the difference between a 'market requirements' and an 'operations resource' view of operations strategy?

- A 'market requirements' perspective of operations strategy sees the main role of operations as satisfying markets. Operations performance objectives and operations decisions should be primarily influenced by a combination of customers' needs and competitors' actions. Both of these may be summarized in terms of the product/service life cycle.

- The 'operations resource' perspective of operations strategy is based on the resource-based view (RBV) of the firm and sees the operation's core competences (or capabilities) as being the main influence on operations strategy. Operations capabilities are developed partly through the strategic decisions taken by the operation. Strategic decision areas in operations are usually divided into structural and infrastructural decisions. Structural decisions are those which define an operation's shape and form. Infrastructural decisions are those which influence the systems and procedures that determine how the operation will work in practice.

➤ How can an operations strategy be put together?

- There are many different procedures which are used by companies, consultancies and academics to formulate operations strategies. Although differing in the stages that they recommend, many of these models have similarities.

- Any operations strategy process should result in strategies that are comprehensive and coherent, provide correspondence, and prioritize the most critical activities or decisions.

Case study
Long Ridge Gliding Club[10]

Long Ridge Gliding Club is a not-for-profit organization run by its members. The large grass airfield is located on the crest of a ridge about 400 metres above sea level. It is an ideal place to practise ridge soaring and cross-country flying. The gliders are launched using a winch machine which can propel them from a standing start to around 110 kilometres per hour (70 mph), 300 metres above the airfield, in just five seconds. The club is housed in a set of old farm buildings with simple but comfortable facilities for members. A bar and basic catering services are provided by the club steward and inexpensive bunk-rooms are available for club members wishing to stay overnight.

The club has a current membership of nearly 150 pilots who range in ability from novice to expert. While some members have their own gliders, the club has a fleet of three single-seater and three twin-seater gliders available to its members. The club also offers trial flights to members of the public. (In order to provide insurance cover they actually sell a three-month membership with a 'free' flight at the start.) These 'casual flyers' can book flights in advance or just turn up and fly on a first-come, first-served basis. The club sells trial-flight gift vouchers which are popular as birthday and Christmas presents. The club's brochure and web site encourage people to:

> 'Experience the friendly atmosphere and excellent facilities and enjoy the thrill of soaring above Long Ridge's dramatic scenery. For just £70 you could soon be in the air. Phone now or just turn up and our knowledgeable staff will be happy to advise you. We have a team of professional instructors dedicated to make this a really memorable experience.'

The average flight for a trial lesson is around 10 minutes. If the conditions are right the customer may be lucky and get a longer flight although at busy times the instructors may feel under pressure to return to the ground to give another lesson. Sometimes when the weather is poor, low cloud and

wind in the wrong direction, almost not fit for flying at all, the instructors still do their best to get people airborne but they are restricted to a 'circuit': a takeoff, immediate circle and land. This only takes two minutes. Circuits are also used to help novice pilots practise landings and takeoffs. At the other end of the scale many of the club's experienced pilots can travel long distances and fly back to the airfield. The club's record for the longest flight is 755 kilometres, taking off from the club's airfield and landing back on the same airfield eight hours later, never having touched the ground. (They take sandwiches and drinks and a bottle they can use to relieve themselves!)

The club has three part-time employees: a club steward, an office administrator and a mechanic. In the summer months the club also employs a winch driver (for launching the gliders) and two qualified flying instructors. Throughout the whole year essential tasks such as maintaining the gliders, getting them out of the hangar and towing them to the launch point, staffing the winches, keeping the flying log, bringing back gliders, and providing look-out cover is undertaken on a voluntary basis by club members. It takes a minimum of five experienced people (club members) to be able to launch one glider. The club's membership includes ten qualified instructors who, together with the two paid summer instructors, provide instruction in two-seater gliders for the club's members and the casual flyers.

When club members come to fly they are expected to arrive by 9.30 am and be prepared to stay all day to help each other and any casual flyers get airborne while they wait their turn to fly. On a typical summer's day there might be ten club members requiring instruction plus four casual flyers and also six members with their own gliders who have to queue up with the others for a launch hoping for a single long-distance flight. In the winter months there would typically be six members, one casual flyer and six experienced pilots. Club members would hope to have three flights on a good day, with durations of between two and forty (average ten) minutes per flight depending on conditions. However, if the weather conditions change they may not get a flight. Last year there were 180 days when flying took place, 140 in the 'summer' season and 40 in the 'winter'. Club members are charged an £8.00 winch fee each time they take to the air. In addition, if they are using one of the club's gliders, they are charged 50p per minute that they are in the air.

Bookings for trial flights and general administration are dealt with by the club's administrator who is based in a cabin close to the car park and works most weekday mornings from 9.00 am to 1.00 pm. An answerphone takes messages at other times. The launch point is out of sight and 1.5 km from the cabin but a safe walking route is signposted. Club members can let themselves onto the airfield and drive to the launch point. At the launch point the casual flyers might have to stand and wait for some time until a club member has time to find out what they want. Even when a flight has been pre-booked casual flyers may then be kept waiting, on the exposed and often windy airfield, for up to two hours before their flight, depending on how many club members are present. Occasionally they will turn up for a pre-booked trial flight and will be turned away because either the weather is unsuitable or there are not enough club members to get a glider into the air. The casual flyers are encouraged to help out with the routine tasks but often seem reluctant to do so. After their flight they are left to find their own way back to their cars.

Income from the casual flyers is seen to be small compared to membership income and launch fees but the club's management committee views casual flying as a 'loss leader' to generate club memberships which are £350 per annum. The club used to generate a regular surplus of around £10,000 per year which is used to upgrade the gliders and other facilities. However, insurance costs have risen dramatically due to their crashing and severely damaging four gliders during the last two years. Two of the accidents resulted in the deaths of one member and one casual flyer and serious injuries to three other members.

The club's committee is under some pressure from members to end trial flights because they reduce the number of flights members can have in a day. Some members have complained that they sometimes spend most of their day working to get casual flyers into the air and miss out on flying themselves. Although they provide a useful source of income for the hard-pressed club (around 700 were sold in the previous year), only a handful have been converted into club memberships.

Questions

1 Evaluate the service to club members and casual flyers by completing a table similar to Table 10.1.

2 Chart the five performance objectives to show the differing expectations of club members and casual flyers and compare these with the actual service delivered.

3 What advice would you give to the chairman?

Problems and applications

These problems and applications will help to improve your analysis of operations. You can find more practice problems as well as worked examples and guided solutions on MyOMLab at www.myomlab.com.

1 Explain how the four perspectives of operations strategy would apply to Ryanair and Flextronics.

2 Compare the operations strategies of Ryanair and a full-service airline such as British Airways or KLM.

3 What do you think are the qualifying and order-winning factors for (a) a top of the range Ferrari, and (b) a Renault Clio?

4 What do you think are the qualifying or order-winning factors for IKEA described in Chapter 1?

5 Search the Internet site of Intel, the best-known microchip manufacturer, and identify what appear to be its main structural and infrastructural decisions in its operations strategy.

6 **(Advanced)** McDonald's has come to epitomize the 'fast-food' industry. When the company started in the 1950s it was the first to establish itself in the market. Now there are hundreds of 'fast-food' brands in the market competing in different ways. Some of the differences between these fast-food chains are obvious. For example, some specialize in chicken products, others in pizza, and so on. However, some differences are less obvious. Originally, McDonald's competed on low price, fast service and a totally standardized service offering. They also offered a very narrow range of items on their menu. Visit a McDonald's restaurant and deduce what you believe to be its most important performance objectives. Then try and identify two other chains which appear to compete in a slightly different way. Then try to identify how these differences in the relative importance of competitive objectives must influence the structural and infrastructural decisions of each chain's operations strategy.

Selected further reading

Boyer, K.K., Swink, M. and Rosenzweig, E.D. (2006) Operations strategy research in the POMS Journal, *Production and Operations Management*, vol. 14, issue 4. A survey of recent research in the area.

Hayes, R.H., Pisano, G.P., Upton, D.M. and Wheelwright, S.C. (2005) *Operations, Strategy, and Technology: Pursuing the Competitive Edge*, Wiley. The gospel according to the Harvard school of operations strategy. Articulate, interesting and informative.

Slack, N. and Lewis, M. (2008) *Operations Strategy*, 2nd edn, Financial Times Prentice Hall, Harlow. What can we say – just brilliant!

Useful web sites

www.aom.pac.edu/bps/ General strategy site of the American Academy of Management.

www.cranfield,ac.uk/som Look for the 'Best factory awards' link. Manufacturing, but interesting.

www.opsman.org Lots of useful stuff.

www.worldbank.org Global issues. Useful for international operations strategy research.

www.weforum.org Global issues, including some operations strategy ones.

www.ft.com Great for industry and company examples.

Now that you have finished reading this chapter, why not visit MyOMLab at www.myomlab.com where you'll find more learning resources to help you make the most of your studies and get a better grade?

Chapter 11

Layout and flow

Key questions

➤ What is 'layout'?
➤ What are the basic layout types used in operations?
➤ What type of layout should an operation choose?
➤ How should each basic layout type be designed in detail?

Introduction

The layout of an operation is concerned with the physical location of its transforming resources. This means deciding where to put all the facilities, machines, equipment and staff in the operation. Layout is often the first thing most of us would notice on entering an operation because it governs its appearance. It also determines the way in which transformed resources – the materials, information and customers – flow through the operation. Relatively small changes in goods in a supermarket, or changing rooms in a sports centre, or the position of a machine in a factory, can affect the flow through the operation which, in turn, affects the costs and general effectiveness of the operation. Figure 11.1 shows the facilities layout activity in the overall model of design in operations.

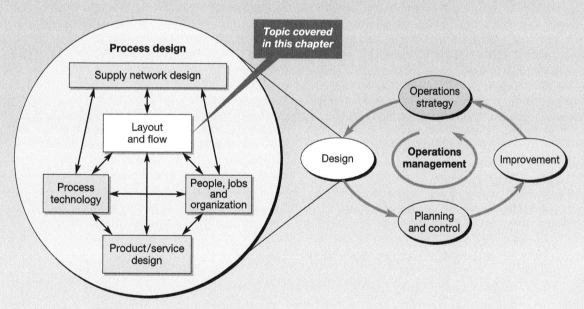

Figure 11.1 This chapter examines layout and flow

Operations in practice Tesco's store flow processes[1]

Successful supermarkets, like Tesco, know that the design of their stores has a huge impact on profitability. They must maximize their revenue per square metre and minimize the costs of operating the store, while keeping customers happy. At a basic level, supermarkets have to get the amount of space allocated to the different areas right. Tesco's 'One in front' campaign, for example, tries to avoid long waiting times by opening additional tills if more than one customer is waiting at a checkout. Tesco also uses technology to understand exactly how customers flow through their stores. The 'Smartlane' system from Irisys, a specialist in intelligent infrared technologies, counts the number and type of customers entering the store (in family or other groups known as 'shopping units'), tracks their movement using infrared sensors, and predicts the likely demand at the checkouts up to an hour in advance. The circulation of customers through the store must be right and the right layout can make customers buy more. Some supermarkets put their entrance on the left-hand side of a building with a layout designed to take customers in a clockwise direction around the store. Aisles are made wide to ensure a relatively slow flow of trolleys so that customers pay more attention to the products on display (and buy more). However, wide aisles can come at the expense of reduced shelf space that would allow a wider range of products to be stocked.

The actual location of all the products is a critical decision, directly affecting the convenience to customers, their level of spontaneous purchase and the cost of filling the shelves. Although the majority of supermarket sales are packaged, tinned or frozen goods, the displays of fruit and vegetables are usually located adjacent to the main entrance, as a signal of freshness and wholesomeness, providing an attractive and welcoming point of entry. Basic products that figure on most people's shopping lists, such as flour, sugar and bread, may be located at the back of the store and apart from each other so that customers have to pass higher-margin

Source: Alamy Images

items as they search. High-margin items are usually put at eye level on shelves (where they are more likely to be seen) and low-margin products lower down or higher up. Some customers also go a few paces up an aisle before they start looking for what they need. Some supermarkets call the shelves occupying the first metre of an aisle 'dead space' – not a place to put impulse-bought goods. But the prime site in a supermarket is the 'gondola-end', the shelves at the end of the aisle. Moving products to this location can increase sales 200 or 300 per cent. It's not surprising that suppliers are willing to pay for their products to be located here. The supermarkets themselves are keen to point out that, although they obviously lay out their stores with customers' buying behaviour in mind, it is counterproductive to be too manipulative. Some commonly held beliefs about supermarket layout are not always true. They deny that they periodically change the location of foodstuffs in order to jolt customers out of their habitual shopping patterns so that they are more attentive to other products and end up buying more. Occasionally layouts are changed, they say, but mainly to accommodate changing, tastes and new ranges.

What is layout?

The 'layout' of an operation or process means how its transformed resources are positioned relative to each other and how its various tasks are allocated to these transforming resources. Together these two decisions will dictate the pattern of flow for transformed resources as they progress through the operation or process (see Figure 11.2). It is an important decision because, if the layout proves wrong, it can lead to over-long or confused flow patterns, customer queues, long process times, inflexible operations, unpredictable flow and high cost. Also, re-laying out an existing operation can cause disruption, leading to customer dissatisfaction or lost operating time. So, because the **layout decision** can be difficult and expensive, operations managers are reluctant to do it too often. Therefore layout must start with a full appreciation of the objectives that the layout should be trying to achieve. However, this is only the starting point of what is a multi-stage process which leads to the final physical layout of the operation.

The layout decision is relatively infrequent but important

What makes a good layout?

To a large extent the objectives of any layout will depend on the strategic objectives of the operation, but there are some general objectives which are relevant to all operations:

- *Inherent safety.* All processes which might constitute a danger to either staff or customers should not be accessible to the unauthorized.
- *Length of flow.* The flow of materials, information or customers should be appropriate for the operation. This usually means minimizing the distance travelled by transformed resources. However, this is not always the case (in a supermarket, for example).
- *Clarity of flow.* All flow of materials and customers should be well signposted, clear and evident to staff and customers alike.
- *Staff conditions.* Staff should be located away from noisy or unpleasant parts of the operation.
- *Management coordination.* Supervision and communication should be assisted by the location of staff and communication devices.
- *Accessibility.* All machines and facilities should be accessible for proper cleaning and maintenance.
- *Use of space.* All layouts should use space appropriately. This usually means minimizing the space used, but sometimes can mean achieving an impression of spacious luxury, as in the entrance lobby of a high-class hotel.
- *Long-term flexibility.* Layouts need to be changed periodically. A good layout will have been devised with the possible future needs of the operation in mind.

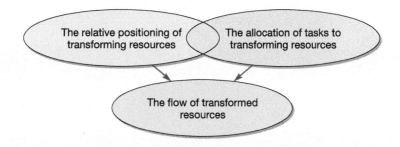

Figure 11.2 Layout involves the relative positioning of transformed resources within operations and processes and the allocation of tasks to the resources, which together dictate the flow of transformed resources through the operation or process

The basic layout types

Most practical layouts are derived from only four **basic layout types**. These are:

- **fixed-position layout**
- **functional layout**
- **cell layout**
- **product layout.**

Layout is related to process type

Process 'types' represent the broad approaches to the organization of processes and activities. Layout is a narrower, but related concept. It is the physical manifestation of a process type, but there is often some overlap between **process types** and the layouts that they could use. As Table 11.1 indicates, a process type does not necessarily imply only one particular basic layout.

Layout is influenced by
process types

Fixed-position layout

Fixed-position layout is in some ways a contradiction in terms, since the transformed resources do not move between the transforming resources. Instead of materials, information or customers flowing through an operation, the recipient of the processing is stationary and the equipment, machinery, plant and people who do the processing move as necessary. This could be because the product or the recipient of the service is too large to be moved conveniently, or it might be too delicate to move, or perhaps it could object to being moved; for example:

- *Motorway construction* – the product is too large to move.
- *Open-heart surgery* – patients are too delicate to move.
- *High-class service restaurant* – customers would object to being moved to where food is prepared.
- *Shipbuilding* – the product is too large to move.
- *Mainframe computer maintenance* – the product is too big and probably also too delicate to move, and the customer might object to bringing it in for repair.

Table 11.1 The relationship between process types and basic layout types

Manufacturing process types	Basic layout types	Service process types
Project processes	Fixed-position layout	Professional services
Jobbing processes		
	Functional layout	Service shops
Batch processes		
	Cell layout	
Mass processes		Mass services
Continuous processes	Product layout	

A construction site is typical of a fixed-position layout in that there is a limited amount of space which must be allocated to the various transforming resources. The main problem in designing this layout will be to allocate areas of the site to the various contractors so that they have adequate space, they can receive and store their deliveries of materials, they can have access to their parts of the project without interfering with each other's movements, they minimize movement, and so on.

Short case
'Factory flow' helps surgery productivity[2]

Even surgery can be seen as a process, and like any process, it can be improved. Normally patients remain stationary with surgeons and other theatre staff performing their tasks around the patient. But this idea has been challenged by John Petri, an Italian consultant orthopaedic surgeon at a hospital in Norfolk in the UK. Frustrated by spending time drinking tea while patients were prepared for surgery, he redesigned the process so now he moves continually between two theatres. While he is operating on a patient in one theatre, his anaesthetist colleagues are preparing a patient for surgery in another theatre. After finishing with the first patient, the surgeon 'scrubs up', moves to the second operating theatre, and

begins the surgery on the second patient. While he is doing this the first patient is moved out of the first operating theatre and the third patient is prepared. This method of overlapping operations in different theatres allows the surgeon to work for five hours at a time rather than the previous standard three-and-a-half-hour session. *'If you were running a factory',* says the surgeon, *'you wouldn't allow your most important and most expensive machine to stand idle. The same is true in a hospital.'* Currently used on hip and knee replacements, this layout would not be suitable for all surgical procedures. But, since its introduction the surgeon's waiting list has fallen to zero and his productivity has doubled. *'For a small increase in running costs we are able to treat many more patients'*, said a spokesperson for the hospital management. *'What is important is that clinicians . . . produce innovative ideas and we demonstrate that they are effective.'*

Assembly line surgery

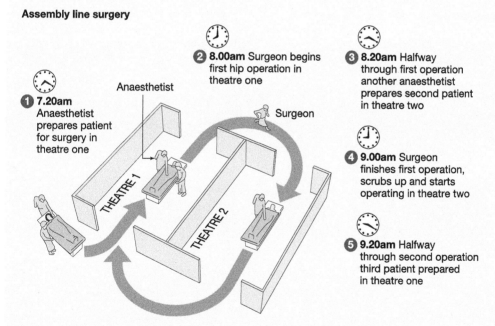

Figure 11.3 Assembly line surgery

Functional layout

Functional layout is so called because it conforms to the needs and convenience of the functions performed by the transforming resources within the processes. (Confusingly, functional layout is also referred to as 'process layout' but this term is being superseded.)

In functional layout, similar resources or processes are located together. This may be because it is convenient to group them together, or that the utilization of transforming resources is improved. It means that when materials, information or customers flow through the operation, their route is determined according to their needs. Different products or customers will have different needs and therefore take different routes. Usually this makes the flow pattern in the operation very complex. Examples of functional layouts include:

- *Hospital* – some processes (e.g. X-ray machines and laboratories) are required by several types of patient; some processes (e.g. general wards) can achieve high staff- and bed-utilization.
- *Machining the parts which go into aircraft engines* – some processes (e.g. heat treatment) need specialist support (heat and fume extraction); some processes (e.g. machining centres) require the same technical support from specialist setter–operators; some processes (e.g. grinding machines) get high machine utilization as all parts which need grinding pass through a single grinding section.
- *Supermarket* – some products, such as tinned goods, are convenient to restock if grouped together. Some areas, such as those holding frozen vegetables, need the common technology of freezer cabinets. Others, such as the areas holding fresh vegetables, might be together because that way they can be made to look attractive to customers (see the opening short case).

Figure 11.4 shows a functional layout in a university library. The various areas – reference books, enquiry desk, journals, and so on – are located in different parts of the operation. The customer is free to move between the areas depending on his or her requirements. The

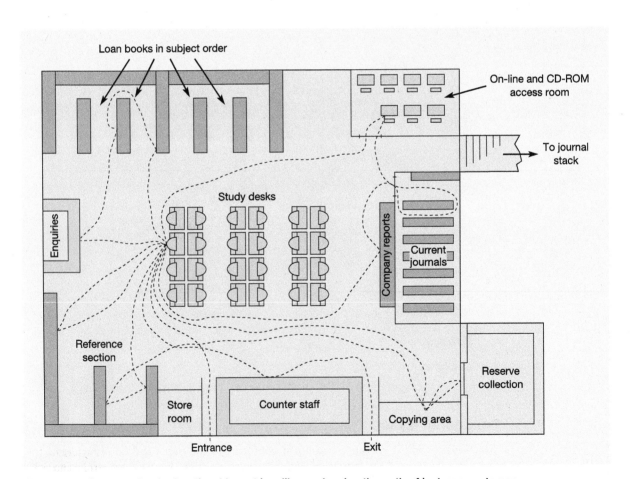

Figure 11.4 An example of a functional layout in a library showing the path of just one customer

figure also shows the route taken by one customer on one visit to the library. If the routes for the customers were superimposed on the plan, the pattern of the traffic between the various parts of the operation would be revealed. The density of this traffic flow is an important piece of information in the detailed design of this type of layout. Changing the location of the various areas in the library will change the pattern of flow for the library as a whole.

Cell layout

A cell layout is one where the transformed resources entering the operation are pre-selected (or pre-select themselves) to move to one part of the operation (or cell) in which all the transforming resources, to meet their immediate processing needs, are located. After being processed in the cell, the transformed resources may go on to another cell. In effect, cell layout is an attempt to bring some order to the complexity of flow which characterizes functional layout. Examples of cell layouts include:

- *Some laptop assembly* – within a contract manufacturer's factory, the assembly of different laptop brands may be done in a special area dedicated to that one brand that has special requirements such as particularly high quality levels.
- *'Lunch' products area in a supermarket* – some customers use the supermarket just to purchase sandwiches, savoury snacks, etc. for their lunch. These products may be located together so that these customers do not have to search around the store.
- *Maternity unit in a hospital* – customers needing maternity attention are a well-defined group who can be treated together and who are unlikely to need the other facilities of the hospital at the same time that they need the maternity unit.

Although the idea of cell layout is often associated with manufacturing, the same principle can be, and is, used in services. In Figure 11.5 the ground floor of a department store is shown, comprising displays of various types of goods in different parts of the store. In this sense the predominant layout of the store is a functional layout. However, some 'themed' products may be put together, such as in the sports shop. This area is a **shop-within-a-shop** which will stock sports clothes, sports shoes, sports bags, sports books and videos, sports equipment and energy drinks, which are also located elsewhere in the store. They have been located in the 'cell' not because they are similar goods (shoes, books and drinks would not usually be located together) but because they are needed to satisfy the needs of a particular type of customer. Enough customers come to the store to buy 'sports goods' in particular to devote an area specifically for them. Also, customers intending to buy sports shoes might also be persuaded to buy other sports goods if they are placed in the same area.

Shop-within-a-shop [margin note]

Product layout

Product layout involves locating the transforming resources entirely for the convenience of the transformed resources. Each product, piece of information or customer follows a prearranged route in which the sequence of activities that are required matches the sequence in which the processes have been located. The transformed resources 'flow' as in a 'line' through the process. This is why this type of layout is sometimes called flow or **line layout**. Flow is predictable and therefore relatively easy to control. Examples of product layout include:

Line layout [margin note]

- *Automobile assembly* – almost all variants of the same model require the same sequence of processes.
- *Loan application processing* – all applications require the same sequence of clerical and decision-making activities.
- *Self-service cafeteria* – generally the sequence of customer requirements (starter, main course, dessert, drink) is common to all customers, but layout also helps control customer flow.

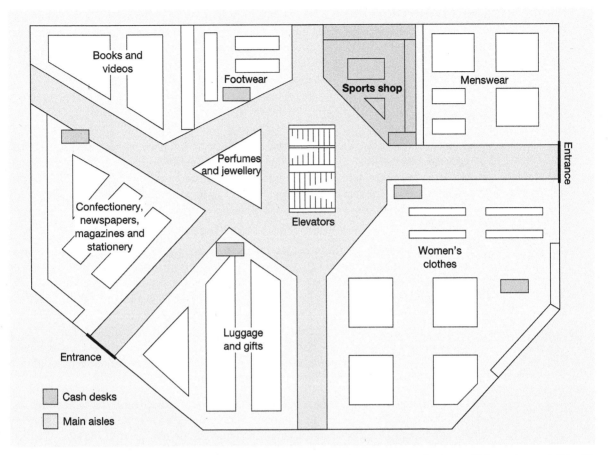

Figure 11.5 The ground floor plan of a department store showing the sports goods shop-within-a-shop retail 'cell'

Figure 11.6 shows the sequence of processes in a paper-making operation. Such an operation would use product layout. Gone are the complexities of flow which characterized functional layouts, and to a lesser extent cell layouts, and although different types of paper are produced in this operation, all types have the same processing requirements.

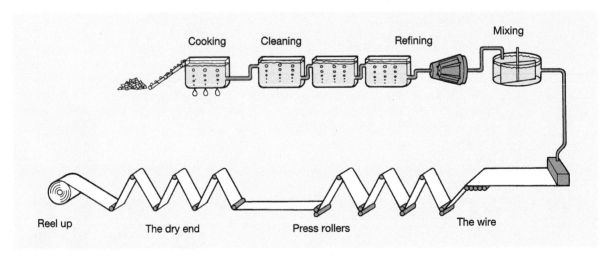

Figure 11.6 The sequence of processes in paper-making; each process will be laid out in the same sequence

Short case
Yamaha tunes its assembly lines

The Yamaha Corporation of Japan, founded in 1887, has grown to become the world's largest manufacturer of musical instruments, as well as producing a whole variety of other goods, from semiconductors and robots through to sporting goods and furniture. In recent years it has developed a reputation for product diversification, an understanding of new markets and, especially, innovative manufacturing methods. For example, it was one of the first piano manufacturers to make up-market grand pianos using assembly line techniques (the picture shows grand pianos being assembled in the same way as motor vehicles). Traditionally, grand pianos (as opposed to the less expensive and better-selling upright pianos) were made using individual build methods which relied on craft skills. The main advantage of this was that skilled workers could accommodate individual variations in the (often inconsistent) materials from which the piano is made. Each individual piano would be constructed around the idiosyncrasies of the material to make a product unique in its tone and tuning. Not so with Yamaha, which, although making some of the highest-quality pianos in the world, emphasizes consistency and reliability, as well as richness of tone.

Mixed layouts

Many operations either design themselves hybrid layouts which combine elements of some or all of the basic layout types, or use the 'pure' basic layout types in different parts of the operation. For example, a hospital would normally be arranged on functional-layout principles, each department representing a particular type of process (the X-ray department, the surgical theatres, the blood-processing laboratory, and so on). Yet within each department, quite different layouts are used. The X-ray department is probably arranged in a functional layout, the surgical theatres in a fixed-position layout, and the blood-processing laboratory in a product layout. Another example is shown in Figure 11.7. Here a restaurant complex is

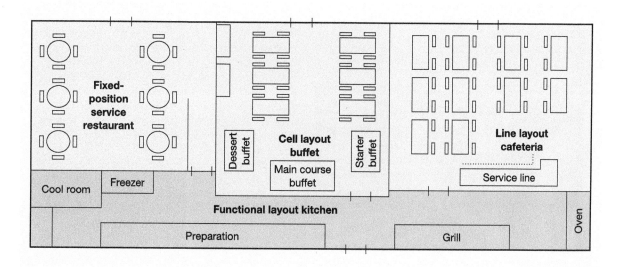

Figure 11.7 A restaurant complex with all four basic layout types

shown with three different types of restaurant and the kitchen which serves them all. The kitchen is arranged in a functional layout, the traditional service restaurant is arranged in a fixed-position layout, the buffet restaurant is arranged in a cell-type layout, while in the cafeteria restaurant, all customers take the same route when being served with their meal. They may not take the opportunity to be served with every dish but they move through the same sequence of processes.

Short case
Chocolate and customers flow through Cadbury's[3]

Flow of chocolate

In the famous Cadbury's chocolate factory at Bourneville, on the outskirts of Birmingham, UK, chocolate products are manufactured to a high degree of consistency and efficiency. Production processes are based on a *product layout*. This has allowed Cadbury's engineers to develop and procure machinery to meet the technical and capacity requirements of each stage of the process. Consider, for example, the production of Cadbury's Dairy Milk bars. First, the standard liquid chocolate is prepared from cocoa beans, fresh milk and sugar using specialized equipment, connected together with pipes and conveyors. These processes operate continuously, day and night, to ensure consistency of both the chocolate itself and the rate of output. Next, the liquid is pumped through heated pipework to the moulding department, where it is automatically dispensed into a moving line of precision-made plastic moulds which form the chocolate bars and vibrate them to remove any trapped air bubbles. The moulds are continuously conveyed into a large refrigerator, allowing sufficient time for the chocolate to harden. The next stage inverts the moulds and shakes out the moulded bars. These then pass directly to a set of highly automated wrapping and packing machines, from where they go to the warehouse.

Flow of customers

Cadbury also has a large visitor centre called 'Cadbury World' alongside the factory (linked to a viewing area

Customers being processed

Source: Cadbury World

which looks onto the packaging area described above). Cadbury World is a permanent exhibition devoted entirely to chocolate and the part Cadbury has played in its fascinating history. Because most of the attractions are indoors, with limited circulation space, the main exhibition and demonstration areas are designed to allow a smooth flow of customers, where possible avoiding bottlenecks and delays. The design is also a 'product' layout with a single route for all customers. Entry to the Exhibition Area is by timed ticket, to ensure a constant flow of input customers, who are free to walk around at their preferred speed, but are constrained to keep to the single track through the sequence of displays. On leaving this section, they are directed upstairs to the Chocolate Packaging Plant, where a guide escorts standard-sized batches of customers to the appropriate positions where they can see the packing processes and a video presentation. The groups are then led down to and around the Demonstration Area, where skilled employees demonstrate small-scale production of handmade chocolates. Finally, visitors are free to roam unaccompanied through a long, winding path of the remaining exhibits.

Cadbury has chosen to use the product layout design for both the production of chocolates and the processing of its visitors. In both cases, volumes are large and the variety offered is limited. Sufficient demand exists for each standard 'product', and the operations objective is to achieve consistent high quality at low cost. Neither operation has much volume flexibility, and both are expensive to change.

Source: Cadbury World

Chocolate being processed

What type of layout should an operation choose?

The volume and variety characteristics of an operation will influence its layout

The importance of flow to an operation will depend on its **volume and variety characteristics.** When volume is very low and variety is relatively high, 'flow' is not a major issue. For example, in telecommunications satellite manufacture, a fixed-position layout is likely to be appropriate because each product is different and because products 'flow' through the operation very infrequently, so it is just not worth arranging facilities to minimize the flow of parts through the operation. With higher volume and lower variety, flow becomes an issue. If the variety is still high, however, an entirely flow-dominated arrangement is difficult because there will be different flow patterns. For example, the library in Figure 11.4 will arrange its different categories of books and its other services partly to minimize the average distance its customers have to 'flow' through the operation. But, because its customers' needs vary, it will arrange its layout to satisfy the majority of its customers (but perhaps inconvenience a minority). When the variety of products or services reduces to the point where a distinct 'category' with similar requirements becomes evident but variety is still not small, cell layout could become appropriate, as in the sports goods cell in Figure 11.5. When variety is relatively small and volume is high, flow can become regularized and a product-based layout is likely to be appropriate, as in an assembly plant (see Figure 11.8).

Selecting a layout type

The volume–variety characteristics of the operation will, to a large extent, narrow the choice down to one or two layout options. The decision as to which layout type to adopt will be influenced by an understanding of their relative advantages and disadvantages. Table 11.2 shows some of the more significant advantages and disadvantages associated with each layout

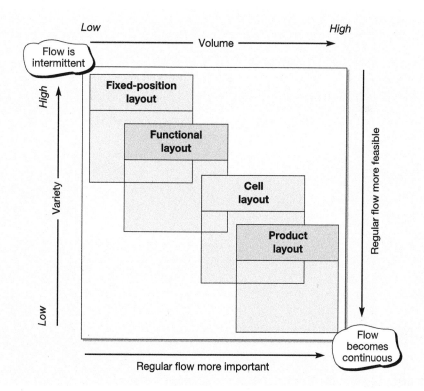

Figure 11.8 The volume–variety process position of an operation influences its layout and, in turn, the flow of transformed resources

Table 11.2 The advantages and disadvantages of the basic layout types

	Advantages	Disadvantages
Fixed-position	Very high mix and product flexibility Product or customer not moved or disturbed High variety of tasks for staff	Very high unit costs Scheduling of space and activities can be difficult Can mean much movement of plant and staff
Functional	High mix and product flexibility Relatively robust in the case of disruptions Relatively easy supervision of equipment or plant	Low facilities utilization Can have very high work-in-progress or customer queuing Complex flow can be difficult to control
Cell	Can give a good compromise between cost and flexibility for relatively high-variety operations Fast throughput Group work can result in good motivation	Can be costly to rearrange existing layout Can need more plant and equipment Can give lower plant utilization
Product	Low unit costs for high volume Gives opportunities for specialization of equipment Materials or customer movement is convenient	Can have low mix flexibility Not very robust if there is disruption Work can be very repetitive

type. It should be stressed, however, that the type of operation will influence their relative importance. For example, a high-volume television manufacturer may find the low-cost characteristics of a product layout attractive, but an amusement theme park may adopt the same layout type primarily because of the way it 'controls' customer flow.

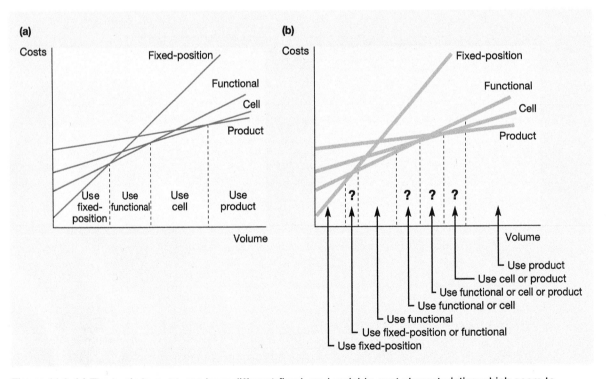

Figure 11.9 (a) The basic layout types have different fixed- and variable-cost characteristics which seem to determine which one to use. (b) In practice the uncertainty about the exact fixed and variable costs of each layout means the decision can rarely be made on cost alone

Of all the characteristics of the various layout types, perhaps the most generally significant are the unit cost implications of layout choice. This is best understood by distinguishing between the fixed- and variable-cost elements of adopting each layout type. For any particular product or service, the fixed costs of physically constructing a fixed-position layout are relatively small compared with any other way of producing the same product or service. However, the variable costs of producing each individual product or service are relatively high compared to the alternative layout types. Fixed costs then tend to increase as one moves from fixed-position, through functional and cell, to product layout. Variable costs per product or service tend to decrease, however. The total costs for each layout type will depend on the volume of products or services produced and are shown in Figure 11.9(a). This seems to show that for any volume there is a lowest-cost basic layout. However, in practice, the cost analysis of layout selection is rarely as clear as this. The exact cost of operating the layout is difficult to forecast and will probably depend on many often-difficult-to-predict factors. Rather than use lines to represent the cost of layout as volume increases, broad bands, within which the real cost is likely to lie, are probably more appropriate (*see* Fig. 11.9(b)). The discrimination between the different layout types is now far less clear. There are ranges of volume for which any of two or three layout types might provide the lowest operating cost. The less certainty there is over the costs, the broader the cost 'bands' will be, and the less clear the choice will be. The probable costs of adopting a particular layout need to be set in the broader context of advantages and disadvantages in Table 11.2.

Detailed design of the layout

Once the basic layout type has been decided, the next step is to decide the detailed design of the layout. Detailed design is the act of operationalizing the broad principles which were implicit in the choice of the basic layout type.

Detailed design in fixed-position layout

In fixed-position arrangements the location of resources will be determined, not on the basis of the flow of transformed resources, but on the convenience of transforming resources themselves. The objective of the detailed design of fixed-position layouts is to achieve a layout for the operation which allows all the transforming resources to maximize their contribution to the transformation process by allowing them to provide an effective 'service' to the transformed resources. The detailed layout of some fixed-position layouts, such as building sites, can become very complicated, especially if the planned schedule of activities is changed frequently. Imagine the chaos on a construction site if heavy trucks continually (and noisily) drove past the site office, delivery trucks for one contractor had to cross other contractors' areas to get to where they were storing their own materials, and the staff who spent most time at the building itself were located furthest away from it. Although there are techniques which help to locate resources on fixed-position layouts, they are not widely used.

Detailed design in functional layout

The detailed design of functional layouts is complex, as is flow in this type of layout. Chief among the factors which lead to this complexity is the very large number of different options. For example, in the very simplest case of just two work centres, there are only two ways of arranging these *relative to each other*. But there are six ways of arranging three centres and 120 ways of arranging five centres. This relationship is a factorial one. For N centres there are factorial N ($N!$) different ways of arranging the centres, where:

$$N! = N \times (N - 1) \times (N - 2) \times \ldots \times (1) \qquad (1)$$

So for a relatively simple functional layout with, say, 20 work centres, there are $20! = 2.433 \times 10^{18}$ ways of arranging the operation. This **combinatorial complexity** of functional layouts makes optimal solutions difficult to achieve in practice. Most functional layouts are designed by a combination of intuition, common sense and systematic trial and error.

Combinatorial complexity

The information for functional layouts

Before starting the process of detailed design in functional layouts there are some essential pieces of information which the designer needs:

- The area required by each work centre;
- The constraints on the shape of the area allocated to each work centre;
- The degree and direction of flow between each work centre (for example, number of journeys, number of loads or cost of flow per distance travelled);
- The desirability of work centres being close together or close to some fixed point in the layout.

Flow record chart

The degree and direction of flow are usually shown on a **flow record chart** like that shown in Figure 11.10(a) which records in this case the number of loads transported between departments. This information could be gathered from routeing information, or where flow is more random, as in a library for example, the information could be collected by observing

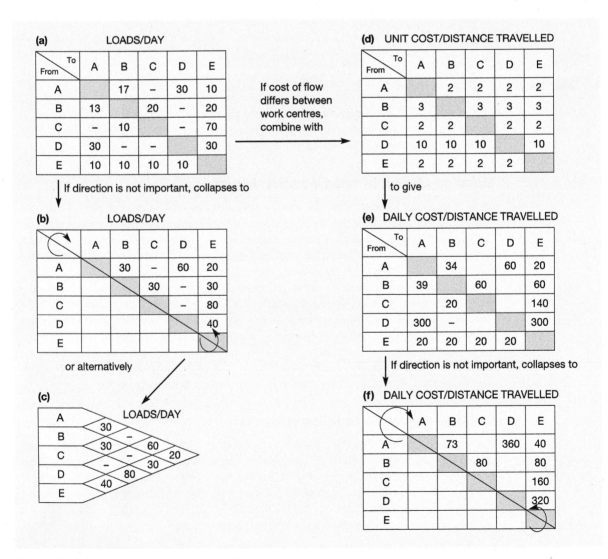

Figure 11.10 Collecting information in functional layout

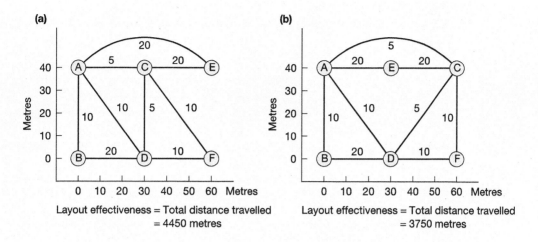

Layout effectiveness = Total distance travelled = 4450 metres

Layout effectiveness = Total distance travelled = 3750 metres

Figure 11.11 (a) and (b) The objective of most functional layouts is to minimize the cost associated with movement in the operation, sometimes simplified to minimizing the total distance travelled

the routes taken by customers over a typical period of time. If the direction of the flow between work centres makes little difference to the layout, the information can be collapsed as shown in Figure 11.10(b), an alternative form of which is shown in Figure 11.10(c). There may be significant differences in the costs of moving materials or customers between different work centres. For example, in Figure 11.10(d) the unit cost of transporting a load between the five work centres is shown. Combining the unit cost and flow data gives the cost-per-distance-travelled data shown in Figure 11.10(e). This has been collapsed as before into Figure 11.10(f).

Minimizing distance travelled

In most examples of functional layout, the prime objective is to minimize the costs to the operation which are associated with flow through the operation. This usually means minimizing the total distance travelled in the operation. For example, Figure 11.11(a) shows a simple six-centre functional layout with the total number of journeys between centres each day. The effectiveness of the layout, at this simple level, can be calculated from:

$$\text{Effectiveness of layout} = \sum F_{ij} D_{ij} \text{ for all } i \neq j$$

where

F_{ij} = the flow in loads or journeys per period of time from work centre i to work centre j
D_{ij} = the distance between work centre i and work centre j.

The lower the effectiveness score, the better the layout. In this example the total of the number of journeys multiplied by the distance for each pair of departments where there is some flow is 4,450 metres. This measure will indicate whether changes to the layout improve its effectiveness (at least in the narrow terms defined here). For example, if centres C and E are exchanged as in Figure 11.11(b) the effectiveness measure becomes 3,750, showing that the new layout now has reduced the total distance travelled in the operation. These calculations assume that all journeys are the same in that their cost to the operation is the same. In some operations this is not so, however. For example, in the hospital some journeys involving healthy staff and relatively fit patients would have little importance compared with other journeys where very sick patients need to be moved from the operating theatres to intensive-care wards. In these cases a cost (or difficulty) element is included in the measure of layout effectiveness:

$$\text{Effectiveness of layout} = \sum F_{ij} D_{ij} C_{ij} \text{ for all } i \neq j$$

where

C_{ij} is the cost per distance travelled of making a journey between departments i and j.

The general functional layout design method

The general approach to determining the location of work centres in a functional layout is as follows:

Step 1 Collect information relating to the work centres and the flow between them.

Step 2 Draw up a schematic layout showing the work centres and the flow between them, putting the work centres with the greatest flow closest to each other.

Step 3 Adjust the schematic layout to take into account the constraints of the area into which the layout must fit.

Step 4 Draw the layout showing the actual work centre areas and distances which materials or customers must travel. Calculate the effectiveness measure of the layout either as total distance travelled or as the cost of movement.

Step 5 Check to see if exchanging any two work centres will reduce the total distance travelled or the cost of movement. If so, make the exchange and return to step 4. If not, make this the final layout.

Worked example

Rotterdam Educational Group (REG) is a company which commissions, designs and manufactures education packs for distance-learning courses and training. It has leased a new building with an area of 1,800 square metres, into which it needs to fit 11 'departments'. Prior to moving into the new building it has conducted an exercise to find the average number of trips taken by its staff between the 11 departments. Although some trips are a little more significant than others (because of the loads carried by staff) it has been decided that all trips will be treated as being of equal value.

Step 1 – Collect information

The areas required by each department together with the average daily number of trips between departments are shown in the flow chart in Figure 11.12. In this example the direction of flow is not relevant and very low flow rates (less than five trips per day) have not been included.

DEPARTMENT	AREA (m²)	CODE
Reception	85	A
Meeting room	160	B
Layout and design	100	C
Editorial	225	D
Printing	200	E
Cutting	75	F
Receiving and shipping	200	G
Binding	120	H
Video production	160	I
Packing	200	J
Audio production	100	K

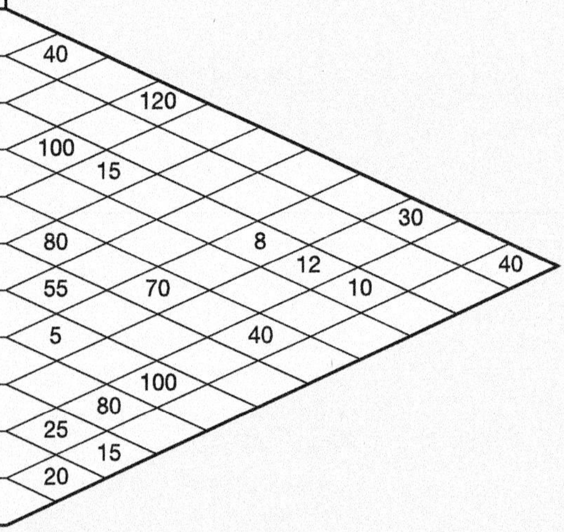

Dimensions of the building = 30 metres × 60 metres

Figure 11.12 Flow information for Rotterdam Educational Group

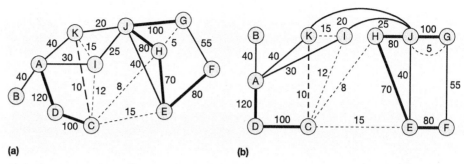

Figure 11.13 (a) Schematic layout placing centres with high traffic levels close to each other, (b) schematic layout adjusted to fit building geometry

Step 2 – Draw schematic layout

Figure 11.13(a) shows a schematic arrangement of departments. The thickest lines represent high flow rates between 70 and 120 trips per day; the medium lines are used for flow rates between 20 and 69 trips per day; and the thinnest lines are for flow rates between 5 and 19 trips per day. The objective here is to arrange the work centres so that those with the thick lines are closest together. The higher the flow rate, the shorter the line should be.

Step 3 – Adjust the schematic layout

If departments were arranged exactly as shown in Figure 11.13(a), the building which housed them would be of an irregular, and therefore high-cost, shape. The layout needs adjusting to take into account the shape of the building. Figure 11.13(b) shows the departments arranged in a more ordered fashion which corresponds to the dimensions of the building.

Step 4 – Draw the layout

Figure 11.14 shows the departments arranged with the actual dimensions of the building and occupying areas which approximate to their required areas. Although the distances between the centroids of departments have changed from Figure 11.14 to accommodate their physical shape, their relative positions are the same. It is at this stage that a quantitative expression of the cost of movement associated with this relative layout can be calculated.

Step 5 – Check by exchanging

The layout in Figure 11.14 seems to be reasonably effective but it is usually worthwhile to check for improvement by exchanging pairs of departments to see if any reduction in total flow can be obtained. For example, departments H and J might be exchanged, and the total distance travelled calculated again to see if any reduction has been achieved.

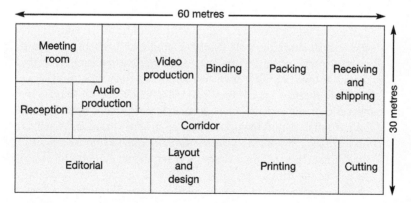

Figure 11.14 Final layout of building

Computer-aided functional layout design

Heuristic procedures

The combinatorial complexity of functional layout has led to the development of several **heuristic procedures** to aid the design process. Heuristic procedures use what have been described as 'short cuts in the reasoning process' and 'rules of thumb' in the search for a reasonable solution. They do not search for an optimal solution (though they might find one by chance) but rather attempt to derive a good suboptimal solution. One such computer-based heuristic procedure is called **CRAFT** (Computerized Relative Allocation of Facilities Technique).[4] The reasoning behind this procedure is that, whereas it is infeasible to evaluate factorial N ($N!$) different layouts when N is large, it is feasible to start with an initial layout and then evaluate all the different ways of exchanging two work centres.

CRAFT

There are

$$\frac{N!}{2!(N-2)!}$$

possible ways of exchanging 2 out of N work centres. So for a 20-work-centre layout, there are 190 ways of exchanging 2 work centres.

Three inputs are required for the CRAFT heuristic: a matrix of the flow between departments; a matrix of the cost associated with transportation between each of the departments; and a spatial array showing an initial layout. From these:

- the location of the centroid of each department is calculated;
- the flow matrix is weighted by the cost matrix, and this weighted flow matrix is multiplied by the distances between departments to obtain the total transportation costs of the initial layout;
- the model then calculates the cost consequence of exchanging every possible pair of departments.

The exchange giving the most improvement is then fixed, and the whole cycle is repeated with the updated cost flow matrix until no further improvement is made by exchanging two departments.

Detailed design in cell layout

Figure 11.15 shows how a functional layout has been divided into four cells, each of which has the resources to process a 'family' of parts. In doing this the operations management has implicitly taken two interrelated decisions regarding:

- the extent and nature of the cells it has chosen to adopt;
- which resources to allocate to which cells.

Production flow analysis

Cluster analysis

Production flow analysis

The detailed design of cellular layouts is difficult, partly because the idea of a cell is itself a compromise between process and product layout. To simplify the task, it is useful to concentrate on either the process or the product aspects of cell layout. If cell designers choose to concentrate on processes, they could use **cluster analysis** to find which processes group naturally together. This involves examining each type of process and asking which other types of processes a product or part using that process is also likely to need. One approach to allocating tasks and machines to cells is **production flow analysis** (PFA), which examines both product requirements and process grouping simultaneously. In Figure 11.16(a) a manufacturing operation has grouped the components it makes into eight families – for example, the components in family 1 require machines 2 and 5. In this state the matrix does not seem to exhibit any natural groupings. If the order of the rows and columns is changed, however, to move the crosses as close as possible to the diagonal of the matrix which goes from top left to bottom right, then a clearer pattern emerges. This is illustrated in Figure 11.16(b) and shows that the machines could conveniently be grouped together in three cells, indicated on the diagram as cells A, B and C. Although this procedure is a particularly useful way to

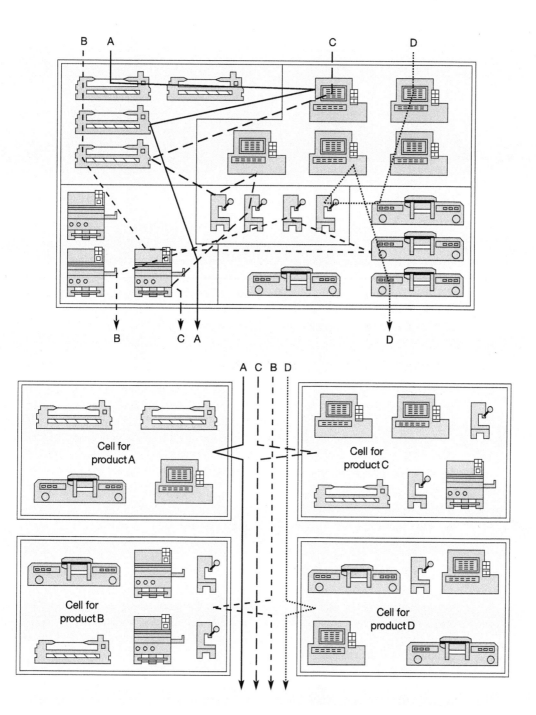

Figure 11.15 Cell layout groups processes together which are necessary for a family of products

allocate machines to cells, the analysis is rarely totally clean. This is the case here where component family 8 needs processing by machines 3 and 8 which have been allocated to cell B. There are some partial solutions for this. More machines could be purchased and put into cell A. This would clearly solve the problem but requires investing capital in a new machine which might be under-utilized. Or, components in family 8 could be sent to cell B after they have been processed in cell A (or even in the middle of their processing route if necessary). This solution avoids the need to purchase another machine but it conflicts partly with the basic idea of cell layout – to achieve a simplification of a previously complex flow. Or, if there are several components like this, it might be necessary to devise a special cell for them (usually

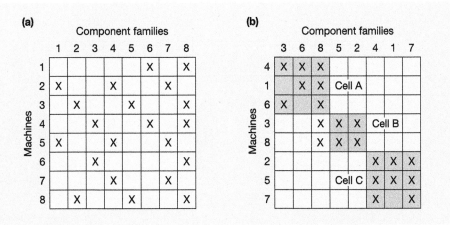

Figure 11.16 (a) and (b) Using production flow analysis to allocate machines to cells

Remainder cell

called a **remainder cell**) which will almost be like a mini-functional layout. This remainder cell does remove the 'inconvenient' components from the rest of the operation, however, leaving it with a more ordered and predictable flow.

Detailed design in product layout

The nature of the product layout design decision is a little different from the other layout types. Rather than 'where to place what', product layout is concerned more with 'what to place where'. Locations are frequently decided upon and then work tasks are allocated to each location. For example, it may have been decided that four stations are needed to make computer cases. The decision then is which of the tasks that go into making the cases should be allocated to each station. The main product layout decisions are as follows:

- What cycle time is needed?
- How many stages are needed?
- How should the task-time variation be dealt with?
- How should the layout be balanced?

The cycle time of product layouts

Cycle time

Cycle time is the time between completed products, pieces of information or customers emerging from the process. Cycle time is a vital factor in the design of product layouts and has a significant influence on most of the other detailed design decisions. It is calculated by considering the likely demand for the products or services over a period and the amount of production time available in that period.

Worked example

Suppose the regional back-office operation of a large bank is designing an operation which will process its mortgage applications. The number of applications to be processed is 160 per week and the time available to process the applications is 40 hours per week.

$$\text{Cycle time for the layout} = \frac{\text{time available}}{\text{number to be processed}} = \frac{40}{160} = \frac{1}{4} \text{ hour}$$

$$= 15 \text{ minutes}$$

So the bank's layout must be capable of processing a completed application once every 15 minutes.

The number of stages

Total work content

The next decision concerns the number of stages in the layout and depends on the cycle time required and the total quantity of work involved in producing the product or service. This latter piece of information is called the **total work content**. The larger the total work content and the smaller the required cycle time, the more stages will be necessary.

> ### Worked example
>
> Suppose the bank in the previous example calculated that the average total work content of processing a mortgage application is 60 minutes. The number of stages needed to produce a processed application every 15 minutes can be calculated as follows:
>
> $$\text{Number of stages} = \frac{\text{total work content}}{\text{required cycle time}}$$
>
> $$= \frac{60 \text{ minutes}}{15 \text{ minutes}}$$
>
> $$= 4 \text{ stages}$$
>
> If this figure had not emerged as a whole number it would have been necessary to round it up to the next largest whole number. It is difficult (although not always impossible) to hire fractions of people to staff the stages.

Task-time variation

Imagine a line of four stages, each contributing a quarter of the total work content of processing the mortgage, and passing the documentation on to the next stage every 15 minutes. In practice, of course, the flow would not be so regular. Each station's allocation of work might on average take 15 minutes, but almost certainly the time will vary each time a mortgage application is processed. This is a general characteristic of all repetitive processing (and indeed of all work performed by humans) and can be caused by such factors as differences between each product or service being processed along the line (in the mortgage-processing example, the time some tasks require will vary depending on the personal circumstances of the person applying for the loan), or slight variations in coordination and effort on the part of staff performing the task. This variation can introduce irregularity into the flow along the line, which in turn can lead to both periodic queues at the stages and lost processing time. It may even prove necessary to introduce more resources into the operation to compensate for the loss of efficiency resulting from work-time variation.

Balancing work-time allocation

Line balancing

One of the most important design decisions in product layout is that of **line balancing**. In the mortgage-processing example we have assumed that the 15 minutes of work content are allocated equally to the four stations. This is nearly always impossible to achieve in practice and some imbalance in the work allocation results. Inevitably this will increase the effective cycle time of the line. If it becomes greater than the required cycle time, it may be necessary to devote extra resources, in the shape of a further stage, to compensate for the imbalance.

Balancing loss

The effectiveness of the line-balancing activity is measured by **balancing loss**. This is the time wasted through the unequal allocation of work as a percentage of the total time invested in processing the product or service.

Balancing techniques[5]

Precedence diagram

There are a number of techniques available to help in the line-balancing task. Again, in practice, the most useful (and most used) 'techniques' are the relatively simple such as the **precedence diagram**. This is a representation of the ordering of the elements which compose the total work content of the product or service. Each element is represented by a circle. The circles are connected by arrows which signify the ordering of the elements. Two rules apply when constructing the diagram:

- the circles which represent the elements are drawn as far to the left as possible;
- none of the arrows which show the precedence of the elements should be vertical.

The precedence diagram, either using circles and arrows or transposed into tabular form, is the most common starting point for most balancing techniques. We do not treat the more complex of these techniques here but it is useful to describe the general approach to balancing product layouts.

Worked example

In Figure 11.17 the work allocations in a four-stage line are illustrated. The total amount of time invested in producing each product or service is four times the cycle time because, for every unit produced, all four stages have been working for the cycle time. When the work is equally allocated between the stages, the total time invested in each product or service produced is $4 \times 2.5 = 10$ minutes. However, when work is unequally allocated, as illustrated, the time invested is $3.0 \times 4 = 12$ minutes, i.e. 2.0 minutes of time, 16.67 per cent of the total, is wasted.

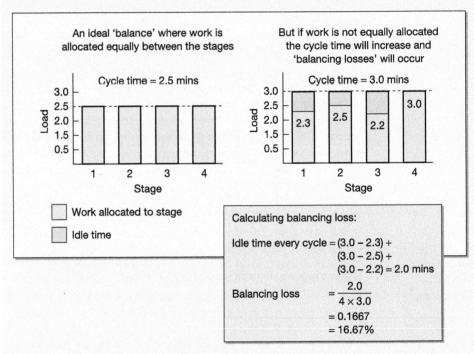

Figure 11.17 Balancing loss is that proportion of the time invested in processing the product or service which is not used productively

This general approach is to allocate elements from the precedence diagram to the first stage, starting from the left, in order of the columns until the work allocated to the stage is as close to, but less than, the cycle time. When that stage is as full of work as is possible without exceeding the cycle time, move on to the next stage, and so on, until all the work elements are allocated. The key issue is how to select an element to be allocated to a stage when more than one element could be chosen. Two heuristic rules have been found to be particularly useful in deciding this:

- Simply choose the largest that will 'fit' into the time remaining at the stage.
- Choose the element with the most 'followers': that is the highest number of elements which can only be allocated when that element has been allocated.

Worked example

Karlstad Kakes (KK) is a manufacturer of speciality cakes, which has recently obtained a contract to supply a major supermarket chain with a speciality cake in the shape of a space rocket. It has been decided that the volumes required by the supermarket warrant a special production line to perform the finishing, decorating and packing of the cake. This line would have to carry out the elements shown in Figure 11.18, which also shows the precedence diagram for the total job. The initial order from the supermarket is for 5,000 cakes a week and the number of hours worked by the factory is 40 per week. From this:

$$\text{The required cycle time} = \frac{40 \text{ hrs} \times 60 \text{ mins}}{5,000} = 0.48 \text{ min}$$

$$\text{The required number of stages} = \frac{1.68 \text{ min (the total work content)}}{0.48 \text{ min (the required cycle time)}} = 3.5 \text{ stages}$$

This means four stages.

Element	a	– De-tin and trim	0.12 mins
Element	b	– Reshape with off-cuts	0.30 mins
Element	c	– Clad in almond fondant	0.36 mins
Element	d	– Clad in white fondant	0.25 mins
Element	e	– Decorate, red icing	0.17 mins
Element	f	– Decorate, green icing	0.05 mins
Element	g	– Decorate, blue icing	0.10 mins
Element	h	– Affix transfers	0.08 mins
Element	i	– Transfer to base and pack	0.25 mins

Total work content = 1.68 mins

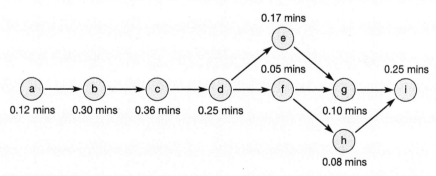

Figure 11.18 Element listing and precedence diagram for Karlstad Kakes

Working from the left on the precedence diagram, elements a and b can be allocated to stage 1. Allocating element c to stage 1 would exceed the cycle time. In fact, only element c can be allocated to stage 2 because including element d would again exceed the cycle time. Element d can be allocated to stage 3. Either element e or element f can also be allocated to stage 3, but not both, or the cycle time would be exceeded. Following the 'largest element' heuristic rule, element e is chosen. The remaining elements then are allocated to stage 4. Figure 11.19 shows the final allocation and the balancing loss of the line.

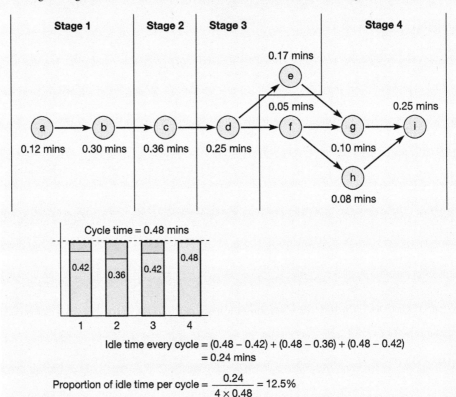

Figure 11.19 Allocation of elements to stages and balancing loss for Karlstad Kakes

Arranging the stages

All the stages necessary to fulfil the requirements of the layout may not be arranged in a sequential 'single line'. Return to the mortgage-processing example, which requires four stages working on the task to maintain a cycle time of one processed application every 15 minutes. The conventional arrangement of the four stages would be to lay them out in one line, each stage having 15 minutes' worth of work. However, nominally, the same output rate could also be achieved by arranging the four stages as two shorter lines, each of two stages with 30 minutes' worth of work each. Alternatively, following this logic to its ultimate conclusion, the stages could be arranged as four parallel stages, each responsible for the whole work content. Figure 11.20 shows these options.

Long thin
Short fat

This may be a simplified example, but it represents a genuine issue. Should the layout be arranged as a single **long thin** line, as several **short fat** parallel lines, or somewhere in between? (Note that 'long' refers to the number of stages and 'fat' to the amount of work allocated to each stage.) In any particular situation there are usually technical constraints which limit either how 'long and thin' or how 'short and fat' the layout can be, but there is usually a range of possible options within which a choice needs to be made. The advantages of each extreme of the long thin to short fat spectrum are very different and help to explain why different arrangements are adopted.

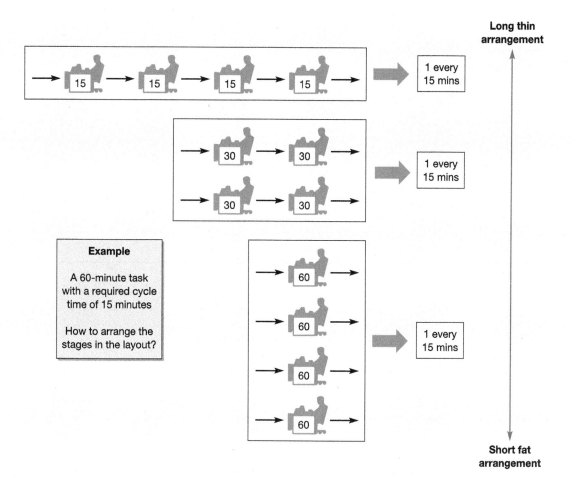

Figure 11.20 The arrangement of stages in product layout can be described on a spectrum from 'long thin' to 'short fat'

The advantages of the long thin arrangement
These include:

- *Controlled flow of materials or customers* – which is easy to manage.
- *Simple materials handling* – especially if a product being manufactured is heavy, large or difficult to move.
- *Lower capital requirements*. If a specialist piece of equipment is needed for one element in the job, only one piece of equipment would need to be purchased; on short fat arrangements every stage would need one.
- *More efficient operation*. If each stage is only performing a small part of the total job, the person at the stage will have a higher proportion of direct productive work as opposed to the non-productive parts of the job, such as picking up tools and materials.

The advantages of the short fat arrangement
These include:

- *Higher mix flexibility*. If the layout needs to process several types of product or service, each stage or line could specialize in different types.

- *Higher volume flexibility.* As volume varies, stages can simply be closed down or started up as required; long thin arrangements would need rebalancing each time the cycle time changed.
- *Higher robustness.* If one stage breaks down or ceases operation in some way, the other parallel stages are unaffected; a long thin arrangement would cease operating completely.
- *Less monotonous work.* In the mortgage example, the staff in the short fat arrangement are repeating their tasks only every hour; in the long thin arrangement it is every 15 minutes.

Summary answers to key questions

Check and improve your understanding of this chapter using self assessment questions and a personalised study plan, audio and video downloads, and an eBook – all at www.myomlab.com.

➤ What are the basic layout types used in operations?

■ There are four basic layout types. They are fixed-position layout, functional layout, cell layout and product layout.

➤ What type of layout should an operation choose?

■ Partly this is influenced by the nature of the process type, which in turn depends on the volume–variety characteristics of the operation. Partly also the decision will depend on the objectives of the operation. Cost and flexibility are particularly affected by the layout decision.

■ The fixed and variable costs implied by each layout differ such that, in theory, one particular layout will have the minimum costs for a particular volume level. However, in practice, uncertainty over the real costs involved in layout makes it difficult to be precise on which is the minimum-cost layout.

➤ What is layout design trying to achieve?

■ In addition to the conventional operations objectives which will be influenced by the layout design, factors of importance include the length and clarity of customer, material or information flow; inherent safety to staff and/or customers; staff comfort; accessibility to staff and customers; the ability to coordinate management decisions; the use of space; and long-term flexibility.

➤ How should each basic layout type be designed in detail?

■ In fixed-position layout the materials or people being transformed do not move but the transforming resources move around them. Techniques are rarely used in this type of layout, but some, such as resource location analysis, bring a systematic approach to minimizing the costs and inconvenience of flow at a fixed-position location.

■ In functional layout all similar transforming resources are grouped together in the operation. The detailed design task is usually (although not always) to minimize the distance travelled by the transformed resources through the operation. Either manual or computer-based methods can be used to devise the detailed design.

■ In cell layout the resources needed for a particular class of product are grouped together in some way. The detailed design task is to group the products or customer types such that convenient cells can be designed around their needs. Techniques such as production flow analysis can be used to allocate products to cells.

■ In product layout, the transforming resources are located in sequence specifically for the convenience of products or product types. The detailed design of product layouts includes a number of decisions, such as the cycle time to which the design must conform, the number of stages in the operation, the way tasks are allocated to the stages in the line, and the arrangement of the stages in the line. The cycle time of each part of the design, together with the number of stages, is a function of where the design lies on the 'long thin' to 'short fat' spectrum of arrangements. This position affects costs, flexibility, robustness and staff attitude to work. The allocation of tasks to stages is called line balancing, which can be performed either manually or through computer-based algorithms.

Case study
Weldon Hand Tools

Weldon Hand Tools, one of the most successful of the European hand tool manufacturers, decided to move into the 'woodworking' tools market. Previously its products had been confined to car maintenance, home decorating and general hand tools. One of the first products which it decided to manufacture was a general-purpose 'smoothing plane', a tool which smoothes and shapes wood. Its product designers devised a suitable design and the company's work measurement engineers estimated the time it would take in standard minutes (the time to perform the task plus allowances for rest etc.) to perform each element in the assembly process. The marketing department also estimated the likely demand (for the whole European market) for the new product. Its sales forecast is shown in Table 11.3.

The marketing department was not totally confident of its forecast, however. *'A substantial proportion of demand is likely to be export sales, which we find difficult to predict. But whatever demand does turn out to be, we will have to react quickly to meet it. The more we enter these parts of the market, the more we are into impulse buying and the more sales we lose if we don't supply.'*

This plane was likely to be the first of several similar planes. A further model had already been approved for launch about one year after this, and two or three further models were in the planning stage. All the planes were similar, merely varying in length and width.

Table 11.3 Sales forecast for smoothing plane

Time period	Volume
Year 1	
1st quarter	98,000 units
2nd quarter	140,000 units
3rd quarter	140,000 units
4th quarter	170,000 units
Year 2	
1st quarter	140,000 units
2nd quarter	170,000 units
3rd quarter	200,000 units
4th quarter	230,000 units

Designing the manufacturing operation

It has been decided to assemble all planes at one of the company's smaller factory sites where a whole workshop is unused. Within the workshop there is plenty of room for expansion if demand proves higher than forecast. All machining and finishing of parts would be performed at the main factory and the parts shipped to the smaller site where they would be assembled at the available workshop. An idea of the assembly task can be gained from the partially exploded view of the product (*see* Fig. 11.21). Table 11.4 gives the 'standard time' for each element of the assembly task. Some of the tasks are described as 'press' operations. These use a simple mechanical press that applies sufficient force for simple bending, riveting or force-fitting operations. This type of press is not an expensive or sophisticated piece of technology.

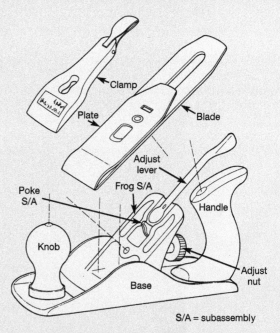

Figure 11.21 Partially exploded view of the new plane

Table 11.4 Standard times for each element of assembly task in standard minutes (SM)

Element	Time in standard minutes (SM)
Press operations	
Assemble poke subassembly	0.12
Fit poke subassembly to frog	0.10
Rivet adjusting lever to frog	0.15
Press adjusting nut screw to frog	0.08
TOTAL PRESS OPERATIONS	0.45
Bench operations	
Fit adjusting nut to frog	0.15
Fit frog screw to frog	0.05
Fit knob to base	0.15
Fit handle to base	0.17
Fit frog subassembly to base	0.15
Assemble blade subassembly	0.08
Assemble blade subassembly, clamp and label to base and adjust	0.20
Make up box and wrap plane, pack and stock	0.20
TOTAL ASSEMBLY AND PACK TIME	1.60

Costs and pricing

The standard costing system at the company involves adding a 150 per cent overhead charge to the direct labour cost of manufacturing the product, and the product would retail for the equivalent of around €35 in Europe where most retailers will sell this type of product for about 70–120 per cent more than they buy it from the manufacturer.

Questions

1 How many staff should the company employ?

2 What type of facilities and technology will the company need to buy in order to assemble this product?

3 Design a layout for the assembly operation (to include the fly press work) including the tasks to be performed at each part of the system.

4 How would the layout need to be adjusted as demand for this and similar products builds up?

Problems and applications

These problems and applications will help to improve your analysis of operations. You can find more practice problems as well as worked examples and guided solutions on MyOMLab at www.myomlab.com.

1 A loan application process involves 8 separate tasks. Task A takes 10 minutes and does not require any other of the tasks to be performed before it can be started. Similarly, Task B can be started without any other task being completed and takes 8 minutes. Task C takes 16 minutes and cannot be performed until Task A has been done. Task D cannot be done until both A and B have been performed and takes 8 minutes. Task E requires tasks C and D to be finished and takes 8 minutes. After task E has been performed, Tasks F and G, taking respectively 5 and 17 minutes, can be performed. Finally (but only after Tasks F and G have been performed), Task H can be performed and takes 11 minutes. Devise a precedence diagram for this process, and, assuming a required cycle time of 18 minutes, determine how many people will be required to perform the task, and if they are arranged in a 'product' layout, how the tasks will be allocated to each person. Calculate the balancing loss for this layout.

2 A simple product has 8 elements (a to h) whose times and immediate predecessors are shown in Table 11.5. Devise a product layout that will produce products at a rate of at least 6 products an hour. How many people will be required for this layout, and what will be its balancing loss?

Table 11.5 The immediate predecessors table for a simple product

Task	Time (mins)	Immediate predecessor task
a	5	–
b	4	a
c	3	b
d	4	b
e	2	c
f	6	c
g	3	d, e, f
h	4	g

Table 11.6 Flow of materials

	D1	D2	D3	D4	D5	D6	D7	D8
D1	\	30						
D2	10	\	15	20				
D3		5	\	12	2		15	
D4		6		\	10	20		
D5				8	\	8	10	12
D6	3				2	\	30	
D7	3					13	\	2
D8				10	6		15	\

3 The flow of materials through eight departments is shown in Table 11.6. Assuming that the direction of the flow of materials is not important, construct a relationship chart, a schematic layout and a suggested layout, given that each department is the same size and the eight departments should be arranged four along each side of a corridor.

4 Sketch the layout of your local shop, coffee bar or sports hall reception area. Observe the area and draw onto your sketch the movements of people through the area over a sufficient period of time to get over 20 observations. Assess the flow in terms of volume, variety and type of layout.

5 Revisit the opening short case in this chapter that examines some of the principles behind supermarket layout. Then visit a supermarket and observe people's behaviour. You may wish to try and observe which areas they move slowly past and which areas they seem to move past without paying attention to the products. (You may have to exercise some discretion when doing this; people generally don't like to be stalked round the supermarket too obviously.) Try and verify, as far as you can, some of the principles that were outlined in the opening short case. If you were to redesign the supermarket what would you recommend?

Selected further reading

This is a relatively technical chapter and, as you would expect, most books on the subject are technical. Here are a few of the more accessible.

Karlsson, C. (1996) Radically new production systems, *International Journal of Operations and Production Management*, vol. 16, no. 11. An interesting paper because it traces the development of Volvo's factory layouts over the years.

Meyers, F.E. and Stephens, M.P. (2000) *Manufacturing Facilities Design and Material Handling*, Prentice-Hall, Upper Saddle River, NJ. Exactly what it says, thorough.

Meller, R.D. and Kai-Yin Gau (1996) The facility layout problem: recent and emerging trends and perspectives, *Journal of Manufacturing Systems*, vol. 15, issue 5, 351–66. A review of the literature in the area.

Useful web sites

www.bpmi.org Site of the Business Process Management Initiative. Some good resources including papers and articles.

www.bptrends.com News site for trends in business process management generally. Some interesting articles.

www.iienet.org The American Institute of Industrial Engineers site. They are an important professional body for process design and related topics.

www.waria.com A Workflow and Reengineering Association web site. Some useful topics.

www.strategosinc.com/plant_layout_elements Some useful briefings, mainly in a manufacturing context.

www.opsman.org Lots of useful stuff.

Now that you have finished reading this chapter, why not visit MyOMLab at www.myomlab.com where you'll find more learning resources to help you make the most of your studies and get a better grade?

Chapter 12

Capacity planning and control

Key questions

➤ What is capacity planning and control?

➤ How are demand and capacity measured?

➤ What are the alternative ways of coping with demand fluctuation?

➤ How can operations plan and control their capacity level?

➤ How can queuing theory be used to plan capacity?

Introduction

Providing the capability to satisfy current and future demand is a fundamental responsibility of operations management. Get the balance between capacity and demand right and the operation can satisfy its customers cost-effectively. Get it wrong and it will fail to satisfy demand, and have excessive costs. Capacity planning and control is also sometimes referred to as *aggregate* planning and control. This is because, at this level of the planning and control, demand and capacity calculations are usually performed on an aggregated basis which does not discriminate between the different products and services that an operation might produce. The essence of the task is to reconcile, at a general and aggregated level, the supply of capacity with the level of demand which it must satisfy (*see* Figure 12.1). This chapter also has a supplement that deals with analytical queuing models, one way of considering capacity planning and control, especially in some service operations.

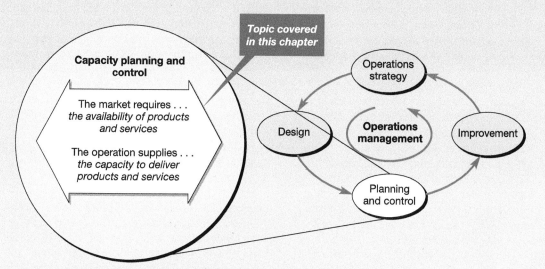

Figure 12.1 This chapter covers capacity planning and control

Check and improve your understanding of this chapter using self assessment questions and a personalised study plan, audio and video downloads, and an eBook – all at www.myomlab.com.

Operations in practice Britvic – delivering drinks to demand[1]

Britvic is amongst Europe's leading soft-drink manufacturers, a major player in a market consuming nearly ten billion litres a year. Annually, Britvic bottles, distributes and sells over 1 billion litres of ready-to-drink soft drinks in around 400 different flavours, shapes and sizes, including brands such as Pepsi, Tango, Robinsons, Aqua Libra, Purdey's and J2O. Every year, Britvic produce enough cans of soft drinks to stretch three times around the world, so it has to be a high-volume and high-speed business. Its six UK factories contain factory lines producing up to 1,500 cans a minute, with distribution organized on a giant scale. At the centre of its distribution network is a National Distribution Centre (NDC) located at Lutterworth, UK. It is designed to operate 24 hours a day throughout the year, handling up to 620 truckloads of soft drinks daily and, together with a national network of 12 depots, it has to ensure that 250,000 outlets in the UK receive their orders on time. Designed and built in collaboration with Wincanton, a specialist supply chain solutions company, which now manages Britvic's NDC, it is capable of holding up to 140 million cans in its 50,000-pallet 'High Bay' warehouse. All information, from initial order to final delivery, is held electronically. Loads are scanned at Britvic factories and fed into the *'Business Planning and Control System'* that creates a schedule of receipts. This information is then fed to the *Warehouse Management System* and when hauliers arrive at the NDC, data are passed over to the *Movement Control System* that controls the retrieval of pallets from the High Bay.

Over the year Britvic distribute over 100 million cases. However, the demand pattern for soft drinks is seasonal, with short-term changes caused by both weather and marketing campaigns. Furthermore, Britvic's service policy of responding whenever customers want them to deliver has a dramatic impact on the NDC and its capacity planning. *'Our busiest periods are during the summer and in the run-up to Christmas, where we expect over 200 trailers in and out each day – that equates to about 3 million cases per week. In the quiet periods, especially after Christmas, we have less than a million cases per week'* (Distribution Manager).

Not only is demand on the NDC seasonal in a general sense, it can vary from 2,000 pallets one day, to 6,000 the next, as a result of short-term weather patterns and variable order patterns from large

Source: Wincanton

customers (supermarkets). Given the lack of space in the High Bay, it is not possible to simply stock up for the busy periods, so flexibility and efficiency are the keys to success.

The NDC uses a number of methods to cope with demand fluctuation. Most importantly is the use and development of technology both within the NDC and out in Britvic's supply chain. High levels of throughput and the ability to respond quickly to demand fluctuations depend on the use of integrated information technology linked to automated 'High Bay' handling technology. *'Without the automation this plant simply couldn't function. You realize how much you need this system when it breaks down! The other day, multiple errors in the system meant that in the space of 6 hours we went from being ahead to having 50 loads waiting to be processed. That equates to 1,350 pallets or nearly 4 million cans.'*

Human resource management is also key in managing capacity. Every morning the shift manager receives orders for the day, although further orders can be placed at any time during the day. The order information allows the multi-skilled workforce to be allocated effectively. The daily meetings also allow any problems to be addressed and dealt with before they become critical. Finally, by outsourcing the NDC management to Wincanton, the site is able to second employees from other Wincanton-owned sites when demand is high. *'Our other sites around the country have different peaks and troughs throughout the year which helps us utilize employee numbers.'*

What is capacity management?

Capacity

The most common use of the word **capacity** is in the static, physical sense of the fixed *volume* of a container, or the space in a building. This meaning of the word is also sometimes used by operations managers. For example, a pharmaceutical manufacturer may invest in new 1,000-litre capacity reactor vessels, a property company purchases a 500-vehicle capacity city-centre car park, and a 'multiplex' cinema is built with 10 screens and a total capacity of 2,500 seats. Although these capacity measures describe the *scale* of these operations, they do not reflect the processing capacities of these investments. To do this we must incorporate a *time* dimension appropriate to the use of assets. So the pharmaceutical company will be concerned with the level of output that can be achieved using the 1,000-litre reactor vessel. If a batch of standard products can be produced every hour, the planned processing capacity could be as high as 24,000 litres per day. If the reaction takes four hours, and two hours are used for cleaning between batches, the vessel may only produce 4,000 litres per day. Similarly, the car park may be fully occupied by office workers during the working day, 'processing' only 500 cars per day. Alternatively, it may be used for shoppers staying on average only one hour, and theatre-goers occupying spaces for three hours in the evening. The processing capacity would then be up to 5,000 cars per day. Thus the definition of the capacity of an operation is the *maximum level of value-added activity over a period of time* that the process can achieve under normal operating conditions.

Capacity constraints

Capacity constraint

Many organizations operate at below their maximum processing capacity, either because there is insufficient demand completely to 'fill' their capacity, or as a deliberate policy, so that the operation can respond quickly to every new order. Often, though, organizations find themselves with some parts of their operation operating below their capacity while other parts are at their capacity 'ceiling'. It is the parts of the operation that are operating at their capacity 'ceiling' which are the **capacity constraint** for the whole operation. It is these parts of the operation that are pushed to their capacity ceiling that act as the constraint on the whole operation. For example, a retail superstore might offer a gift-wrapping service which at normal times can cope with all requests for its services without delaying customers unduly. At Christmas, however, the demand for gift wrapping might increase proportionally far more than the overall increase in custom for the store as a whole. Unless extra resources are provided to increase the capacity of this micro-operation, it could constrain the capacity of the whole store.

Planning and controlling capacity

Long-term capacity strategy

Capacity planning and control is the task of setting the effective capacity of the operation so that it can respond to the demands placed upon it. This usually means deciding how the operation should react to fluctuations in demand. These strategies were concerned with introducing (or deleting) major increments of physical capacity. We called this task **long-term capacity strategy**. In this chapter we are treating the shorter timescale where capacity decisions are being made largely within the constraints of the physical capacity limits set by the operation's long-term capacity strategy.

Medium- and short-term capacity

Medium term capacity planning and control

Having established long-term capacity, operations managers must decide how to adjust the capacity of the operation in the **medium term**. This usually involves an assessment of the demand forecasts over a period of 2–18 months ahead, during which time planned output can be varied, for example, by changing the number of hours the equipment is used. In practice, however, few forecasts are accurate, and most operations also need to respond to changes in demand which occur over a shorter timescale. Hotels and restaurants have unexpected and apparently random changes in demand from night to night, but also know from experience that certain days are on average busier than others. So operations managers also have to make **short-term capacity** adjustments, which enable them to flex output for a short period, either on a predicted basis (for example, bank checkouts are always busy at lunchtimes) or at short notice (for example, a sunny warm day at a theme park).

Short-term capacity planning and control

Aggregate demand and capacity

Aggregate planning and control

The important characteristic of capacity planning and control, as we are treating it here, is that it is concerned with setting capacity levels over the medium and short terms in **aggregated** terms. That is, it is making overall, broad capacity decisions, but is not concerned with all of the detail of the individual products and services offered. This is what 'aggregated' means – different products and services are bundled together in order to get a broad view of demand and capacity. This may mean some degree of approximation, especially if the mix of products or services being produced varies significantly (as we shall see later in this chapter). Nevertheless, as a first step in planning and control, aggregation is necessary. For example, a hotel might think of demand and capacity in terms of 'room nights per month', which ignores the number of guests in each room and their individual requirements, but is a good first approximation. A woollen knitwear factory might measure demand and capacity in the number of units (garments) it is capable of making per month, ignoring size, colour or style variations. Aluminium producers could use tonnes per month, ignoring types of alloy, gauge and batch size variation. The ultimate aggregation measure is money. For example, retail stores, which sell an exceptionally wide variety of products, use revenue per month, ignoring variation in spend, number of items bought, the gross margin of each item and the number of items per customer transaction. If all this seems very approximate, remember that most operations have sufficient experience of dealing with aggregated data to find it useful.

The objectives of capacity planning and control

The decisions taken by operations managers in devising their capacity plans will affect several different aspects of performance:

- *Costs* will be affected by the balance between capacity and demand (or output level if that is different). Capacity levels in excess of demand could mean under-utilization of capacity and therefore high unit cost.
- *Revenues* will also be affected by the balance between capacity and demand, but in the opposite way. Capacity levels equal to or higher than demand at any point in time will ensure that all demand is satisfied and no revenue lost.
- *Working capital* will be affected if an operation decides to build up finished goods inventory prior to demand. This might allow demand to be satisfied, but the organization will have to fund the inventory until it can be sold.
- *Quality* of goods or services might be affected by a capacity plan which involved large fluctuations in capacity levels, by hiring temporary staff for example. The new staff and the disruption to the routine working of the operation could increase the probability of errors being made.
- *Speed* of response to customer demand could be enhanced, either by the build-up of inventories (allowing customers to be satisfied directly from the inventory rather than having to wait for items to be manufactured) or by the deliberate provision of surplus capacity to avoid queuing.
- *Dependability* of supply will also be affected by how close demand levels are to capacity. The closer demand gets to the operation's capacity ceiling, the less able it is to cope with any unexpected disruptions and the less dependable its deliveries of goods and services could be.

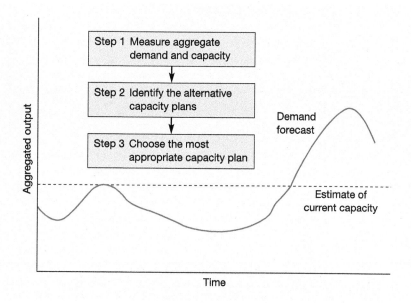

Figure 12.2 The steps in capacity planning and control

- *Flexibility*, especially volume flexibility, will be enhanced by surplus capacity. If demand and capacity are in balance, the operation will not be able to respond to any unexpected increase in demand.

The steps of capacity planning and control

The sequence of capacity planning and control decisions which need to be taken by operations managers is illustrated in Figure 12.2. Typically, operations managers are faced with a forecast of demand which is unlikely to be either certain or constant. They will also have some idea of their own ability to meet this demand. Nevertheless, before any further decisions are taken, they must have quantitative data on both capacity and demand. So the first step will be to *measure the aggregate demand and capacity* levels for the planning period. The second step will be to *identify the alternative capacity plans* which could be adopted in response to the demand fluctuations. The third step will be to *choose the most appropriate capacity plan* for their circumstances.

Measuring demand and capacity

Forecasting demand fluctuations

Forecasting is a key input to capacity planning and control

Although demand forecasting is usually the responsibility of the sales and/or marketing functions, it is a very important input into the **capacity planning and control** decision, and so is of interest to operations managers. After all, without an estimate of future demand it is not possible to plan effectively for future events, only to react to them. It is therefore important to understand the basis and rationale for these demand forecasts. As far as capacity planning and control is concerned, there are three requirements from a demand forecast.

It is expressed in terms which are useful for capacity planning and control

If forecasts are expressed only in money terms and give no indication of the demands that will be placed on an operation's capacity, they will need to be translated into realistic expectations of demand, expressed in the same units as the capacity (for example, machine hours per year, operatives required, space, etc.).

It is as accurate as possible

In capacity planning and control, the accuracy of a forecast is important because, whereas demand can change instantaneously, there is a lag between deciding to change capacity and the change taking effect. Thus many operations managers are faced with a dilemma. In order to attempt to meet demand, they must often decide output in advance, based on a forecast which might change before the demand occurs, or worse, prove not to reflect actual demand at all.

It gives an indication of relative uncertainty

Decisions to operate extra hours and recruit extra staff are usually based on forecast levels of demand, which could in practice differ considerably from actual demand, leading to unnecessary costs or unsatisfactory customer service. For example, a forecast of demand levels in a supermarket may show initially slow business that builds up to a lunchtime rush. After this, demand slows, only to build up again for the early evening rush, and it finally falls again at the end of trading. The supermarket manager can use this forecast to adjust (say) checkout capacity throughout the day. But although this may be an accurate average demand forecast, no single day will exactly conform to this pattern. Of equal importance is an estimate of how much actual demand could differ from the average. This can be found by examining demand statistics to build up a distribution of demand at each point in the day. The importance of this is that the manager now has an understanding of when it will be important to have reserve staff, perhaps filling shelves, but on call to staff the checkouts should demand warrant it. Generally, the advantage of probabilistic forecasts such as this is that it allows operations managers to make a judgement between possible plans that would virtually guarantee the operation's ability to meet actual demand, and plans that minimize costs. Ideally, this judgement should be influenced by the nature of the way the business wins orders: price-sensitive markets may require a risk-avoiding cost minimization plan that does not always satisfy peak demand, whereas markets that value responsiveness and service quality may justify a more generous provision of operational capacity.

Seasonality of demand

In many organizations, capacity planning and control is concerned largely with coping with seasonal demand fluctuations. Almost all products and services have some **demand seasonality** and some also have **supply seasonality**, usually where the inputs are seasonal agricultural products – for example, in processing frozen vegetables. These fluctuations in demand or supply may be reasonably forecastable, but some are usually also affected by unexpected variations in the weather and by changing economic conditions. Figure 12.3 gives some examples of seasonality, and the short case 'Producing while the sun shines' discusses the sometimes unexpected link between weather conditions and demand levels.

Demand seasonality
Supply seasonality

Consider the four different types of operation described previously: a wool knitwear factor, a city hotel, a supermarket and an aluminium producer. Their demand patterns are shown in Figure 12.4. The woollen knitwear business and the city hotel both have seasonal sales demand patterns, but for different reasons: the woollen knitwear business because of climatic patterns (cold winters, warm summers) and the hotel because of demand from business people, who take vacations from work at Christmas and in the summer. The retail supermarket is a little less seasonal, but is affected by pre-vacation peaks and reduced sales during vacation periods. The aluminium producer shows virtually no seasonality, but is showing a steady growth in sales over the forecast period.

Weekly and daily demand fluctuations

Seasonality of demand occurs over a year, but similar predictable variations in demand can also occur for some products and services on a shorter cycle. The daily and weekly demand patterns of a supermarket will fluctuate, with some degree of predictability. Demand might be low in the morning, higher in the afternoon, with peaks at lunchtime and after work in the evening. Demand might be low on Monday and Tuesday, build up during the latter part

Figure 12.3 Many types of operation have to cope with seasonal demand

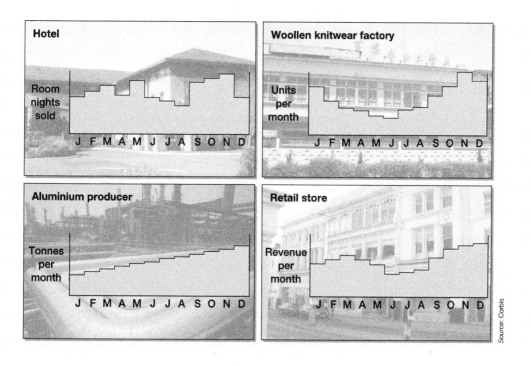

Figure 12.4 Aggregate demand fluctuations for four organizations

of the week and reach a peak on Friday and Saturday. Banks, public offices, telephone sales organizations and electricity utilities all have weekly and daily, or even hourly, demand patterns which require capacity adjustment. The extent to which an operation will have to cope with very short-term demand fluctuations is partly determined by how long its customers are prepared to wait for their products or services. An operation whose customers are incapable of, or unwilling to, wait will have to plan for very short-term demand fluctuations. Emergency services, for example, will need to understand the hourly variation in the demand for their services and plan capacity accordingly.

Short case
Producing while the sun shines[2]

Source: Alamy/Medical-on-line

The sales of some products are profoundly affected by the weather. Sunglasses, sunscreen, waterproof clothing and ice cream are all obvious examples. Yet the range of operations interested in weather forecasting has expanded significantly. Energy utilities, soft drink producers and fresh food producers and retailers are all keen to purchase the latest weather forecasts. But so are operations such as banking call centres and mobile phone operators. It would appear that the demand for telephone banking falls dramatically when the sun shines, as does the use of mobile phones. A motorway catering group was surprised to find that their sales of hot meals fell predictably by €110,000 per day for each degree temperature rise above 20 °C. Similarly, insurance companies have found it wise to sell their products when the weather is poor and likely customers are trapped indoors rather than relaxing outside in the sun, refusing to worry about the future. In the not-for-profit sector new understanding is being developed on the link between various illnesses and temperature. Here temperature is often used as a predictor of demand. So, for example, coronary thrombosis cases peak two days after a drop in temperature, for strokes the delay is around five days, while deaths from respiratory infections peak twelve days from a temperature drop. Knowing this, hospital managers can plan for changes in their demand.

Because of this, meteorological services around the world now sell increasingly sophisticated forecasts to a wide range of companies. In the UK, the Meteorological Office offers an internet-based service for its customers.

It is also used to help insurance specialists price insurance policies to provide compensation against weather-related risk. Complex financial products called 'weather derivates' are now available to compensate for weather-related uncertainty. So, for example, an energy company could buy a financial option before winter where the seller pays the company a guaranteed sum of money if the temperature rises above a certain level. If the weather is mild and energy sales are low, the company gets compensation. If the weather is cold, the company loses the premium it has paid to the seller but makes up for it by selling more power at higher prices. However, as meteorologists point out, it is up to the individual businesses to use the information wisely. Only they have the experience to assess the full impact of weather on their operation. So, for example, supermarkets know that a rise in temperature will impact on the sales of cottage cheese (whereas, unaccountably, the sales of cottage cheese with pineapple chunks are not affected).

Measuring capacity

The main problem with measuring capacity is the complexity of most operations. Only when the operation is highly standardized and repetitive is capacity easy to define unambiguously. So if a television factory produces only one basic model, the weekly capacity could be described as 2,000 Model A televisions. A government office may have the capacity to print and post 500,000 tax forms per week. A fast ride at a theme park might be designed to process batches of 60 people every three minutes – a capacity to convey 1,200 people per hour. In each case,

Output capacity measure   an **output capacity measure** is the most appropriate measure because the output from the operation does not vary in its nature. For many operations, however, the definition of capacity is not so obvious. When a much wider range of outputs places varying demands

Input capacity measures   on the process, for instance, output measures of capacity are less useful. Here **input capacity measures** are frequently used to define capacity. Almost every type of operation could use a mixture of both input and output measures, but in practice, most choose to use one or the other (*see* Table 12.1).

Capacity depends on activity mix

The hospital measures its capacity in terms of its resources, partly because there is not a clear relationship between the number of beds it has and the number of patients it treats. If all

Table 12.1 Input and output capacity measures for different operations

Operation	Input measure of capacity	Output measure of capacity
Air-conditioner plant	Machine hours available	**Number of units per week**
Hospital	**Beds available**	Number of patients treated per week
Theatre	**Number of seats**	Number of customers entertained per week
University	**Number of students**	Students graduated per year
Retail store	**Sales floor area**	Number of items sold per day
Airline	**Number of seats available on the sector**	Number of passengers per week
Electricity company	Generator size	**Megawatts of electricity generated**
Brewery	Volume of fermentation tanks	**Litres per week**

Note: The most commonly used measure is shown in bold.

its patients required relatively minor treatment with only short stays in hospital, it could treat many people per week. Alternatively, if most of its patients required long periods of observation or recuperation, it could treat far fewer. Output depends on the mix of activities in which the hospital is engaged and, because most hospitals perform many different types of activities, output is difficult to predict. Certainly it is difficult to compare directly the capacity of hospitals which have very different activities.

Worked example

Suppose an air-conditioner factory produces three different models of air-conditioner unit: the de luxe, the standard and the economy. The de luxe model can be assembled in 1.5 hours, the standard in 1 hour and the economy in 0.75 hour. The assembly area in the factory has 800 staff hours of assembly time available each week.

If demand for de luxe, standard and economy units is in the ratio 2:3:2, the time needed to assemble $2 + 3 + 2 = 7$ units is:

$$(2 \times 1.5) + (3 \times 1) + (2 \times 0.75) = 7.5 \text{ hours}$$

The number of units produced per week is:

$$\frac{800}{7.5} \times 7 = 746.7 \text{ units}$$

If demand changes to a ratio of de luxe, economy, standard units of 1:2:4, the time needed to assemble $1 + 2 + 4 = 7$ units is:

$$(1 \times 1.5) + (2 \times 1) + (4 \times 0.75) = 6.5 \text{ hours}$$

Now the number of units produced per week is:

$$\frac{800}{6.5} \times 7 = 861.5 \text{ units}$$

Design capacity and effective capacity

The theoretical capacity of an operation – the capacity which its technical designers had in mind when they commissioned the operation – cannot always be achieved in practice. For example, a company coating photographic paper will have several coating lines which deposit thin layers of chemicals onto rolls of paper at high speed. Each line will be capable of running at a particular speed. Multiplying the maximum coating speed by the operating time of the plant gives the theoretical **design capacity** of the line. But in reality the line cannot be

Design capacity

run continuously at its maximum rate. Different products will have different coating requirements, so the line will need to be stopped while it is changed over. Maintenance will need to be performed on the line, which will take out further productive time. Technical scheduling difficulties might mean further lost time. Not all of these losses are the operations manager's fault; they have occurred because of the market and technical demands on the operation. The actual capacity which remains, after such losses are accounted for, is called the **effective capacity** of operation. These causes of reduction in capacity will not be the only losses in the operation. Such factors as quality problems, machine breakdowns, absenteeism and other avoidable problems will all take their toll. This means that the *actual output* of the line will be even lower than the effective capacity. The ratio of the output actually achieved by an operation to its design capacity, and the ratio of output to effective capacity are called, respectively, the **utilization** and the **efficiency** of the plant:

Effective capacity

Utilization
Efficiency

$$\text{Utilization} = \frac{\text{actual output}}{\text{design capacity}}$$

$$\text{Efficiency} = \frac{\text{actual output}}{\text{effective capacity}}$$

Worked example

Suppose the photographic paper manufacturer has a coating line with a design capacity of 200 square metres per minute, and the line is operated on a 24-hour day, 7 days per week (168 hours per week) basis.

Design capacity is $200 \times 60 \times 24 \times 7 = 2.016$ million square metres per week. The records for a week's production show the following lost production time:

1	Product changeovers (set-ups)	20 hrs
2	Regular preventative maintenance	16 hrs
3	No work scheduled	8 hrs
4	Quality sampling checks	8 hrs
5	Shift change times	7 hrs
6	Maintenance breakdown	18 hrs
7	Quality failure investigation	20 hrs
8	Coating material stockouts	8 hrs
9	Labour shortages	6 hrs
10	Waiting for paper rolls	6 hrs

During this week the actual output was only 582,000 square metres.

The first five categories of lost production occur as a consequence of reasonably unavoidable, planned occurrences and amount to a total of 59 hours. The last five categories are unplanned, and avoidable, losses and amount to 58 hours.

Measured in hours of production.

$$\text{Design capacity} = 168 \text{ hours per week}$$

$$\text{Effective capacity} = 168 - 59 = 109 \text{ hrs}$$

$$\text{Actual output} = 168 - 59 - 58 = 51 \text{ hrs}$$

$$\text{Utilization} = \frac{\text{actual output}}{\text{design capacity}} = \frac{51 \text{ hrs}}{168 \text{ hrs}} = 0.304 (30\%)$$

$$\text{Efficiency} = \frac{\text{actual output}}{\text{effective capacity}} = \frac{51 \text{ hrs}}{109 \text{ hrs}} = 0.468 (47\%)$$

Critical commentary

For such an important topic, there is surprisingly little standardization in how capacity is measured. Not only is a reasonably accurate measure of capacity needed for operations planning and control, it is also needed to decide whether it is worth investing in extra physical capacity such as machines. Yet not all practitioners would agree with the way in which design and effective capacity have been defined or measured in the previous worked example. For example, some would argue that the first five categories do *not* occur as 'a consequence of reasonably unavoidable, planned occurrences'. Product changeover set-ups can be reduced, allocating work in a different manner between processes could reduce the amount of time when no work is scheduled, even re-examining preventive maintenance schedules could lead to a reduction in lost time. One school of thought is that whatever capacity efficiency measures are used, they should be useful as diagnostic measures which can highlight the root causes of inefficient use of capacity. The idea of overall equipment effectiveness (OEE) described next is often put forward as a useful way of measuring capacity efficiencies.

Overall equipment effectiveness[3]

Overall equipment effectiveness

The **overall equipment effectiveness** (OEE) measure is an increasingly popular method of judging the effectiveness of operations equipment. It is based on three aspects of performance:

- *the time* that equipment is available to operate;
- *the quality* of the product or service it produces;
- *the speed*, or throughput rate, of the equipment.

Overall equipment effectiveness is calculated by multiplying an availability rate by a performance (or speed) rate multiplied by a quality rate. Some of the reduction in available capacity of a piece of equipment (or any process) is caused by time losses such as set-up and changeover losses (when the equipment or process is being prepared for its next activity), and breakdown failures when the machine is being repaired. Some capacity is lost through

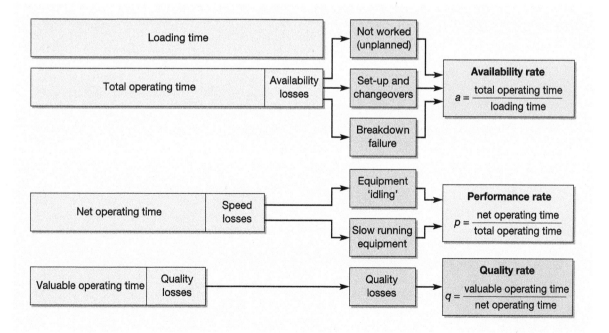

Figure 12.5 Operating equipment effectiveness

speed losses such as when equipment is idling (for example when it is temporarily waiting for work from another process) and when equipment is being run below its optimum work rate. Finally, not everything processed by a piece of equipment will be error-free. So some capacity is lost through quality losses.

Taking the notation in Figure 12.5,

$$OEE = a \times p \times q$$

For equipment to operate effectively, it needs to achieve high levels of performance against all three of these dimensions. Viewed in isolation, these individual metrics are important indicators of plant performance, but they do not give a complete picture of the machine's *overall* effectiveness. This can only be understood by looking at the combined effect of the three measures, calculated by multiplying the three individual metrics together. All these losses to the OEE performance can be expressed in terms of units of time – the design cycle time to produce one good part. So, a reject of one part has an equivalent time loss. In effect, this means that an OEE represents the valuable operating time as a percentage of the design capacity.

Worked example

In a typical 7-day period, the planning department programmes a particular machine to work for 150 hours – its loading time. Changeovers and set-ups take an average of 10 hours and breakdown failures average 5 hours every 7 days. The time when the machine cannot work because it is waiting for material to be delivered from other parts of the process is 5 hours on average and during the period when the machine is running, it averages 90 per cent of its rated speed. Three per cent of the parts processed by the machine are subsequently found to be defective in some way.

$$
\begin{aligned}
\text{Maximum time available} &= 7 \times 24 \text{ hours} \\
&= 168 \text{ hours}
\end{aligned}
$$

$$\text{Loading time} = 150 \text{ hours}$$

$$
\begin{aligned}
\text{Availability losses} &= 10 \text{ hours (set-ups)} + 5 \text{ hrs (breakdowns)} \\
&= 15 \text{ hours}
\end{aligned}
$$

$$
\begin{aligned}
\text{So, Total operating time} &= \text{Loading time} - \text{Availability} \\
&= 150 \text{ hours} - 15 \text{ hours} \\
&= 135 \text{ hours}
\end{aligned}
$$

$$
\begin{aligned}
\text{Speed losses} &= 5 \text{ hours (idling)} + ((135 - 5) \times 0.1)(10\% \text{ of remaining time}) \\
&= 18 \text{ hours}
\end{aligned}
$$

$$
\begin{aligned}
\text{So, Net operating time} &= \text{Total operating time} - \text{Speed losses} \\
&= 135 - 18 \\
&= 117 \text{ hours}
\end{aligned}
$$

$$
\begin{aligned}
\text{Quality losses} &= 117 \text{ (Net operating time)} \times 0.03 \text{ (Error rate)} \\
&= 3.51 \text{ hours}
\end{aligned}
$$

$$
\begin{aligned}
\text{So, Valuable operating time} &= \text{Net operating time} - \text{Quality losses} \\
&= 117 - 3.51 \\
&= 113.49 \text{ hours}
\end{aligned}
$$

$$
\begin{aligned}
\text{Therefore, availability rate} = a &= \frac{\text{Total operating time}}{\text{Loading time}} \\
&= \frac{135}{150} = 90\%
\end{aligned}
$$

and, performance rate = p = $\dfrac{\text{Net operating time}}{\text{Total operating time}}$

$$= \frac{117}{135} = 86.67$$

and quality rate = q = $\dfrac{\text{Valuable operating time}}{\text{Net operating time}}$

$$= \frac{113.49}{117} = 97\%$$

OEE $(a \times p \times q)$ = 75.6%

Short case
British Airways London Eye

The British Airways London Eye is the world's largest observation wheel and one of the UK's most spectacular tourist attractions. The 32 passenger capsules, fixed on the perimeter of the 135 metre diameter rim, each hold 25 people. The wheel rotates continuously, so entry requires customers to step into the capsules which are moving at 0.26 metre per second, which is a quarter of normal walking speed. One complete 360 degree rotation takes 30 minutes, at the end of which the doors open and passengers disembark. Boarding and disembarkation are separated on the specially designed platform which is built out over the river. The attraction has a 'timed admissions booking system' (TABS) for both individual and group bookings. This allocates requests for 'flights' on the basis of half-hour time slots. At the time of writing, the BA London Eye is open every day except Christmas Day. Admission is from 10.00 am to 9.30 pm (for the 9.30 to 10.00 pm slot) in the summer, from the beginning of April to mid-September. For the rest of the year, the winter season, admission begins at 10.00 am, and last admissions are for the 5.30 to 6.00 pm slot.

Source: British Airways London Eye

The BA London Eye forecasts anticipated that 2.2 million passengers would fly the London Eye in 2000, excluding January, which was reserved for final testing and admission of invited guests only. An early press release told journalists that the London Eye would rotate an average of 6,000 revolutions per year.

The alternative capacity plans

With an understanding of both demand and capacity, the next step is to consider the alternative methods of responding to demand fluctuations. There are three 'pure' options available for coping with such variation:

Level capacity plan
Chase demand plan
Demand management

- Ignore the fluctuations and keep activity levels constant (**level capacity plan**).
- Adjust capacity to reflect the fluctuations in demand (**chase demand plan**).
- Attempt to change demand to fit capacity availability (**demand management**).

In practice, most organizations will use a mixture of all of these 'pure' plans, although often one plan might dominate. The Short case 'Seasonal salads' describes how one operation pursues some of these options.

Short case
Seasonal salads

Lettuce is an all-year-round ingredient for most salads, but both the harvesting of the crop and its demand are seasonal. Lettuces are perishable and must be kept in cold stores and transported in refrigerated vehicles. Even then the product only stays fresh for a maximum of a week. In most north European countries, demand continues throughout the winter at around half the summer levels, but outdoor crops cannot be grown during the winter months. Glasshouse cultivation is possible but expensive.

One of Europe's largest lettuce growers is G's Fresh Salads, based in the UK. Their supermarket customers require fresh produce to be delivered 364 days a year, but because of the limitations of the English growing season, the company has developed other sources of supply in Europe. It acquired a farm and packhouse in the Murcia region of south-eastern Spain, which provides the bulk of salad crops during the winter, transported daily to the UK by a fleet of refrigerated trucks. Further top-up produce is imported by air from around the world.

Sales forecasts are agreed with the individual supermarkets well in advance, allowing the planting and growing programmes to be matched to the anticipated level of sales. However, the programme is only a rough guide. The supermarkets may change their orders right up to the afternoon of the preceding day. Weather is a

dominant factor. First, it determines supply – how well the crop grows and how easy it is to harvest. Second, it influences sales – cold, wet periods during the summer discourage the eating of salads, whereas hot spells boost demand greatly.

Figure 12.6 illustrates this. The Iceberg lettuce sales programme is shown, and compared with the actual English-grown and Spanish-grown sales. The fluctuating nature of the actual sales is the result of a combination of weather-related availability and supermarket demand. These do not always match. When demand is higher than expected, the picking rigs and their crews continue

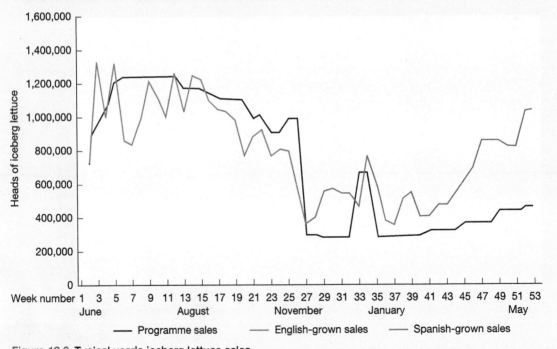

Figure 12.6 Typical year's iceberg lettuce sales

to work into the middle of night, under floodlights. Another capacity problem is the operation's staffing levels. It relies on temporary seasonal harvesting and packing staff to supplement the full-time employees for both the English and Spanish seasons. Since most of the crop is transported to the UK in bulk, a large permanent staff is maintained for packing and distribution in the UK. The majority of the Spanish workforce is temporary, with only a small number retained during the

extremely hot summer to grow and harvest other crops such as melons.

The specialist lettuce harvesting machines (the 'rigs') are shipped over to Spain every year at the end of the English season, so that the company can achieve maximum utilization from all this expensive capital equipment. These rigs not only enable very high productivity of the pickers, but also ensure the best possible conditions for quality packing and rapid transportation to the cold stores.

Level capacity plan

In a level capacity plan, the processing capacity is set at a uniform level throughout the planning period, regardless of the fluctuations in forecast demand. This means that the same number of staff operate the same processes and should therefore be capable of producing the same aggregate output in each period. Where non-perishable materials are processed, but not immediately sold, they can be transferred to finished goods inventory in anticipation of sales at a later time. Thus this plan is feasible (but not necessarily desirable) for our examples of the woollen knitwear company and the aluminium producer (*see* Fig. 12.7).

Level capacity plans of this type can achieve the objectives of stable employment patterns, high process utilization, and usually also high productivity with low unit costs. Unfortunately, they can also create considerable inventory which has to be financed and stored. Perhaps the biggest problem, however, is that decisions have to be taken as to what to produce for inventory rather than for immediate sale. Will green woollen sweaters knitted in July still be fashionable in October? Could a particular aluminium alloy in a specific sectional shape still be sold months after it has been produced? Most firms operating this plan, therefore, give priority to only creating inventory where future sales are relatively certain and unlikely to be affected by changes in fashion or design. Clearly, such plans are not suitable for 'perishable' products, such as foods and some pharmaceuticals, for products where fashion changes rapidly and unpredictably (for example, popular music CDs, fashion garments), or for customized products.

A level capacity plan could also be used by the hotel and supermarket, although this would not be the usual approach of such organizations, because it usually results in a waste of staff resources, reflected in low productivity. Because service cannot be stored as inventory, a level capacity plan would involve running the operation at a uniformly high level of capacity

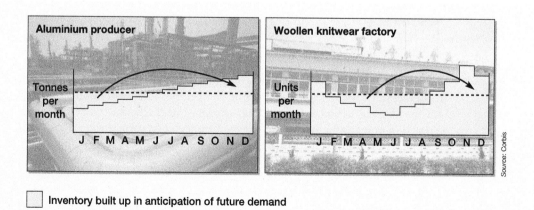

☐ Inventory built up in anticipation of future demand

Figure 12.7 Level capacity plans which use anticipation inventory to supply future demand

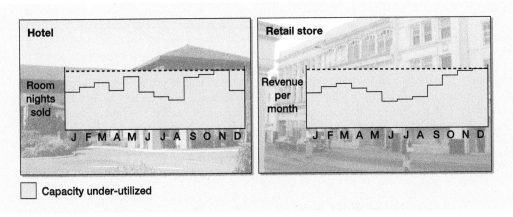

Capacity under-utilized

Figure 12.8 Level capacity plans with under-utilization of capacity

availability. The hotel would employ sufficient staff to service all the rooms, to run a full restaurant, and to staff the reception even in months when demand was expected to be well below capacity. Similarly, the supermarket would plan to staff all the checkouts, warehousing operations, and so on, even in quiet periods (*see* Fig. 12.8).

Low utilization can make level capacity plans prohibitively expensive in many service operations, but may be considered appropriate where the opportunity costs of individual lost sales are very high. For example, in the high-margin retailing of jewellery and in (real) estate agents. It is also possible to set the capacity somewhat below the forecast peak demand level in order to reduce the degree of under-utilization. However, in the periods where demand is expected to exceed planned capacity, customer service may deteriorate. Customers may have to queue for long periods or may be 'processed' faster and less sensitively. While this is obviously far from ideal, the benefits to the organization of stability and productivity may outweigh the disadvantages of upsetting some customers.

Chase demand plan

The opposite of a level capacity plan is one which attempts to match capacity closely to the varying levels of forecast demand. This is much more difficult to achieve than a level capacity plan, as different numbers of staff, different working hours, and even different amounts of equipment may be necessary in each period. For this reason, pure chase demand plans are unlikely to appeal to operations which manufacture standard, non-perishable products. Also, where manufacturing operations are particularly capital-intensive, the chase demand policy would require a level of physical capacity, all of which would only be used occasionally. It is for this reason that such a plan is less likely to be appropriate for the aluminium producer than for the woollen garment manufacturer (*see* Fig. 12.9). A pure chase demand plan is more usually adopted by operations which cannot store their output, such as customer-processing operations or manufacturers of perishable products. It avoids the wasteful provision of excess staff that occurs with a level capacity plan, and yet should satisfy customer demand throughout the planned period. Where output can be stored, the chase demand policy might be adopted in order to minimize or eliminate finished goods inventory.

Sometimes it is difficult to achieve very large variations in capacity from period to period. If the changes in forecast demand are as large as those in the hotel example (*see* Fig. 12.10), significantly different levels of staffing will be required throughout the year. This would mean employing part-time and temporary staff, requiring permanent employees to work longer hours, or even bringing in contract labour. The operations managers will then have the difficult task of ensuring that quality standards and safety procedures are still adhered to, and that the customer service levels are maintained.

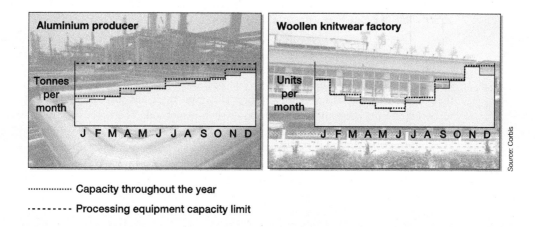

.... Capacity throughout the year

-------- Processing equipment capacity limit

Figure 12.9 Chase demand capacity plans with changes in capacity which reflect changes in demand

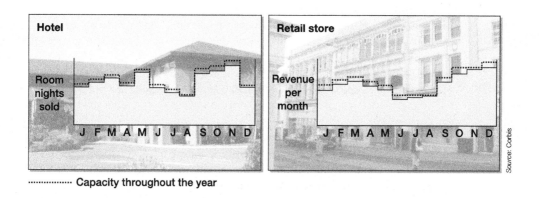

.... Capacity throughout the year

Figure 12.10 Chase demand capacity plans with changes in capacity which reflect changes in demand

Methods of adjusting capacity

The chase demand approach requires that capacity is adjusted by some means. There are a number of different methods for achieving this, although they may not all be feasible for all types of operation. Some of these methods are listed below.

Overtime and idle time

Often the quickest and most convenient method of adjusting capacity is by varying the number of productive hours worked by the staff in the operation. When demand is higher than nominal capacity, **overtime** is worked, and when demand is lower than nominal capacity the amount of time spent by staff on productive work can be reduced. In the latter case, it may be possible for staff to engage in some other activity such as cleaning or maintenance. This method is only useful if the timing of the extra productive capacity matches that of the demand. For example, there is little to be gained in asking a retail operation's staff to work extra hours in the evening if all the extra demand is occurring during their normal working period. The costs associated with this method are either the extra payment which is normally necessary to secure the agreement of staff to work overtime, or in the case of **idle time**, the costs of paying staff who are not engaged in direct productive work. Further, there might be costs associated with the fixed costs of keeping the operation heated, lit and secure over the extra period staff are working. There is also a limit to the amount of extra working time which any workforce can deliver before productivity levels decrease. **Annualized hours** approaches,

Overtime

Idle time

Annualized hours

as described below in the Short case 'Working by the year', are one way of flexing working hours without excessive extra costs.

Varying the size of the workforce

If capacity is largely governed by workforce size, one way to adjust it is to adjust the size of the workforce. This is done by hiring extra staff during periods of high demand and laying them off as demand falls, or **hire and fire**. However, there are cost and ethical implications to be taken into account before adopting such a method. The costs of hiring extra staff include those associated with recruitment, as well as the costs of low productivity while new staff go through the learning curve. The costs of lay-off may include possible severance payments, but might also include the loss of morale in the operation and loss of goodwill in the local labour market. At a micro-operation level, one method of coping with peaks in demand in one area of an operation is to build sufficient flexibility into job design and job demarcation so that staff can transfer across from less busy parts of the operation. For example, the French hotel chain Novotel has trained some of its kitchen staff to escort customers from the reception area up to their rooms. The peak times for registering new customers coincide with the least busy times in the kitchen and restaurant areas.

Hire and fire

Using part-time staff

A variation on the previous strategy is to recruit **part-time staff**, that is, for less than the normal working day. This method is extensively used in service operations such as supermarkets and fast-food restaurants but is also used by some manufacturers to staff an evening shift after the normal working day. However, if the fixed costs of employment for each employee, irrespective of how long he or she works, are high then using this method may not be worthwhile.

Part-time staff

Subcontracting

In periods of high demand, an operation might buy capacity from other organizations, called **subcontracting**. This might enable the operation to meet its own demand without the extra expense of investing in capacity which will not be needed after the peak in demand has passed. Again, there are costs associated with this method. The most obvious one is that subcontracting can be very expensive. The subcontractor will also want to make sufficient margin out of the business. A subcontractor may not be as motivated to deliver on time or to the desired levels of quality. Finally, there is the risk that the subcontractors might themselves decide to enter the same market.

Subcontracting

Critical commentary

To many, the idea of fluctuating the workforce to match demand, either by using part-time staff or by hiring and firing, is more than just controversial. It is regarded as unethical. It is any business's responsibility, they argue, to engage in a set of activities which are capable of sustaining employment at a steady level. Hiring and firing merely for seasonal fluctuations, which can be predicted in advance, is treating human beings in a totally unacceptable manner. Even hiring people on a short-term contract, in practice, leads to them being offered poorer conditions of service and leads to a state of permanent anxiety as to whether they will keep their jobs. On a more practical note, it is pointed out that, in an increasingly global business world where companies may have sites in different countries, those countries that allow hiring and firing are more likely to have their plants 'downsized' than those where legislation makes this difficult.

Manage demand plan

Demand management
Change demand

The most obvious mechanism of **demand management** is to **change demand** through price. Although this is probably the most widely applied approach in demand management, it is less common for products than for services. For example, some city hotels offer low-cost 'city break' vacation packages in the months when fewer business visitors are expected. Skiing and camping holidays are cheapest at the beginning and end of the season and are particularly expensive during school vacations. Discounts are given by photo-processing firms during winter periods, but never around summer holidays. Ice cream is 'on offer' in many supermarkets during the winter. The objective is invariably to stimulate off-peak demand and to constrain peak demand, in order to smooth demand as much as possible. Organizations can also attempt to increase demand in low periods by appropriate advertising. For example, turkey growers in the UK and the USA make vigorous attempts to promote their products at times other than Christmas and Thanksgiving.

Short case
Working by the year[4]

One method of fluctuating capacity as demand varies throughout the year without many of the costs associated with overtime or hiring temporary staff is called the Annual Hours Work Plan. This involves staff contracting to work a set number of hours per year rather than a set number of hours per week. The advantage of this is that the amount of staff time available to an organization can be varied throughout the year to reflect the real state of demand. Annual hours plans can also be useful when supply varies throughout the year. For example, a UK cheese factory of Express Foods, like all cheese factories, must cope with processing very different quantities of milk at different times of the year. In spring and during early summer, cows produce large quantities of milk, but in late summer and autumn the supply of milk slows to a trickle. Before the introduction of annualized hours, the factory

had relied on overtime and hiring temporary workers during the busy season. Now the staff are contracted to work a set number of hours a year with rotas agreed more than a year in advance and after consultation with the union. This means that at the end of July staff broadly know what days and hours they will be working up to September of the following year. If an emergency should arise, the company can call in people from a group of 'super crew' who work more flexible hours in return for higher pay but can do any job in the factory.

However, not all experiments with annualized hours have been as successful as that at Express Foods. In cases where demand is very unpredictable, staff can be asked to come in to work at very short notice. This can cause considerable disruption to social and family life. For example, at one news-broadcasting company, the scheme caused problems. Journalists and camera crew who went to cover a foreign crisis found that they had worked so many hours they were asked to take the whole of one month off to compensate. Since they had no holiday plans, many would have preferred to work.

Alternative products and services

Alternative products

Sometimes, a more radical approach is required to fill periods of low demand such as developing **alternative products** or services which can be produced on existing processes, but have different demand patterns throughout the year (see the Short case 'Getting the message' for an example of this approach). Most universities fill their accommodation and lecture theatres with conferences and company meetings during vacations. Ski resorts provide organized mountain activity holidays in the summer. Some garden tractor companies in the US now make snow movers in the autumn and winter. The apparent benefits of filling capacity in this way must be weighted against the risks of damaging the core product or service, and the operation must be fully capable of serving both markets. Some universities have been criticized for providing sub-standard, badly decorated accommodation which met the needs of impecunious undergraduates, but which failed to impress executives at a trade conference.

Mixed plans

Each of the three 'pure' plans is applied only where its advantages strongly outweigh its disadvantages. For many organizations, however, these 'pure' approaches do not match their required combination of competitive and operational objectives. Most operations managers are required simultaneously to reduce costs and inventory, to minimize capital investment, and yet to provide a responsive and customer-oriented approach at all times. For this reason, most organizations choose to follow a mixture of the three approaches. This can be best illustrated by the woollen knitwear company example (*see* Fig. 12.11). Here some of the peak demand has been brought forward by the company offering discounts to selected retail

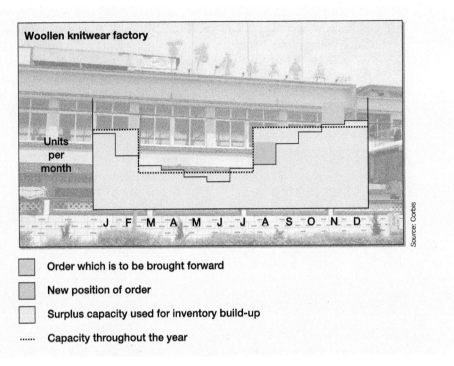

Order which is to be brought forward

New position of order

Surplus capacity used for inventory build-up

...... Capacity throughout the year

Figure 12.11 A mixed capacity plan for the woollen knitwear factory

customers (manage demand plan). Capacity has also been adjusted at two points in the year to reflect the broad changes in demand (chase demand plan). Yet the adjustment in capacity is not sufficient to avoid totally the build-up of inventories (level capacity plan).

Yield management

In operations which have relatively fixed capacities, such as airlines and hotels, it is important to use the capacity of the operation for generating revenue to its full potential. One approach used by such operations is called **yield management**.[5] This is really a collection of methods, some of which we have already discussed, which can be used to ensure that an operation maximizes its potential to generate profit. Yield management is especially useful where:

● capacity is relatively fixed;
● the market can be fairly clearly segmented;
● the service cannot be stored in any way;
● the services are sold in advance;
● the marginal cost of making a sale is relatively low.

Airlines, for example, fit all these criteria. They adopt a collection of methods to try to maximize the yield (i.e. profit) from their capacity. These include the following:

● *Over-booking capacity.* Not every passenger who has booked a place on a flight will actually show up for the flight. If the airline did not fill this seat it would lose the revenue from it. Because of this, airlines regularly book more passengers onto flights than the capacity of the aircraft can cope with. If they over-book by the exact number of passengers who fail to show up, they have maximized their revenue under the circumstances. Of course, if more passengers show up than they expect, the airline will have a number of upset passengers to deal with (although they may be able to offer financial inducements for the passengers to take another flight). If they fail to over-book sufficiently, they will have empty seats. By studying past data on flight demand, airlines try to balance the risks of over-booking and under-booking.

Yield management

Short case
Getting the message[6]

Companies which traditionally operate in seasonal markets can demonstrate some considerable ingenuity in their attempts to develop counter-seasonal products. One of the most successful industries in this respect has been the greetings card industry. Mother's Day, Father's Day, Halloween, Valentine's Day and other occasions have all been promoted as times to send (and buy) appropriately designed cards. Now, having run out of occasions to promote, greetings card manufacturers have moved on to 'non-occasion' cards, which can be sent at any time. These have the considerable advantage of being less seasonal, thus making the companies' seasonality less marked.

Hallmark Cards, the market leader in North America, has been the pioneer in developing non-occasion cards. Their cards include those intended to be sent from a parent to a child with messages such as 'Would a hug help?', 'Sorry I made you feel bad' and 'You're perfectly wonderful – it's your room that's a mess'. Other cards deal with more serious adult themes such as friendship ('You're more than a friend, you're just like family') or even alcoholism ('This is hard to say, but I think you're a much neater person when you're not drinking'). Now Hallmark Cards has founded a 'loyalty marketing group' that 'helps companies communicate with their customers at an emotional level'. It promotes the use of greetings cards for corporate use, to show that customers and

employees are valued. Whatever else these products may be, they are not seasonal!

- *Price discounting.* At quiet times, when demand is unlikely to fill capacity, airlines will also sell heavily discounted tickets to agents who then themselves take the risk of finding customers for them. In effect, this is using the price mechanism to affect demand.
- *Varying service types.* Discounting and other methods of affecting demand are also adjusted depending on the demand for particular types of service. For example, the relative demand for first-, business- and economy-class seats varies throughout the year. There is no point discounting tickets in a class for which demand will be high. Yield management also tries to adjust the availability of the different classes of seat to reflect their demand. They will also vary the number of seats available in each class by upgrading or even changing the configuration of airline seats.

Choosing a capacity planning and control approach

Before an operation can decide which of the capacity plans to adopt, it must be aware of the consequences of adopting each plan in its own set of circumstances. Two methods are particularly useful in helping to assess the consequences of adopting particular capacity plans:

Cumulative
representations
Queuing theory

- **cumulative representations** of demand and capacity;
- **queuing theory.**

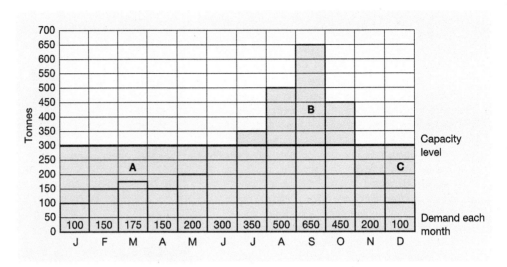

Figure 12.12 If the over-capacity areas (A+C) are greater than the under-capacity area (B), the capacity level seems adequate to meet demand. This may not necessarily be the case, however

Cumulative representations

Figure 12.12 shows the forecast aggregated demand for a chocolate factory which makes confectionery products. Demand for its products in the shops is greatest at Christmas. To meet this demand and allow time for the products to work their way through the distribution system, the factory must supply a demand which peaks in September, as shown. One method of assessing whether a particular level of capacity can satisfy the demand would be to calculate the degree of over-capacity below the graph which represents the capacity levels (areas A and C) and the degree of under-capacity above the graph (area B). If the total over-capacity is greater than the total under-capacity for a particular level of capacity, then that capacity could be regarded as adequate to satisfy demand fully, the assumption being that inventory has been accumulated in the periods of over-capacity. However, there are two problems with this approach. The first is that each month shown in Figure 12.12 may not have the same amount of productive time. Some months (August, for example) may contain vacation periods which reduce the availability of capacity. The second problem is that a capacity level which seems adequate may only be able to supply products *after* the demand for them has occurred. For example, if the period of under-capacity occurred at the beginning of the year, no inventory could have accumulated to meet demand. A far superior way of assessing capacity plans is first to plot demand on a *cumulative* basis. This is shown as the thicker line in Figure 12.13.

The cumulative representation of demand immediately reveals more information. First, it shows that although total demand peaks in September, because of the restricted number of available productive days, the peak demand per productive day occurs a month earlier in August. Second, it shows that the fluctuation in demand over the year is even greater than it seemed. The ratio of monthly peak demand to monthly lowest demand is 6.5:1, but the ratio of peak to lowest demand per productive day is 10:1. Demand per productive day is more relevant to operations managers, because productive days represent the time element of capacity.

The most useful consequence of plotting demand on a cumulative basis is that, by plotting capacity on the same graph, the feasibility and consequences of a capacity plan can be assessed. Figure 12.13 also shows a level capacity plan which produces at a rate of 14.03 tonnes per productive day. This meets cumulative demand by the end of the year. It would also pass our earlier test of total over-capacity being the same as or greater than under-capacity.

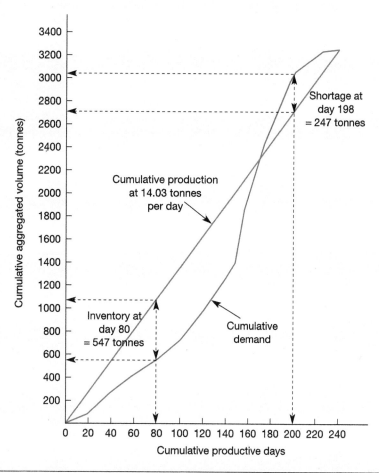

	J	F	M	A	M	J	J	A	S	O	N	D
Demand (tonnes/month)	100	150	175	150	200	300	350	500	650	450	200	100
Productive days	20	18	21	21	22	22	21	10	21	22	21	18
Demand (tonnes/day)	5	8.33	8.33	7.14	9.52	13.64	16.67	50	30.95	20.46	9.52	5.56
Cumulative days	20	38	59	80	102	124	145	155	176	198	219	237
Cumulative demand	100	250	425	575	775	1075	1425	1925	2575	3025	3225	3325
Cumulative production (tonnes)	281	533	828	1122	1431	1740	2023	2175	2469	2778	3073	3325
Ending inventory (tonnes)	181	283	403	547	656	715	609	250	(106)	(247)	(150)	0

Figure 12.13 A level capacity plan which produces shortages in spite of meeting demand at the end of the year

However, if one of the aims of the plan is to supply demand when it occurs, the plan is inadequate. Up to around day 168, the line representing cumulative production is above that representing cumulative demand. This means that at any time during this period, more product has been produced by the factory than has been demanded from it. In fact the vertical distance between the two lines is the level of inventory at that point in time. So by day 80, 1,122 tonnes have been produced but only 575 tonnes have been demanded. The surplus of production above demand, or inventory, is therefore 547 tonnes. When the cumulative demand line lies above the cumulative production line, the reverse is true. The vertical distance between the two lines now indicates the shortage, or lack of supply. So by day 198, 3,025 tonnes have been demanded but only 2,778 tonnes produced. The shortage is therefore 247 tonnes.

For any capacity plan to meet demand as it occurs, its cumulative production line must always lie above the cumulative demand line. This makes it a straightforward task to judge the adequacy of a plan, simply by looking at its cumulative representation. An impression of the inventory implications can also be gained from a cumulative representation by judging the area between the cumulative production and demand curves. This represents the amount of inventory carried over the period. Figure 12.14 illustrates an adequate level capacity plan for the chocolate manufacturer, together with the costs of carrying inventory. It is assumed that inventory costs £2 per tonne per day to keep in storage. The average inventory each month is taken to be the average of the beginning- and end-of-month inventory levels, and the

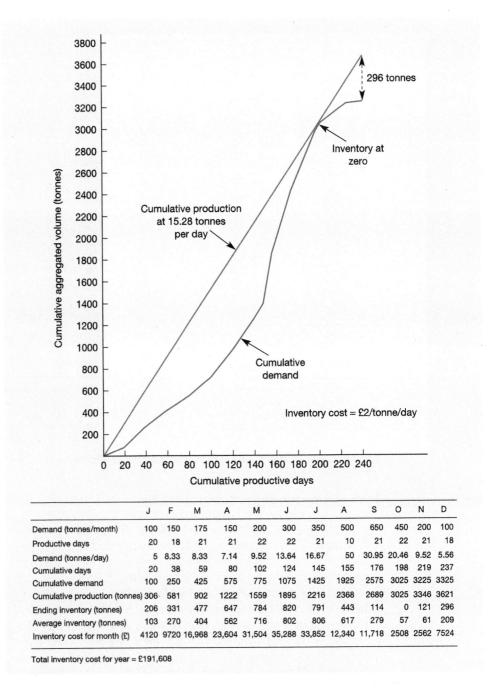

	J	F	M	A	M	J	J	A	S	O	N	D
Demand (tonnes/month)	100	150	175	150	200	300	350	500	650	450	200	100
Productive days	20	18	21	21	22	22	21	10	21	22	21	18
Demand (tonnes/day)	5	8.33	8.33	7.14	9.52	13.64	16.67	50	30.95	20.46	9.52	5.56
Cumulative days	20	38	59	80	102	124	145	155	176	198	219	237
Cumulative demand	100	250	425	575	775	1075	1425	1925	2575	3025	3225	3325
Cumulative production (tonnes)	306	581	902	1222	1559	1895	2216	2368	2689	3025	3346	3621
Ending inventory (tonnes)	206	331	477	647	784	820	791	443	114	0	121	296
Average inventory (tonnes)	103	270	404	562	716	802	806	617	279	57	61	209
Inventory cost for month (£)	4120	9720	16,968	23,604	31,504	35,288	33,852	12,340	11,718	2508	2562	7524

Total inventory cost for year = £191,608

Figure 12.14 A level capacity plan which meets demand at all times during the year

inventory-carrying cost each month is the product of the average inventory, the inventory cost per day per tonne and the number of days in the month.

Comparing plans on a cumulative basis

Chase demand plans can also be illustrated on a cumulative representation. Rather than the cumulative production line having a constant gradient, it would have a varying gradient representing the production rate at any point in time. If a pure demand chase plan was adopted, the cumulative production line would match the cumulative demand line. The gap between the two lines would be zero and hence inventory would be zero. Although this would eliminate inventory-carrying costs, as we discussed earlier, there would be costs associated with changing capacity levels. Usually, the marginal cost of making a capacity change increases with the size of the change. For example, if the chocolate manufacturer wishes to increase capacity by 5 per cent, this can be achieved by requesting its staff to work overtime – a simple, fast and relatively inexpensive option. If the change is 15 per cent, overtime cannot provide sufficient extra capacity and temporary staff will need to be employed – a more expensive solution which also would take more time. Increases in capacity of above 15 per cent might only be achieved by subcontracting some work out. This would be even more expensive. The cost of the change will also be affected by the point from which the change is being made, as well as the direction of the change. Usually, it is less expensive to change capacity towards what is regarded as the 'normal' capacity level than away from it.

Worked example

Suppose the chocolate manufacturer, which has been operating the level capacity plan as shown in Figure 12.15, is unhappy with the inventory costs of this approach. It decides to explore two alternative plans, both involving some degree of demand chasing.

Plan 1

- Organize and staff the factory for a 'normal' capacity level of 8.7 tonnes per day.
- Produce at 8.7 tonnes per day for the first 124 days of the year, then increase capacity to 29 tonnes per day by heavy use of overtime, hiring temporary staff and some subcontracting.
- Produce at 29 tonnes per day until day 194, then reduce capacity back to 8.7 tonnes per day for the rest of the year.

The costs of changing capacity by such a large amount (the ratio of peak to normal capacity is 3.33:1) are calculated by the company as being:

Cost of changing from 8.7 tonnes/day to 29 tonnes/day = £110,000
Cost of changing from 29 tonnes/day to 8.7 tonnes/day = £60,000

Plan 2

- Organize and staff the factory for a 'normal' capacity level of 12.4 tonnes per day.
- Produce at 12.4 tonnes per day for the first 150 days of the year, then increase capacity to 29 tonnes per day by overtime and hiring some temporary staff.
- Produce at 29 tonnes/day until day 190, then reduce capacity back to 12.4 tonnes per day for the rest of the year.

The costs of changing capacity in this plan are smaller because the degree of change is smaller (a peak to normal capacity ratio of 2.34:1), and they are calculated by the company as being:

Cost of changing from 12.4 tonnes/day to 29 tonnes/day = £35,000
Cost of changing from 29 tonnes/day to 12.4 tonnes/day = £15,000

→

Figure 12.15 illustrates both plans on a cumulative basis. Plan 1, which envisaged two drastic changes in capacity, has high capacity change costs but, because its production levels are close to demand levels, it has low inventory carrying costs. Plan 2 sacrifices some of the inventory cost advantage of Plan 1 but saves more in terms of capacity change costs.

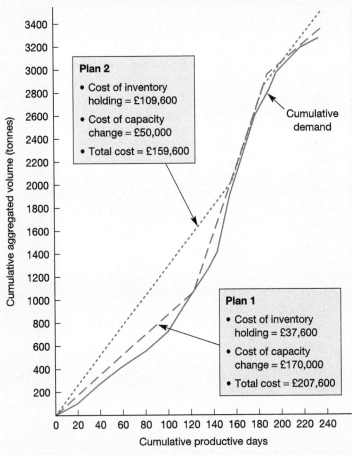

Plan 2
- Cost of inventory holding = £109,600
- Cost of capacity change = £50,000
- Total cost = £159,600

Cumulative demand

Plan 1
- Cost of inventory holding = £37,600
- Cost of capacity change = £170,000
- Total cost = £207,600

Figure 12.15 Comparing two alternative capacity plans

Capacity planning as a queuing problem

Cumulative representations of capacity plans are useful where the operation has the ability to store its finished goods as inventory. However, for operations where it is not possible to produce products and services *before* demand for them has occurred, a cumulative representation would tell us relatively little. The cumulative 'production' could never be above the cumulative demand line. At best, it could show when an operation failed to meets its demand. So the vertical gap between the cumulative demand and production lines would indicate the amount of demand unsatisfied. Some of this demand would look elsewhere to be satisfied, but some would wait. This is why, for operations which, by their nature, cannot store their output, such as most service operations, capacity planning and control is best considered using waiting or **queuing theory**.

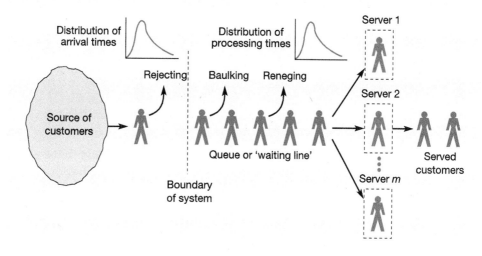

Figure 12.16 The general form of the capacity decision in queuing systems

Queuing or 'waiting line' management

When we were illustrating the use of cumulative representations for capacity planning and control, our assumption was that, generally, any production plan should aim to meet demand at any point in time (the cumulative production line must be above the cumulative demand line). Looking at the issue as a queuing problem (in many parts of the world queuing concepts are referred to as 'waiting line' concepts) accepts that, while sometime demand may be satisfied instantly, at other times customers may have to wait. This is particularly true when the arrival of individual demands on an operation are difficult to predict, or the time to produce a product or service is uncertain, or both. These circumstances make providing adequate capacity at all points in time particularly difficult. Figure 12.16 shows the general form of this capacity issue. Customers arrive according to some probability distribution and wait to be processed (unless part of the operation is idle); when they have reached the front of the queue, they are processed by one of the n parallel 'servers' (their processing time also being described by a probability distribution), after which they leave the operation. There are many examples of this kind of system. Table 12.2 illustrates some of these. All of these examples can be described by a common set of elements that define their queuing behaviour.

Calling population

The source of customers – sometimes called the **calling population** – is the source of supply of customers. In queue management 'customers' are not always human. 'Customers' could for example be trucks arriving at a weighbridge, orders arriving to be processed or machines waiting to be serviced, etc. The source of customers for queuing system can be either *finite* or *infinite*. A finite source has a known number of possible customers. For example, if one

Table 12.2 Examples of operations which have parallel processors

Operation	Arrivals	Processing capacity
Bank	Customers	Tellers
Supermarket	Shoppers	Checkouts
Hospital clinic	Patients	Doctors
Graphic artist	Commissions	Artists
Custom cake decorators	Orders	Cake decorators
Ambulance service	Emergencies	Ambulances with crews
Telephone switchboard	Calls	Telephonists
Maintenance department	Breakdowns	Maintenance staff

maintenance person serves four assembly lines, the number of customers for the maintenance person is known, i.e. four. There will be a certain probability that one of the assembly lines will break down and need repairing. However, if one line really does break down the probability of another line needing repair is reduced because there are now only three lines to break down. So, with a finite source of customers the probability of a customer arriving depends on the number of customers already being serviced. By contrast, an infinite customer source assume that there is a large number of potential customers so that it is always possible for another customer to arrive no matter how many are being serviced. Most queuing systems that deal with outside markets have infinite, or 'close-to-infinite', customer sources.

Arrival rate

The arrival rate is the rate at which customers needing to be served arrive at the server or servers. Rarely do customers arrive at a steady and predictable rate. Usually there is variability in their arrival rate. Because of this it is necessary to describe arrival rates in terms of probability distributions. The important issue here is that, in queuing systems, it is normal that at times no customers will arrive and at other times many will arrive relatively close together.

Queue

The queue – customers waiting to be served form the queue or waiting line itself. If there is relatively little limit on how many customers can queue at any time, we can assume that, for all practical purposes, an infinite queue is possible. Sometimes, however, there is a limit to how many customers can be in the queue at any one time.

Rejecting

Rejecting – if the number of customers in a queue is already at the maximum number allowed, then the customer could be rejected by the system. For example, during periods of heavy demand some web sites will not allow customers to access part of the site until the demand on its services has declined.

Baulking

Baulking – when a customer is a human being with free will (and the ability to get annoyed) he or she may refuse to join the queue and wait for service if it is judged to be too long. In queuing terms this is called baulking.

Reneging

Reneging – this is similar to baulking but here the customer has queued for a certain length of time and then (perhaps being dissatisfied with the rate of progress) leaves the queue and therefore the chance of being served.

Queue discipline

Queue discipline – this is the set of rules that determine the order in which customers waiting in the queue are served. Most simple queues, such as those in a shop, use a *first-come first-served* queue discipline.

Servers

Servers – a server is the facility that processes the customers in the queue. In any queuing system there may be any number of servers configured in different ways. In Figure 12.16 servers are configured in parallel, but some may have servers in a series arrangement. For example, on entering a self-service restaurant you may queue to collect a tray and cutlery, move on to the serving area where you queue again to order and collect a meal, move on to a drinks area where you queue once more to order and collect a drink, and then finally queue to pay for the meal. In this case you have passed through four servers (even though the first one was not staffed) in a series arrangement. Of course, many queue systems are complex arrangements of series and parallel connections. There is also likely to be variation in how long it takes to process each customer. Even if customers do not have differing needs, human servers will vary in the time they take to perform repetitive serving tasks. Therefore processing time, like arrival time, is usually described by a probability distribution.

Balancing capacity and demand

The dilemma in managing the capacity of a queuing system is how many servers to have available at any point in time in order to avoid unacceptably long queuing times or unacceptably low utilization of the servers. Because of the probabilistic arrival and processing times, only rarely will the arrival of customers match the ability of the operation to cope with them. Sometimes, if several customers arrive in quick succession and require longer-than-average processing times, queues will build up in front of the operation. At other times, when customers arrive less frequently than average and also require shorter-than-average processing times, some of the servers in the system will be idle. So even when the average capacity (processing capability) of the operation matches the average demand (arrival rate) on the system, both queues and idle time will occur.

If the operation has too few servers (that is, capacity is set at too low a level), queues will build up to a level where customers become dissatisfied with the time they are having to wait, although the utilization level of the servers will be high. If too many servers are in place (that is, capacity is set at too high a level), the time which customers can expect to wait will not be long but the utilization of the servers will be low. This is why the capacity planning and control problem for this type of operation is often presented as a trade-off between customer waiting time and system utilization. What is certainly important in making capacity decisions is being able to predict both of these factors for a given queuing system. The supplement to this chapter details some of the more simple mathematical approaches to understanding queue behaviour.

Variability in demand or supply

Variability reduces effective capacity

The variability, either in demand or capacity, as discussed above, will reduce the ability of an operation to process its inputs. That is, it will **reduce its effective capacity**. The greater the variability in arrival time or activity time at a process the more the process will suffer both high throughput times and reduced utilization. This principle holds true for whole operations, and because long throughput times mean that queues will build up in the operation, high variability also affects inventory levels. This is illustrated in Figure 12.17. The implication of this is that the greater the variability, the more extra capacity will need to be provided to compensate for the reduced utilization of available capacity. Therefore, operations with high levels of variability will tend to set their base level of capacity relatively high in order to provide this extra capacity.

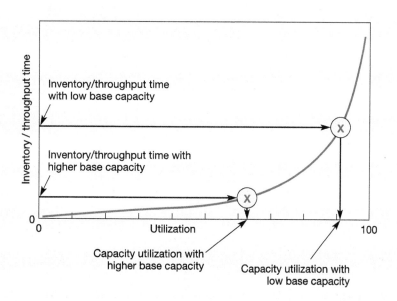

Figure 12.17 The effect of variability on the utilization of capacity

Customer perceptions of queuing

If the 'customers' waiting in a queue are real human customers, an important aspect of how they judge the service they receive from a queuing system is how they perceive the time spent queuing. It is well known that if you are told that you'll be waiting in a queue for twenty minutes and you are actually serviced in ten minutes, your perception of the queuing experience will be more positive than if you were told that you would be waiting ten minutes but the queue actually took twenty minutes. Because of this, the management of queuing systems usually involves attempting to manage customers' perceptions and expectations in some way (see the Short case on Madame Tussaud's for an example of this). One expert in queuing has come up with a number of principles that influence how customers perceive waiting times.[7]

- Time spent idle is perceived as longer than time spent occupied.
- The wait before a service starts is perceived as more tedious than a wait within the service process.
- Anxiety and/or uncertainty heightens the perception that time spent waiting is long.
- A wait of unknown duration is perceived as more tedious than a wait whose duration is known.
- An unexplained wait is perceived as more tedious than a wait that is explained.
- The higher the value of the service for the customer, the longer the wait that will be tolerated.
- Waiting on one's own is more tedious than waiting in a group (unless you really don't like the others in the group).

Short case
Managing queues at Madame Tussaud's, Amsterdam

A short holiday in Amsterdam would not be complete without a visit to Madame Tussaud's, located on four upper floors of the city's most prominent department store in Dam Square. With 600,000 visitors each year, this is the third most popular tourist attraction in Amsterdam, after the flower market and canal trips. On busy days in the summer, the centre can just manage to handle 5,000 visitors. On a wet day in January, however, there may only be 300 visitors throughout the whole day. The centre is open for admission, seven days a week, from 10.00 am to 5.30 pm. In the streets outside, orderly queues of expectant tourists snake along the pavement, looking in at the displays in the store windows. In this public open space, Tussaud's can do little to entertain the visitors, but entrepreneurial buskers and street artists are quick to capitalize on a captive market. On reaching the entrance lobby, individuals, families and groups purchase their admission tickets. The lobby is in the shape of a large horseshoe, with the ticket sales booth in the centre. On winter days or at quiet spells, there will only be one sales assistant, but on busier days, visitors can pay at either side of the ticket booth, to speed up the process. Having paid, the visitors assemble in the

Source: Madame Tussaud's

lobby outside the two lifts. While waiting in this area, a photographer wanders around offering to take photos of the visitors standing next to life-sized wax figures of famous people. They may also be entertained by living look-alikes of famous personalities who act as guides to groups of visitors in batches of around 25 customers (the capacity of each of the two lifts which takes visitors up to the facility). The lifts arrive every four minutes and customers simultaneously disembark, forming one group of about 50 customers, who stay together throughout the session.

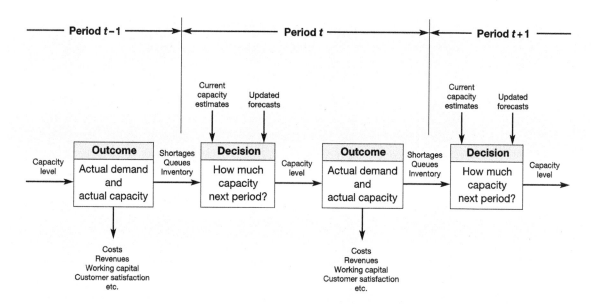

Figure 12.18 Capacity planning and control as a dynamic sequence of decisions

The dynamics of capacity planning and control

Our emphasis so far has been on the planning aspects of capacity management. In practice, the management of capacity is a far more dynamic process which involves controlling and reacting to *actual* demand and *actual* capacity as it occurs. The capacity control process can be seen as a sequence of partially reactive capacity decision processes as shown in Figure 12.18. At the beginning of each period, operations management considers its forecasts of demand, its understanding of current capacity and, if appropriate, how much inventory has been carried forward from the previous period. Based on all this information, it makes plans for the following period's capacity. During the next period, demand might or might not be as forecast and the actual capacity of the operation might or might not turn out as planned. But whatever the actual conditions during that period, at the beginning of the next period the same types of decisions must be made, in the light of the new circumstances.

Summary answers to key questions

Check and improve your understanding of this chapter using self assessment questions and a personalised study plan, audio and video downloads, and an eBook – all at www.myomlab.com.

➤ What is capacity planning and control?

■ It is the way operations organize the level of value-added activity which they can achieve under normal operating conditions over a period of time.

■ It is usual to distinguish between long-, medium- and short-term capacity decisions. Medium- and short-term capacity management where the capacity level of the organization is adjusted within the fixed physical limits which are set by long-term capacity decisions is sometimes called aggregate planning and control.

- Almost all operations have some kind of fluctuation in demand (or seasonality) caused by some combination of climatic, festive, behavioural, political, financial or social factors.

➤ How are demand and capacity measured?

- Either by the availability of its input resources or by the output which is produced. Which of these measures is used partly depends on how stable is the mix of outputs. If it is difficult to aggregate the different types of output from an operation, input measures are usually preferred.
- The usage of capacity is measured by the factors 'utilization' and 'efficiency'. A more recent measure is that of overall operations effectiveness (OEE).

➤ What are the alternative ways of coping with demand fluctuation?

- Output can be kept level, in effect ignoring demand fluctuations. This will result in under-utilization of capacity where outputs cannot be stored, or the build-up of inventories where output can be stored.
- Output can chase demand by fluctuating the output level through some combination of overtime, varying the size of the workforce, using part-time staff and subcontracting.
- Demand can be changed, either by influencing the market through such measures as advertising and promotion, or by developing alternative products with a counter-seasonal demand pattern.
- Most operations use a mix of all these three 'pure' strategies.

➤ How can operations plan and control their capacity level?

- Representing demand and output in the form of cumulative representations allows the feasibility of alternative capacity plans to be assessed.
- In many operations, especially service operations, a queuing approach can be used to explore capacity strategies.

➤ How can queuing theory be used to plan capacity?

- By considering the capacity decision as a dynamic decision which periodically updates the decisions and assumptions upon which decisions are based.

Case study
Holly farm

In 2003, Charles and Gillian Giles decided to open up their farm to the paying public, in response to diminishing profits from their milk and cereals activities. They invested all their savings into building a 40-space car park and an area with spaces for six 40-seater buses, a safe viewing area for the milking parlour, special trailers for passengers to be transported around the farm on guided tours, a permanent exhibition of equipment, a 'rare breeds' paddock, a children's adventure playground, a picnic area, a maize maze and a farm shop. Behind the farm shop they built a small 'factory' making real dairy ice cream, which also provided for public viewing. Ingredients for the ice cream, pasteurized cream and eggs, sugar, flavourings, etc., were bought out, although this was not obvious to the viewing public.

The maize maze at Holly Farm

Gillian took responsibility for all these new activities and Charles continued to run the commercial farming business. Through advertising, giving lectures to local schools and local organizations, the number of visitors to the farm increased steadily. By 2006 Gillian became so involved in running her business that she was unable to give so much time to these promotional activities, and the number of paying visitors levelled out at around 15,000 per year. Although the farm opened to the public at 11.00 am and closed at 7.00 pm after milking was finished, up to 90 per cent of visitors in cars or coaches would arrive later than 12.30 pm, picnic until around 2.00 pm, and tour the farm until about 4.00 pm. By that time, around 20 per cent would have visited the farm shop and left, but the remainder would wait to view the milking, then visit the shop to purchase ice cream and other produce, and then depart.

Gillian opened the farm to the public each year from April to October inclusive. Demand would be too low outside this period, the conditions were often unsuitable for regular tractor rides, and most of the animals had to be kept inside. Early experience had confirmed that mid-week demand was too low to justify opening, but Friday to Monday was commercially viable, with almost exactly twice as many visitors on Saturdays and Sundays as on Fridays or Mondays. Gillian summed up the situation. *'I have decided to attempt to increase the number of farm visitors in 2008 by 50 per cent. This would not only improve our return on "farm tours" assets, but also would help the farm shop to achieve its targets, and the extra sales of ice cream would help to keep the "factory" at full output. The real problem is whether to promote sales to coach firms or to intensify local advertising to attract more families in cars. We could also consider tie-ups with schools for educational visits, but I would not want to use my farm guide staff on any extra weekdays, as Charles needs them three days per week for "real" farming work. However, most of the farm workers are glad of this extra of work as if fits in well with their family life, and helps them to save up for the luxuries most farm workers cannot afford.'*

The milking parlour

With 150 cows to milk, Charles invested in a 'carousel' parlour where cows are milked on a slow-moving turntable. Milking usually lasts from 4.30 pm to 7.00 pm, during which time visitors can view from a purpose-built gallery which has space and explanatory tape recordings, via headphones, for twelve people. Gillian has found that on average spectators like to watch for ten minutes, including five minutes for the explanatory tape. *'We're sometimes a bit busy on Saturdays and Sundays and a queue often develops before 4.00 pm as some people want to see the milking and then go home. Unfortunately, neither Charles nor the cows are prepared to start earlier. However, most people are patient and everybody gets their turn to see this bit of high technology. In a busy period, up to 80 people per hour pass through the gallery.'*

The ice cream 'factory'

The factory is operated 48 weeks per year, four days per week, eight hours per day, throughout the year. The three employees, farm workers' wives, are expected to work in line with farm opening from April to October, but hours and days are by negotiation in other months. All output is in one-litre plastic boxes, of which 350 are made every day, which is the maximum mixing and fast-freezing capacity. Although extra mixing hours would create more unfrozen ice cream, the present equipment cannot safely and fully fast-freeze more than 350 litres over a 24-hour period. Ice cream that is not fully frozen cannot be transferred to the finished goods freezer, as slower freezing spoils the texture of the product. As it takes about one hour to clean out between flavours, only one of the four flavours is made on any day. The finished goods freezer holds a maximum of 10,000 litres, but to allow stock rotation, it cannot in practice be loaded to above 7,000 litres. Ideally no ice cream should be held more than six weeks at the factory, as the total recommended storage time is only twelve weeks prior to retail sale (there is no preservative used). Finished goods inventory at the end of December 2007 was 3,600 litres.

Gillian's most recent figures indicated that all flavours cost about £4.00 per litre to produce (variable cost of materials, packaging and labour). The factory layout is by process with material preparation and weighing sections, mixing area, packing equipment, and separate freezing equipment. It is operated as a batch process.

Ice cream sales

The majority of output is sold through regional speciality shops and food sections of department stores. These outlets are given a standard discount of 25 per cent to allow a 33 per cent mark-up to the normal retail price of £8.00 per litre. Minimum order quantity is 100 litres, and deliveries are made by Gillian in the van on Tuesdays. Also, having been shown around the farm and 'factory', a large proportion of visitors buy ice cream at the farm shop, and take it away in well-insulated containers that keep it from melting for up to two hours in the summer. Gillian commented 'These are virtually captive customers. We have analysed this demand and found that on average one out of two coach customers buys a one-litre box. On average, a car comes with four occupants, and two 1-litre boxes are purchased. The farm shop retail price is £2.00 per box, which gives us a much better margin than for our sales to shops.'

In addition, a separate, fenced, road entrance allows local customers to purchase goods at a separate counter of the farm shop without payment for, or access to, the other farm facilities. 'This is a surprisingly regular source of sales. We believe this is because householders make very infrequent visits to stock up their freezers almost regardless of the time of year, or the weather. We also know that local hotels also buy a lot this way, and their use of ice cream is year-round, with a peak only at Christmas when there are a larger number of banquets.' All sales in this category are at the full retail price (£8.00). The finished product is sold to three categories of buyers. See Table 12.3. (Note – (a) no separate record is kept of those sales to the paying farm visitors and those to the 'Farm Shop only', (b) the selling prices and discounts for 2008 will be as for 2007, (c) Gillian considered that 2007 was reasonably typical in terms of weather, although rainfall was a little higher than average during July and August.)

Table 12.3 Analysis of annual sales of ice cream (£000s) from 2003 to 2007, and forecast sales for 2008

	2003	2004	2005	2006	2007	2008 forecast
Retail shops	32	104	156	248	300	260
Farm shop total	40	64	80	100	108	160
Total	72	168	236	348	408	420

Table 12.4 gives details of visitors to the farm and ice cream sales in 2007. Gillian's concluding comments were 'We have a long way to go to make this enterprise meet our expectations. We will probably make only a small return on capital employed in 2007, so must do all we can to increase our profitability. Neither of us wants to put more capital into the business, as we would have to borrow at interest rates of up to 15 per cent. We must make our investment work better. As a first step, I have decided to increase the number of natural flavours of our ice cream to ten in 2008 (currently only four) to try and defend the delicatessen trade against a competitor's aggressive marketing campaign. I don't expect that to fully halt the decline in our sales to these outlets, and this is reflected in our sales forecast.'

Questions

1 Evaluate Gillian's proposal to increase the number of farm visitors in 2008 by 50 per cent. (You may wish to consider: What are the main capacity constraints within these businesses? Should she promote coach company visits, even if this involves offering a discount on the admission charges? Should she pursue increasing visitors by car or school parties? In what other ways is Gillian able to manage capacity? What other information would help Gillian to take these decisions?)

2 What factors should Gillian consider when deciding to increase the number of flavours from four to ten?

(Note: For any calculations, assume that each month consists of four weeks. The effects of statutory holidays should be ignored for the purpose of this initial analysis.)

Table 12.4 Records of farm visitors and ice cream sales (in £000) in 2007

	Jan	Feb	Mar	Apr	May	June	July	Aug	Sept	Oct	Nov	Dec	TOTAL
Total number of paying farm visitors	0	0	0	1,200	1,800	2,800	3,200	3,400	1,800	600	0	0	14,800
Monthly ice cream sales	18	20.2	35	26.8	36	50.2	50.6	49.2	39	25.6	17.4	40	408.8

Problems and applications

These problems and applications will help to improve your analysis of operations. You can find more practice problems as well as worked examples and guided solutions on MyOMLab at www.myomlab.com.

1 A local government office issues hunting licences. Demand for these licences is relatively slow in the first part of the year but then increases after the middle of the year before slowing down again towards the end of the year. The department works a 220-day year on a 5-days-a-week basis. Between working days 0 and 100, demand is 25 per cent of demand during the peak period which lasts between day 100 and day 150. After 150 demand reduces to about 12 per cent of the demand during the peak period. In total, the department processes 10,000 applications per year. The department has 2 permanent members of staff who are capable of processing 15 licence applications per day. If an untrained temporary member of staff can only process 10 licences per day, how many temporary staff should the department recruit between days 100 and 150?

2 In the example above, if a new computer system is installed that allows experienced staff to increase their work rate to 20 applications per day, and untrained staff to 15 applications per day, (a) does the department still need 2 permanent staff, and (b) how many temporary members of staff will be needed between days 100 and 150?

3 A field service organization repairs and maintains printing equipment for a large number of customers. It offers one level of service to all its customers and employs 30 staff. The operation's marketing vice-president has decided that in future the company will offer 3 standards of service, platinum, gold and silver. It is estimated that platinum-service customers will require 50 per cent more time from the company's field service engineers than the current service. The current service is to be called 'the gold service'. The silver service is likely to require about 80 per cent of the time of the gold service. If future demand is estimated to be 20 per cent platinum, 70 per cent gold and 10 per cent silver service, how many staff will be needed to fulfil demand?

4 Look again at the principles which govern customers' perceptions of the queuing experience. For the following operations, apply the principles to minimize the perceived negative effects of queuing.

(a) A cinema
(b) A doctor's surgery
(c) Waiting to board an aircraft.

5 Consider how airlines cope with balancing capacity and demand. In particular, consider the role of yield management. Do this by visiting the web site of a low-cost airline, and for a number of flights price the fare that is being charged by the airline from tomorrow onwards. In other words, how much would it cost if you needed to fly tomorrow, how much if you needed to fly next week, how much if you needed to fly in 2 weeks, etc. Plot the results for different flights and debate the findings.

6 Calculate the overall equipment efficiency (OEE) of the following facilities by investigating their use.

(a) A lecture theatre
(b) A cinema
(c) A coffee machine

Discuss whether it is worth trying to increase the OEE of these facilities and, if it is, how you would go about it.

Selected further reading

Brandimarte, P. and Villa, A. (1999) *Modelling Manufacturing Systems: From Aggregate Planning to Real Time Control*, Springer, New York, NY. Very academic although it does contain some interesting pieces if you need to get 'under the skin' of the subject.

Hopp, W.J. and Spearman, M.L. (2000) *Factory Physics*, 2nd edn, McGraw-Hill, New York, NY. Very mathematical indeed, but includes some interesting maths on queuing theory.

Olhager, J., Rudberg, M. and Wikner, J. (2001) Long-term capacity management: linking the perspectives from manufacturing strategy and sales and operations planning, *International Journal of Production Economics*, vol. 69, issue 2, 215–25. Academic article, but interesting.

Vollmann, T., Berry, W., Whybark, D.C. and Jacobs, F.R. (2004) *Manufacturing Planning and Control Systems for Supply Chain Management: The Definitive Guide for Professionals*, McGraw-Hill Higher Education. The latest version of the 'bible' of manufacturing planning and control. It's exhaustive in its coverage of all aspects of planning and control including aggregate planning.

Useful web sites

www.dti.gov.uk/er/index Web site of the Employment Relations Directorate which has developed a framework for employers and employees which promotes a skilled and flexible labour market founded on principles of partnership.

www.worksmart.org.uk/index.php This site is from the Trades Union Congress. Its aim is 'to help today's working people get the best out of the world of work'.

www.opsman.org Lots of useful stuff.

www.eoc-law.org.uk/ This web site aims to provide a resource for legal advisers and representatives who are conducting claims on behalf of applicants in sex discrimination and equal pay cases in England and Wales. This site covers employment-related sex discrimination only.

www.dol.gov/index.htm US Department of Labor's site with information regarding using part-time employees.

www.downtimecentral.com/ Lots of information on operational equipment efficiency (OEE).

Now that you have finished reading this chapter, why not visit MyOMLab at www.myomlab.com where you'll find more learning resources to help you make the most of your studies and get a better grade?

Chapter 13

Supply chain planning and control

Key questions

- What is supply chain management?
- What are the activities of supply chain management?
- What are the types of relationship between operations in supply chains?
- How do supply chains behave in practice?
- How can supply chains be improved?

Introduction

Operations managers have to look beyond an internal view if they want to manage their operations effectively. As operations outsource many of their activities and buy more of their services and materials from outside specialists, the way they manage the supply of products and services to their operations becomes increasingly important, as does the integration of their distribution activities. Even beyond this immediate supply chain, there are benefits from managing the flow between customers' customers and suppliers' suppliers. This activity is now commonly termed *supply chain management*. This chapter considers the more 'infrastructural' issues of planning and controlling the individual chains in the supply network.

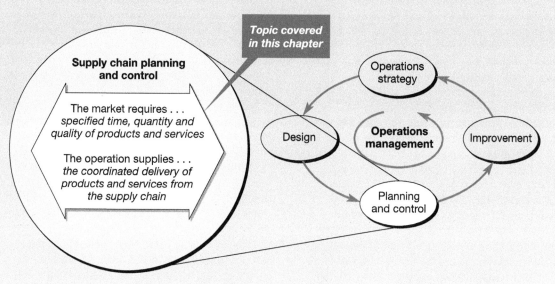

Figure 13.1 This chapter covers supply chain planning and control

Operations in practice Siemens 'SCOR' a success[1]

by Carsten Dittrich, University of Southern Denmark

Siemens AG, with over 450,000 people, sales of around €70 billion and operating in more than 190 countries, is one of the world's top five electrical engineering and electronics companies, producing products from mobile phones to power plants. For over a decade Siemens has used the Supply-Chain Operations Reference (SCOR) model to improve its supply chain efficiency and process performance. (The SCOR model is explained later in this chapter.) The implementation of the model was initially intended to support the company's move to a considerably stronger focus on e-business. Teams of more than 250 internal change agents were formed to start to review strategies, opportunities and challenges.

Siemens initially developed what they called their 'Generic Business Process' version of the SCOR model so that it could be applied in all their markets. However, Siemens soon realized that different kinds of business required different supply chain solutions. For example, Siemens used SCOR to streamline the Make-to-Order processes of its 'Siemens Medical Solutions' business whose computed tomography (CT) devices are made in Germany and China. This was a particularly difficult business involving 'make-to-order' functions such as the global management of customer orders, comprehensive and complex material management, customization and production, technical support, worldwide dispatch and logistics, and installation at the customer's site. Yet while Siemens was the clear innovation leader, before the SCOR initiative its inflexible and bureaucratic processes had resulted in long waits for customers, high levels of inventory and high costs. The CT supply chain was not connected, with little common understanding of how processes should work or what its supply objectives should be. Internal operations managers in the supply chain answered to headquarters rather than to end-customers and conflicting performance objectives led to fluctuating demands throughout the chain. It was the SCOR process that helped Siemens

Source: Alamy Images

tackle these problems directly. Order management and planning and control processes moved from individual and fragmented order handling to the management of all worldwide customer orders; sourcing was simplified and integrated using 22 'A suppliers' rather than the 250 used previously, production of small quantities was organized according to customer specifications, strategic partnerships were developed with service providers, quick installation of systems directly delivered to customer sites using qualified CT factory personal was implemented, and 'reverse logistics' employed to refurbish used systems.

The improvements in supply chain performance were spectacular. Order to delivery time reduced from 22 weeks to 2 weeks, the simplified and transparent order on the factories allowed two production lines to do the work of the four used previously, factory throughput time was reduced from 13 days to 6 days, flexibility was increased tremendously to a level of ± 50% orders per month, inventory levels were reduced significantly, enabling CT to divest a warehouse, direct shipments non-stop from the factory to the customer enabled delivery to customer sites within 5 working days and also allowed customers to track shipments.

What is supply chain management?

Supply chain management is the management of the interconnection of organizations that relate to each other through upstream and downstream linkages between the processes that produce value to the ultimate consumer in the form of products and services. It is a holistic approach to managing across company boundaries. The term '**supply network**' refers to all the operations that are linked together so as to provide goods and services through to the end-customers. In this chapter we deal with the 'ongoing' flow of goods and services through this network along individual channels or strands of that network. In large organizations there can be many hundreds of strands of linked operations passing through the operation. These strands are more commonly referred to as **supply chains**. An analogy often used to describe supply chains is that of the 'pipeline'. Just as liquids flow through a pipeline, so physical goods (and services, but the metaphor is more difficult to imagine) flow down a supply chain. Long pipelines will, of course, contain more liquid than short ones. So, the time taken for liquid to flow all the way through a long pipeline will be longer than if the pipeline were shorter. Stocks of inventory held in the supply chain can be thought of as analogous to storage tanks. On the journey through the **supply chain pipeline**, products are processed by different operations in the chain and also stored at different points.

A supply network is all the operations linked together to provide goods and services through to the end-customers

A supply chain is a strand of linked operations

Supply chain pipeline

Supply chain management objectives

All supply chain management shares one common, and central, objective – to satisfy the end-customer. All stages in a chain must eventually include consideration of the final customer, no matter how far an individual operation is from the end-customer. When a customer decides to make a purchase, he or she triggers action back along the whole chain. All the businesses in the supply chain pass on portions of that end-customer's money to each other, each retaining a margin for the value it has added. Each operation in the chain should be satisfying its own customer, but also making sure that eventually the end-customer is also satisfied.

For a demonstration of how end-customer perceptions of supply satisfaction can be very different from that of a single operation, examine the customer 'decision tree' in Figure 13.2. It charts the hypothetical progress of a hundred customers requiring service (or products) from a business (for example, a printer requiring paper from an industrial paper stockist). Supply performance, as seen by the core operation (the warehouse), is represented by the shaded part of the diagram. It has received 20 orders, 18 of which were 'produced' (shipped to customers) as promised (on time, and in full). However, originally 100 customers may have requested service, 20 of who found the business did not have appropriate products (did not stock the right paper), 10 of whom could not be served because the products were not available (out of stock), 50 of whom were not satisfied with the price and/or delivery (of whom 10 placed an order notwithstanding). Of the 20 orders received, 18 were produced as promised (shipped) but 2 were not received as promised (delayed or damaged in transport). So what seems a 90 per cent supply performance is in fact an 8 per cent performance from the customer's perspective. And this is just one operation. Include the cumulative effect of similar reductions in performance for all the operations in a chain, and the probability that the end-customer is adequately served could become remote. The point here is that the performance both of the supply chain as a whole, and its constituent operations, should be judged in terms of how all end-customer needs are satisfied.

Supply chain objectives

Meeting the requirements of end-customers requires the supply chain to achieve appropriate levels of the five operations performance objectives: quality, speed, dependability, flexibility and cost.

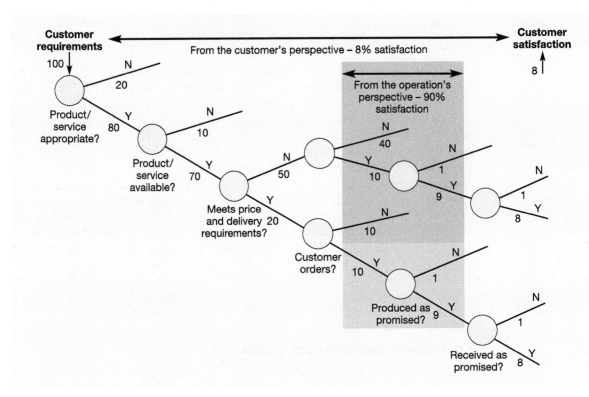

Figure 13.2 Taking a customer perspective of supply chain performance can lead to very different conclusions

Quality – the quality of a product or service when it reaches the customer is a function of the quality performance of every operation in the chain that supplied it. Errors in each stage of the chain can multiply in their effect on end-customer service, so if each of 7 stages in a supply chain has a 1 per cent error rate, only 93.2 per cent of products or services will be of good quality on reaching the end-customer (i.e. 0.99^7). This is why, only by every stage taking some responsibility for its own *and its suppliers'* performance, can a supply chain achieve high end-customer quality.

Speed has two meanings in a supply chain context. The first is how fast customers can be served, an important element in any business's ability to compete. However, fast customer response can be achieved simply by over-resourcing or over-stocking within the supply chain. For example, very large stocks in a retail operation can reduce the chances of stock-out to almost zero, so reducing customer waiting time virtually to zero. Similarly, an accounting firm may be able to respond quickly to customer demand by having a very large number of accountants on standby waiting for demand that may (or may not) occur. An alternative perspective on speed is the time taken for goods and services to move through the chain. So, for example, products that move quickly down a supply chain will spend little time as inventory because to achieve fast throughput time, material cannot dwell for significant periods as inventory. This in turn reduces inventory-related costs in the supply chain.

Dependability – like speed, one can almost guarantee 'on-time' delivery by keeping excessive resources, such as inventory, within the chain. However, dependability of throughput time is a much more desirable aim because it reduces uncertainty within the chain. If the individual operations in a chain do not deliver as promised on time, there will be a tendency for customers to over-order, or order early, in order to provide some kind of insurance against late delivery. This is why delivery dependability is often measured as 'on time, in full' in supply chains.

Flexibility – in a supply chain context is usually taken to mean the chain's ability to cope with changes and disturbances. Very often this is referred to as supply chain agility. The concept of agility includes previously discussed issues such as focusing on the end-customer and ensuring fast throughput and responsiveness to customer needs. But, in addition, agile supply chains are sufficiently flexible to cope with changes, either in the nature of customer demand or in the supply capabilities of operations within the chain.

Cost – in addition to the costs incurred within each operation, the supply chain as a whole incurs additional costs that derive from each operation in a chain doing business with each other. These may include such things as the costs of finding appropriate suppliers, setting up contractual agreements, monitoring supply performance, transporting products between operations, holding inventories, and so on. Many developments in supply chain management, such as partnership agreements or reducing the number of suppliers, are attempts to minimize transaction costs.

The activities of supply chain management

Some of the terms used in supply chain management are not universally applied. Furthermore, some of the concepts behind the terminology overlap in the sense that they refer to common parts of the total supply network. This is why it is useful first of all to distinguish between the different terms we shall use in this chapter. These are illustrated in Figure 13.3. *Supply chain management* coordinates all the operations on the supply side and the demand side. *Purchasing and supply management* deals with the operation's interface with its supply markets. *Physical distribution management* may mean supplying immediate customers, while *logistics* is an extension that often refers to materials and information flow down through a distribution channel, to the retail store or consumers (increasingly common because of the growth of internet-based retailing). The term *third-party logistics* (TPL) indicates outsourcing

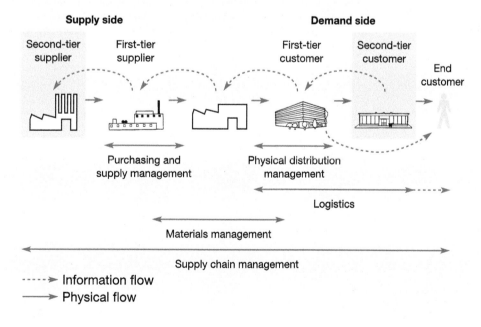

Figure 13.3 Some of the terms used to describe the management of different parts of the supply chain

to a specialist logistics company. *Materials management* is a more limited term and refers to the flow of materials and information only through the immediate supply chain.

Purchasing (procurement) and supply management

Purchasing

At the supply end of the business, **purchasing** (sometimes called 'procurement') buys in materials and services from suppliers. Typically the volume and value of these purchases are increasing as organizations concentrate on their 'core tasks'. Purchasing managers provide a vital link between the operation itself and its suppliers. They must understand the requirements of all the processes within the operation and also the capabilities of the suppliers (sometimes thousands in number) who could potentially provide products and services for the operation. Purchasing can have a very significant impact on any operation's costs, and therefore profits. To illustrate the impact that price-conscious purchasing can have on profits, consider a simple manufacturing operation with the following financial details:

Total sales	£10,000,000
Purchased services and materials	£7,000,000
Salaries	£2,000,000
Overheads	£500,000

Therefore, profit = £500,000. Profits could be doubled to £1 million by any of the following:

- increase sales revenue by up to 100 per cent
- decrease salaries by 25 per cent
- decrease overheads by 100 per cent
- decrease purchase costs by 7.1 per cent.

A doubling of sales revenue does sometimes occur in very fast-growing markets, but this would be regarded by most sales and marketing managers as an exceedingly ambitious target. Decreasing the salaries bill by a quarter is likely to require substantial alternative investment – for example, in automation – or reflects a dramatic reduction in medium- to long-term sales. Similarly, a reduction in overheads by 100 per cent is unlikely to be possible over the short-to-medium term without compromising the business. However, reducing purchase costs by 7.1 per cent, although a challenging objective, is usually far more of a realistic option than the other actions. The reason purchase price savings can have such a dramatic impact on total profitability is that purchase costs are such a large proportion of total costs. The higher the proportion of purchase costs, the more profitability can be improved in this way. Figure 13.4 illustrates this.

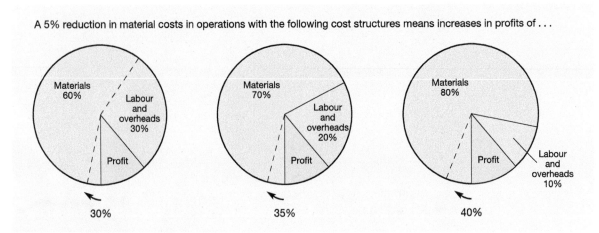

Figure 13.4 The larger the level of material costs as a proportion of total costs, the greater the effect on profitability of a reduction in material costs

Ford Motors' team value management[2]

Purchasing managers are a vital link between an operation and its suppliers. But they work best when teamed up with mainstream operations managers who know what the operation really needs, especially if, between them, they take a role that challenges previous assumptions. That is the basis behind Ford Motor Company's 'team value management' (TVM) approach. Reputedly, it all started when Ford's Head of Global Purchasing, David Thursfield, discovered that a roof rack designed for one of Ford's smaller cars was made of plastic-coated aluminium and capable of bearing a 100 kg load. This prompted the questions, *'Why is this rack covered in plastic? Why would anyone want to put 100 kg on the roof of a car that small?'* He found that no one had ever questioned the original specification. When Ford switched to using steel roof racks capable of bearing a smaller weight, they halved the cost. *'It is important'*, he says, *'to check whether the company is getting the best price for parts and raw material that provide the appropriate level of performance without being too expensive.'* The savings in a large company such as Ford can be huge. Often in multinationals,

Source: Getty Images/Getty Images News

each part of the business makes sourcing and design decisions independently and does not exploit opportunities for cross-usage of components. The TVM approach is designed to bring together engineering and purchasing staff and identify where cost can be taken out of purchased parts and where there is opportunity for parts commonality between different models. When a company's global purchasing budget is $75bn like Ford's, the potential for cost savings is significant.

Supplier selection

Choosing appropriate suppliers should involve trading off alternative attributes. Rarely are potential suppliers so clearly superior to their competitors that the decision is self-evident. Most businesses find it best to adopt some kind of supplier 'scoring' or assessment procedure. This should be capable of rating alternative suppliers in terms of factors such as those in Table 13.1.

Supplier selection

Choosing **suppliers** should involve evaluating the relative importance of all these factors. So, for example, a business might choose a supplier that, although more expensive than alternative suppliers, has an excellent reputation for on-time delivery, because that is more appropriate to the way the business competes itself, or because the high level of supply

Table 13.1 Factors for rating alternative suppliers

Short-term ability to supply	*Longer-term ability to supply*
Range of products or services provided	Potential for innovation
Quality of products or services	Ease of doing business
Responsiveness	Willingness to share risk
Dependability of supply	Long-term commitment to supply
Delivery and volume flexibility	Ability to transfer knowledge as well as products and services
Total cost of being supplied	Technical capability
Ability to supply in the required quantity	Operations capability Financial capability Managerial capability

dependability allows the business to hold lower stock levels, which may even save costs overall. Other trade-offs may be more difficult to calculate. For example, a potential supplier may have high levels of technical capability, but may be financially weak, with a small but finite risk of going out of business. Other suppliers may have little track record of supplying the products or services required, but show the managerial talent and energy for potential customers to view developing a supply relationship as an investment in future capability.

Worked example

A hotel chain has decided to change its supplier of cleaning supplies because its current supplier has become unreliable in its delivery performance. The two alternative suppliers that it is considering have been evaluated, on a 1–10 scale, against the criteria shown in Table 13.2. That also shows the relative importance of each criterion, also on a 1–10 scale. Based on this evaluation, Supplier B has the superior overall score.

Table 13.2 Weighted supplier selection criteria for the hotel chain

Factor	Weight	Supplier A score	Supplier B score
Cost performance	10	8 (8 × 10 = 80)	5 (5 × 10 = 50)
Quality record	10	7 (7 × 10 = 70)	9 (9 × 10 = 90)
Delivery speed promised	7	5 (5 × 7 = 35)	5 (5 × 7 = 35)
Delivery speed achieved	7	4 (4 × 7 = 28)	8 (8 × 7 = 56)
Dependability record	8	6 (6 × 8 = 48)	8 (8 × 8 = 64)
Range provided	5	8 (8 × 5 = 40)	5 (5 × 5 = 25)
Innovation capability	4	6 (6 × 4 = 24)	9 (9 × 4 = 36)
Total weighted score		325	356

Single- and multi-sourcing

An important decision facing most purchasing managers is whether to source each individual product or service from one or more than one supplier, known, respectively, as **single-sourcing** and **multi-sourcing**. Some of the advantages and disadvantages of single- and multi-sourcing are shown in Table 13.3.

Single-sourcing
Multi-sourcing

Table 13.3 Advantages and disadvantages of single- and multi-sourcing

	Single-sourcing	Multi-sourcing
Advantages	• Potentially better quality because more SQA possibilities • Strong relationships which are more durable • Greater dependency encourages more commitment and effort • Better communication • Easier to cooperate on new product/service development • More scale economies • Higher confidentiality	• Purchaser can drive price down by competitive tendering • Can switch sources in case of supply failure • Wide sources of knowledge and expertise to tap
Disadvantages	• More vulnerable to disruption if a failure to supply occurs • Individual supplier more affected by volume fluctuations • Supplier might exert upward pressure on prices if no alternative supplier is available	• Difficult to encourage commitment by supplier • Less easy to develop effective SQA • More effort needed to communicate • Suppliers less likely to invest in new processes • More difficult to obtain scale economies

It may seem as though companies that multi-source do so exclusively for their own short-term benefit. However, this is not always the case: multi-sourcing can bring benefits to both supplier and purchaser in the long term. For example, Robert Bosch GmbH, the German automotive components business, required that subcontractors do no more than 20 per cent of their total business with them. This was to prevent suppliers becoming too dependent and allow volumes to be fluctuated without pushing the supplier into bankruptcy. However, there has been a trend for purchasing functions to reduce the number of companies supplying any one part or service.

Purchasing, the Internet and e-procurement

For some years, electronic means have been used by businesses to confirm purchased orders and ensure payment to suppliers. The rapid development of the Internet, however, opened up the potential for far more fundamental changes in purchasing behaviour. Partly this was as the result of supplier information made available through the Internet. By making it easier to search for alternative suppliers, the Internet changed the economics of the search process and offers the potential for wider searches. It also changed the economics of scale in purchasing. For example, purchasers requiring relatively low volumes find it easier to group together in order to create orders of sufficient size to warrant lower prices.

E-procurement

E-procurement is the generic term used to describe the use of electronic methods in every stage of the purchasing process from identification of requirement through to payment, and potentially to contract management.[3] Many of the large automotive, engineering and petrochemical companies, for example, have adopted such an approach. Typical of these companies' motives are those put forward by Shell Services International, part of the petro-chemical giant:[4]

> 'Procurement is an obvious first step in e-commerce. First, buying through the web is so slick and cheap compared to doing it almost any other way. Second, it allows you to aggregate, spend and ask: Why am I spending this money, or shouldn't I be getting a bigger discount? Third, it encourages new services like credit, insurance and accreditation to be built around it.'

Generally the benefits of e-procurement are taken to include the following.

- It promotes efficiency improvements (the way people work) in purchasing processes.
- It improves commercial relationships with suppliers.
- It reduces the transaction costs of doing business for suppliers.
- It opens up the marketplace to increased competition and therefore keeps prices competitive.
- It improves a business's ability to manage their supply chain more efficiently.

The benefits of e-procurement go beyond reducing costs

Note how lowering prices (purchase costs to the buyer) is only one of **the benefits of e-procurement**. The cost savings from purchased goods may be the most visible advantages of e-procurement, but some managers say that it is just the tip of the iceberg. It can also be far more efficient because purchasing staff are no longer chasing purchase orders and performing routine administrative tasks. Much of the advantage and time savings comes from the decreased need to re-enter information, from streamlining the interaction with suppliers and from having a central repository for data with everything contained in one system. Purchasing staff can negotiate with vendors faster and more effectively. Online auctions can compress negotiations from months to one or two hours, or even minutes.

Electronic marketplaces

E-procurement has grown largely because of the development over the last ten years of electronic marketplaces (also sometimes called infomediaries or cybermediaries). These operations which have emerged in business-to-business commerce offer services to both buyers and sellers. They have been defined as, 'an information system that allows buyers and sellers to exchange information about prices and product (and service) offerings, and the firm operating the electronic marketplace acts as in intermediary'.[5] They can be categorized as consortium, private or third party.

- A private e-marketplace is where buyers or sellers conduct business in the market only with their partners and suppliers by previous arrangement.
- The consortium e-marketplace is where several large businesses combine to create an e-marketplace controlled by the consortium.
- A third-party e-marketplace is where an independent party creates an unbiased, market-driven e-marketplace for buyers and sellers in an industry.

The scope of e-procurement

The influence of the Internet on purchasing behaviour is not confined to when the trade actually takes place over the Internet. It is also an important source of purchasing information, even if the purchase is actually made by using more traditional methods. Also, even though many businesses have gained advantages by using e-procurement, it does not mean that everything should be bought electronically. When businesses purchase very large amounts of strategically important products or services, it will negotiate multimillion-euro deals, which involve months of discussion, arranging for deliveries up to a year ahead. In such environments, e-procurement adds little value. Deciding whether to invest in e-procurement applications (which can be expensive), say some authorities, depends on what is being bought. For example, simple office supplies such as pens, paper clips and copier paper may be appropriate for e-procurement, but complex, made-to-order engineered components are not. Four questions seem to influence whether e-procurement will be appropriate:[6]

- *Is the value of the spend high or low?* High spending on purchased products and services gives more potential for savings from e-procurement.
- *Is the product or commodity highly substitutable or not?* When products and services are 'substitutable' (there are alternatives), e-procurement can identify and find lower-cost alternatives.
- *Is there a lot of competition or a little?* When several suppliers are competing, e-procurement can manage the process of choosing a preferred supplier more effectively and with more transparency.
- *How efficient are your internal processes?* When purchasing processes are relatively inefficient, e-procurement's potential to reduce processing costs can be realized.

Global sourcing

Global sourcing

One of the major supply chain developments of recent years has been the expansion in the proportion of products and (occasionally) services which businesses are willing to source from outside their home country; this is called **global sourcing**. It is the process of identifying, evaluating, negotiating and configuring supply across multiple geographies. Traditionally, even companies that exported their goods and services all over the world (that is, they were international on their demand side) still sourced the majority of their supplies locally (that is, they were not international on their supply side). This has changed – companies are now increasingly willing to look further afield for their supplies, and for very good reasons. Most companies report a 10 per cent to 35 per cent cost savings by sourcing from low-cost-country suppliers.[7] There are a number of other factors promoting global sourcing:

- The formation of trading blocs in different parts of the world has had the effect of lowering tariff barriers, at least within those blocs. For example, the single market developments within the European Union (EU), the North American Free Trade Agreement (NAFTA) and the South American Trade Group (MERCOSUR) have all made it easier to trade internationally within the regions.

- Transportation infrastructures are considerably more sophisticated and cheaper than they once were. Super-efficient port operations in Rotterdam and Singapore, for example, integrated road–rail systems, jointly developed autoroute systems, and cheaper air freight have all reduced some of the cost barriers to international trade.
- Perhaps most significantly, far tougher world competition has forced companies to look to reducing their total costs. Given that in many industries bought-in items are the largest single part of operations costs, an obvious strategy is to source from wherever is cheapest.

There are, of course, problems with global sourcing. The risks of increased complexity and increased distance need managing carefully. Suppliers that are a significant distance away need to transport their products across long distances. The risks of delays and hold-ups can be far greater than when sourcing locally. Also, negotiating with suppliers whose native language is different from one's own makes communication more difficult and can lead to misunderstandings over contract terms. Therefore global sourcing decisions require businesses to balance cost, performance, service and risk factors, not all of which are obvious. These factors are important in global sourcing because of non-price or 'hidden' cost factors such as cross-border freight and handling fees, complex inventory stocking and handling requirements, and even more complex administrative, documentation and regulatory requirements. The factors that must be understood and included in evaluating global sourcing opportunities are as follows.

- *Purchase price* – the total price, including transaction and other costs related to the actual product or service delivered
- *Transportation costs* – transportation and freight costs, including fuel surcharges and other costs of moving products or services from where they are produced to where they are required
- *Inventory carrying costs* – storage, handling, insurance, depreciation, obsolescence and other costs associated with maintaining inventories, including the opportunity costs of working capital
- *Cross-border taxes, tariffs and duty costs* – sometimes called 'landed costs', which are the sum of duties, shipping, insurance and other fees and taxes for door-to-door delivery
- *Supply performance* – the cost of late or out-of-specification deliveries, which, if not managed properly, can offset any price gains attained by shifting to an offshore source
- *Supply and operational risks* – including geopolitical factors, such as changes in country leadership, trade policy changes, the instability caused by war and/or terrorism or natural disasters and disease, all of which may disrupt supply.

Global sourcing and social responsibility

Although the responsibility of operations to ensure that they only deal with ethical suppliers has always been important, the expansion of global sourcing has brought the issue into sharper focus. Local suppliers can (to some extent) be monitored relatively easily. However, when suppliers are located around the world, often in countries with different traditions and ethical standards, monitoring becomes more difficult. Not only that, but there may be genuinely different views of what is regarded as ethical practice. Social, cultural and religious differences can easily make for mutual incomprehension regarding each other's ethical perspective. This is why many companies are putting significant effort into articulating and clarifying their supplier selection policies. The short case on Levi Strauss's policy is typical of an enlightened organization's approach to global sourcing.

Short case
Extracts from Levi Strauss's global sourcing policy[8]

Our Global Sourcing and Operating Guidelines help us to select business partners who follow workplace standards and business practices that are consistent with our company's values. These requirements are applied to every contractor who manufactures or finishes products for Levi Strauss & Co. Trained inspectors closely audit and monitor compliance among approximately 600 cutting, sewing, and finishing contractors in more than 60 countries . . . The numerous countries where Levi Strauss & Co. has existing or future business interests present a variety of cultural, political, social and economic circumstances . . . The Country Assessment Guidelines help us assess any issue that might present concern in light of the ethical principles we have set for ourselves. Specifically, we assess . . . the . . . Health and Safety Conditions Human Rights Environment, the Legal System and the Political, Economic and Social Environment that would protect the company's commercial interests and brand/corporate image. The company's employment standards state that they will only do business with partners who adhere to the following guidelines:

- *Child Labor*: Use of child labor is not permissible. Workers can be no less than 15 years of age and not younger than the compulsory age to be in school. We will not utilize partners who use child labor in any of their facilities.
- *Prison Labor/Forced Labor*: We will not utilize prison or forced labor in contracting relationships in the manufacture and finishing of our products. We will not utilize or purchase materials from a business partner utilizing prison or forced labor.
- *Disciplinary Practices*: We will not utilize business partners who use corporal punishment or other forms of mental or physical coercion.
- *Working Hours*: While permitting flexibility in scheduling, we will identify local legal limits on work hours and seek business partners who do not

exceed them except for appropriately compensated overtime. Employees should be allowed at least one day off in seven.
- *Wages and Benefits*: We will only do business with partners who provide wages and benefits that comply with any applicable law and match the prevailing local manufacturing or finishing industry practices.
- *Freedom of Association*: We respect workers' rights to form and join organizations of their choice and to bargain collectively. We expect our suppliers to respect the right to free association and the right to organize and bargain collectively without unlawful interference.
- *Discrimination*: While we recognize and respect cultural differences, we believe that workers should be employed on the basis of their ability to do the job, rather than on the basis of personal characteristics or beliefs. We will favor business partners who share this value.
- *Health and Safety*: We will only utilize business partners who provide workers with a safe and healthy work environment. Business partners who provide residential facilities for their workers must provide safe and healthy facilities.

Physical distribution management and the Internet

Physical distribution management

Logistics

Distribution

In supply chains dealing with tangible products, the products need to be transported to customers. This is called **physical distribution management**, but sometimes the term **logistics**, or simply **distribution**, is used. The potential offered by Internet communications in physical distribution management has had two major effects. The first is to make information available more readily along the distribution chain. This means that the transport companies, warehouses, suppliers and customers that make up the chain can share knowledge of where goods are in the chain. This allows the operations within the chain to coordinate their activities more readily, with potentially significant cost savings. For example, an important issue for

Back-loading

transportation companies is **back-loading**. When the company is contracted to transport goods from A to B, its vehicles may have to return from B to A empty. Back-loading means finding a potential customer that wants their goods transported from B to A in the right time frame. Companies which can fill their vehicles on both the outward and return journeys will have significantly lower costs per distance travelled than those whose vehicles are empty for half the total journey.

The second impact of the Internet has been in the 'business to consumer' (B2C, *see* the discussion on supply chain relationships later) part of the supply chain. While the last few years have seen an increase in the number of goods bought by consumers online, most goods still have to be physically transported to the customer. Often early e-retailers ran into

Order fulfilment

major problems in the **order fulfilment** task of actually supplying their customers. Partly this was because many traditional warehouse and distribution operations were not designed for e-commerce fulfilment. Supplying a conventional retail operation requires relatively large vehicles to move relatively large quantities of goods from warehouses to shops. Distributing to individual customers requires a large number of smaller deliveries.

Short case
TDG serving the whole supply chain[9]

Source: TDG Logistics

TDG are specialists in providing *third-party* logistics services to the growing number of manufacturers and retailers that choose not to do their own distribution. Instead they outsource to companies like TDG, which have operations spread across 250 sites that cover the UK, Ireland, France, Spain, Poland and Holland, employ 8,000 employees and use 1,600 vehicles. They provided European logistics services through their own operations in the Netherlands and Ireland and, with the support of alliance partners, in several other European companies.

'There are a number of different types of company providing distribution services', says David Garman, Chief Executive Officer of TDG, 'each with different propositions for the market. At the simplest level, there are the "haulage" and "storage" businesses. These companies either move goods around or they store them in warehouses. Clients plan what has to be done and it is done to order. One level up from the haulage or storage operations are the physical distribution companies, who bring haulage and storage together. These companies collect clients' products, put them into storage facilities and deliver them to the end-customer as and when required. After that there are the companies who offer contract logistics. As a contract logistics service provider you are likely to be dealing with the more sophisticated clients who are looking for better quality facilities and management and the capability to deal with more complex operations. One level further up is the market for supply chain management services. To do this you have to be able to manage supply chains from end to end, or at least

some significant part of the whole chain. Doing this requires a much greater degree of analytical and modelling capability, business process reengineering and consultancy skills.'

TDG, along with other prominent logistics companies, describes itself as a 'lead logistics provider' or LLP, This means that they can provide the consultancy-led, analytical and strategic services integrated with a sound base of practical experience in running successful 'on-the-road' operations. 'In 1999 TDG was a UK distribution company', says David Garman, 'now we are a European contract logistics provider with a vision to becoming a full supply chain management company. Providing such services requires sophisticated operations capability, especially in terms of information technology and management dynamism. Because our sites are physically dispersed with our vehicles at any time spread around the motorways of Europe, IT is fundamental to this industry. It gives you visibility of your operation. We need the best operations managers, supported by the best IT.'

Types of relationships in supply chains

One of the key issues within a supply chain is how relationships with immediate suppliers and customers should be managed. The behaviour of the supply chain as a whole is, after all, made up of the relationships which are formed between individual pairs of operations in the chain. It is important, therefore, to have some framework which helps us to understand the different ways in which supply chain relationships can be developed.

Business or consumer relationships?

Business to business

Business to consumer

Consumer to business

Customer to customer

The growth in e-commerce has established broad categorization of supply chain relationships. This happened because Internet companies have categorized market sectors defined by who is supplying whom. Figure 13.5 illustrates this categorization, and distinguishes between relationships that are the final link in the supply chain, involving the ultimate consumer, and those involving two commercial businesses. So, **business-to-business** (B2B) relationships are by far the most common in a supply chain context and include some of the e-procurement exchange networks discussed earlier. **Business-to-consumer** (B2C) relationships include both 'bricks and mortar' retailers and online retailers. **Consumer-to-business** (C2B) relationships involve consumers posting their needs on the web (sometimes stating the price they are willing to pay), companies then deciding whether to offer. **Customer-to-customer** (C2C) or peer-to-peer (P2P) relationships include the online exchange and auction services and file sharing services. In this chapter we deal almost exclusively with B2B relationships.

Types of business-to-business relationship

A convenient way of categorizing supply chain relationships is to examine the extent and nature of what a company chooses to buy in from suppliers. Two dimensions are particularly important – *what* the company chooses to outsource, and *who* it chooses to supply it. In terms of what is outsourced, key questions are, 'how many activities are outsourced (from doing everything in-house at one extreme, to outsourcing everything at the other extreme), and

	Relationship – to . . .	
	Business	**Consumer (Peer)**
Business	**B2B** *Relationship* • Most common, all but the last link in the supply chain *E-commerce examples* • Electronic marketplaces • e.g. b2b Index	**B2C** *Relationship* • Retail operations • Comparison web sites *E-commerce examples* • Online retailers • e.g. Amazon.com
Consumer (Peer)	**C2B** *Relationship* • Consumers offer, business responds *E-commerce examples* • Usually focused on specialist area • e.g. Google Adsense	**C2C (P2P)** *Relationship* • Originally one of the driving forces behind the modern Internet (ARPANET) *E-commerce examples* • File sharing networks (legal and illegal) • e.g. Napster, Gnutella

Relationship – from . . .

Figure 13.5 The business–consumer relationship matrix

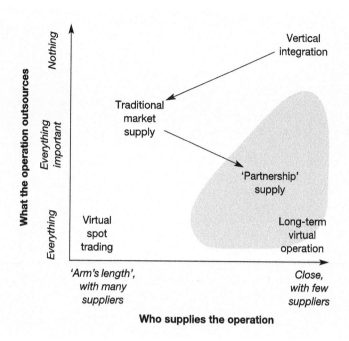

Figure 13.6 Types of supply chain relationship

'how important are the activities outsourced (from outsourcing only trivial activities at one extreme, to outsourcing even core activities at the other extreme)? In terms of who is chosen to supply products and services, again two questions are important, 'how many suppliers will be used by the operation (from using many suppliers to perform the same set of activities at one extreme, through to only one supplier for each activity at the other extreme), and 'how close are the relationships (from 'arm's length' relationships at one extreme, through to close and intimate relationships at the other extreme)? Figure 13.6 illustrates this way of characterizing relationships. It also identifies some of the more common types of relationship and shows some of the trends in how supply chain relationships have moved.

Short case
Northern Foods wins a slice of the in-flight meals business[10]

The companies that provide airline catering services are in a tough business. Meals must be of a quality that is appropriate for the class and type of flight, yet the airlines that are their customers are always looking to keep costs as low as possible, menus must change frequently (3-monthly) and the airlines must respond promptly to customer feedback. If this were not enough, forecasting passenger numbers is particularly difficult. Catering suppliers are advised of the likely numbers of passengers for each flight several days in advance, but the actual minimum number of passengers for each class is only fixed six hours before take-off (although numbers can still be increased after this, due to late sales). Also, flight arrivals are sometimes delayed, putting pressure on everyone to reduce the turnaround time, and upsetting work schedules. And even when a flight lands on time

Specialized companies have developed that prepare food in specialized factories, often for several airlines.

no more than 40 minutes are allowed before the flight is ready for take-off again, so complete preparation and a well-ordered sequence of working is essential. It is a specialized business, and in order to maintain a fast, responsive and agile service, airline caterers have traditionally produced food on, or near, airport sites using their own chefs and staff to cook and tray-set meals. The catering companies' suppliers are also usually airline specialists who themselves are located near the caterers so that they can offer very short response times.

The companies that provide catering services may also provide related services. For example, LSG Sky Chefs (a subsidiary of Deutsche Lufthansa AG) is a provider of tailor-made in-flight services for all types of airlines around the world. Their main areas of service are Airline Catering, In-flight Equipment and Logistics and In-flight Management. They are also large, employing 30,000 people at 200 customer service centres in 49 countries. In 2007 they produced 418 million meals for more than 300 airlines, representing more than 30 per cent of the global airline catering market.

But the airline sector has over recent years suffered a series of shocks including 9/11, oil price volatility, financial crises and world recession. This has meant that airlines are reviewing their catering supply solutions. In December 2008 Gate Gourmet, the world's largest independent provider of airline catering lost the contract to supply British Airways' short-haul flights out of Heathrow to new entrants into the airline catering market, a consortium of Northern Foods, a leading food producer, whose normal business is supplying retailers with own-label and branded food, and DHL, a subsidiary of Deutsche Post and the market-leading international express and logistics company. DHL is already a large supplier to 'airside' caterers at Heathrow and already has its own premises at the airport. Northern Foods will make the food at its existing factories and deliver it to DHL, which will assemble onto airline catering trays and transfer them onto aircraft. The new contract is the first time that Northern Foods, whose biggest customer is Marks and Spencer, the UK retail chain, has developed new business outside its normal supermarket customer base. It said it was 'delighted to have been chosen by BA based on the quality of our food'.

Traditional market supply relationships

The very opposite of performing an operation in-house is to purchase goods and services from outside in a 'pure' market fashion, often seeking the 'best' supplier every time it is necessary to purchase. Each transaction effectively becomes a separate decision. The **relationship** between buyer and seller, therefore, can be very short-term. Once the goods or services are delivered and payment is made, there may be no further trading between the parties. The advantages of traditional market supplier relationships are usually seen as follows:

Short-term transactional relationships

- They maintain competition between alternative suppliers. This promotes a constant drive between suppliers to provide best value.
- A supplier specializing in a small number of products or services (or perhaps just one), but supplying them to many customers, can gain natural economies of scale. This enables the supplier to offer the products and services at a lower price than would be obtained if customers performed the activities themselves on a smaller scale.
- There is inherent flexibility in outsourced supplies. If demand changes, customers can simply change the number and type of suppliers. This is a far faster and simpler alternative to having to redirect their internal activities.
- Innovations can be exploited no matter where they originate. Specialist suppliers are more likely to come up with innovative products and services which can be bought in faster and cheaper than would be the case if the company were itself trying to innovate.
- They help operations to concentrate on their core activities. One business cannot be good at everything. It is sensible therefore to concentrate on the important activities and outsource the rest.

There are, however, disadvantages in buying in a totally 'free market' manner:

- There may be supply uncertainties. Once an order has been placed, it is difficult to maintain control over how that order is fulfilled.
- Choosing who to buy from takes time and effort. Gathering sufficient information and making decisions continually are, in themselves, activities which need to be resourced.

- There are strategic risks in subcontracting activities to other businesses. An over-reliance on outsourcing can 'hollow out' the company, leaving it with no internal capabilities which it can exploit in its markets.

Short-term relationships may be used on a trial basis when new companies are being considered as more regular suppliers. Also, many purchases which are made by operations are one-off or very irregular. For example, the replacement of all the windows in a company's office block would typically involve this type of competitive-tendering market relationship. In some public-sector operations, purchasing is still based on short-term contracts. This is mainly because of the need to prove that public money is being spent as judiciously as possible. However, this short-term, price-oriented type of relationship can have a downside in terms of ongoing support and reliability. This may mean that a short-term 'least-cost' purchase decision will lead to long-term high cost.

Virtual operations

Virtual operation

An extreme form of outsourcing operational activities is that of the **virtual operation**. Virtual operations do relatively little themselves, but rely on a network of suppliers that can provide products and services on demand. A network may be formed for only one project and then disbanded once that project ends. For example, some software and Internet companies are virtual in the sense that they buy in all the services needed for a particular development. This may include not only the specific software development skills but also such things as project management, testing, applications prototyping, marketing, physical production, and so on. Much of the Hollywood film industry also operates in this way. A production company may buy and develop an idea for a movie, but it is created, edited and distributed by a loose network of agents, actors, technicians, studios and distribution companies. The advantage of virtual operations is their flexibility and the fact that the risks of investing in production facilities are far lower than in a conventional operation. However, without any solid base of resources, a company may find it difficult to hold onto and develop a unique core of technical expertise. The resources used by virtual companies will almost certainly be available to competitors. In effect, the core competence of a virtual operation can only lie in the way it is able to manage its supply network.

'Partnership' supply relationships

Partnership relationships

Partnership relationships in supply chains are sometimes seen as a compromise between vertical integration on the one hand (owning the resources which supply you) and pure market relationships on the other (having only a transactional relationship with those who supply you). Although to some extent this is true, partnership relationships are not only a simple mixture of vertical integration and market trading, although they do attempt to achieve some of the closeness and coordination efficiencies of vertical integration, but at the same time attempt to achieve a relationship that has a constant incentive to improve. Partnership relationships are defined as: *'relatively enduring inter-firm cooperative agreements, involving flows and linkages that use resources and/or governance structures from autonomous organizations, for the joint accomplishment of individual goals linked to the corporate mission of each sponsoring firm'.*[11] What this means is that suppliers and customers are expected to cooperate, even to the extent of sharing skills and resources, to achieve joint benefits beyond those they could have achieved by acting alone. At the heart of the concept of partnership lies the issue of the *closeness* of the relationship. Partnerships are close relationships, the degree of which is influenced by a number of factors, as follows:

- *Sharing success.* An attitude of shared success means that both partners work together in order to increase the total amount of joint benefit they receive, rather than manoeuvring to maximize their own individual contribution.

- *Long-term expectations.* Partnership relationships imply relatively long-term commitments, but not necessarily permanent ones.
- *Multiple points of contact.* Communication between partners is not only through formal channels, but may take place between many individuals in both organizations.
- *Joint learning.* Partners in a relationship are committed to learn from each other's experience and perceptions of the other operations in the chain.
- *Few relationships.* Although partnership relationships do not necessarily imply single sourcing by customers, they do imply a commitment on the part of both parties to limit the number of customers or suppliers with whom they do business. It is difficult to maintain close relationships with many different trading partners.
- *Joint coordination of activities.* Because there are fewer relationships, it becomes possible jointly to coordinate activities such as the flow of materials or service, payment, and so on.
- *Information transparency.* An open and efficient information exchange is seen as a key element in partnerships because it helps to build confidence between the partners.
- *Joint problem-solving.* Although partnerships do not always run smoothly, jointly approaching problems can increase closeness over time.
- *Trust.* This is probably the key element in partnership relationships. In this context, trust means the willingness of one party to relate to the other on the understanding that the relationship will be beneficial to both, even though that cannot be guaranteed. Trust is widely held to be both the key issue in successful partnerships, but also, by far, the most difficult element to develop and maintain.

Customer relationship management (CRM)

There is a story (which may or may not be true) that is often quoted to demonstrate the importance of using information technology to analyse customer information. It goes like this: Wal-Mart, the huge US-based supermarket chain, did an analysis of customers' buying habits and found a statistically significant correlation between purchases of beer and purchases of diapers (nappies), especially on Friday evenings. The reason? Fathers were going to the supermarket to buy nappies for their babies, and because fatherhood restricted their ability to go out for a drink as often, they would also buy beer. Supposedly this led the supermarket to start locating nappies next to the beer in their stores, resulting in increased sales of both.

Customer relationship management

Whether it is true or not, it does illustrate the potential of analysing data to understand customers. This is the basis of **customer relationship management** (CRM). It is a method of learning more about customers' needs and behaviours in order to develop stronger relationships with them. Although CRM usually depends on information technology, it is misleading to see it as a 'technology'. Rather it is a process that helps us to understand customers' needs and develop ways of meeting those needs while maximizing profitability. CRM brings together all the disparate information about customers so as to gain insight into their behaviour and their value to the business. It helps to sell products and services more effectively and increase revenues by:

- Providing services and products that are exactly what your customers want
- Retaining existing customers and discovering new ones
- Offering better customer service
- Cross-selling products more effectively.

CRM tries to help organizations understand who their customers are and what their value is over a lifetime. It does this by building a number of steps into its customer interface processes. First, the business must determine the needs of its customers and how best to meet those needs. For example, banks may keep track of its customers' age and lifestyle so that it can offer appropriate products like mortgages or pensions to them when they fit their needs. Second, the business must examine all the different ways and parts of the organization where customer-related information is collected, stored and used. Businesses may interact with customers in different ways and through different people. For example, sales people, call centres, technical staff, operations and distribution managers may all, at different times, have contact with customers. CRM systems should integrate these data. Third, all customer-related data must be analysed to obtain a holistic view of each customer and identify where service can be improved.

Critical commentary

Despite its name, some critics of CRM argue that the greatest shortcoming is that it is insufficiently concerned with directly helping customers. CRM systems are sold to executives as a way to increase efficiency, force standardized processes and gain better insight into the state of the business. But they rarely address the need to help organizations resolve customer problems, answer customer questions faster, or help them solve their own problems. This may explain the trend towards a shift in focus from automating internal front-office functions to streamlining processes such as online customer support.

Supply chain behaviour

A fundamental question in supply chain management is: 'How should supply chains be managed when operations compete in different ways in different markets?' One answer, proposed by Professor Marshall Fisher of Wharton Business School, is to organize the supply chains serving those individual markets in different ways.[12] He points out that many companies have seemingly similar products which, in fact, compete in different ways. Shoe manufacturers may produce classics which change little over the years, as well as fashions which last only one or two seasons. Chocolate manufacturers have stable lines which have been sold for 50 years, but also product 'specials' associated with an event or film release, maybe selling only for a few months. Demand for the former products will be relatively stable and predictable, but demand for the latter will be far more uncertain. Also, the profit margin commanded by the innovative product will probably be higher than that of the more functional product. However, the price (and therefore the margin) of the innovative product may drop rapidly once it has become unfashionable in the market.

Efficient supply chains
Responsive supply chains

The supply chain policies which are seen to be appropriate for functional products and innovative products are termed by Fisher **efficient supply chain** policies and **responsive supply chain** policies, respectively. Efficient supply chain policies include keeping inventories low, especially in the downstream parts of the network, so as to maintain fast throughput and reduce the amount of working capital tied up in the inventory. What inventory there is in the network is concentrated mainly in the manufacturing operation, where it can keep utilization high and therefore manufacturing costs low. Information must flow quickly up and down the chain from retail outlets back up to the manufacturer so that schedules can be given the maximum amount of time to adjust efficiently. The chain is then managed to make sure that products flow as quickly as possible down the chain to replenish what few stocks are kept downstream. By contrast, responsive supply chain policy stresses high service levels and responsive supply to the end-customer. The inventory in the network will be deployed as closely as possible to the customer. In this way, the chain can still supply even when dramatic changes occur in customer demand. Fast throughput from the upstream parts of the chain will still be needed to replenish downstream stocks. But those downstream stocks are needed to ensure high levels of availability to end-customers. Figure 13.7 illustrates how the different supply chain policies match the different market requirements implied by functional and innovative products.

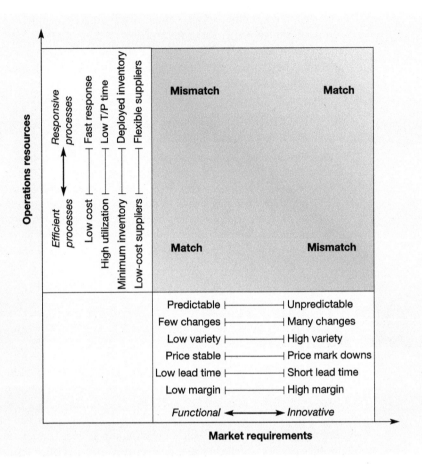

Figure 13.7 Matching the operations resources in the supply chain with market requirements

Source: Adapted from Fisher, M.C. (1997) What is the right supply chain for your product? *Harvard Business Review*, March–April, 105–16.

The bullwhip effect – supply chain dynamics

The '**bullwhip effect**', is used to describe how a small disturbance at the downstream end of a supply chain causes increasingly large disturbances, errors, inaccuracies and volatility as it works its way upstream. Its main cause is an understandable desire by the different links in the supply chain to manage their production rates and inventory levels sensibly. To demonstrate this, examine the production rate and stock levels for the supply chain shown in Table 13.4. This is a four-stage supply chain where an original equipment manufacturer (OEM) is served by three tiers of suppliers. The demand from the OEM's market has been running at a rate of 100 items per period, but in period 2 demand reduces to 95 items. All stages in the supply chain work on the principle that they will keep in stock one period's demand (a simplification but not a gross one). The 'stock' column shows the starting stock at the beginning, and the finish stock at the end, of the period. At the beginning of period 2, the OEM has 100 units in stock. Demand in period 2 is 95 and the OEM must produce enough to finish up at the end of the period with 95 in stock (this being the new demand rate). To do this, it need only manufacture 90 items; these, together with 5 items taken out of the starting stock, will supply demand and leave a finished stock of 95 items and the OEM can operate at a steady rate of 95 items per period. Note, however, that a change in demand of only 5 items has produced a fluctuation of 10 items in the OEM's production rate.

Now carry this same logic through to the first-tier supplier. At the beginning of period 2, the second-tier supplier has 100 items in stock. The demand which it has to supply in period 2 is derived from the production rate of the OEM. This has dropped down to 90 in period 2. The

Table 13.4 Fluctuations of production levels along supply chain in response to small change in end-customer demand

Period	Third-tier supplier		Second-tier supplier		First-tier supplier		Original equipment mfr		Demand
	Prodn.	Stock	Prodn.	Stock	Prodn.	Stock	Prodn.	Stock	
1	100	100 100	100	100 100	100	100 100	100	100 100	100
2	20	100 60	60	100 80	80	100 90	90	100 95	95
3	180	60 120	120	80 100	100	90 95	95	95 95	95
4	60	120 90	90	100 95	95	95 95	95	95 95	95
5	100	90 95	95	95 95	95	95 95	95	95 95	95
6	95	95 95	95	95 95	95	95 95	95	95 95	95

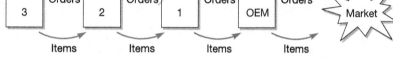

(Note all operations keep one period's inventory.)

first-tier supplier therefore has to produce sufficient to supply the demand of 90 and leave one month's demand (now 90 items) as its finish stock. A production rate of 80 items per month will achieve this. It will therefore start period 3 with an opening stock of 90 items, but the demand from the OEM has now risen to 95 items. It therefore has to produce sufficient to fulfil this demand of 95 items and leave 95 items in stock. To do this, it must produce 100 items in period 3. This logic can be extended right back to the third-tier supplier. The further back up the supply chain an operation is placed, the more drastic are the fluctuations caused by the relatively small change in demand from the final customer. The decision of how much to produce each month was governed by the following relationship:

Total available for sale in any period = Total required in the same period
Starting stock + Production rate = Demand + Closing stock
Starting stock + Production rate = 2 × Demand (because closing stock must be equal to demand)
Production rate = 2 × Demand − Starting stock

This relatively simple exercise does not include any time lag between a demand occurring in one part of the supply chain and it being transmitted to its supplier. In practice there will be such a lag, and this will make the fluctuations even more marked.

Miscommunication in the supply chain

Whenever two operations in a supply chain arrange for one to provide products or services to the other, there is the potential for misunderstanding and miscommunication. This may be caused simply by not being sufficiently clear about what a customer expects or what a supplier is capable of delivering. There may also be more subtle reasons stemming from differences in perception of seemingly clear agreements. The effect is analogous to the children's game of 'Chinese whispers'. The first child whispers a message to the next child who, whether he or she has heard it clearly or not, whispers an interpretation to the next child, and so on. The more children the message passes between, the more distorted it tends to become. The last

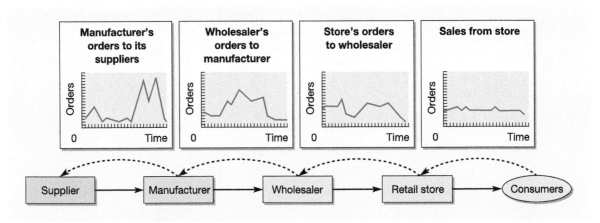

Figure 13.8 Typical supply chain dynamics

child says out loud what the message is, and the children are amused by the distortion of the original message. Figure 13.8 shows the bullwhip effect in a typical supply chain, with relatively small fluctuations in the market cause increasing volatility further back in the chain.

Supply chain improvement

Increasingly important in supply chain practice are attempts to improve supply chain performance. These are usually attempts to understand the complexity of supply chain processes; others focus on coordinating activities throughout the chain.

The SCOR model

The Supply Chain Operations Reference model (SCOR) is a broad, but highly structured and systematic, framework to supply chain improvement that has been developed by the Supply Chain Council (SCC), a global non-profit consortium. The framework uses a methodology, diagnostic and benchmarking tools that are increasingly widely accepted for evaluating and comparing supply chain activities and their performance. Just as important, the SCOR model allows its users to improve, and communicate supply chain management practices within and between all interested parties in their supply chain by using a standard language and a set of structured definitions. The SCC also provides a benchmarking database by which companies can compare their supply chain performance to others in their industries and training classes. Companies that have used the model include BP, AstraZeneca, Shell, SAP AG, Siemens AG and Bayer. The model uses three well-known individual techniques turned into an integrated approach. These are:

● Business process modelling
● Benchmarking performance
● Best practice analysis.

Business process modelling

SCOR does not represent organizations or functions, but rather processes. Each basic 'link' in the supply chain is made up of five types of process, each process being a 'supplier–customer' relationship, see Figure 13.9.

● 'Source' is the procurement, delivery, receipt and transfer of raw material items, sub-assemblies, products and/or services.

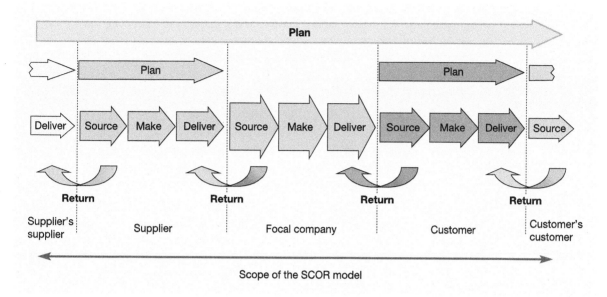

Figure 13.9 Matching the operations resources in the supply chain with market requirements

- 'Make' is the transformation process of adding value to products and services through mixing production operations processes.
- 'Deliver' processes perform all customer-facing order management and fulfilment activities including outbound logistics.
- 'Plan' processes manage each of these customer–supplier links and balance the activity of the supply chain. They are the supply and demand reconciliation process, which includes prioritization when needed.
- 'Return' processes look after the reverse logistics flow of moving material back from end-customers upstream in the supply chain because of product defects or post-delivery customer support.

All these processes are modelled at increasingly detailed levels from level 1 through to more detailed process modelling at level 3.

Benchmarking performance

Performance metrics in the SCOR model are also structured by level, as is process analysis. Level 1 metrics are the yardsticks by which an organization can measure how successful it is in achieving its desired positioning within the competitive environment, as measured by the performance of a particular supply chain. These level 1 metrics are the key performance indicators (KPIs) of the chain and are created from lower-level diagnostic metrics (called level 2 and level 3 metrics) which are calculated on the performance of lower-level processes. Some metrics do not 'roll up' to level 1, these are intended to diagnose variations in performance against plan.

Best practice analysis

Best practice analysis follows the benchmarking activity that should have measured the performance of the supply chain processes and identified the main performance gaps. Best practice analysis identifies the activities that need to be performed to close the gaps. SCC members have identified more than 400 'best practices' derived from their experience. The definition of a 'best practice' in the SCOR model is one that:

- Is current – neither untested (emerging) nor outdated.
- Is structured – it has clearly defined goals, scope and processes.

- Is proven – there has been some clearly demonstrated success.
- Is repeatable – it has been demonstrated to be effective in various contexts.
- Has an unambiguous method – the practice can be connected to business processes, operations strategy, technology, supply relationships, and information or knowledge management systems.
- Has a positive impact on results – operations improvement can be linked to KPIs.

The SCOR roadmap

The SCOR model can be implemented by using a five-phase project 'roadmap'. Within this roadmap lies a collection of tools and techniques that both help to implement and support the SCOR framework. In fact many of these tools are commonly used management decision tools such as Pareto charts, cause–effect diagrams, maps of material flow and brainstorming.

Phase 1: Discover – Involves supply-chain definition and prioritization where a 'Project Charter' sets the scope for the project. This identifies logic groupings of supply chains within the scope of the project. The priorities, based on a weighted rating method, determine which supply chains should be dealt with first. This phase also identifies the resources that are required, identified and secured through business process owners or actors.

Phase 2: Analyse – Using data from benchmarking and competitive analysis, the appropriate level of performance metrics are identified; that will define the strategic requirements of each supply chain.

Phase 3: Material flow design – In this phase the project teams have their first go at creating a common understanding of how processes can be developed. The current state of processes is identified and an initial analysis attempts to see where there are opportunities for improvement.

Phase 4: Work and information flow design – The project teams collect and analyse the work involved in all relevant processes (plan, source, make, deliver and return) and map the productivity and yield of all transactions.

Phase 5: Implementation planning – This is the final and preparation phase for communicating the findings of the project. Its purpose is to transfer the knowledge of the SCOR team(s) to individual implementation or deployment teams.

Benefits of the SCOR model

Claimed benefits from using the SCOR model include improved process understanding and performance, improved supply chain performance, increased customer satisfaction and retention, a decrease in required capital, better profitability and return on investment, and increased productivity. And, although most of these results could arguably be expected when any company starts focusing on business processes improvements, SCOR proponents argue that using the model gives an above average and supply focused improvement.

Critical commentary

Although the SCOR model is increasingly being adopted, it has been criticized for under-emphasizing people issues. The SCOR model assumes, but does not explicitly address, the human resource base skill set, notwithstanding the model's heavy reliance on supply chain knowledge to understand the model and methodology properly. Often external expertise is needed to support the process. This, along with the nature of the SCC membership, also implies that the SCOR model may be appropriate only for relatively large companies that are more likely to have the necessary business capabilities to implement the model. Many small to medium-sized companies may find difficulty in handle full-scale model implementation. Some critics would also argue that the model lacks a link to the financial plans of a company, making it very difficult to highlight the benefits obtainable, as well as inhibiting senior management support.

The effects of e-business on supply chain management practice[13]

New information technology applications combined with internet-based e-business have transformed supply chain management practice. Largely, this is because they provide better and faster information to all stages in the supply chain. Information is the lifeblood of supply chain management. Without appropriate information, supply chain managers cannot make the decisions that coordinate activities and flows through the chain. Without appropriate information, each stage in the supply chain has relatively few cues to tell them what is happening elsewhere in the chain. To some extent, they are 'driving blind' and having to rely on the most obvious of mismatches between the activities of different stages in the chain (such as excess inventory) to inform their decisions. Conversely, with accurate and 'near real-time' information, the disparate elements in supply chains can integrate their efforts to the benefit of the whole chain and, eventually, the end-customer. Just as importantly, the collection, analysis and distribution of information using e-business technologies is far less expensive to arrange than previous, less automated methods. Table 13.5 summarizes some of the effects of e-business on three important aspects of supply chain management – business and market information flow, product and service flow, and the cash flow that comes as a result of product and service flow.

Table 13.5 Some effects of e-business on supply chain management practice

	Market/sales information flow	Product/service flow	Cash flow
Supply-chain-related activities	Understanding customers' needs Designing appropriate products / services Demand forecasting	Purchasing Inventory management Throughput / waiting times Distribution	Supplier payments Customer invoicing Customer receipts
Beneficial effects of e-business practices	Better customer relationship management Monitoring real-time demand On-line customization Ability to coordinate output with demand	Lower purchasing administration costs Better purchasing deals Reduced bullwhip effect Reduced inventory More efficient distribution	Faster movement of cash Automated cash movement Integration of financial information with sales and operations activities

Information-sharing

One of the reasons for the fluctuations in output described in the example earlier was that each operation in the chain reacted to the orders placed by its immediate customer. None of the operations had an overview of what was happening throughout the chain. If information had been available and **shared throughout the chain**, it is unlikely that such wild fluctuations would have occurred. It is sensible therefore to try to transmit information throughout the chain so that all the operations can monitor true demand, free of these distortions. An obvious improvement is to make information on end-customer demand available to upstream operations. Electronic point-of-sale (EPOS) systems used by many retailers attempt to do this. Sales data from checkouts or cash registers are consolidated and transmitted to the warehouses, transportation companies and supplier manufacturing operations that form their supply chain. Similarly, electronic data interchange (EDI) helps to share information (*see* the short case on Seven-Eleven Japan). EDI can also affect the economic order quantities shipped between operations in the supply chain.

Information sharing helps improve supply chain performance

Short case
Seven-Eleven Japan's agile supply chain[14]

Source: Getty Images

Seven-Eleven Japan (SEJ) is that country's largest and most successful retailer. The average amount of stock in an SEJ store is between 7 and 8.4 days of demand, a remarkably fast stock turnover for any retailer. Industry analysts see SEJ's agile supply chain management as being the driving force behind its success. It is an agility that is supported by a fully integrated information system that provides visibility of the whole supply chain and ensures fast replenishment of goods in its stores customized exactly to the needs of individual stores. As a customer comes to the checkout counter the assistant first keys in the customer's gender and approximate age and then scans the bar codes of the purchased goods. This sales data is transmitted to the Seven-Eleven headquarters through its own high-speed lines. Simultaneously, the store's own computer system records and analyzes the information so that store managers and headquarters have immediate point-of-sale information. This allows both store managers and headquarters to, hour by hour, analyze sales trends, any stock-outs, types of customer buying certain products, and so on. The headquarters computer aggregates all this data by region, product and time so that all parts of the supply chain, from suppliers through to the stores, have the information by the next morning. Every Monday, the company chairman and top executives review all performance information for the previous week and develop plans for the up-coming week. These plans are presented on Tuesday morning to SEJ's 'operations field counsellors' each of which is responsible for facilitating performance improvement in around eight stores. On Tuesday afternoon the field counsellors for each region meet to decide how they will implement the overall plans

for their region. On Tuesday night the counsellors fly back to their regions and by next morning are visiting their stores to deliver the messages developed at headquarters which will help the stores implement their plans. SEJ's physical distribution is also organized on an agile basis. The distribution company maintains radio communications with all drivers and SEJ's headquarters keeps track of all delivery activities. Delivery times and routes are planned in great detail and published in the form of a delivery time-table. On average each delivery takes only one and half minutes at each store, and drivers are expected to make their deliveries within ten minutes of scheduled time. If a delivery is late by more than thirty minutes the distribution company has to pay the store a fine equivalent to the gross profit on the goods being delivered. The agility of the whole supply system also allows SEJ headquarters and the distribution company to respond to disruptions. For example, on the day of the Kobe earthquake, SEJ used 7 helicopters and 125 motor cycles to rush through a delivery of 64,000 rice balls to earthquake victims.

Channel alignment

Channel alignment helps improve supply chain performance

Channel alignment means the adjustment of scheduling, material movements, stock levels, pricing and other sales strategies so as to bring all the operations in the chain into line with **each other**. This goes beyond the provision of information. It means that the systems and methods of planning and control decision-making are harmonized through the chain. For example, even when using the same information, differences in forecasting methods or purchasing practices can lead to fluctuations in orders between operations in the chain. One way of avoiding this is to allow an upstream supplier to manage the inventories of its downstream customer. This is known as **vendor-managed inventory** (VMI). So, for example, a packaging supplier could take responsibility for the stocks of packaging materials held by a food manufacturing customer. In turn, the food manufacturer takes responsibility for the stocks of its products which are held in its customer's, the supermarket's warehouses.

Vendor-managed inventory

Operational efficiency

'Operational efficiency' means the efforts that each operation in the chain can make to reduce its own complexity, reduce the cost of doing business with other operations in the chain and increase throughput time. The cumulative effect of these individual activities is to simplify throughput in the whole **chain**. For example, imagine a chain of operations whose performance level is relatively poor: quality defects are frequent, the lead time to order products and services is long, and delivery is unreliable and so on. The behaviour of the chain would be a continual sequence of errors and effort wasted in replanning to compensate for the errors. Poor quality would mean extra and unplanned orders being placed, and unreliable delivery and slow delivery lead times would mean high safety stocks. Just as important, most operations managers' time would be spent coping with the inefficiency. By contrast, a chain whose operations had high levels of operations performance would be more predictable and have faster throughput, both of which would help to minimize supply chain fluctuations.

One of the most important approaches to improving the operational efficiency of supply chains is known as **time compression**. This means speeding up the flow of materials down the chain and the flow of information back up the chain. The supply chain dynamics effect we observed in Table 13.4 was due partly to the slowness of information moving back up the chain. Figure 13.10 illustrates the advantages of supply chain time compression in terms of its overall impact on profitability.[15]

Operational efficiency helps improve supply chain performance

Supply chain time compression

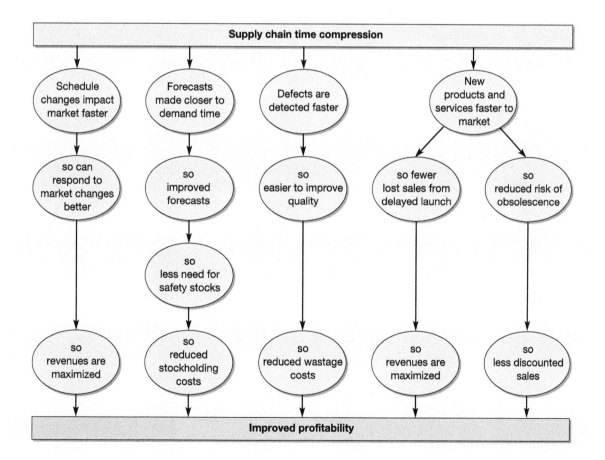

Figure 13.10 Supply chain time compression can both reduce costs and increase revenues
Source: Based on Towill

Supply chain vulnerability

Supply chain risk

One of the consequences of the agile supply chain concept has been to take more seriously the possibility of **supply chain risk** and disruption. The concept of agility includes consideration of how supply chains have to cope with common disruptions such as late deliveries, quality problems, incorrect information, and so on. Yet far more dramatic events can disrupt supply chains. Global sourcing means that parts are shipped around the world on their journey through the supply chain. Microchips manufactured in Taiwan could be assembled to printed circuit boards in Shanghai which are then finally assembled into a computer in Ireland. Perhaps most significantly, there tends to be far less inventory in supply chains that could buffer interruptions to supply. According to Professor Martin Christopher, an authority on supply chain management, '*Potentially the risk of disruption has increased dramatically as the result of a too-narrow focus on supply chain efficiency at the expense of effectiveness. Unless management recognizes the challenge and acts upon it, the implications for us all could be chilling.*'[16] These 'chilling' effects can arise as a result of disruptions such as natural disasters, terrorist incidents, industrial or direct action such as strikes and protests, accidents such as fire in a vital component supplier's plant, and so on. Of course, many of these disruptions have always been present in business. It is the increased vulnerability of supply chains that has made many companies place more emphasis on understanding supply chain risks.

Summary answers to key questions

Check and improve your understanding of this chapter using self assessment questions and a personalised study plan, audio and video downloads, and an eBook – all at www.myomlab.com.

➤ What are supply chain management and its related activities?

- Supply chain management is a broad concept which includes the management of the entire supply chain from the supplier of raw material to the end-customer.

- Its component activities include purchasing, physical distribution management, logistics, materials management and customer relationship management (CRM).

➤ What are the types of relationship between operations in supply chains?

- Supply networks are made up of individual pairs of buyer–supplier relationships. The use of Internet technology in these relationships has led to a categorization based on a distinction between business and consumer partners. Business-to-business (B2B) relationships are of the most interest in operations management terms. They can be characterized on two dimensions – what is outsourced to a supplier, and the number and closeness of the relationships.

- Traditional market supplier relationships are where a purchaser chooses suppliers on an individual periodic basis. No long-term relationship is usually implied by such 'transactional' relationships, but it makes it difficult to build internal capabilities.

- Virtual operations are an extreme form of outsourcing where an operation does relatively little itself and subcontracts almost all its activities.

- Partnership supplier relationships involve customers forming long-term relationships with suppliers. In return for the stability of demand, suppliers are expected to commit to high levels of service. True partnerships are difficult to sustain and rely heavily on the degree of trust which is allowed to build up between partners.

- Customer relationship management (CRM) is a method of learning more about customers' needs and behaviours in order to develop stronger relationships with them. It brings together all information about customers to gain insight into their behaviour and their value to the business.

➤ What is the 'natural' pattern of behaviour in supply chains?

- Marshall Fisher distinguishes between functional markets and innovative markets. He argues that functional markets, which are relatively predictable, require efficient supply chains, whereas innovative markets, which are less predictable, require 'responsive' supply chains.

- Supply chains exhibit a dynamic behaviour known as the 'bullwhip' effect. This shows how small changes at the demand end of a supply chain are progressively amplified for operations further back in the chain.

➤ How can supply chains be improved?

- The Supply Chain Operations Reference model (SCOR) is a highly structured framework for supply chain improvement that has been developed by the Supply Chain Council (SCC).

- The model uses three well-known individual techniques turned into an integrated approach. These are:
  - Business process modelling
  - Benchmarking performance
  - Best practice analysis.

- To reduce the 'bullwhip' effect, operations can adopt some mixture of three coordination strategies:
  - information-sharing: the efficient distribution of information throughout the chain can reduce demand fluctuations along the chain by linking all operations to the source of demand;
  - channel alignment: this means adopting the same or similar decision-making processes throughout the chain to coordinate how and when decisions are made;
  - operational efficiency: this means eliminating sources of inefficiency or ineffectiveness in the chain; of particular importance is 'time compression', which attempts to increase the throughput speed of the operations in the chain.

- Increasingly, supply risks are being managed as a countermeasure to their vulnerability.

Case study
Supplying fast fashion[17]

Garment retailing has changed. No longer is there a standard look that all retailers adhere to for a whole season. Fashion is fast, complex and furious. Different trends overlap and fashion ideas that are not even on a store's radar screen can become 'must haves' within six months. Many retail businesses with their own brands, such as H&M and Zara, sell up-to-the-minute fashionability at low prices, in stores that are clearly focused on one particular market. In the world of fast fashion catwalk designs speed their way into high-street stores at prices anyone can afford. The quality of the garment means that it may only last one season, but fast-fashion customers don't want yesterday's trends. As *Newsweek* puts it, *'being a "quicker picker-upper" is what made fashion retailers H&M and Zara successful. [They] thrive by practicing the new science of "fast fashion"; compressing product development cycles as much as six times.'*

H&M – established in Sweden in 1947, now sells clothes and cosmetics in over 1,000 stores in 20 countries around the world. The business concept is 'fashion and quality at the best price'. With more than 40,000 employees, and revenues of around SEK 60,000 million, its biggest market is Germany, followed by Sweden and the UK. H&M are seen by many as the originator of the fast fashion concept. Certainly they have years of experience at driving down the price of up-to-the-minute fashions. *'We ensure the best price,'* they say, *'by having few middlemen, buying large volumes, having extensive experience of the clothing industry, having a great knowledge of which goods should be bought from which markets, having efficient distribution systems, and being cost-conscious at every stage'.*

Zara – the first store opened almost by accident in 1975 when Amancio Ortega Gaona, a women's pyjama manufacturer, was left with a large cancelled order. The shop he opened was intended only as an outlet for cancelled orders. Now, Inditex, the holding group that includes the Zara brand, has over 1,300 stores in 39 countries with sales of over €3 billion. The Zara brand accounts for over 75 per cent of the group's total retail sales, and is still based in northwest Spain. By 2003 it had become the world's fastest-growing volume garment retailer. The Inditex group also has several other branded chains including Pull and Bear, and Massimo Dutti. In total it employs almost 40,000 people in a business that is known for a high degree of vertical integration compared with most fast-fashion companies. The company believes that it is their integration along the supply chain that allows them to respond to customer demand fast and flexibly while keeping stock to a minimum.

But the retail operations that customers see are only the end part of the supply chain that feeds them. And these have also changed.

At its simplest level, the fast-fashion supply chain has four stages. First, the garments are designed, after which they are manufactured; they are then distributed to the retail outlets where they are displayed and sold in retail operations designed to reflect the businesses' brand values. In this short case we examine two fast-fashion operations, Hennes and Mauritz (known as H&M) and Zara, together with United Colors of Benetton (UCB), a similar chain, but with a different market positioning.

Benetton – almost fifty years ago Luciano Benetton took the world of fashion by storm by selling the bright, casual sweaters designed by his sister across Europe (and later the rest of the world), promoted by controversial advertising. By 2005 the Benetton Group was present in 120 countries throughout the world. Selling casual garments, mainly under its United Colors of Benetton (UCB) and its more fashion-oriented Sisley brands, it produces 110 million garments a year, over 90 per cent of them in Europe. Its retail network of over 5,000 stores produces revenue of around €2 billion. Benetton products are seen as less 'high fashion' but higher quality and durability, with higher prices, than H&M and Zara.

Design

All three businesses emphasize the importance of design in this market. Although not *haute couture,* capturing design trends is vital to success. Even the boundary between high and fast fashion is starting to blur. In 2004 H&M recruited high-fashion designer Karl Lagerfeld, previously noted for his work with more exclusive brands. For H&M his designs were priced for value rather than exclusivity, *'Why do I work for H&M? Because I believe in inexpensive clothes, not "cheap" clothes'*, said Lagerfeld. Yet most of H&M's products come from over a hundred designers in Stockholm who work with a team of 50 pattern designers, around 100 buyers and a number of budget controllers. The department's task is to find the optimum balance between the three components making up H&M's business concept – fashion, price and quality. Buying volumes and delivery dates are then decided.

Zara's design functions are organized in a different way from most similar companies'. Conventionally, the design input comes from three *separate* functions: the designers themselves, market specialists, and buyers who place orders on to suppliers. At Zara the design stage is split into three product areas: women's, men's and children's garments.

In each area, designers, market specialists and buyers are co-located in design halls that also contain small workshops for trying out prototype designs. The market specialists in all three design halls are in regular contact with Zara retail stores, discussing customer reaction to new designs. In this way, the retail stores are not the end of the whole supply chain but the beginning of the design stage of the chain. Zara's around 300 designers, whose average age is 26, produce approximately 40,000 items per year of which about 10,000 go into production.

Benetton also has around 300 designers, who not only design for all their brands, but also are engaged in researching new materials and clothing concepts. Since 2000 the company has moved to standardize their range globally. At one time more than 20 per cent of its ranges were customized to the specific needs of each country, now only between 5 and 10 per cent of garments are customized. This reduced the number of individual designs offered globally by over 30 per cent, strengthening the global brand image and reducing production costs.

Both H&M and Zara have moved away from the traditional industry practice of offering two 'collections' a year, for Spring/Summer and Autumn/Winter. Their 'seasonless cycle' involves the continual introduction of new products on a rolling basis throughout the year. This allows designers to learn from customers' reactions to their new products and incorporate them quickly into more new products. The most extreme version of this idea is practised by Zara. A garment will be designed and a batch manufactured and 'pulsed' through the supply chain. Often the design is never repeated; it may be modified and another batch produced, but there are no 'continuing' designs as such. Even Benetton have increased the proportion of what they call 'flash' collections, small collections that are put into its stores during the season.

Manufacturing

At one time Benetton focused its production on its Italian plants. Then it significantly increased its production outside Italy to take advantage of lower labour costs. Non-Italian operations include factories in North Africa, Eastern Europe and Asia. Yet each location operates in a very similar manner. A central, Benetton-owned, operation performs some manufacturing operations (especially those requiring expensive technology) and coordinates the more labour-intensive production activities that are performed by a network of smaller contractors (often owned and managed by ex-Benetton employees). These contractors may in turn subcontract some of their activities. The company's central facility in Italy allocates production to each of the non-Italian networks, deciding what and how much each is to produce. There is some specialization, for example, jackets are made in Eastern Europe while T-shirts are made in Spain. Benetton also has a controlling share in its main supplier of raw materials, to ensure fast supply to its factories. Benetton are also known for the practice of dyeing garments after

assembly rather than using dyed thread or fabric. This postpones decisions about colours until late in the supply process so that there is a greater chance of producing what is needed by the market.

H&M does not have any factories of its own, but instead works with around 750 suppliers. Around half of production takes place in Europe and the rest mainly in Asia. It has 21 production offices around the world that between them are responsible for coordinating the suppliers who produce over half a billion items a year for H&M. The relationship between production offices and suppliers is vital, because it allows fabrics to be bought in early. The actual dyeing and cutting of the garments can then be decided at a later stage in the production The later an order can be placed on suppliers, the less the risk of buying the wrong thing. Average supply lead times vary from three weeks up to six months, depending on the nature of the goods. However, *'The most important thing'*, they say, *'is to find the optimal time to order each item. Short lead times are not always best. With some high-volume fashion basics, it is to our advantage to place orders far in advance. Trendier garments require considerably shorter lead times.'*

Zara's lead times are said to be the fastest in the industry, with a 'catwalk to rack' time of as little of as 15 days. According to one analyst this is because they *'owned most of the manufacturing capability used to make their products, which they use as a means of exciting and stimulating customer demand'*. About half of Zara's products are produced in its network of 20 Spanish factories, which, like at Benetton, tended to concentrate on the more capital-intensive operations such as cutting and dyeing. Subcontractors are used for most labour-intensive operations like sewing. Zara buy around 40 per cent of its fabric from its own wholly owned subsidiary, most of which is in undyed form for dyeing after assembly. Most Zara factories and their subcontractors work on a single-shift system to retain some volume flexibility.

Distribution

Both Benetton and Zara have invested in highly automated warehouses, close to their main production centres that store, pack and assemble individual orders for their retail networks. These automated warehouses represent a major investment for both companies. In 2001, Zara caused some press comment by announcing that it would open a second automated warehouse even though, by its own calculations, it was only using about half its existing warehouse capacity. More recently, Benetton caused some controversy by announcing that it was exploring the use of RFID tags to track its garments.

At H&M, while the stock management is primarily handled internally, physical distribution is subcontracted. A large part of the flow of goods is routed from production site to the retail country via H&M's transit terminal in Hamburg. Upon arrival the goods are inspected and allocated to the stores or to the centralized store stockroom. The centralized store stockroom, within H&M referred to as 'Call-Off warehouse' replenishes stores on item level according to what is selling.

Retail

All H&M stores (average size, 1,300 square metres) are owned and solely run by H&M. The aim is to 'create a comfortable and inspiring atmosphere in the store that makes it simple for customers to find what they want and to feel at home'. This is similar to Zara stores, although they tend to be smaller (average size, 800 square metres). Perhaps the most remarkable characteristic of Zara stores is that garments rarely stay in the store for longer than 2 weeks. Because product designs are often not repeated and are produced in relatively small batches, the range of garments displayed in the store can change radically every two or three weeks. This encourages customers both to avoid delaying a purchase and to revisit the store frequently.

Since 2000 Benetton has been reshaping its retail operations. At one time the vast majority of Benetton retail outlets were small shops run by third parties. Now these small stores have been joined by several, Benetton-owned and -operated, larger stores (1,500 to 3,000 square metres). These mega-stores can display the whole range of Benetton products and reinforce the Benetton shopping experience.

Question

Compare and contrast the approaches taken by H&M, Benetton and Zara to managing their supply chains.

Problems and applications

These problems and applications will help to improve your analysis of operations. You can find more practice problems as well as worked examples and guided solutions on MyOMLab at www.myomlab.com.

1 'Look, why should we waste our time dealing with suppliers who can merely deliver good product, on time, and in full? There are any number of suppliers who can do that. What we are interested in is developing a set of suppliers who will be able to supply us with suitable components for the generation of products that comes after the next products we launch. It's the underlying capability of suppliers that we are really interested in.'

(a) Devise a set of criteria that this manager could use to evaluate alternative suppliers.

(b) Suggest ways in which she could determine how to weight each criterion.

2 Three managers are attending a seminar on 'Getting More Value from Your Purchasing Function'. One manager is from a large retail bank, one is from a general hospital and the third is from a printing company. At the seminar they were discussing their problems during coffee.

'This is really useful; I think that even a relatively small reduction in our bought-in supplies bill could have a major impact on the profitability of our printing company.'

'Yes, I agree the hospital will also benefit from an exercise that would reduce the bought-in supplies bill. At the moment it accounts for almost 30 per cent of all our expenditure.'

'Yes, at the bank we spend almost 20 per cent of our expenditure on bought-in supplies. Given that our profit is 20 per cent of our total revenue, any saving in bought-in supplies would be valuable.'

'I have to say that profits are not so high in the printing industry. Our profits are only 10 per cent of sales revenue. However, with bought-in supplies accounting for 70 per cent of our total costs, I am sure that any reduction in bought-in supplies costs will be useful.'

Which of these three managers would benefit most from a 5 per cent reduction in their bought-in supplies bill?

3 The example of the bullwhip effect shown in Table 13.4 shows how a simple 5 per cent reduction in demand at the end of supply chain causes fluctuations that increase in severity the further back an operation is placed in the chain.

(a) Using the same logic and the same rules (i.e. all operations keep one period's inventory), what would the effect on the chain be if demand fluctuated period by period between 100 and 95? That is, period 1 has a demand of 100, period 2 has a demand of 95, period 3 a demand of 100, period 4 a demand of 95, and so on?

(b) What happens if all operations in the supply chain decided to keep only half of the period's demand as inventory?

4 If you were the owner of a small local retail shop, what criteria would you use to select suppliers for the goods which you wish to stock in your shop? Visit three shops which are local to you and ask the owners how they select their suppliers. In what way were their answers different from what you thought they might be?

5 Visit a C2C auction site (for example eBay) and analyse the function of the site in terms of the way it facilitates transactions. What does such a site have to get right to be successful?

Selected further reading

Andersen, M. and Skjoett-Larsen, T. (2009) Corporate social responsibility in global supply chains, *Supply Chain Management: An International Journal*, vol. 14, issue 2, 75–86. A good review of the topic.

Christopher, M. (2004) *Logistics and Supply Chain Management: Creating Value-adding Networks*, Financial Times Prentice Hall, Harlow. Updated version of a classic that gives a comprehensive treatment on supply chain management from a distribution perspective by one of the gurus of supply chain management.

Fisher, M.L. (1997) What is the right supply chain for your product?, *Harvard Business Review*, vol. 75, no. 2.

A particularly influential article that explores the issue of how supply chains are not all the same.

Green, K.W. Jr, Whitten, D. and Inman, R.A. (2008) The impact of logistics performance on organizational performance in a supply chain context, *Supply Chain Management: An International Journal*, vol. 13, issue 4, 317–27. What it says in the title.

Harrison, A. and van Hoek, R. (2002) *Logistics Management and Strategy*, Financial Times Prentice Hall, Harlow. A short but readable book that explains many of the modern ideas in supply chain management including lean supply chains and agile supply chains.

Useful web sites

www.cio.com/research/scm/edit/012202_scm Site of CIO's Supply Chain Management Research Center. Topics include procurement and fulfilment, with case studies.

www.stanford.edu/group/scforum/ Stanford University's supply chain forum. Interesting debate.

www.rfidc.com/ Site of the RFID Centre that contains RFID demonstrations and articles to download.

www.spychips.com/ Vehemently anti-RFID site. If you want to understand the nature of some activists' concern over RFID, this site provides the arguments.

www.cips.org/ The Chartered Institute of Purchasing and Supply (CIPS) is an international organization, serving the purchasing and supply profession and dedicated to promoting best practice. Some good links.

www.opsman.org Lots of useful stuff.

Now that you have finished reading this chapter, why not visit MyOMLab at www.myomlab.com where you'll find more learning resources to help you make the most of your studies and get a better grade?

Index